THE WESTERN HERITAGE

to 1500

STEWART C. EASTON

HOLT, RINEHART AND WINSTON, INC.

New York · Chicago · San Francisco · Toronto · London

Binding
The Parthenon, Athens
(COURTESY OF KENNETH L. CULVER)

This book consists of twelve chapters from
The Western Heritage *by Stewart C. Easton.*

Library of Congress
Catalog Card Number: 66–10212

2652857

Printed in the
United States of America

1 2 3 4 5 6 7 8 9

PREFACE

This edition entitled *The Western Heritage to 1500* consists of the first twelve chapters of the author's *The Western Heritage,* second edition, published in 1966. The last chapters of *The Western Heritage* have already been published as a separate volume and can of course be used in conjunction with this book.

The present volume has been published separately in order to accommodate those instructors and students who desire a shorter account of ancient and medieval history than is found in the author's much more detailed *The Heritage of the Past to 1500* (second edition, 1964). It is perhaps worth noting that the present volume is less than half the length of the earlier work, and much that the author considers worth knowing necessarily has had to be omitted. But since the tendency in Western Civilization courses has been to concentrate more on the modern period—and there is obviously much to be said for this procedure, especially when these courses constitute all the history many students will take in college—it was thought worth while to abbreviate the earlier material and present it in the form of a relatively brief survey in a single volume.

The book has been designed on a rather rigorously topical basis, and there is more interpretation than is customary in textbooks. It is, of course, much easier to give merely a compendium of facts and to leave all the interpretation to the instructor. It must be admitted that some instructors prefer this kind of text. Obviously not all teachers will agree with all the author's interpretations. But where the teacher disagrees he is free to take up the issue with his students in the knowledge that they will already have one suggested interpretation at their disposal. This will make for a livelier class discussion than if the student had only the bare facts and was compelled to rely upon the instructor for the only interpretation available to him. On the other hand, when the instructor agrees with the author's interpretation, he does not have to start from the beginning and interpret all the facts, but is given the opportunity to add from his own store of knowledge the details that were necessarily omitted from the book for reasons of space. Students also should not feel it to be their duty to agree with the author or accept his interpretations as final because the interpretations are printed in a published book. A book is chosen for study by an instructor because he believes the facts are accurate and the views are worthy of serious consideration and may give rise to intelligent thought and discussion.

A choice of suitable paperbacks and a few hardcover books for use with this text appears at the end of each chapter. A few remarks are appended to almost all the books mentioned, for the purpose of giving the student some guidance on their scope and contents. A study guide to accompany the complete *Western Heritage* was prepared by Professor Malcolm Moule of the University of the Pacific, Stockton, California, and was published in 1966. This guide will be found useful also by those who study only the period covered in this volume.

I am indebted to many persons and organizations for help in finding appropriate illustrations, as indicated in the credit lines. Special thanks are due to Miss Mary M. Kenway of the Pierpont Morgan Library in New York, who helped unearth the pictures in the book taken from medieval manuscripts, and to the staff of the Metropolitan Museum of Art.

The contribution made to the book by my wife, both by way of suggestions, encouragement, and criticism, and in the typing of much of the manuscript, deserves a special and unique acknowledgment. Though it is formally acknowledged here in the printed page, it can add little to what I have said to her many times over in private.

STEWART C. EASTON

Tucson, Arizona
February 1967

CONTENTS

I • Before History

II • The Ancient World

III • The Centuries of Transition

IV • The Middle Ages

MAPS

I · BEFORE HISTORY

A prehistoric fresco from the Lascaux Caves, Dordogne, France. Central subject of the left wall in the Nave. Huge engraved Cow, painted in black.

Chronological Chart

AGES OF PREHISTORY

Type of Man	Cultural Epoch	Geological Epoch	Approx. Date (B.C.)*
Pithecanthropus (Java man)	Lower Paleolithic (Food gathering)	Pleistocene Age	500,000
Sinanthropus (Peking man)	Lower Paleolithic (Food gathering)	Pleistocene Age	500,000
Neanderthal	Lower Paleolithic (Food gathering)	Pleistocene Age	150,000
Neanderthaloid	Lower Paleolithic (Food gathering)	Pleistocene Age	150,000
Homo-Sapiens (Cro-Magnon, etc.)	Upper Paleolithic	Pleistocene Age	50,000
	Mesolithic	Holocene (recent age)	8,000
	Neolithic Revolution (Food growing —Middle East and Europe)	Holocene (recent age)	5500 or later
	Followed by: Copper Age		ca. 4500
	Bronze Age		ca. 3500
	Iron Age		ca. 1800

* All the dates above are in dispute, and no consensus is to be found among archaeologists. All that the chart gives is a relative time scale, which will certainly be modified by further research.

ONE

The Foundations of an Organized Society

❖ **The economic and political foundations of a society**

ECONOMIC REQUIREMENTS

In all ages and in all societies the human being has had certain fundamental needs. These arise from the very fact that he is a human being, living in a society. No man can live for more than a limited period by himself; even if he could survive alone for his own lifetime, he could not reproduce his kind. He must therefore have some relations with his fellow men, and these relations are necessarily regulated by custom and usually by law. As a producer and consumer, he has an economic part to play in the life of his society. Lastly, he has certain nonmaterial needs, which he pursues with greater or lesser intensity in accordance with the opportunities provided by his society and the dictates of his own personal individuality.

The basic economic requirements of human beings are food, shelter, and clothing. In prehistoric societies their pursuit must have consumed such an enormous proportion of available human energies that there was little left for other activities. Food could be obtained from animals and wild plants, which were hunted or harvested in accordance with the skills and techniques available to the society. Such an economy may be termed a natural one—man was dependent entirely upon what was provided for him by nature, especially if he clothed himself in animal skins and lived in caves. When nature failed him, he moved on to a more favorable location, where he continued to live in a natural economy.

At the next stage of development, called the Neolithic Revolution, man ceased to be totally dependent upon nature and began in some degree to control it. He learned to breed and tend animals, so that they were always available to him for food when he needed them, and he taught them to work for him and supplement his own labor. He learned to plant crops and harvest them, laying down seeds in some spot cleared for the purpose and in which such plants did not grow by nature. He learned to build himself a home where none had been provided by nature, and he even discovered how to grow special crops such as flax from which he could make himself clothing.

Having learned in some degree to control and harness nature, man at last found himself both with leisure to produce luxuries that made life more pleasant and comfortable, and with a surplus of crops beyond the consuming needs of his society. He was able to offer these surpluses of manufactured luxuries and of crops for human consumption in exchange for goods produced by other men outside his immediate group. This *trade*, evidences of which have been found as early as the Neolithic age, was ultimately supplemented and fed by the products of *industry*. Industrial production is characterized by a more extensive division of labor under which some members of the society, freed from direct agricultural work, specialize in manufacturing a varied assortment of articles to be consumed at home or to be traded in exchange for foreign products. An economically advanced society is characterized by the diversity of products manufactured and by effective organization of production to take advantage of specialized skills and minimize the waste of human energies in unnecessary labor.

Protection through government and law   It used to be thought that man in a state of nature was forced to compete with all other human beings for his very subsistence, or, in the famous words of Thomas Hobbes, that his life was "solitary, poor, nasty, brutish, and short." We have no record of such a way of life, either in early times, or among present-day "primitive" men. And it no longer seems as probable to us as it did in the nineteenth century, under the influence of the biological ideas of Darwin, that human survival was a matter of success in the constant struggle for existence, if this struggle is conceived of as a struggle between human beings. It now seems much more probable that survival has always been due to successful cooperation between human beings to resist the always dangerous forces of nature.

This cooperation must necessarily have involved banding together for the purposes of mutual protection, still the primary purpose of all government. If a social unit, even one as small as a family, is unable to evolve an acceptable system, under which the authority to maintain internal order and resist external aggression is vested in one or more of its members, it will soon disintegrate. The first requirement therefore of any government is that it should possess power to enforce its will upon individuals. This coercive power inherent in all governments may be backed by police forces for domestic use and military forces to repel external aggression. Whatever the form of government it must also possess some moral authority and be acceptable either to a majority of the people or to a minority that commands enough moral or material resources to enable it to coerce the majority. No government, whether by one man or by many, can survive without some support and acceptance.

A government, to be accepted by even a mi-nority of the people, cannot behave in an arbitrary and unpredictable manner. It must make clear what its policy is in matters of daily concern to the people. This need for certainty is satisfied by the establishment of law, which explains to the people what is expected of them and decrees penalties for the behavior it defines as unacceptable. Law is essentially the regulation of the public behavior of human beings in an organized society, and it is enforced by the power of the government, as long as the government is able to maintain its authority.

From very early times men have considered that laws should be made in accordance with an abstraction called justice. But, as there has never been any agreed conception of justice at any time in history, individuals in each society have arrived at their own conceptions of justice by their own thought and have tried to modify the law accordingly. Justice has remained a valuable ideal, but in fact it has been the enforceable law that has prevailed rather than the abstract and unenforceable ideal. Most law-givers in early societies claimed that they received the law from the gods and that their laws were therefore just; hence they decreed severe penalties for anyone who should attempt, from his feeble human thinking, to change them. In ancient Egypt there was no written law until a very late date. The Pharaoh who, as a god, was supposed to "know the hearts of men," could judge cases in the light of his intuitive and immediate perception of justice.

Evolution of political institutions—From clans and tribes to the national state   It is possible that in some far-off age the self-sufficient family may also have been the political unit, with one member exercising an authority recognized and accepted by the other members. This state of affairs, however, presupposes the self-sufficiency of the one family, and such self-sufficiency is unlikely at any time or in any place. The clan, or union of a small number of families, sometimes closely connected by blood relationship, perhaps through a recent common ancestor, is known as a historical social unit. A larger unit is the tribe, composed of several clans. Still larger units of government are city-states; empires, which sometimes rule over wide areas subdued by warfare; and in our own times, national states.

When the tribal units emerge into the light of history, there is usually a chieftain occupying the position of the head of the tribal government, advised by other minor chiefs or heads of families, and sometimes by the whole body of adults, who form an assembly whose advice is called for on special occasions and whose consent is necessary for important decisions. Such a government is a primitive democracy, of which we find evidence in Mesopotamia at an early date, and traces of which are found among other peoples, such as the primitive Greeks, Romans, and Germans of the West. In other societies we find at an early time the institution of kingship, in which the ruler has already been granted the power to govern without the formality of consultation with his subjects. In some Greek city-states kingship gave place to democracy; while in Rome after the expulsion of the kings, rule was exercised by elected consuls advised by a senate.

Common to all these forms of government are systems of law and officials who carry out the policies of the government. From the very primitive to the most advanced and modern forms of government the most important function is always the provision of protection to the governed; and though modern governments have undertaken multifarious subsidiary tasks, essentially they perform these tasks instead of the people themselves because the people have requested or allowed them to do so—tasks supposedly for their benefit which, in their view, can best be performed by common rather than private effort and under direction from above. The modern political and economic theory known as socialism emphasizes the importance of the role of the government in providing for the people what they are unable to provide for themselves.

Historical forms of government—Monarchy, oligarchy, democracy The essential requirement of government is, then, that it be effective and that its authority in the area entrusted to it should be accepted. Many forms of government may fulfill these criteria, and many forms are known to history; human inventiveness may yet devise new combinations. The Greek philosopher Aristotle recognized three types of what he thought of as good governments: monarchy, aristocracy (rule by "the best"), and constitutional government. These could degenerate into tyranny, oligarchy (rule by the few, not necessarily the best), and democracy (rule by the propertyless many). Whether or not we accept his judgment of good and bad governments, the classification itself is useful and fairly comprehensive.

Each of the governments may exist in pure or mixed forms. Monarchy may consist of rule by a king or a single ruler under some other title and his chosen advisers, with the responsibility ultimately resting with the ruler, or it may be a rule limited by the legal or moral necessity for him to consult his advisers, by whom he may be overruled. The latter is a limited or constitutional monarchy, and within this classification there are many degrees of limitation, down to the point where the "advisers" rule, and the king is merely a respected figurehead and symbol of unity, as in England. An oligarchy may be elected, or it may be entitled to rule by hereditary right; and it may have to consult the people in certain matters and submit to being overruled on occasion. A democracy may be direct, as in Athens, or representative as in modern states, the representatives subject to re-election or recall. The form of government, then, is always subject to change and modification in accordance with the needs of the time and the wishes of the people governed, but whatever the form and whatever the label— some modern labels are devised purely with the aim of confusing—a government's first task is to govern. If it cannot do this, it will inevitably be replaced by one that can.

THE "CULTURE" OF A SOCIETY

The common elements of all cultures—The accumulated heritage from the past Together the social organization, political institutions, economic activities, law, science, art, religion, and thought are called the culture of a society. The cave paintings of the Old Stone age and the mass-production techniques of the twentieth century are equally an expression of the cultural creativeness of these particular societies. They are the work of men living in the society, making use of the physical environment provided for them by nature. Their creativeness is limited by the natural conditions, but not determined by them. The men of the Old Stone age could hardly have progressed at a single leap to the mass-production technique of the twentieth century or to its representative political government, since cultural inventiveness had first to traverse all the intermediate stages, and the institutions of society had to be modified with each innovation. Men had first to live in settled communities and develop institutions fit for such communities; they had to make the necessary technical inventions for communication, transportation, and production, and again slowly develop social institutions that could release and take advantage of natural human inventiveness.

But it is not necessary for each society to start again from scratch, inventing its techniques from the beginning. It can take advantage of the achievements of its predecessors. Once the Neolithic Revolution had taken place and agriculture was seen to be an improvement over the earlier food gathering, this fundamental invention became a part of the permanent possession of mankind, and any new society could build on the foundations laid by Neolithic man. Cultural change, therefore, is cumulative. The thoughts of mankind have been, as it were, built into the world—and the world has been changed by them, forever. Only if all knowledge of human deeds in the last seven thousand years were lost, would it be necessary for mankind to return to the conditions of the Old Stone age and start again.

The uniqueness of each culture　Although each society does build on the foundations laid by its predecessors and exploits its cultural heritage, it is also, in a sense, unique. The men of ancient Egypt developed a political institution, the divine kingship, that they were unwilling to abandon, yet which was not successfully copied by other societies; they developed an art that had little influence on subsequent art in other countries and yet has been considered by many to be a fitting expression of the Egyp-

tian attitude toward life. This attitude toward life seems to be the unique element in every society, which gives it its characteristic form. While the ancient Egyptians denied the fact of change, regarding it as illusory, and had therefore no interest in progress, we in the twentieth century not only recognize the fact of change but try to take advantage of it and help it on by our efforts. We set ourselves goals that we try to achieve; then, having achieved them, we set ourselves ever more distant goals and strive toward them. To the Egyptians the moon was a goddess, not an area for potential human colonization.

But no society before ours had any conception of progress such as we have. Many societies looked back to a golden age in the past that they longed to recapture, and even the Greeks, whose ideas were in so many ways similar to ours, lacked that sense of the importance of building for the future that is characteristic of modern Western civilization. It is necessary, therefore, in studying civilization as it was manifested in a particular society, to try to discover its own characteristic attitude toward life and to view its cultural achievements in the light of this attitude, while at the same time noting those cultural advances that it made and passed on to its successors as part of the total cultural heritage of mankind.

The diffusion of culture　Cultural advances first made within a particular society may be taken up by other societies and spread throughout the entire world. But they must be able to find their proper place in the receiving society; they must find a fertile ground for reception and propagation. The divine kingship of Egypt would not have fitted into the existing contemporary society in Mesopotamia, and even if the Mesopotamian peoples had known of it, they would hardly have tried to graft it onto their existing native institutions. On the other hand, the Christian and other religions have been diffused through many countries where they supplied answers to the problems that the inhabitants of those countries had been trying to solve and where they fitted in with the psychological predisposition of the peoples. The system of parliamentary government whose origins are to be found in medieval England was gradually diffused throughout Europe and, especially since World War I, has spread into many countries of the world that desired to accept a form of government that had apparently proved itself to be effective in the war itself. But in other places it has so far failed to take root because of the tenacity of existing institutions.

Technical inventions do not, as a rule, meet with the same opposition as religious or political innovations and can be passed from one society to another with less disturbance. There are thousands of examples of such diffusion of inventions from the earliest times to the present. Probably the idea of food growing and the domestication of animals spread throughout the world from some center in the Near East, though the possibility of the separate invention of such a fundamental idea cannot be ruled out. The invention of writing was probably diffused from the ancient land of Sumer, though the earliest receivers, the Egyptians, modified and improved upon the Sumerian practice, using their own pictures and symbols, and developing new writing materials available to them but not to the Sumerians. It is not known by how many millenniums the use of language preceded the written symbols, but the languages of peoples in historic times have many resemblances to each other that prove their diffusion from one people to another. Other inventions such as printing, gunpowder, and the cultivation of the silkworm can be traced in some detail by the historian from their first use in one country to their full development in another.

Each society, then, receives by diffusion some of its cultural heritage, to which it adds the products of its own genius. A society may even invent unnecessarily for itself things that have already been developed elsewhere, unknown to it, which it could have received by diffusion if it had had wider cultural contacts. On the other hand, not all knowledge available to any one people has been preserved or transmitted to others. The ancient Sumerians knew all the basic forms of architecture, but the Egyptians and Greeks did not make use of them; medieval European technical knowledge—as, for instance, of the rotation of crops—was in many ways markedly inferior to that of several earlier peoples. The Renaissance Italians had to reinvent many commercial aids known to the Hellenistic world. Each civilization does not accept the entire cultural heritage of its predecessors and build on it; it accepts only what fits its own environment and its own way of living. Even our immense technical achievements, valuable as we may think them—and likely to bring great material benefits if adopted by the peoples we consider backward—may not be universally acceptable. History has yet to show to what extent Western technology will be accepted by a people like, say, the Hindus whose religion teaches a different view of the relation between the material and the spiritual and the relative importance to be assigned to this world and the hereafter. To receive and use what we are willing to transmit to them, perhaps their whole scheme of values must be altered, and their civilization may fall into decay rather than adopt such an alien scheme of values as ours.

❖ The rise and fall of civilizations

THEORIES OF HISTORY—SPENGLER AND TOYNBEE

In recent centuries the attention of the historian has been especially concentrated on the rise and fall of the many civilizations that have been known in the past. Why, he asks, has a civilization or a society known some sudden period of great creativeness, and why, then, does life seem to have gone from it and the cultural leadership of mankind, which it held for a brief season, to have passed from it into other hands? Many have been the answers propounded, but none has gained universal assent. It may indeed be that no answer can ever be given in material terms and that no explanation will ever be satisfactory because in fact there *is* no explanation of universal validity.

Two philosopher-historians of the twentieth century, Oswald Spengler and Arnold Toynbee, have especially concerned themselves with this problem. Spengler in *The Decline of the West* tried to show that the life of a society followed certain laws of growth and decay analogous to those found in the plant world. Each culture passes through stages that he calls spring, summer, and autumn. As it nears the end of its natural span, it passes over into its winter phase, which Spengler called "civilization," characterized by "Caesarism," the cult of the grandiose and huge, and the revival of dead religious forms that in the springtime of the culture had been filled with life. Clearly there is some empirical evidence for his theory, but Spengler scarcely made any effort to explain why cultures should behave in this manner— and, like so many historicists, he can justly be accused of frequently tailoring his evidence to fit his theory.

Arnold Toynbee, who, like Spengler, occasionally chooses his facts somewhat capriciously and has created a rather arbitrary list of what he thinks of as civilizations (in the normal use of that word), has tried to explain in *A Study of History* the arresting of progress as a failure to respond creatively to a challenge presented by certain difficulties that had to be faced by the society. Toynbee, of course, thus assumed that a society ought to evolve and make progress, and that if it failed to do so, it was in some way not fulfilling its proper tasks. It is doubtful if this is a fair assumption, as there is no inherent reason why a society should wish to progress and should not be simply content with its present way of life, as apparently the ancient Egyptians were. The desire to progress is a typically modern and Western ideal, and should not be assumed as part of the make-up of earlier peoples; though perhaps when we look back upon the history of mankind from our vantage point we are not unjustified in observing that they *did not* make progress, even if there is no reason why they should have wished to do so. The value of Toynbee's approach is a moral one. He wishes to remind us that change is always with us, whether we will it or not, and as human beings we have to learn how to deal with it by being willing and ready to change ourselves and our outlook in order to cope with the new situations that ever confront us. A few further remarks on Toynbee's theory of history will appear in Chapter 3, with special reference to the ancient civilizations that preceded the Greek.

THE NECESSITY FOR OBJECTIVITY AND IMAGINATION IN HISTORICAL STUDY

The moralist's approach to history, however, is not one to be wholeheartedly recommended. It obscures too much and it tends to prevent a true appreciation of the past. The student of history should strive to see each society and civilization first in its own terms, and should try to appreciate its outlook and attitude toward life, carefully refraining from value judgments based on experience in our own society—should see, for instance, whether to be a slave was the same thing in ancient Egypt, in fifth-century Athens or Sparta, and in the nineteenth-century southern states of America. The student of history might well conclude that it was a totally different thing to be the slave of an Egyptian Pharaoh in the days before individual freedom and self-realization had become an ideal.

Our student should not, like the nineteenth-century social philosopher and political scientist Karl Marx and his followers, overhastily transfer his knowledge of Western European class struggles into the ancient world and assume, for example, that the breakdown of Egyptian government after the Old Kingdom was in any way the equivalent of the French or Russian revolutions. He should try to avoid being taken in by the use of the same word to describe events that occurred in totally different cultural contexts. Such a procedure requires the exercise of historical imagination, and this can only be acquired by study, life experience, and hard effort. But the effort is well worthwhile, for it enlarges the horizons and develops that perspective which can be of the utmost value in ordinary affairs.

The student should also try to see the indebtedness of one civilization to another, trace the progress of cultural assimilation and transmission, and see how each people, as Goethe put it, has stood upon the shoulders of its predecessors. Such understanding may lead him to a sense of responsibility toward his own heritage from the past and to the determination to pass this heritage on to posterity substantially unimpaired and, if possible, increased.

The general form of this book has been

designed to show the separate characteristics of each society and civilization considered, and to reveal the cumulative heritage of mankind and how all the achievements of mankind in our society have their roots far back in the past—and also how impossible it would have been for us to have reached our present heights if the slow tedious work of developing intellectual and physical tools had not been done for us by those giants who went before us, who had so little to work with and such a long road to travel. When we tend to neglect this debt and overestimate ourselves and our achievements, it is perhaps wise for us to stop for a moment, think, and remember once more that "we are the heirs of all the ages."

Suggestions for further reading

Because of the wealth of material available in inexpensive paper-bound editions, the reading list at the end of each chapter is in two sections, paperbound books and hard-cover books. For the paperbound books, the only bibliographical information given is the name of the series. Many bookstores carry leading series in stock and if the volumes you want are not on their shelves will be glad to order them for you. If you are unable to order a book through your bookstore, you can find the publisher's address in a volume entitled *Paperbound Books in Print*, which is on hand at most bookstores and libraries. For the hard-cover editions, full bibliographical information is given to assist you in finding the book you want in the library or in ordering it from a bookstore.

PAPER-BOUND BOOKS

Bury, John Bagnell. *The Idea of Progress*. Dover. A classic study, first published in 1920, of how men have come to the belief that some progress is to be discerned in history. Mostly concerned with the idea of progress during the eighteenth-century Enlightenment, but including a good section on the nineteenth century.

Clough, Shepard B. *The Rise and Fall of Civilization*. Columbia University Press. Interesting and well-written interpretation, stressing heavily the material advancement of man and its influence on his culture.

Collingwood, R. G. *The Idea of History*. Galaxy. The author's contributions to the philosophy of history, as collected in this posthumous volume, have been much discussed and influential. Collingwood emphasizes the relativity of all historical judgments.

Fromm, Erich. *Marx's Concept of Man*. Ungar. In the process of analyzing several of Marx's lesser known works, the author explains much of Marx's attitude toward history.

Gustavson, Carl G. *A Preface to History*. McGraw-Hill. Interesting introduction to the study of history, its meaning and purpose.

Hegel, G. W. F. *Lectures on the Philosophy of History*, trans. from the German by J. Sibree. Dover. Seminal lectures by the early nineteenth-century German idealist philosopher, virtually the founder of the modern philosophy of history. The least formidable of Hegel's writings for the beginner. Examples are stimulating and interesting.

Hughes, H. Stuart. *Oswald Spengler: A Critical Estimate*. Scribner. Useful digest of Spengler's *The Decline of the West* (2 vols. New York: Alfred A. Knopf, Inc., 1945). Good introduction to Spengler's theories.

Löwith, Karl. *Meaning in History: the Theological Implications of the Philosophy of History*. Phoenix. Interesting and sometimes profound study, first published in 1949, of what some influential writers, from St. Augustine to Marx, have thought about history and its meaning.

Muller, Herbert J. *The Uses of the Past*. Mentor and Galaxy. A series of brief, sympathetic studies of several past societies and their enduring achievements. Examples chosen to illustrate differences between past civilizations and the modern West. Provocative on the issue of what may really be learned from the past. See also Muller's *The Loom of History* (Mentor).

Popper, Karl R. *The Open Society and Its Enemies*. 2 vols. Torchbooks. Severe but enlightening criticism of historicism, especially hard on Plato and Hegel. First volume is called *The Spell of Plato*, the second, *The Rise of Oracular Philosophy*, two suggestive titles which accurately reveal the author's point of view. Analysis of Marx and Marxism is especially interesting.

Stern, Fritz, ed. *The Varieties of History: from Voltaire to the Present*. Meridian. Useful anthology of historical writing from earliest examples to the present.

Toynbee, Arnold. *A Study of History*. Galaxy. The

ten volumes of Toynbee's work are now appearing in paper-bound editions, and are preferable to the hard-cover abridgment by D. C. Somervell (vols. I–VI and vols. VII–X, New York: Oxford University Press, 1947, 1957) since the latter, though honest and careful, is sometimes misleading because it omits many illustrations of Toynbee's theory. The theory of challenge and response appears in vol. I, but vol. IV will probably be found of most general interest, as Toynbee is at his best when he is considering the decline of civilizations and is trying to find reasons for it.

HARD-COVER BOOKS

Bloch, Marc. *The Historian's Craft.* New York: Alfred A. Knopf, Inc., 1953. Unfinished work by a leading French historian killed in World War II. Thoughtful consideration of the tasks of a historian, especially useful for its evaluation of the different kinds of historical sources.

Carr, Edward Hallett. *What is History?* New York: Alfred A. Knopf, Inc., 1962. Important and stimulating series of lectures, entertaining as well as instructive, on the tasks of the historian and the different viewpoints held on such matters as historical causation, the idea of progress, and the like. This book and that of Bloch are two of the most useful books on the subject as introductions for the would-be historian and the student.

Einstein, Lewis. *Historical Change.* Cambridge, England: Cambridge University Press, 1946. Stimulating discussion of how changes have come about in history. Written under the influence of World War II, but much is still extremely relevant.

Highet, Gilbert. *The Migration of Ideas.* New York: Oxford University Press, 1954. Stimulating little book on how culture and ideas are diffused, with thought-provoking illustrations from all periods of history.

Namier, Lewis B. *Avenues of History.* New York: The Macmillan Company, 1952. Influential British historian's essays on his specialty. First essay especially valuable on the task of the historian and the functions of historical study.

TWO

Prehistoric Man

❖ Difficulties of studying prehistory

It is now believed that a creature recognizable as man has walked the earth for more than half a million years. He has not always lived in the same areas of the earth, for at different times the movements of glaciers and changes of climate have made some regions uninhabitable. But at no time in the last half million years was the whole earth uninhabitable, and immense periods of time have separated the great glacial epochs from each other. Yet it is, at the most, ten thousand—probably not more than eight thousand—years ago that man first began to grow his own food and domesticate the useful animals.

This presents to us at once the great question—Why so long? Could prehistoric man not have taken this supreme step earlier, and started on the road to civilization many thousands of years before 8000 B.C.?

To this fundamental question it is impossible to give an answer. The truth is that we know very little indeed about prehistoric man. The unremitting labors of archaeologists and anthropologists, fruitful though these have been, have only scratched the surface of our almost total ignorance. Besides, no two experts are ever in agreement on all points in their interpretation of the meager data available.

It is necessary to stress this point because all that will be said in this chapter is still in the realm of opinion. It is possible that in two hundred years none of it will be acceptable to our less ignorant descendants. No one should think

that prehistory or even ancient history stands still. On the contrary, the older the history, the more it can gain from archaeology and from the discovery and re-interpretation of documents and inscriptions unknown or neglected before. Every discovery of a new fossil of early man is important; every discovery of a cave, every excavation of an early camp site, may alter in fundamental points some of our reconstructed history of early man—whereas even the discovery of a hitherto unknown manuscript or a painting of Leonardo da Vinci would not alter in any important respect our knowledge of the general history of the Italian Renaissance.

❖ The first beginnings of man

THE EVOLUTION OF MAN AS A SPECIES

The evolutionary theory of the origin of man has been greatly modified since Darwin first propounded it in crude form in the middle of the nineteenth century. There are still many inconvenient facts which seem very difficult to explain on the basis of natural selection; and the entire theory, if viewed dispassionately, often seems to a layman so extraordinarily *unlikely* as an explanation of how the present bewildering diversity of natural phenomena, including human beings, did evolve, as to suggest a willful perversity in present-day men. In this age, on principle, we are inclined to prefer even the most far-fetched of material explanations to the possibility of any kind of divine guidance or intervention, or the fulfillment of any divine purpose. Chance and probability appear to us so much more scientific, and therefore more credible, than a superhuman power and wisdom which could *direct* the course of evolution. This much, however, may be said for the currently fashionable neo-Darwinian theory—it cannot be disproved, and it explains reasonably well what we know of early man and of his biological inheritance from the animal world. Whether it is likely to be true can only be left to the judgment of the individual.

According to this theory, those species of living organisms which were best fitted to survive in their environment did survive, and were gradually modified in form by the process of mutation, a process which can be observed in the laboratory in the case of certain animals. The ancestors of man were not those most specialized and suitable for a particular environment. On the contrary, they were more "generalized" and adaptable. From time to time new mutations appeared in the species, and those creatures that could survive best in a changed environment did so, and propagated, while the older, less adaptable species died out. The huge animals became overspecialized and incapable of adaptation, perhaps in a modified environment, and so became extinct; while the smaller, unspecialized creatures, forced to adapt themselves or perish, developed mutations with survival value. Thus, it is suggested, the ancestors of man first came on to dry land from the ocean, lived for countless aeons in trees, and at last descended to the earth and began to walk upright, in the process increasing their brain capacity. So we arrive at the first real toolmaking men, of whom the oldest specimen known to us is *Zinjanthropus*, a hominid from central Africa.

EVIDENCE FOR THE ACTIVITIES OF EARLY MAN

Before we deal with the early men known to us from archaeology it should be stated clearly that it is not permissible to use evidence from people who are living today under primitive conditions and assume at once that they are living in the same way as our ancestors of the

Old Stone age. It is not impossible that these contemporary "primitive" men, though they now use tools recognizably similar to those discovered in ancient deposits, have lost certain knowledge their ancestors once possessed. Their culture would then represent a decline from some higher stage. On the other hand, they may have made some slight progress in ten thousand years, though not as much as civilized man. We can only use our knowledge of these contemporaries of ours to create an imaginative picture of what stone age men were like, and of the life they lived. But it remains an imaginative picture, which may or may not be true to reality, and it cannot be used as evidence in any way the equal of the inferences we may make from the actual remains discovered by archaeologists.

We have just said that the archaeologist has to make inferences. By this it is meant that he unearths objects, not written records; and the objects tell no clear story by themselves. We have before us, say, a dead body painted with ocher in a corner of a cave, and there are tools beside the body, and perhaps food. We infer some kind of primitive religion from the juxtaposition of these objects, but we cannot be certain of the existence of this religion. It has been suggested that such finds prove the existence of a belief in a future life, in which the soul is supposed to return to earth to use the tools he used once in life and to eat the food left for him; or, alternatively, that he needs these things for his use in a future life. But such a conclusion as this can never be proved true, and, as a result, archaeologists are frequently at odds with each other, and wide agreement is rare. Perhaps the tools were considered to be a part of the man's personality; perhaps they were believed to bring bad luck upon anyone who used them after he was dead. The food might be a simple remnant of a funeral feast partaken of by the survivors. The ocher may have been a primitive cosmetic, and the smearing of the corpse a ceremony of no more significance than the attentions lavished upon the American dead by "morticians" in the twentieth century. The objects alone tell us little beyond the fact that such or such objects were in use. All the rest is inference.

As if it were not unfortunate enough for

the historian to be compelled to treat with skepticism all conclusions drawn from his knowledge of the present-day world, the simple material evidence provided by archaeological finds must be interpreted for him by archaeologists and anthropologists who differ greatly among themselves. And with good reason, for these men have at their disposal only random finds—an infinitesimal percentage of the human beings who lived and died in the ancient times they are studying. Seldom indeed does an anthropologist have even a full skeleton at his disposal. He may have a jawbone and a thighbone, found in the same area, but he must then decide if they belong together. One very famous "man," endowed with a name, about whom *Life* magazine built a highly circumstantial story, complete with pictures, in 1955, was nothing but an unusual jawbone that could not belong to any known human species. Through the science of comparative anatomy an entire organism was imagined into which the jaw could fit. Thus "Kanam" man came into existence, and was duly photographed by *Life*'s camermen. The information that follows should therefore be regarded only as a summary of present archaeological opinion, fragmentary and incomplete, quite certain to be considerably modified and added to as more discoveries are made.

Until comparatively recently the oldest known human remains were those of a number of *Pithecanthropi* (ape-men), found in Java. But excavations of recent years have tended to show that Africa, not Asia, was the cradle of the human race, and there have been numerous finds of creatures that are close to the dividing line between men and apes, about which there will surely be controversy for many years to come.[1] The two main groups of East Asian

Pithecanthropi, formerly regarded as belonging to different species (Java man and Peking man) are now considered to be of the same species, and of much the same age, though more information is available about the life habits of the latter. They were toolmakers, used fire (perhaps, but not certainly, for cooking), and probably ate the marrow of their fellow men. Some anthropologists claim that Peking man shows certain physical characteristics of later Mongolian peoples; others believe that the Australian aborigines are descended from Java man. Still others assert that ancient men found in Rhodesia, more recent than Java or Peking men, are the ancestors of the South African Bushman. Most anthropologists, however, fight shy of this type of theory, and the majority do not even recognize the better known Neanderthal man as the direct ancestor of any men of the present day. Some very ancient skulls from England and France (Swanscombe and Fontchévade) appear to resemble those of modern men more than does that of Neanderthal man, giving rise to a theory that the *Homo sapiens* of modern times has a far more ancient ancestry than had hitherto been supposed. As a further illustration of the difficulties of attaining certainty in this disputed field, actual fakes of ancient men have been perpetrated and, for periods of time, accepted as genuine. Such was "Piltdown man," accepted by most anthropologists, though not by all, for several decades, until a more refined technique of chemical analysis revealed the fraud as recently as 1953.

Neanderthal man (from 150,000 B.C. onward) is known to archaeologists from a considerable number of finds, the first of which was in the Neander gorge near Dusseldorf, Germany, in 1856. Many subsequent finds have

[1] The anatomical dividing line between man and ape will probably always be a matter for dispute. Although recent investigations of chimpanzees have shown that these animals make use of some aids to food gathering that may be thought of as tools, the use of tools in general, and above all their improvement in the light of experience, is pre-eminently a human activity, and the easiest way of determining whether fossilized primates were indeed men and not animals is by determining if they used tools. When no tools can be associated with a particular fossil, a study of the anatomical structure can provide information, such as the capacity of the brain case, the size and massiveness of the jaw, whether the creature walked upright, and similar important details that may in total amount to a strong probability that it was a man and not an animal. *Pithecanthropus erectus* or Java man has been classified as a man although no tools are associated with him. But obviously a man can better be judged by his artifacts than by his physical structure.

provided us with a considerable amount of information about this type of man, who has been found also in North Africa and southwestern Asia, and probably survived to as late as 40,000 B.C. The brain capacity of Neanderthal men comes close to that of modern men, though in other respects they resemble the Asiatic *Pithecanthropi* more than they resemble *Homo sapiens*. Their skulls were large, thick walled, and low vaulted, with huge brow ridges, a broad nose, massive chinless jaws, and large teeth. Clumsy legs and arms suggest a not fully upright posture—not unlike the general picture of cave men as popularized in so many comic strips.

Neanderthal men used flaked tools, scrapers, and small hand axes, seeming especially to favor the triangular or heart-shaped forms. Their tools were strictly utilitarian and, unlike the tools of their successors, show no signs of having been modeled with any aesthetic purpose in view. They made very little use of bone or antler, but in their successful hunting, which enabled their species to survive, they probably used wooden spears, stone balls, and pit traps to destroy their prey. In spite of his failure to make any significant innovations in tool technique, Neanderthal man for the first time, as far as we know, paid considerable attention to the burial of his dead. Corpses have been discovered on which elaborate care was expended. Tools and funeral offerings were found with them, and the bodies in some instances were painted with red ocher. A Neanderthaloid child was buried in Siberia together with horns from mountain goats, which appear to have been placed upright around the corpse. Such practices clearly indicate the growth of ceremonial customs and rituals of the kind we associate with religion.

The period when Neanderthal man roamed the earth is generally called the Lower Paleolithic age—lower because in fossil deposits the lower remains are earlier, and Paleolithic (Old Stone) because all implements were made of either bone or stone. The classification by implements has become conventional, but it is not satisfactory unless one wishes to speak only of the tools used. The development in tools that took place from the Paleolithic to the Neolithic (New Stone) age was far less important than the epoch-making change from food gathering to food producing which characterized these periods.

The whole of the Lower Paleolithic period is placed within the geological age known as the Pleistocene. Most authorities recognize four glaciations for Europe and America during this time. The glaciers stretched down as far south as France, making the climate within their range bitterly cold. When they receded, the climate was as warm as, or perhaps even warmer than, now. It is possible that even at the present time we are in an interglacial period, since it is only about 50,000 years since the last glaciers (Würm glaciation) began to recede, not a long time for an interglacial period. The glaciers had perhaps not receded to their present position until almost the end of the Upper Paleolithic age.

❖ **Upper Paleolithic period**

During the course of the Würm glaciation *Homo sapiens*, anatomically the same as present-day man, suddenly appeared in great numbers; and it may be assumed that not very long afterward mankind became differentiated into the races we know today, the Caucasoid, Negroid, Mongoloid, and their subdivisions. From the evidence at present available these "modern" men first appeared in western Asia, especially in Palestine, and from there spread to Europe, where so many sites have been uncovered that it is possible to distinguish a number of successive cultural periods, all marked by the appearance of the superior stone knives characteristic of the Upper Paleolithic age everywhere. Greatest of these cultures was the so-called Magdalenian (from about 15,000 to perhaps as late as 8,000 B.C.), which produced the most beautiful of the polychrome paintings of southern France and northern Spain.

Controversy has raged fiercely about these paintings, which are mostly of animals, ever since they were first discovered, and they were pronounced fakes by the pundits of the late nineteenth century. Although no one now regards them as anything but genuine, there are many other problems connected with them. Paintings were sometimes superimposed one upon another; they are often on the walls near the roof of the caves. They obviously were not made to be admired by human beings. How did the artists obtain enough light to be able to make their paintings in dim, almost inaccessible corners? No primitive torch could give our own artists enough light to duplicate them, even if they could manage, as these early artists manifestly could, to do without living models. There are paintings which are so far from the ground that elaborate scaffolding must have been erected, since the floor does not seem to have sunk since Paleolithic times.

All Upper Paleolithic peoples lived primarily by hunting, and they devoted far more inventiveness to it than did earlier peoples. They made extensive use of bone and antler, from which they fashioned barbed spears, fish gorgets and harpoons with detachable heads and barbs like curved teeth (Magdalenian). From stone they made chisels, gouges, and awls, which could be used to work the bone and for carving and engraving. The tools themselves were often made in an artistic manner. The Magdalenian peoples used an eyed needle made of bone. Several of these peoples made the first mechanical aids to hunting, a spear thrower and the bow and arrow, both of which permitted hunting from a distance, thus revolutionizing their way of life.

But more revolutionary still were the first man-made houses, which date from the Upper Paleolithic period and probably belonged to mammoth hunters of the Gravettian culture in Czechoslovakia, Russia, and Siberia, where suitable natural caves were scarce. The houses so far excavated appear to have been each used by several families. One was oval in shape, measuring about 40 feet in length with five hearths. It is not known what was used for roofing material, if anything, possibly skins weighed down by branches much like a tent. Another house was surrounded by a wide circular wall made of limestone and clay. In Czechoslovakia coal, which was close to the surface in that area, was already in use for fuel. Other houses of the same period were made by digging a kind of cellar and apparently using logs for the roof and as support for the sides.

❖ **Mesolithic period, *ca.* 8000 B.C.**

The period following the decline of the great ages of cave painting but preceding the Neolithic Revolution is called the Mesolithic age. In many respects this is an exceptionally interesting epoch. The Würm glaciation had come to an end, and the more favorable climatic conditions made for easier living. *Homo sapiens* was slowly peopling the earth, and a great variety of new occupations became possible, notably those connected with the sea. As far as can be determined at the present time, the two major centers of Mesolithic culture were in the lands to the east of the Mediterranean, especially Palestine (Natufian culture), and in the northern plains of Europe (Maglemosian culture). Southern Europe appears to have contributed little that was new in this period.

The Natufian culture appears to have been originally based on hunting. But as time went on the Natufians, as is evident from their sickles and reaping knives, began to harvest natural grasses that grew in the area. No evidence as yet suggests that these grasses were planted or that grain was ever stored. But pestles and mortars, and querns (the Mexican *metate*) have been found in which the grain was pounded and beaten. Both the Natufians and Maglemosians domesticated the dog, the first animal known to have been tamed as a helper of man. Probably the first dogs were scavengers around the Mesolithic settlements, and were later utilized in the hunt.

The Natufian, like other Mesolithic cultures, is marked by the wide use of microliths, small sharpened stones used with weapons such as spearheads and reed arrows. The blades of Natufian bone sickles contained several such microliths set in grooves in the bone. Late

Natufian culture, which shades over into the Neolithic, has been brought to light in the successive deposits of the ancient "city" of Jericho, built around an important desert oasis. Here at one period the people lived in round huts with sunken floors and walls built of brick, the whole surrounded by a stone wall with inner stairways and round towers obviously used for defensive purposes—even though here as elsewhere there is very little evidence for much warfare either in Mesolithic or Neolithic times. At a later stage the houses were made up of rectangular rooms set around a courtyard, and it is estimated that Jericho may have had a population as large as 3,000. There is some evidence that the Natufian villages also kept herds of goats, in which case it is likely that wild goats were the second species of animal to be domesticated. The Jericho area, indeed, is certainly one of the centers where the Neolithic Revolution began, though whether it holds absolute priority in time has yet to be determined.

The Maglemosian culture (Denmark) in northern Europe was a hunting culture like its predecessors, but far more use was made of maritime resources, possibly because in the changed climate hunting in the forests had become more difficult. It is evident that large numbers of these Mesolithic men lived by fishing as well as by hunting. The use of microliths (very small stones) for hafting axes and similar tools as well as for harpoon barbs is well authenticated, and the hafted axes must have been valuable for the necessary work of felling the forests. Hard igneous rocks were worked for the first time to obtain sharp points and cutting edges. Far more tools were now made of bone and antler, including improved fish spears and harpoons and fishhooks not too different from those used today. The Maglemosian peoples also used fish nets and fish traps, and some of their neighbors were already using a sleigh. But as yet there is no evidence to show that this Mesolithic culture of the Maglemosians developed into the Neolithic. The Neolithic Revolution arrived in these hunting areas of northern Europe several millenniums after it had been spread throughout much of the East.

❖ **The Neolithic Revolution**

BEGINNINGS OF AGRICULTURE

We now come to what is perhaps the most important revolution in history. It may be truly called a revolution because it changed the way of life of the peoples of the world in a fundamental manner, making possible all subsequent civilizations. Yet, as will be recognized from our account of the Mesolithic, it was not truly a sudden change but grew gradually out of the practices of those peoples who had settled down in communities even before they had learned to plant and harvest crops.

When man lived by food gathering and hunting, he was dependent upon his environment. His sole influence upon this environment consisted in his depredations. He could not repair any damage he did to it; his only remedy was to move away. In this respect his life was like that of the animals. If it were not for his art, we should be tempted to say that he was still only one of the animals, less specialized and able to make use of tools beyond their capacity but not yet fully able to use his superior mind to take control of his environment. Control became possible with the conscious growing of plants.

It requires acute observation to see *how* a plant grows, to perceive the sequence of cause and effect between the seed and the plant. Then it requires experiment to take a seed, to plant it, and at last to see it grow, fulfilling the presumption of the experiment. This was the act of someone we may legitimately think of as the first scientist, some nameless leader. The Neolithic Revolution thus was a social and intellectual revolution rather than a technical one. Man could have continued, as certain tribes still existing today have continued, to make his living only by food gathering. But he did not. For hundreds of thousands of years he had lived in the same old way, never settling down permanently, building no cities, producing no surplus for a leisured population. Now all these activities became possible.

DIFFUSION OF THE NEOLITHIC REVOLUTION

From the evidence at present available, it seems likely that the Revolution spread by diffusion from its original center in the Near East, being first taken up by local communities and gradually penetrating further afield, reaching parts of eastern Europe soon after 5000 B.C. and Britain about 3000 B.C. In some parts of Europe the older food-gathering, hunting culture persisted until much later times.

The Jericho culture, already mentioned, is at present the earliest known Neolithic culture (about 7000 B.C.). Two other centers, the Belt Cave culture in Iran just south of the Caspian Sea and the Jarmo culture near the source of the Tigris in the Kurdish hills, appear to have originated somewhat later than Jericho. However, these centers had become full Neolithic cultures by 6000 B.C., with at first domesticated sheep and goats and no evidence of agriculture, then shortly afterward pigs and cows and a wide range of domesticated plants including wheat and barley. The Belt Cave peoples lived in two large caves, whereas the Jarmo and Jericho peoples lived in substantial villages. These three centers are the major sites excavated so far, and it seems extremely likely that others will be found in this general area where it appears most probable that the Neolithic Revolution originated.

Fired pottery became a widespread industry throughout the Asiatic and later the Egyptian Neolithic areas. Once the technique had been invented the potters quickly began to improve the form of their wares and to paint and decorate them. It is generally believed that women were the first potters and during the later stages of the Neolithic period were the bearers of such artistic traditions as there were. There is no certain evidence of the use of a potter's wheel until several millenniums later; but some mechanical method of turning the pottery while it was being molded was probably in use. The great art of the Upper Paleolithic was never repeated. Only in the production of exceptionally beautiful battle axes, some of them decorated, and in the painting of pottery, usually in abstract and geometrical patterns, did Neolithic man display much artistry.

Textile weaving and basketry were the new crafts of this age. Rope nets had long been used for fishing, but weaving was new and required the prior invention of spinning. In most of the earlier examples of weaving, flax was used as the raw material, leading in dynastic Egypt to the production of beautiful linen garments. Basketry, which made use of whatever local materials were available, appeared even before Neolithic times, but was greatly developed during this age when the need arose for containers for the new farming life. Tools were not greatly changed except for the addition of reaping knives, sickles, and hoes. The digging stick was used for preparing the ground. The ox-drawn wooden plow appeared at least as early as 3000 B.C. in Mesopotamia, in Egypt, and probably

Megaliths at Carnac (Brittany). Note the size of the stones in relation to the size of the man in the left foreground. (COURTESY AMERICAN MUSEUM OF NATURAL HISTORY)

Aerial view of Stonehenge (England). Note how this view emphasizes the fact that these megaliths make up a temple. Beneath the stones at the outer edge of the circle are remains of burials. (COURTESY BRITISH INFORMATION SERVICES)

in India, where it is mentioned in written records. None have survived from an earlier date than this.

While bronze was coming into use and written records were for the first time being produced in Mesopotamia, the Neolithic Revolution was gradually being diffused throughout Europe, most of which remained Neolithic (that is, without metal and without written records) for several millenniums more.

One feature of the Late Neolithic age in Europe has given rise to controversy at least since the twelfth century A.D., though recent research with scientific techniques has given us new clues. Any visitor to Brittany, Wales, or Salisbury Plain in England is sure to have seen menhirs, large single pillars of stone, and the circles of such stones, which are called cromlechs. Stone slabs or blocks, with other slabs serving as a roof, making a kind of chamber of stones, are not uncommon; these are known as dolmens. The controversy has concerned the purpose of these monuments (which are collectively called megaliths, "large stones"), and most authorities agree that the stones are in

some way connected with the very ancient and natural religion of sun worship.

By far the most impressive of all the Neolithic monuments is Stonehenge on Salisbury Plain in England. This is a circle of megaliths, and while it is clearly an ancient temple, recent research suggests also that the stones were arranged in such a way as to form the first known calendar. Close to Stonehenge are burial pits which probably antedate the stone circle itself. The bodies were cremated and the remains buried in these pits.

SIGNIFICANCE OF THE NEOLITHIC REVOLUTION

It will by this time be clear that the Neolithic Revolution was perhaps the most important event in the history of man. The next revolution of comparable importance took place in the nineteenth century, when man first began to use extensively the power of machinery rather than the labor of his own hands and back. From Neolithic times to the Industrial Revolution a condition of universal plenty was never possible, even if man had been able to achieve the social organization required. Every human being can do only a limited amount of work himself in a day. He can produce only a limited surplus, which cannot keep any very large number of people fed and clothed who are not themselves engaged in actual production. The leisured classes in such circumstances must always be strictly limited in number. Improvement in transportation and organization can distribute very widely the surplus of the many producers. But this total surplus can never be very great. This inconvenient fact has conditioned all civilization between the Neolithic and Industrial revolutions. A small class of leisured people, with their needs and even luxuries provided for, have been the intellectual and cultural leaders in civilization. In our own times, with machines capable of performing so many tasks formerly done by human energy, plenty for all has at last and for the first time become theoretically possible.

Before the Neolithic Revolution man was condemned to live from hand to mouth. He had no means for preserving his food, which had to be killed and eaten as he needed it. He took whatever crops were provided for him by his environment. With the Neolithic Revolution it was possible for some favored people to be spared the manual labor of farming because each farmer could now produce a small surplus over and above his immediate needs, and this could be used for the support of nonmanual workers. Moreover, it was possible even for the farmer himself to spend at least some of his time in thinking and in cultural activities not immediately connected with his bodily sustenance. Men were now free to turn their attention toward new goals—the better organization of production, the improvement of their social order, and the increase of their technical knowledge, which would in time be used for the production of a new range of materials and manufactures.

❖ **The beginnings of metallurgy**

Traditionally three metals have given their names to successive ages in history—the Copper (Chalcolithic), the Bronze, and the Iron ages. With these we leave the Paleolithic and Neolithic ages behind us. But it should be recognized that metal tools and weapons, which were much more expensive, did not at once replace stone tools. All were used for special purposes, and not until iron metallurgy, making use of a cheap and plentiful raw material, had become extremely widespread did the use of stone tools die out.

Recent investigations have made a convincing case both for the areas where the different phases of metallurgy began and the means by which the necessary discoveries were probably made. Copper is in short supply in the river valleys, which are the sites of the great early civilizations. But it was readily available in immediately usable form from the mountains of Anatolia eastward into Iran. By the middle of the fourth millennium B.C. copper tools were known, hammered out of raw copper by stone tools. In order to smelt copper a temperature of slightly over 1000 degrees centigrade is necessary. Such a temperature cannot be obtained in a camp fire or even an ordinary charcoal pot. But the heat in a pottery kiln certainly exceeds this figure, and it seems extremely likely that copper would at some time be dropped into such a kiln, with the result that it would be smelted and become much more amenable to hammering and molding into tools.

It seems likely that the discovery of bronze was due to the fortuitous fact that the copper obtained by the city-states of Sumer from Oman on the Persian Gulf contained as much as 14 per cent tin. If such copper ore was smelted in a kiln, bronze would be the result, and though for many years tin, mostly obtained later from cassiterite, was probably not recognized as the necessary component for the bronze alloy, in due time major efforts were made to discover cassiterite, and its sources were mined on behalf of the Bronze age peoples.

Ancient tradition credits the Hittites with the discovery of iron smelting, and archaeology suggests that the metal was first smelted in the Hittite homeland of Anatolia. Elsewhere meteoric iron was used when available long before smelting. But early in the second millennium B.C. the Hittites had learned its secret and established a tight monopoly both over the process and over the export of iron products. Iron, however, has no advantages over bronze until it has been smelted at higher temperatures than copper and bronze, and carbonized. Moreover, it is a longer process, requiring heating and reheating as well as hammering and beating. The "steeling" of iron can be achieved in a charcoal fire by the use of a blast of air of a certain strength; it can also be achieved by the use of a wooden pole charred by immersion in a fire. Both of these processes could be discovered by chance and repeated at will once the cause and effect sequence was observed, as long as an efficient bellows was also available (blowpipes were used earlier) to raise the heat of the charcoal fire.

But it is not surprising that it took several centuries before the technique was mastered, and another two or three before the secrets were learned outside its country of origin. But iron making spread eventually throughout Europe. The Peoples of the Sea who invaded Egypt in the time of Rameses III possessed it. So did the Philistines on their arrival in Palestine. So also did the Dorians who destroyed the Bronze age civilization of Mycenae. The accessibility of iron ores and their cheapness eventually brought the Bronze age to an end, giving place to the Iron age, which has lasted until our own century.

Suggestions for further reading

PAPER-BOUND BOOKS

Childe, V. Gordon. *Man Makes Himself*. Mentor. Written as long ago as 1936, this little book by a pioneer archaeologist and prehistorian is still useful, though the information in it needs to be supplemented from other sources.

Clark, Grahame. *World Prehistory: An Outline*. Cambridge University Press. Up-to-date (1961) survey in brief compass; little interpretation.

Cleator, P. E. *Lost Languages*. Mentor. Concerned with the origin and development of writing and language, containing many useful illustrations.

Heizer, Robert, ed. *Man's Discovery of His Past: Literary Landmarks in Archaeology*. Spectrum. Interesting collection of readings from leading archaeologists.

Kuhn, Herbert. *On the Track of Prehistoric Man*. Vintage. Devoted entirely to cave art, this translation from the German provides an excellent picture of what is to be found in the dif-

ferent caves and gives some of the theories put forward to explain the paintings, drawings, and sculptures.

Laming, Annette. *Lascaux: Paintings and Engravings*. Penguin. Illustrated booklet giving an account of prehistoric cave paintings in southern France.

Leakey, L. S. B. *Adam's Ancestors: The Evolution of Man and His Culture*. Torchbooks. By the archaeologist who excavated most of the recent sites on the African continent. Especially good on the way prehistoric man made his stone tools, but more limited in scope than Clark.

Macgowan, Kenneth, and Hester, Joseph A., Jr. *Early Man in the New World*. Anchor.

Mongait, A. L. *Archaeology in the U.S.S.R.* Penguin. Informative on the recent discoveries in European and Asiatic Russia which have added much to our knowledge of prehistoric man, especially in Upper Paleolithic times.

Tax, Sol, ed. *Anthropology Today*. Phoenix. Useful collection of readings from anthropologists.

Wendt, Herbert. *In Search of Adam*. Collier. Sprightly account of the progress of archaeology and its successes and failures.

Woolley, Leonard. *Digging Up the Past*. Penguin. Useful introduction to the work of archaeologists.

HARD-COVER BOOKS

Ceram, C. W. *Gods, Graves and Scholars*. New York: Alfred A. Knopf, Inc., 1951. Ever popular work on the achievement of archaeologists.

Coon, Carleton S. *The Story of Man: From the First Human to Primitive Culture and Beyond*, 2d ed. rev. New York: Alfred A. Knopf, Inc., 1962. An anthropologist's account of early man and his society. One of the best in the field, solidly based on our knowledge of the prehistoric finds, but not free from illegitimate inferences from our knowledge of present-day "primitive" man.

Hawkes, Jacquetta, and Woolley, Leonard. *Prehistory and the Beginnings of Civilization*, vol. I of the UNESCO History of Mankind. New York: Harper & Row, Publishers, 1963. The well-written summary of present knowledge of prehistoric man by Jacquetta Hawkes, which occupies the first half of this book, is made even more valuable by the extensive comments in the notes by scholars who differ with the author in specific areas and draw attention to theories and explanations other than those which appear in the text.

II · THE ANCIENT WORLD

The Pyramids at Gizeh at the time of the inundation of the Nile. (PHOTO BY FUZANI)

View of the Parthenon on the Acropolis at Athens.

The Colosseum, a Roman amphitheatre, constructed by the first two Flavian emperors.

Chronological Chart

THE ANCIENT WORLD

Egypt	Mesopotamia	Hebrews	Greeks	Romans	Century
Neolithic age	Neolithic age				6000–3000 B.C.
Old Kingdom	Sumerian cities		Bronze Age in Crete		3000
Middle Kingdom	Amorite conquest of Babylonia	Wanderings of Patriarchs (?)	Height of Minoan civilization	Early invasions of Italy by Indo-Europeans	2000
Hyksos invasion and conquest	Hammurabi's Code				1800
	Kassite rule of Babylonia	Family of Jacob migrates to Egypt (?)			1700
			Mycenaean civilization		1600
Establishment of New Kingdom (1580)					1500
Akhenaton (1377–1360)			Conquest of Crete by Mycenaeans		1400
Rameses II (1301–1234)		Exodus of Israelites (?)			1300
		Era of Judges (1225–1020)	Dorian invasions (1200–1000)		1200
Rameses III (1198–1167)			Fall of Troy (ca. 1184)		1100
		Saul (1020–1004) David (1004–965)	Greek settlements in Asia Minor	Terramare peoples in Italy	1000
		Division of Kingdom of Israel (926)		Etruscans in Italy	900
	Assyrian conquest of Babylon (910)		Homeric poems (850)		800
			Great Age of Miletus (750–550)	Traditional date of founding of Rome (753)	
		Samaria conquered by Assyrians (721)			700

Egypt	Mesopotamia	Hebrews	Greeks	Romans	Century
	Height of Assyrian Empire			Etruscan rule in Rome (616–509)	
Conquest by Assyria (670)			Draconian Code (Athens–621)		
	Fall of Assyria (606)	Conquest of Judea by Nebuchadnezzar (586)			
	Cyrus, King of Medes, later of Persians (549–530)	Exile in Babylon (586–538)	Lycurgan reforms (Sparta–ca. 610)	Establishment of Roman Republic (509)	600 / 500
Conquest by Persia (525)					
	Darius I (522–486)				
	Alexander the Great (336–323)	Return to Jerusalem (538)	Persian invasions (490–479)	Rome as leader of Latin League (490–430)	400
Conquest by Alexander (332)		Conquest by Alexander (332)	Peloponnesian War (431–404)		
Ptolemy I (323–283)					
	Conquest by Alexander (332)			Samnite Wars (327–290)	300
	Seleucus I (305-280)			Second Punic War (218–201)	200
		Conquest by Antiochus III (198)			
		Revolt of Maccabees (167)	Macedonia becomes Roman province—Greece under Roman rule (146)		
Caesar in Egypt (48–47)				First Triumvirate (60)	100
	Reorganization of Asia by Pompey (66–62)	Conquest by Pompey (63)		Second Triumvirate (43)	
				Reign of Augustus (31 B.C.–A.D. 14)	
Death of Cleopatra (30)					0 B.C. A.D. 0
		Revolt of Judea and fall of Jerusalem (66–70)		Reign of Vespasian (69–79)	
. . . . . Part of Roman Empire					100

THREE

The Heritage of the Ancient Near East

❖ **Egypt**

THE OLD KINGDOM (*ca.* 3000–2200 B.C.)

It has already been indicated in the last chapter that the Neolithic Revolution first occurred in western Asia. The earliest Neolithic communities known to us are to be found there. It is, however, in Mesopotamia that we can first justly speak of civilization, with the beginnings of that kind of culture that can grow only in cities, where there is enough labor available for specialization and enough leisure for strictly cultural pursuits. We should therefore properly start this history of civilization by dealing with the urban culture of Mesopotamia and the city-states that fostered it.

Yet in a chapter to be devoted mainly to the achievements of three peoples—the Egyptians, the peoples of Mesopotamia, and the Hebrews—the latter two have such a clear connection that it seems preferable to study Egypt first, in spite of the fact that cultural diffusion, as far as it can be traced, is from Mesopotamia to Egypt rather than the other way round, and Mesopotamia rather than Egypt may more justly be looked upon as the "cradle of civilization."

Egypt was undoubtedly one of the great civilizations of the world, if only because it persisted so long. At least 2,500 years separate the First Dynasty of Egypt from its inglorious end at the hands of the conquering Persians in 525 B.C. During the whole of that period there was little outward change. The fundamental concepts which underlie the Egyptian outlook, as it is reflected in its institutions and way of life, persist throughout the period. It takes a close and discerning eye to detect those changes that were occurring under the surface, a change from a fundamental optimism to a resigned pessimism, from a concern with this life to an overwhelming concern with the hereafter, from the unquestioned supremacy of the Pharaoh as king-god to a rule by the Pharaoh as titular god by courtesy of an all-powerful priesthood.

These changes can be only briefly indicated in a single chapter devoted to the pre-Greek world.

Ancient Egypt is worth studying for its own sake, in part because of its strangeness. Its fundamental ideas, though alien to ours, nevertheless served to give it a stability our own dynamic Western civilization has hitherto lacked. It is worth studying not because it bequeathed so much to later civilizations but precisely because it did not. The Hebrews derived their cultural heritage almost entirely from the Mesopotamian civilization. They answered questions propounded by the Mesopotamian peoples in a manner which has been found satisfactory by subsequent peoples and has been incorporated even into our own Western tradition by way of Christianity. The Hebrews always believed they had, in their own phrase, "spoiled the Egyptians," but they had not. Egyptian civilization continued to satisfy the Egyptian people. It had a survival value unique in history; and yet few achievements can be attributed to it that were thought by later peoples to be worth their while to imitate.

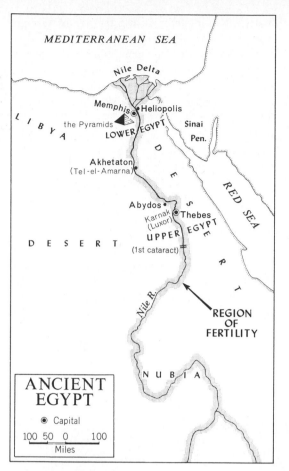

ANCIENT EGYPT

● Capital

100 50 0 100
Miles

he knew *Ma'at.* Literally the word means "harmony," the harmony of the universe, and thus comes to mean, for the Egyptian, everything that is harmonious and in accordance with reality, especially truth and justice. From the earliest times, therefore, the government of Egypt was in the form of a divine monarchy. During his lifetime the king was regarded as Horus, son of Osiris. After death he became Osiris—or perhaps we should say "an" Osiris, since all the monarchs of ancient Egypt were called Osiris after their burial. As Osiris, lord of the afterlife, he was able to help his servants who had been faithful to him on earth, and continued to aid the living. Meanwhile, his successor became a Horus in his turn.

Possessed of authority, perception, and knowledge of heavenly and earthly truth, the king-god was far above man. He made no code of laws; his word, based on his perception, was law. His ministers knew how to judge because he knew their hearts when he chose them for their positions. The whole land of Egypt belonged to him, though in practice, in the Old and Middle Kingdoms, he appears to have taken no material advantage of such ownership. He "made disclosures" rather than asked for advice.

Why the paradox? Was it because Egyptian conditions were peculiar to Egypt and thus its inventions were not transferable elsewhere? Why was the institution of the infallible king-god, the key institution of Egypt, so different from other Oriental despotisms?

Egypt has in ancient and modern times been called the "gift of the Nile." The Nile is a predictable river. It overflows regularly every year, bringing with it not only the life-giving water, but fertile silt which continually enriches the soil of Egypt. Some years the flow is not as high as in others, but always there is an inundation, which appeared to the Egyptians to be the work of heavenly powers. Specifically, these powers were believed to reside in the Pharaoh. He did not predict the rise of the Nile, he *caused* it. This was by no means the limit of his heavenly powers. He knew the hearts of men, he had access to the wisdom of the spiritual world. To use the untranslatable Egyptian term,

Diorite statue of Khafre, with Horus Falcon behind him. The statue depicts the Pharaoh with the majesty of a god and no sign of human failings.

It does not seem that the people of Egypt groaned under such despotism; indeed there is something to be said for this kind of rule as providing a framework for a certain kind of freedom. There is no doubt that men felt themselves free to rise as far as their talents would take them. When all are equally low in comparison with the monarch, among his servants there is a kind of equality of opportunity as well as equality of status. And from extant inscriptions written by servants of the monarch we can observe a certain pride of achievement, even though the success is correctly ascribed to the favor of the Pharaoh earned by their deeds on his behalf.

We have been accustomed to think of the building of the Pyramids during the Old Kingdom as the work of hundreds of thousands of slaves, since that is the tale given us by the much-read Herodotus, the Greek traveler, who made inquiries from the Egyptian priests more than two thousand years later. Yet there is no contemporary evidence for slavery in the Old Kingdom. Slavery became extensive only in the later New Kingdom, during the age of foreign conquests. Far more probable is the theory that the Pyramids, started during the lifetime of the Pharaoh and completed only after his death, were an act of faith, a labor devoted to ensuring the ascent of the Pharaoh to the heavenly world after his death (we know from the Pyramid texts that this was one of their functions), thus enabling him to continue his beneficent work for the Egyptian people even after he had joined his fellow gods in the heavens. The Pyramids of the Old Kingdom, built with jeweler's precision, with the four corners of the base oriented exactly toward the four points of the compass, were also, of course, a wonderful make-work for the thousands of skilled and unskilled laborers who had little to do at a time when the annual flood was at its height, when the materials could be floated on barges right up to the base of the Pyramid.

In the Old Kingdom of Egypt it would seem that the people enjoyed themselves, that they expected the afterlife to be just like this one, secure in the knowledge that if they had served

Model of the Great Pyramid complex, constructed by The Metropolitan Museum of Art. Note the impressive mortuary temples leading up to the pyramid itself. (COURTESY THE METROPOLITAN MUSEUM OF ART)

well in this life the Pharaoh would ensure their continued service in the hereafter. There seems to have been no special attention paid to ceremonial burial with support from spells and charms, so characteristic of the later period of Egypt that we associate it particularly with the Egyptians. In short, since the Nile did indeed bless the people of Egypt and provide them with an easy living and reasonable prosperity at a time when there was no overpopulation, when there were no foreign invaders and Egypt was a secure and self-sufficient community, it is not surprising that all Old Kingdom art breathes an air of confidence and self-satisfaction. It is perhaps also not surprising that the great creative achievements of Egyptian civilization—the hieroglyphic and hieratic writing, the use of papyrus paper, the Pyramids, the characteristic art forms, and the divine monarchy—were all the work of the Old Kingdom. The belief in the eternal stability of the world, the fundamental changelessness of a static universe, likewise was formulated and accepted at this time; and not all the vicissitudes of later eras ever served altogether to dispel this belief.

FIRST INTERMEDIATE PERIOD
(*ca.* 2200–2000 B.C.)

But change at last did come into this changeless land. A Pharaoh named Pepi II lived to an advanced age and apparently lost his grip on the government. Already before his death some of the nobles of Upper Egypt became virtually independent, while foreigners infiltrated into Lower Egypt from the sea and the desert. For almost two hundred years the divine monarch controlled only a small part of Egypt. The old capital of Memphis in Lower Egypt and the later capital of Thebes in Upper Egypt were alike lost to the titular Pharaoh, who now ruled only a small territory around Heracleopolis.

What is of interest to us in this period is the effect change had upon the people who experienced it. From documents of the period we learn that it was widely said that *Ma'at* (order and harmony) had disappeared from the world, everything was topsy-turvy and upside down.

The land, said a priest, "spins around like a potter's wheel." There is no evidence that it was a planned revolution, although its effects were revolutionary in the deepest sense. Possibly the nobles, now independent, rejoiced, but as far as we can judge the people were shocked. When a divine government fails, what is to take its place?

During this time the nobles began to appropriate to themselves texts that had previously been used only for the dead Pharaoh. They began to use the royal funerary customs for themselves, and soon we find what are called "coffin texts" rather than Pyramid texts. The Egyptians, who had scarcely believed that foreigners were human beings at all, now realized to their cost that these foreigners had to be dealt with as if they were. We possess a dialogue between one of the Pharaohs of this time and a minister, in which the minister presumes even to criticize his master for not having given sufficient attention to his land in spite of his heavenly knowledge. The Pharaoh can only agree that he ought to have known and done better.

But at last the anarchy was over. A prince of Thebes in Upper Egypt reunified the country under his control and established Thebes as the capital. The writers breathed a sigh of relief. *Ma'at* had been restored to the land. So the Middle Kingdom began, under the leadership of the great Pharaoh Amenemhat I.

THE MIDDLE KINGDOM (*ca.* 2000–1792 B.C.)

The Middle Kingdom represented essentially an attempt to restore the conditions of the Old Kingdom. The intermediate period was forgotten and *Ma'at* prevailed again. Once more there were peace and prosperity in the land. But the recent troubles had had a peculiar effect on the monarchy.

The Pharaoh was revered as a king-god as before. All the ceremonial and ritual of the divine monarchy was retained. But the Pharaoh himself may well not have believed the myth any longer. How should he, after the failure of the monarch in the two previous centuries? We see from the texts a new concern for social justice, the Pharaoh regarding himself as a

Chronological Chart

Egypt

Neolithic Age	ca. 5000–3000	New Kingdom: Period of Empire —Dynasties XVIII–XX	1570–1090
Old Kingdom: Dynasties I–VI	ca. 3000–2200	Conquest of Syria and part of Mesopotamia	1468
First Intermediate Period: Dynasties VII–XI	ca. 2200–2000	Religious revolution of Akhenaton	ca. 1377–1360
Reconquest of north by Theban princes	2050–2000	Restoration by Tutankhamon	ca. 1360
Middle Kingdom: Dynasty XII	ca. 2000–1792	Rameses II (captivity and exodus of Israelites?)	1301–1234
Second Intermediate Period: Hyksos Invasion—Dynasties XIII–XVII	ca. 1800–1550	New Kingdom: Post-imperial period—Dynasties XXI–XXX	ca. 1090–525
		Conquest by Assyria	ca. 670
Reconquest of Egypt by Theban princes	1580–1550	Conquest by Persia	525
		Conquest by Alexander the Great	332

Mesopotamia

Neolithic Age	ca. 5000–4500	Battle of Carchemish—End of Assyrian Empire and annihilation of Assyrians	606
Early Copper Age	ca. 4500–3000		
Invention of writing	ca. 3500	Chaldeans and New Babylonians	
Early Sumerian cities (Bronze Age)	3000–2400	Conquest of Jerusalem by Nebuchadnezzar	586
		Fall of Babylon to Persians	538
Semitic conquests of Mesopotamia			
Akkadians (Sargon)	2400–2200	Persian Empire	
Guti	2200–2000	Zoroaster the Prophet	ca. 600
Amorites	2000–1750	Cyrus of Persia accepted as king by Medes	549
Hammurabi Code	1800	Conquest of Egypt (Cambyses)	525
Kassites	1750–910	Reorganization of Persia by Darius I	522–486
Assyrian Empire		First Persian expedition to Greece (Darius)	490
Conquest of Babylon	910		
Conquest of Samaria and deportation of Ten Tribes	721	Second Persian expedition to Greece (Xerxes)	480–479
Conquest of Egypt by Esar-Haddon	670	Persian influence in Greece	410–338
Fall of Nineveh to Medes, Chaldeans, and Scythians	612	Conquest of Persia by Alexander the Great	330

Hebrews

Wanderings of Hebrew patriarchs (?)	2000–1700	Period of Judges in Israel	1225–1020
		Saul, king of Israel	1020–1004
Family of Jacob migrates to Egypt (?)	1700	David	1004–965
Exodus of Hebrews from Egypt (?)	1260	Solomon	965–926
		Division of kingdom of Israel	926

Hebrews

Fall of Samaria to Assyrians	721	Conquest by Romans under Pompey, ruled by family of Herods, clients of Romans	63
Fall of Jerusalem; Exile in Babylon	586	Direct rule by Romans	A.D. 6–41
Return of Jews to Jerusalem	538		
Building of the new temple	520–516	Jewish revolt against Romans	66–70
Conquest of Palestine by Alexander the Great (part of Ptolemy I's domain)	332	Destruction of Jerusalem by Titus	70
		Jerusalem rebuilt under name of Aelia Capitolina; Jews not permitted to live in it; Judaea remains Roman province	135
Palestine conquered by Antiochus III of Syria	198		
Revolt of Maccabees against Antiochus IV	167		

Dates (except those for the last four entries) are before Christ. Earlier dates are disputed; others may be a year out.

Chief authority used: G. E. Wright and F. V. Filson, eds., *Westminster Historical Atlas to the Bible* (Philadelphia: Westminster Press, 1945), and J. A. Wilson, *The Burden of Egypt* (Chicago: The University of Chicago Press, 1951), pp. vii–viii.

---

shepherd of the people rather than their unquestioned master. The royal sculpture now depicts these monarchs as careworn individuals rather than majestic supermen.

In the Middle Kingdom also texts appear stressing that the afterlife with the blessed will be a reward for good deeds performed upon earth. But at the same time far more attention was already being paid to ceremonial funerary practices for as many of the people as could afford them. There is a great necropolis at Abydos where nobles and commoners are buried together. Clearly it was no longer believed, as in the Old Kingdom, that the Pharaoh had the power to take those of his servants with him into the afterworld who had served him well. The people evidently began to believe, as they so clearly believed in the New Kingdom, that they had to look out for their own personal immortality, and could no longer rely upon their divine monarch for this service.

SECOND INTERMEDIATE PERIOD AND THE NEW KINGDOM (1792–525 B.C.)

Rise of Egyptian Empire The period of prosperity and peace during the Middle King-dom was rudely broken by a new series of invasions by a people known to history as the Hyksos, whose origins are obscure. This conquest was a real conquest by foreigners, not by native Egyptians; and though the Hyksos rulers usurped the Egyptian throne and tried to behave in every way like their Egyptian predecessors, it is clear that they were never accepted as legitimate rulers, however well they in fact ruled the land. Over parts of Upper Egypt their rule was only nominal, however, and in due course it was again a prince of Upper Egypt, Ahmose I, who drove them out and re-established the divine monarchy. The rest of the period of Egyptian independence is called the New Kingdom, though in fact many of the rulers in later centuries were also foreigners who usurped the throne.

The new rulers of Egypt, determined that never again should there be any such conquest as that of the Hyksos, finally decided on an expansion of their own. Under Thutmose III the Egyptians conquered Palestine and Mesopotamia as far as the Euphrates. The results for Egypt were far from an unmixed blessing. The Egyptians came into contact with foreigners, losing forever their sense of isolation and self-

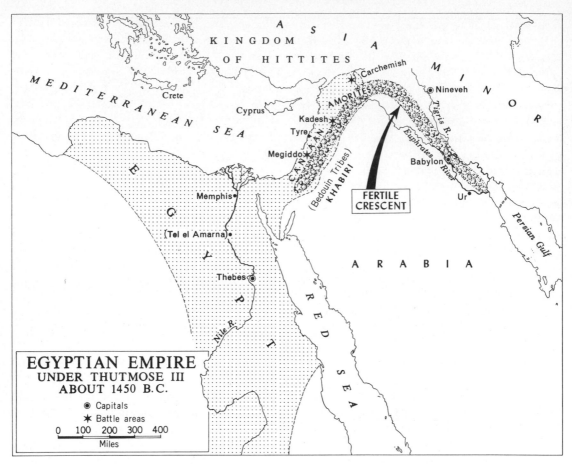

EGYPTIAN EMPIRE
UNDER THUTMOSE III
ABOUT 1450 B.C.

◉ Capitals
✶ Battle areas

0   100   200   300   400
Miles

sufficiency; prisoners of war were brought into Egypt and put to work on the great monuments built by the victors. It was during the New Kingdom that the Israelites were enslaved and forced to "make bricks without straw." As always when there are many slaves in a country the wages of free labor declined catastrophically, and there was a distinct cleavage between rich and poor that had been missing before.

The religious and political revolution of Akhenaton It was not unnatural that this period should have seen the rise of the priesthood to increased power. Not only did the imperial war-god Amon-Re receive the patronage of the warrior Pharaohs, but the popular religion of Osiris, which was concerned with individual resurrection in the hereafter, became stronger than ever before. This popular religion maintained its hold to the very end of Egyptian independence, so that it was possible for Herod-

otus to describe the Egyptians as the "most religious of peoples." It may be surmised that the conditions of the present life on earth were such that a blessed afterlife seemed more than ever desirable and worth making sacrifices on earth to attain. The priesthood was not slow to respond. They were willing to mummify the bodies of all who could pay for the service, and they sold spells and charms to accompany the dead man on his journey into the afterworld. Especially in the late period of the empire, when all was not going so well with the Egyptians as during their first expansion, there is noticeable a great increase in superstition and fear of the dangers of the afterlife. No longer, as in the Old Kingdom and for a long time thereafter, was there a confident expectation of a continuance of the good life after death. On the contrary, there was a fear of monsters, a fear of being made to walk upside down or of doing forced labor, a fear that the soul would not properly separate from the body, and above all a fear that one would not know the right answers to the questions asked by the inquisitors in the underworld. A "declaration of innocence" had to be made to them in the proper form. For a consideration the priests were willing to supply to the faithful charms and spells which would enable them to pass the ordeal safely.

It is not surprising, then, that a religious reformer should have arisen, who tried to take away some of the power of both Amon-Re and Osiris and of their priesthoods. This was the Pharaoh Akhenaton (*ca.* 1377–1360 B.C.), or Amenhotep IV, as he was known prior to his apostasy. This reformer was able to suppress the imperial religion of Amon-Re for the duration of his reign, and substitute the worship of the sun disk, the Aton, whom Akhenaton regarded as the one true god. Thus his religion, like the new art of his period, was naturalistic. The

Pharaoh and his family are portrayed as human beings with ordinary human passions and pleasures, an extraordinary change from the traditional formalism of Egyptian art. The Pharaoh built himself a city which he named after his god, and there he took his courtiers and those who were willing to follow him, while the priesthood bided its time. Akhenaton seems also to have attempted to suppress or at least keep within bounds the growth of the popular Osirian religion, though here we have little evidence to show how far he was successful.

Decline and fall of the New Kingdom Unfortunately for his successors, Akhenaton was so deeply absorbed in his political and religious reform that he neglected to secure his empire. There is extant a large number of letters written to him by his generals, demanding that he bestow on the empire some of his attention. But

The New Kingdom Pharaoh Thutmose III destroying his enemies. Note the gigantic size of the Pharaoh and the conventional puniness of his enemies.

The Pharaoh Akhenaton worshiping. Note how he himself offers worship to the sun god Aton, whose rays enfold him, while his family, at a lower eminence, appear to be worshiping the Pharaoh rather than Aton. (COURTESY CAIRO MUSEUM)

he paid no heed, and when he died peacefully at an early age, almost all classes in the empire were against the regime, and it seems probable that only the special sanctity of the throne prevented an armed revolt. The new Pharaoh, seeing the way the wind was blowing, quickly came to terms with the priesthood. The old religion was restored and the name of Akhenaton blotted from the Egyptian records. Soon afterward an army general succeeded to the throne.

    Thereafter it was difficult for the monarchs to keep the empire intact. Rameses II, a great builder and, in his own opinion, a great warrior, exhausted the resources of Egypt in wars against the rising Hittites in the north (a war concluded

by the first extant treaty in history), and in his building program. Soon thereafter the Egyptians were confined within their own borders. Several foreign monarchs occupied the Egyptian throne, there was a short-lived conquest of Egypt by the rulers of Assyria, and finally, in 525 B.C., a conquest by the Persians. Two hundred years later Egypt was again won by Alexander the Great, whose successors, the Ptolemies, were Macedonians, as was Cleopatra, the last of their line. Finally, Egypt fell to the Romans. As the Hebrew Ezekiel had prophesied, no more princes of the land of Egypt arose (until the twentieth century A.D.).

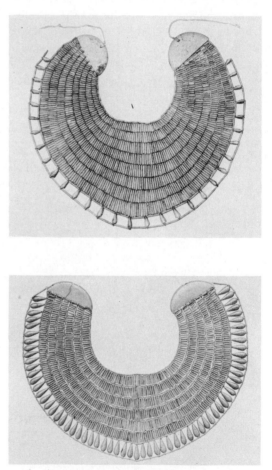

Two collars of beads. The one at the top dates from the XIth Dynasty, the one at the bottom from the XVIIIth. More than seven hundred years separate these two collars, yet the design is the same, suggesting something of Egyptian conservatism. (COURTESY THE METROPOLITAN MUSEUM OF ART)

THE VALUES OF EGYPT—HER LEGACY TO LATER CIVILIZATIONS

The Greeks considered Egypt the repository of all ancient wisdom, and they accorded to her a respect which was perhaps undeserved. While we may now admire the civilization of the Egyptians, it sometimes makes us impatient that they made so little progress, that the great achievements of the Old Kingdom were not treated as the beginning of an ascending path, a fine start to be built upon rather than a Golden Age of glory to be looked back upon and forever imitated. It was a civilization that looked backward and decayed, as distinct from the picture familiar to us of a Western civilization that looks forward and strives forward, but is chaotic and unstable. If we assume that it is an inborn characteristic of man to wish to advance, it is perhaps well to realize that it was not a characteristic of the ancient Egyptians. Toynbee, in studying Egyptian civilization, was hard put to it to discover his challenges and responses and succeeded in devising a pattern satisfactory to him only by doing grave violence to the facts of Egyptian history. The Marxian interpretation of history finds little confirmation in Egypt. We are thus left with a phenomenon which seems ultimately to be explained only in terms of itself—that the Egyptians, unlike ourselves, neither wished to advance nor succeeded in doing so after a brilliant start. Yet their civilization endured for twenty-five centuries.

❖ Mesopotamia

THE SUMERIANS

Primitive democracy—The temple community Mesopotamian civilization, on the other hand, was far from stable. This instability parallels, and may in part be explained by, the difference between the rivers of Mesopotamia and the Egyptian Nile. The Tigris and the Euphrates did not overflow regularly, though it was possible to use them for irrigation. The climate was far from equable. Sometimes there were severe rainstorms and hailstorms, which

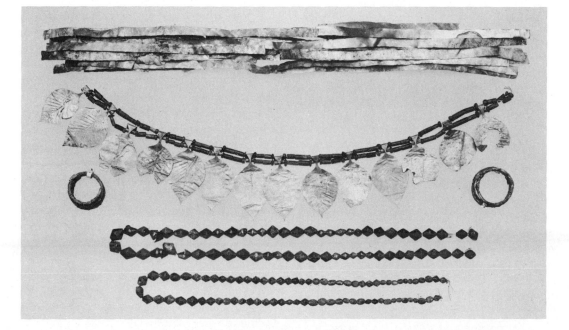

Jewelry from the graves of two ladies-in-waiting of the Queen of Ur, 3500–2500 B.C. Made of gold, carnelian, and lapis lazuli, this jewelry is the oldest known in the world up to the present time, but the skill shown presupposes long development in craftsmanship from prehistoric times. (COURTESY THE METROPOLITAN MUSEUM OF ART)

destroyed the crops; sometimes it was so hot as to be almost unbearable. The country, which was marked by no obvious boundaries, lay wide open to invasion from all sides, and history reveals a constant flow of conquerors who ruled the land between the two rivers. But, as in Egypt, the basic components of the culture and the vast majority of its inventions were provided by the first people to settle in the land from without. These were the Sumerians, a people whose origins are still obscure, known to themselves simply as the "black-headed people."

When they first become known to history they lived in self-governing communities in the lower part of the valleys of the Tigris and Euphrates rivers. There is evidence that government of these states evolved from what may be called a primitive democracy, or rule by elders with the consent of the people, to temple communities where the city-god was the official owner and ruler of the city but governed through an official called a *sangu,* or steward, who managed the god's property and performed the functions of both priest and king. When the small temple communities, perhaps described best as large villages, coalesced into larger units, this official became an *ensi,* presumably with several sangus under him and each responsible for his own smaller community and its temple. When for purposes of defense or for other reasons a number of cities united, then a true king or *lugal* ruled over them, without disrupting the local administration that had preceded his advent. The ensi may therefore best be considered as the ruler of a city-state, while the lugal ruled either a league of city-states or one city-state dominating a number of smaller ones. Even in the largest of the Sumerian governmental entities and in all the regimes that succeeded them, the ruler continued to exercise what was in theory a stewardship in relation to the gods. In theory it was always the gods who ruled in Mesopotamian countries, while the king was only their representative or steward on earth. The Mesopotamian ruler was never a god himself, as in Egypt, though there are some texts extant which suggest that certain kings did attribute to themselves divine qualities.

Scientific and literary achievements The Sumerians are almost certainly the inventors of writing, although it was the Egyptian method of writing on papyrus with picture signs that was taken over by later peoples, rather than the more cumbersome Sumerian method of cutting wedges into clay and baking the clay. The Sumerian cuneiform signs, however, did evolve from pictures in the same way as the Egyptian script, although quite early the Sumerian pictures became so stylized as to be unrecognizable as pictures. The Sumerians developed also the characteristic *ziggurat* form for their temples, and this was used by the later Babylonians, Assyrians, and Chaldeans. The most famous *ziggurat* is the temple of Marduk described by Herodotus in the Babylon of his day, famous for its Hanging Gardens. The Sumerians were skilled architects and knew all the basic architectural forms used by later peoples—the dome, the arch, and the vault. Building largely in brick, they displayed much ingenuity in using this material in different ways to solve their architectural problems. Finally, the Sumerians

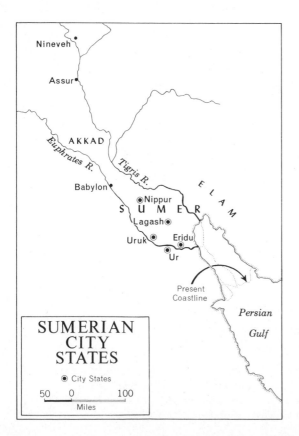

SUMERIAN CITY STATES

◉ City States

50   0   100
      Miles

are noted for their mathematical system, no doubt developed because of their commercial needs, which was based on the number 60 rather than 10 (our own decimal system), but was a true positional system like ours and unlike the systems of the Greeks and Romans. The mathematical tradition thus begun by the Sumerians persisted throughout Mesopotamian history. Successors of the Sumerians divided the circle into six units of 60 degrees, and the great astronomical achievements of the later Chaldeans, which provided the raw material for Hellenistic science, were solidly based on the work done so early in history by the Sumerians.

The Sumerian city-states also developed the first written law known to us. The famous Hammurabi Code granted to the Babylonians by the Amorite king Hammurabi at a much later date is drawn from various Sumerian codes known to us only in fragmentary form. These fragments, however, are quite enough to show that already long before Hammurabi the customs of the different states had been crystallized into law, and appropriate penalties and means of enforcement had been devised.

Cuneiform tablet recording expenditure and distribution of grain and animals. (COURTESY THE METROPOLITAN MUSEUM OF ART)

The fundamental myths of the peoples of Mesopotamia also derive from the Sumerians. The Creation story, known to us best in the Hammurabi version, dates from Sumerian times, although only a few fragments remain from the earlier period. In the Hammurabi version Marduk, the supreme Babylonian god, destroys Tiamat, the goddess of chaos, then creates the world and man, who is created solely for the purpose of working for the gods and thus setting the gods free from labor. The Flood story, to be found in the Epic of Gilgamesh and copied by the Hebrews with alterations, was likewise Sumerian. It may therefore be appropriate to deal here with the Sumerian attitude to life as evidenced in these stories and other extant Sumerian literature, rather than describe this attitude as it appears in the later Babylonian and Assyrian literature. The details may be changed amongst these later peoples, but the framework laid down by the early Sumerians persists, and there is no fundamental change before the conquest of Mesopotamia by Cyrus the Persian and its incorporation into the huge Persian Empire.

Attitude to life If a generalization can be made of the Mesopotamian attitude to life it may be said that it was basically pessimistic, as distinct from the initial optimism of the Egyptians. The Creation story shows that man's purpose in the universe is solely to serve the gods, to set the gods free from the labor they had hitherto performed. Man has no rights against the gods, who may be as arbitrary and unjust as they wish. Man has no recourse against them. The gods expect men to do their will. Unfortunately, however, they did not trouble to inform men of just what was desired of them. It was the primary duty of the king, as we have seen, to act as the representative of the gods on earth, primarily of the city-god to whom the city owed especial allegiance. The king, therefore, had the responsibility of finding out what the gods required of their people. There is a very interesting cylinder seal extant on which are recorded the efforts of an ensi of Lagash, named Gudea, to discover just what kind of temple should be built to the city-god and his spouse. Gudea had first been informed of the god's wishes in a dream, but he made a considerable effort to check his interpretation by various means. When the state was too large for the king to be expected to carry out such a task himself, it became necessary to have a professional priesthood, whose chief task it was to examine whatever signs were available to determine the will of the gods and communicate it to the king, who himself would usually have to perform the particular duties demanded. Thus grew up various practices of divination, such as examining the livers of freshly killed chickens kept for the purpose, watching the flight of birds, interpreting dreams, and, finally, observing the movements of the heavenly bodies, which had the great advantage that they could be predicted a long time in advance. This latter, of course, gave rise to astrology, and ultimately, as a by-product, to true astronomy.

Even the great kings of Assyria, terrifying and powerful conquerors as they appeared to others, were nevertheless constrained to obey the orders of the gods. Their only recourse against the priesthood was to query their interpretations. This it was possible to some extent to do, since the various interpretations were written down in books which could be consulted as well by the king as by the priests. There are texts extant of state letters of the Assyrian monarchs to their priests in which it is asked whether the interpretation is correct that the king must undergo a ritual shaving or stay in a reed hut in the desert for a time. The king, in Mesopotamian thought, besides being their monarch, was a kind of scapegoat for the people. Ritual atonement had first of all to be performed by him, and sometimes by him alone on behalf of the people. All such notions stemmed from the belief that the king was a representative of the gods on earth, that his power was not absolute but limited by a necessary submission to the will of the gods, and that both he and his people were expected to make their primary duty in life the carrying out of the gods' behests. All such ideas are to be found again in Hebrew thought, significantly changed but, in spite of the change, easily recognizable.

The Epic of Gilgamesh, the first of the great poems of quest (cf. the Odyssey, Parzifal) throws more light on the Sumerian attitude toward the gods. Though many themes are intermingled in the poem, the central theme is the search for the plant of immortality by Gilgamesh, the king of Uruk. Faced with the death of a beloved friend, Gilgamesh asks himself why men die, and whether there is any way of attaining immortality without death. At last he finds the plant of immortality, only to have it stolen by a serpent, so that thereafter the serpent has immortality (sheds its skin), while man does not. There is no reason given, as there is no true reason why the god Enlil should have wished to destroy mankind in the Flood, a subsidiary story also to be found in the Epic of Gilgamesh. The same question of why man must die is asked by Gilgamesh in another poem which is authentically Sumerian, though only known in a fragment. Here Gilgamesh is told that the gods have given him valor and renown in the world, but this is to be his only solace. There is no immortality. Unlike the Egyptians, who pictured the afterlife as similar to life on earth, the Mesopotamian afterlife is pictured as a dreary existence for shades. This conception of the afterlife is faithfully reflected in the Hebrew picture of Sheol.

All Mesopotamian thought accepts the idea that man is rewarded or punished on earth in accordance with his earthly deeds. He does not, like the Egyptian, have to buy spells or charms. The king and all the people are expected to know what the gods desire and to perform what is required of them. The gods do not require deeds that are ethical, as the Hebrew prophets insisted; they do not ask, like Micah, for man "to do justly and to love mercy and to walk humbly with thy god." They have certain duties to perform, and it is the task of the king and priests to discover what those duties are. Appropriate sacrifices and rituals must be performed. If they are not performed the gods will punish, even though the people were never given any clear indication what, actually, was demanded. Thus, in essence, they are punished for their ignorance. The Hebrews likewise thought that God required the keeping of the Law, the performance of certain rituals, behavior according to certain recognized norms of conduct. The Hebrews likewise were punished if they did not obey the commands of God. But there was a great difference between the attitude of God and the attitude of the Mesopotamian gods. The latter kept men in ignorance, and treated them as slaves who were not expected to know the reasons for their punishment; whereas the Hebrew God was a loving father who instructed his children and tried to bring them up in the way they should go. Thus again we see how the Mesopotamian peoples raised the problem but did not solve it. Their assumption was that the gods made demands of man and expected obedience; they did not attain to the Hebrew thought that God laid down eternal laws of behavior and punished disobedience to them—still less that God asked ethical behavior from man over and beyond the prescribed dictates of the Law.

The Mesopotamian peoples also were bedeviled by the fact that there were so many gods, whose demands might be contradictory. There was no supreme god, although the god Marduk of Babylon sometimes in the texts approaches this position. There were not only the great gods, representing natural forces, but there were local gods for particular cities and even personal gods, possessed of little power but sometimes able to intercede on behalf of their worshipers. A late prayer points up the dilemma in no uncertain terms when the penitent asks that the fury of not only his own god and goddess be quieted toward him, but also the fury of all the gods whom he "knows or does not know," and for all the transgressions which he "knows or does not know." And the last Chaldean king of Babylon is shown to us as trying to make an image which will be a composite of all the gods in an apparent last desperate effort to achieve some kind of unity. This incident, of course, is referred to in the famous passage in the Book of Daniel where the three Hebrews alone in the city refuse to worship this image and are cast into the "burning fiery furnace." (Daniel: 3)

AMORITE CONQUEST

The Sumerian city-states submitted to their first conquest when a certain Sargon of Agade unified them from the north (*ca.* 2400 B.C.) and introduced them to the Semitic language of Akkadian, which was ultimately to supersede the older Sumerian. After Sargon's death, however, the Sumerian cities regained their independence, though intermittently they had to submit to another northern tribe known as the Guti. However, about 2000 B.C. a more permanent conquest ensued, with the capture of the village of Babylon by the Amorites, a desert people. Babylon was elevated into the capital of the whole territory, and later Amorite rulers made what had been the land of Sumer into a considerable empire stretching far to the north of the territory of the old city-states. Thereafter it is more accurate to speak of the Babylonian Empire, by which term the whole of the Mesopotamian civilization is more commonly known.

Hammurabi Code—General characteristics Hammurabi is the most famous of the Amorite kings of Babylon. He derives his fame largely from the Code which bears his name, though, as has been suggested earlier, it was by no

A stela showing Hammurabi receiving his code of laws from the sun god Shamash, who was also the god of justice. The code itself is inscribed on the stela. (COURTESY THE LOUVRE)

means original with him. It seems clear that the king regarded his Code as one of the means of unifying his motley empire. The Code therefore is a composite of many Sumerian codes, with the addition of new material especially suitable for an imperial structure. No doubt this accounts for the unevenness of the Code, which in some parts is enlightened, even by modern standards, while in others it appears to us to be both barbarous and based on a very peculiar kind of logic. Most often quoted are sections like that which requires that if a house collapses, killing the son of the owner, the son of the architect who built the house shall be put to death, not the architect himself—for whom it might in our day be considered an excessive penalty, though not inherently an unjust one.

Nature of Babylonian justice Certain features of Babylonian society do emerge clearly from the Code. Justice was unequal. The population was divided into three classes: nobles, free commoners, and serfs and slaves. Crimes against nobles were dealt with more severely than those against the lower classes; but nobles themselves were also in many cases dealt with more severely if they had committed the crime. Property seems to have been rated above human life, crimes against property usually being treated more severely. Even accidental homicide was regarded as a crime against the victim's family and compensated accordingly. Murder was not a crime against the state but against the person. Aliens were treated liberally; women held a relatively high position; and there were extensive regulations for industry and trade, as might be expected in a commercial civilization. Noteworthy is the fact that private tenure of land seems to have been the rule, unlike the system described for the Sumerian city-states. Peasants were sharecroppers or serfs as before; but, in addition to the priests, the government and nobles now owned the land. This probably reflects the changed conditions under a conquering house of invaders, who would not necessarily respect the arrangements made by deities for their sustenance, even while they accepted the general divine order decreed by them. The sharecroppers were protected by law against eviction before the end of the contract year—

as before under the regime of the gods—and against obligation to pay full rent if the crop failed.

Social provisions There are many provisions governing marriage in the Code. Evidently, marriage was a legal contract in Babylonia. Though the wife was the legal property of her husband and brought a marriage gift to him, she had some rights, being permitted to return to her father if ill-treated by her husband. Although marriage was ordinarily for life, divorce was permissible; the bridal gift would be returned with her, and she would keep the custody of the children. Women were allowed to engage in business, and had as many business rights as men. However, if the husband fell into debt, the wife could be sold as payment for it. There are severe penalties for adultery and other sexual offenses.

Significance and influence If we knew more about the earlier law codes and, as said earlier, if we knew how it was administered, we could comment with more confidence upon the significance of this Code and how far it represented an advance upon earlier thinking. But the correspondence of Hammurabi shows at least that he took his duties very seriously. Quite trivial disputes he investigated himself, and there are several instances of his sending back cases for retrial, as well as handing down decisions himself. There can be little doubt that the parts of the Code which stem from Hammurabi and Babylon represent a codification of existing practices in the commercial civilization of Babylonia. It cannot, however, be described truly as the first secular legislation. It is significant that it was represented as having divine sanction and as being unalterable, and that it was enforced by the authority of both the ruler and the gods. Legislation that was truly secular, and subject to change by duly authorized legislators, did not arise until the time of the Romans. Even the Greeks entrusted their basic legislation to individuals who were expected to consult the Delphic oracle before they promulgated it. Men who proposed to modify the laws ran the risk of severe penalties if their proposals were rejected.

It is certain that both the Hammurabi Code and the whole Mesopotamian legal tradition had a marked influence upon the Hebrew law of a far later epoch, especially upon those parts of the Hebrew codes which seem to be the most ancient. Here no fewer than thirty-five provisions out of fifty are similar. Even the language in both has marked resemblances. The probable explanation is the influence the legal tradition had upon Canaanites and other peoples of Palestine rather than any direct borrowing by the Hebrews. The Hebrews would naturally adopt some of the customs of the Canaanites; and if, as seems probable, there were already Israelites in Palestine before the exodus of the captives from Egypt, during the reunion of the two branches of the people after the exodus each branch would absorb something of the customs and laws from the other.

THE ASSYRIAN EMPIRE (910–606 B.C.)

Not long after the reign of Hammurabi Babylonia again fell upon evil times, the city of Babylon falling to the barbarian Kassites who held it precariously until its conquest in 910 B.C. by the Assyrians, whose empire deserves more than a passing mention. The Assyrians had long been resident in northern Babylonia, and at times had been subjected to Babylonian rule. Toward the end of the first millennium B.C., however, a number of Assyrian rulers began to establish a military tradition, training their not very numerous people for war. It was not long before the trained Assyrian army began to expand and conquer its neighbors. The Assyrian rulers adopted a policy of extreme harshness, for which they have been known in all subsequent times—in part because their final defeat

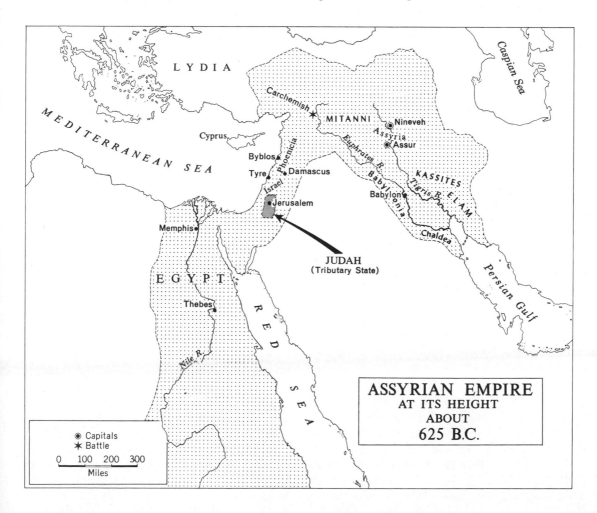

ASSYRIAN EMPIRE
AT ITS HEIGHT
ABOUT
625 B.C.

and extinction as a people invites the easy attention of the moralist. At the height of their power the Assyrians had conquered as far south as Egypt, had forced Judah to pay tribute, and had deported the peoples of northern Israel, exchanging them for other peoples from their extensive empire (the "lost ten tribes of Israel").

Their conquests and methods, however, so aroused their neighbors, as well as the half-subdued peoples in their empire, that a coalition was formed against them. This coalition the Assyrians could defeat in battle, but not without some losses which they could not afford. In the end Nineveh, their capital, was captured (612 B.C.)—celebrated in the Bible by the book of the prophet Nahum—and the Assyrians were exterminated. Though the Babylonians survived, there has been no trace of any Assyrian people as a people since that time. In spite of their fate, however, the Assyrians undoubtedly did prepare the way for later, better organized, and more humane empires in the territory they had conquered. They did improve communications, if only to ensure the collection of the tribute they imposed on their victims; and, very important

to us, they collected in the great library of Assurbanipal in Nineveh cuneiform documents from all over the Near East. Since no ancient people dared to lay sacrilegious hands upon the "cursed" site of Nineveh, they were left undisturbed until modern archaeologists discovered them in the middle of the nineteenth century.

THE CHALDEAN EMPIRE (612–538 B.C.)

When the coalition succeeded in destroying Nineveh, the lion's share of the reconquered territory fell to the Babylonians, who founded a new empire, usually called the Chaldean Empire. Babylon was rebuilt, with a new temple of Marduk. Trade recovered and the whole empire attained to a prosperity that it had not known before. It was during this period that the leaders of Judah were carried away captive into Babylon, with such important results for the future of Judaism. The greatest intellectual achievement of the Chaldean Empire was the revival and development of mathematics and astronomy, although the latter science was strictly subordinated to astrology. Correct observations were made of the stars and their movements,

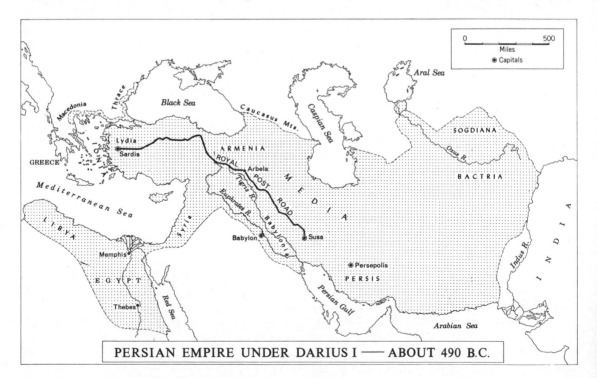

PERSIAN EMPIRE UNDER DARIUS I — ABOUT 490 B.C.

however, and correct predictions could be made with the aid of mathematics. The attitude of the Chaldean people toward their gods and toward life in general does not seem to have undergone any significant change. There was a great deal of personal piety, and there were many questionings of the purposes of the gods and of what they expected of man. There are a number of penitential psalms, but no significantly new thought on any of these matters. A change in Babylonian religion had to wait until the Persian monarchs introduced the higher religion of Zoroastrianism, with its altogether different theology, its advanced ethical teachings, and its idea of a future life.

THE PERSIAN EMPIRE (549–330 B.C.)

Conquest and organization of Near East
Following the breakup of the Assyrian Empire the territory to the east of Babylonia fell into the hands of a people called the Medes, who expanded into the east and incorporated the Persians for a time into their empire. However, an enterprising and able Persian prince named Cyrus in 549 B.C. revolted from the Medes, and after a brief struggle was accepted by them as king. Then the unified Medes and Persians swept westward, conquering Babylonia and Asia Minor. Successors of Cyrus eventually added Egypt to the empire. Thus arose the first of the great Oriental empires to be compared in any way with the empire of Alexander or the Romans. This Persian Empire was thoroughly organized by Darius I, who also sent an expedition against Greece which was defeated at the battle of Marathon in 490 B.C. A subsequent larger expedition sent by his son Xerxes met the same fate, and thereafter the Persians were content for a time with a toehold in Thrace and then with interference in the internal affairs of Greece through the use of money and diplomacy.

Though rather ramshackle in its composition, the Persian Empire did bring the benefits of peace and some degree of civilization to the peoples who composed it. The empire was organized into satrapies under satraps, or governors, responsible to the monarch. The satraps in later times exercised a considerable degree of independence, but they could always be deposed by the monarch when necessary. The Persians as a rule did not attempt to interfere with local customs, and even the Persian religion seems to have been accepted rather than imposed. The monarch had at his disposal a band of picked nobles called the Immortals, who constituted a force of shock troops. The huge motley army of Xerxes which invaded Greece in 480 B.C. was apparently something unusual for Persia, accounting for the many years spent in preparing the expedition. The difficulty of organizing such an army, with its component parts belonging to different races and speaking different languages, was also no doubt largely responsible for the weakness of the defense offered to the conquering Macedonian Alexander the Great in the late fourth century B.C.

Zoroastrianism The religion brought by the Persians into their empire has little relation to what they found there. The prophet Zoroaster, its supposed founder, is a rather mysterious figure, and may have lived, if he lived at all, as late as the sixth or seventh century B.C. or many centuries earlier. In any case he should not be thought of as having inaugurated an altogether new religion. Perhaps he performed something of the work of Buddha in India, in that he clarified the ethics of the existing religion and to some degree systematized its theology. Zoroastrianism was deeply concerned, as the older religions were not, with the problem of good and evil—ethical good and evil, and not merely the failure to observe prescribed ritual practices or to understand what the gods required of man.

The world had been created by Ahura-Mazda, the god of light. But though he would ultimately triumph, he was not omnipotent, and was engaged in a constant struggle with the god of darkness, Aingra-Manu, or Ahriman, who was the embodiment of all wickedness, treachery, and deceit and was possessed of almost equal powers. Each of these gods had his attendant host of spirits ceaselessly working for him. It was man's duty—within limits he had free choice—to aid the god of light in his struggle with the god of darkness and help to overcome him. The Persian kings all claimed their position by the grace of Ahura-Mazda and were required as their duty to support the rule of light upon earth, administer justice, and rule according to righteousness. The priests of Zarathustra, usually called the Magi, kept alive the sacred fire, the symbol of Ahura-Mazda, in their temples.

Zoroastrianism contained a definite and clear belief in a future life. In the process of time the good powers would overcome the evil, and then a messiah would be born to prepare the end of the world. The last great day would then come when Ahriman would be finally vanquished, and the souls of the dead would be judged according to their deeds. The just would at once enter paradise, while the wicked would be case into Hell with their master, Ahriman. There they would serve him until they too would be redeemed in a far distant future. There can be little doubt that the Christian story of the Wise Men of the East who visited the infant Jesus in Bethlehem to worship him was intended to show that the priests of Zarathustra had recognized in him the Messiah whom they awaited.

The sins which lead to damnation are cataloged: pride, gluttony, sloth, and other of the Christian "deadly sins." Likewise the virtues: keeping contracts, obeying rulers, tilling the soil, showing mercy, giving alms, and not doing to others what one did not wish done to oneself. Early Zoroastrianism, unlike the later religions which developed from it and stressed the evil nature of the material world, did not approve of asceticism, self-inflicted suffering, or excessive fasting and grief.

Successors of Zoroastrianism—Mithraism, Manichaeism, medieval heresies The elements of this new revealed religion which affected later Judaism and Christianity are obvious; and many of its features found their fruition elsewhere than in those religions which developed directly from it. In Mithraism, which in the Roman Empire presented such competition to Christianity during the first centuries of the Christian Era, there is far more stress laid on Mithras the Redeemer, as also upon the evil nature of the world, than in Zoroastrianism,

with a resultant emphasis on the corrupt nature of mankind and the means of overcoming it in self-mortification. By the time of the rise of Manichaeism in the third century A.D. the world is seen as altogether corrupted by the god of darkness, and matter itself is conceived of as evil. From this teaching came the beliefs of the Cathari and Albigensians in medieval Europe. But these religions and their influence upon Christianity will be kept for a brief discussion in a later chapter.

CONCLUSION—THE INFLUENCE OF MESOPOTAMIA

We have now traced the history of Mesopotamia until the coming of the Greeks. The greatest direct contribution of these peoples to Western civilization was probably their science, which became mingled with Greek science and so was passed on to the West after the conquests of Alexander. The art of writing was discovered by them; they did important work in mathematics; and they laid the foundations of astronomy. Indirectly, their work was of the greatest importance for the Hebrews, since they gave them their basic law; and from them sprang the whole tradition of submission and obedience to the gods who ruled the universe. The Persians, with their conception of the Last Judgment and rewards and punishments in the next world, and their new thoughts on the nature of good and evil, added an ethical emphasis which affected both later Hebrew thought and Christianity. The Assyrians provided a great object lesson on the dangers of undiluted imperialism, which was appreciated and profited from by the Persians who followed them.

In bulk the contribution of Mesopotamia does not begin to compare with the legacy of the Greeks and Romans, though it probably surpasses the legacy of Egypt; but in the depth of its influence it is surpassed by few civilizations. Without the pioneer work of the Mesopotamian peoples in science and religion the lives of all later peoples would have been substantially different. Mesopotamia itself did not cease to be a center of civilization, but again rose to power and influence under the Parthians, the Sassanid Persians, and the Muslim Abba-

sids. But by this time the independent civilizations of the West were growing up and the
civilizations of the Near East had only a minor
influence upon them. When Harun-al-Rashid of
Bagdad and Charlemagne of Aachen exchanged
courtesies in the eighth century A.D., each knew
almost nothing of the other. The East and West
had embarked on their independent journeys.

❖ The Hebrews—the kingdoms of Israel and Judah

REASONS FOR STUDYING HEBREW HISTORY

The third Near-Eastern civilization that
merits detailed discussion, even in a brief one-
chapter survey, is distinguished from the two
already dealt with by the fact that its achievements lie entirely within the realm of religion
and religious literature. The Hebrews produced
no great art, no distinctive method of government; they had no material inventions whatever
to their credit. Yet their influence on later peoples has far surpassed that of Egypt or Mesopotamia. Hebrew religious thought is still
believed to be truth by a sizable percentage
of twentieth-century men and women. Aside
from Judaism itself, both Christianity and Islam
have adopted a considerable portion of the
Hebrew religious insights as their own. In such
a chapter as this the Hittites, who for many
centuries possessed a great empire in Asia
Minor and surrounding lands, may be dis-
missed, along with the Lydians, who succeeded
them in western Asia Minor and are credited
with the invention of coinage, and also the
Phoenicians and Aramaeans who performed a
notable service as traders by sea and land
respectively. The Hebrews, however, require a

*The earliest coined money in the world. Invention
attributed to the Lydians, three of whose coins
are shown here.* (COURTESY THE METROPOLITAN
MUSEUM OF ART)

more than perfunctory consideration, even
though their history as such could be paralleled
by many other minor peoples, and though their
independence lasted for a paltry few centuries.

Hebrew history would not be worth considering at all if it were not for the fact that it
is familiar to millions of Westerners through
the medium of the Bible, and for the remarkable fact that the Hebrews were the first people
who systematically recorded their history and
strove to give it meaning. Events that merely
happened were for the first time given significance by the priestly chroniclers of the Hebrews.
They were significant because God was the
ruler of history. If the Hebrews were defeated
in battle by the Egyptians, then it was because
God had willed it; and the deed was a reply
to an act of disobedience on the part of the
Hebrews. If two men were swallowed up in an
earthquake, it was because they had sinned
against the Lord. This effort to interpret what
we might call natural events, or events to be
explained wholly by natural causes, was unique
at the time, though the method had a future; it
was believed to be a proper method of historical
interpretation until very recently, and still forms
the basis for many philosophies of history even
in our own century.

The facts of Hebrew history are still and
probably will forever be in dispute. On the
whole the Bible has been confirmed as good
history by archaeological research more than
it has been refuted. Nevertheless, since it is
so highly selective, the historical method of
the chroniclers leaves a great deal to be desired. Reigns of which we should like to have
heard more have been passed over in a few
words because there was little of religious significance to be recorded. The sojourn of a
relatively small number of Hebrews in Egypt
was religiously of supreme importance, and
hence, from a purely historical point of view,
is given a disproportionate amount of space.

However, history as such is not what we
look for in the Bible. The interpretation is, to
us, of supreme importance too. The historical
background against which Hebrew religion developed is of importance, but it is not for us
the crucial thing. So the history itself may be
given in a few bald lines.

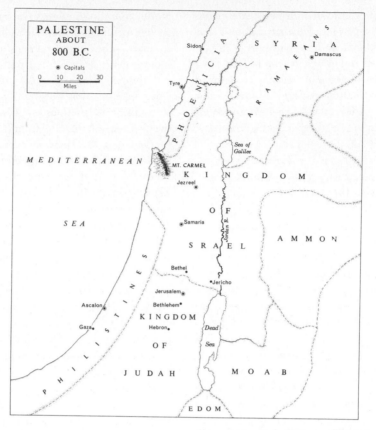

PALESTINE
ABOUT
800 B.C.

⊚ Capitals

0   10   20   30
Miles

HISTORY OF HEBREW KINGDOMS

Hebrew civilization may be said to start with Abraham, according to the Biblical record. He it was who began the religion of Yahweh in Palestine. His grandson Jacob led a number Hebrews into Egypt at the time of a famine in Palestine. Outstaying their welcome, this band of Hebrews was enslaved by a later Pharaoh and made to work on his building program. In due course a leader arose among them named Moses, who was able to revive in the people a renewed belief in their ancestral God, Yahweh, and, against the persistent opposition of the Pharaoh, led them out into the wilderness, where they remained for forty years. During this period Moses gave them the Law of Yahweh, which, again after some opposition, he was able to make prevail as the Law of the whole people. Trained as warriors and held together by their religion and their Law, the people of Israel were led by Joshua into the land of Canaan (Palestine), which after a long time they finally succeeded in subduing against the opposition of

the existing inhabitants. The kingdom was unified under the rule of a warrior-king named David, who had been chosen and anointed as king by the prophet-priest Samuel (*ca.* 1000 B.C.).

The unified kingdom of Israel and Judah survived for only one generation after David. David's son Solomon tried to live like an Oriental monarch on resources suitable for a minor kingdom, and he built the first temple at Jerusalem with the aid of the Phoenician monarch, with whom he had an alliance. The cost was heavy, for he had to permit Israelites to work at forced labor for King Hiram of Phoenicia. This bargain resulted in a rebellion on his death, and thereafter the kingdom was split. The larger and agriculturally better favored northern kingdom of Israel (or Ephraim) was in a politically precarious position, surrounded by stronger nations. The only recourse for Israel was to enter into alliances with one or the other of them, necessitating the toleration or even acceptance of the gods of the foreign princess who sat on the throne. This practice brought down upon the kings of Israel the wrath of the priests and prophets, who claimed that Yahweh was being neglected. It is significant that in the priestly account not one king of Israel did "that which was right in the sight of the Lord." The system of alliances finally collapsed with the rise of Assyria, which succeeded in defeating all the neighbors of Israel, and in 721 B.C. besieged and captured Samaria, the northern capital. Thereafter the people of the northern kingdom were scattered, and an alien people, not worshipers of Yahweh, were brought into the country by the Assyrians to take their place.

Judah meanwhile had to some degree maintained its worship of Yahweh, and the temple at Jerusalem in Judah remained the center of the Hebrew religion. Moreover, the country was poor and did not excite the cupidity of its neighbors to the same degree as Israel. Thus it was permitted to survive by the Assyrians on condition of paying tribute, and not until the Chaldean Empire arose on the ruins of Assyria did Judah have to submit to the yoke of the foreigner. The last few kings of Judah were set up by the Babylonians as their puppets. But, under constant pressure from their priests to refuse obedience to their Babylonian overlords, they soon fell into disfavor and were deposed. As a result of constant rebellions, the Babylonians finally decided to take the leaders of Judah as captives into Babylon. They destroyed the temple and put an end to Hebrew independence (586 B.C.). The exiles in Babylon, however, did not despair. They were held together by priests and prophets, and when the Persians at length put an end to Babylonian independence, the Hebrews, or Jews (as they may now be called), were allowed to return to Palestine and rebuild their temple. This condition of limited self-government under Persian auspices was rudely shattered when Alexander the Great conquered the Near East. One of his successors tried forcibly to Hellenize the Jews, causing a revolt of the orthodox led by the family of the Maccabees. The revolt succeeding, the Jews again had a period of independence until they were conquered by the Romans, who created the province of Judaea in 6 A.D. A later revolt in the seventh decade of the century led to the final destruction of the temple and the scattering of the people. Until the twentieth century there was never again an independent state of Israel or Judah.

Monotheism The Hebrews are, of course, credited above all with the formulation of monotheism, the worship of one God; and this monotheism has been transmitted both to Christianity and to Islam, so that it is the fundamental religious belief of the West. But it is not always recognized that they are also responsible for the precise definition of the nature of sin; and their thought upon the question of sin and punishment has permeated Western thought as deeply as has the concept of monotheism itself. The evolution of Hebrew thought on these two subjects will therefore be treated in some detail in this chapter.

The Hebrews did not come all at once to their idea of a transcendent God ruling the universe. In the period of the desert wanderings we find them given the commandment that they are to have no other gods besides Yahweh, but there is as yet no suggestion that other gods do not exist. He is their special God, their protector and rock of defense, who will keep his promises to his chosen people; but as yet nothing more. It is only in relatively late times that the great prophets picture him as the God of the universe, with all peoples alike subjected to him, and the gods of other peoples as nothing but idols of wood and stone. They were perhaps driven to this conclusion through their belief that God used foreigners to punish his own people, and thus must control these foreigners also.

In early times also it is clear that the Hebrews believed in a rather primitive anthropomorphism, that Yahweh could walk the earth and talk to men, that he needed an earthly habitation. By the time of the end of the kingdom of Judah the priests were emphasizing that God could be neither seen nor heard by human beings, but that he was a spirit, infinitely remote from man though caring for him like a father, dwelling in heaven and not on earth. Ultimately both these concepts—the unity and the spiritual nature of God—were fully accepted by the Jews, and it was in this form that the Hebrew ideas about God were transmitted to subsequent ages.

The supreme consequence of the Hebrew concept is in the field of morality. Because God is a person, he can take part in human affairs, guiding them, rewarding and punishing his children, thus upholding the moral order.

The Hebrew God, being one, not a force of nature but a transcendent being, separate from the world, could act as ruler and governor, first of his chosen people and then of the whole world. He could issue a law which instructed the people in exactly what was required of them, could define disobedience to the law as sin, and could take steps to see that he was obeyed. The law thus removed any doubt in the sinner's mind as to what he was expected to do and what was forbidden him, while holding out the hope that if he fulfilled these duties toward God, he would be prosperous and happy. We shall see in the next section how the Hebrews were forced to modify this simple concept in the light of their actual experience.

Ethics and morality   Hebrew monotheism, then, with its consequent belief that God rewarded and punished men in accordance with their deeds, has been of incalculable importance in the religious and psychological history of mankind. Nevertheless, the traditional Hebrew concept of morality, enforced by God in his capacity as judge, was not to be the last word of the Hebrew thinkers. Some of the prophets saw that the commands of the Law limited morality within a too rigid framework. When Micah spoke of the task of man as to "do justice, love mercy, and walk humbly with thy God," he extended the boundaries of those actions favored by God to less circumscribed activities. And Jeremiah had an inkling of the need for escape from the bondage of the Law when he made this promise in the name of the Lord: "Behold I will make a new covenant with the house of Israel . . . . I will put my law in their inward parts and in their hearts will I write it . . . . And they shall teach no more every man his neighbor and his brothers, saying, 'Know the Lord'; for they shall all know me from the least to the greatest of them."[1]

_____
[1] Jeremiah 31:31–34.

Divine activity in the world   The third great development in Hebrew thought concerns the total activity of God in the world. In early times the whole concept of God expressed in Hebrew writings was as protector of the Children of Israel, his chosen and peculiar people. But if he was all-powerful, then he did not have to fight with other nations; he would deliver them into the hands of Israel. What, then, did this deduction mean, from the point of view of other nations? Was he not their God also? Once this problem is posed—and it did not arise so long as Yahweh was only one God among many—the answer must follow. But it did arise when the logical consequences of his supreme power were considered. If his power were not supreme, then he had to fight on behalf of Israel against the gods of their enemies. If he was supreme, then he was their *enemies'* protector too; or else they were left without a true God at all, which would be unjust. There was no way out of the dilemma; the other nations must somehow fit into the world order. It was all very well to denounce Assyria and Egypt, call their gods false gods, and prophesy destruction for them. But could any prophet with a sense of justice allow such a one-sided arrangement and say it was the work of a just God?

A medieval impression of Jonah praying to God for deliverance from the belly of the whale. Evidently the illustrator's knowledge of zoology left something to be desired! From a manuscript, Pseudo-Rudolf von Ems, Weltchronik, *ca. 1400.* (COURTESY THE PIERPONT MORGAN LIBRARY. Ms. 769, folio 223)

The answer might be, and was, given in terms of Israel's mission. God was using the foreign nations for purposes of his own, for the disciplining of Israel. He could have prevented the Assyrians from oppressing Israel, as he prevented them from taking Jerusalem in the time of Hezekiah; or he could use them to punish Israel's sin, as when the northern kingdom was deported. But to the more thoughtful among the prophets even this seemed rather a cavalier treatment of foreign nations. Were they not judged and punished for their sins; or did only Israel's sins count?

The question is no sooner posed in this manner than it must be answered in the only way possible. If Yahweh were indeed the God of the whole earth, then all the peoples were responsible to him equally, even if Israel had special tasks and special responsibilities as the only people of the earth to whom he had revealed himself and his Law. But the Assyrians were responsible when they broke the ordinary unrevealed natural law, and could be punished for it.

So we have the Book of Jonah, which tells how the prophet was sent to Nineveh to urge the Assyrians to repent. It is nothing short of astounding how daring this thought was that a prophet from the despised nation of Israel should go up to the capital of the mightiest world empire at the height of its power and prophesy its destruction (if it did not repent). The writer shows that Jonah was well aware of his temerity. For at first he did not dare to go, but took a ship going in the opposite direction. Then the Lord sent a storm upon the ship and did not calm it until the sailors had cast Jonah into the sea. Here he was swallowed by a whale, and not released from the belly of the whale until he had repented and promised to fulfill his mission. So at last he went up to Nineveh and preached. And, lo and behold, the Assyrians did repent, and the Lord spared them.

But the story does not end here. Jonah is angry because God has forgiven the Assyrians, thus making him a false prophet. So he sulks in the sun by the gate of the city. A gourd grows to protect him from the sun, and then, at God's command, the gourd withers, showing him by this sign that God has everything in his power,

and that Jonah himself would not survive against God's will. The book ends with the stern rebuke, "Should I not have compassion on Nineveh, that great city, in which are more than a hundred and twenty thousand people who know not their right hands from the left, and also many cattle?" Their ignorance saved them, for they had not been chosen and so had not known of God; when at last they were warned and heard, then God turned from his original purpose.

It should not be thought from this emphasis on the logical thought of the Hebrews that there was anything cold or abstract about their religion or their God. On the contrary, their whole thinking represented God as a person impossibly high above man, but recognizably akin to him, and with the feelings of man. It was thus possible not only to worship God but to love him, and God loved man in return. To the Hebrews man was in a real sense the son of God, who must occasionally be corrected, but always with a fatherly hand. "Those I love I rebuke and chasten," says the writer of the Proverbs. But the emphasis was not always on the chastening. "I taught Ephraim to walk, I took him in my arms . . . with human bonds I drew him, with cords of love. How shall I give you up, Ephraim, how shall I let you go, Israel? My heart turns within me, all my tenderness is kindled. I will not perform my fierce anger. I will not turn about to destroy Ephraim. For I am God and not man."[2]

Sin and punishment It has already been suggested that later Hebrew thought was disturbed by the discrepancy between the promises made by God to his people—seen by the Hebrews as a special Covenant between God and his chosen people—and the experience of life on earth as they knew it. If they obeyed the Law they should have been rewarded, and if they ceased to obey it, then they should have been punished. But only rarely did this happen; and it was the apparent happiness of the ungodly, and the undoubted occasional suffering of the manifestly righteous, that may have persuaded the later Hebrews to adopt the idea of a future life where justice would be vindicated.

[2] Hosea 11:3–8.

It does not seem that the Covenant itself was ever seriously questioned. But later thinkers realized that it could not comprise the whole duty of man, nor could the simple theory of rewards and punishments on earth suffice. More thought was needed on this central problem of the relationship between God and man, and much of the profoundest thought of mankind went into the effort to understand it. This thought, embodied in the Old Testament, became part of the imperishable heritage of Western man.

God had created man, not as a slave of God, but in the image of God. He had made man only a little lower than the Elohim (one of the Hebrew words for God, but sometimes translated by the timorous, who do not appreciate the grandeur of the Hebrew aspiration, as "angels"); he was God's special favorite among all living creatures, a child of God. And God was for man a Rock of Defense. If this were so, and God was all-just, all-righteous, and all-powerful, demanding equal righteousness from man, how could he sometimes seem not to care, and deliver man over to destructive forces of nature or to his earthly enemies? Was this the protection to which he was entitled by the Covenant?

The answer varied in different stages of Hebrew civilization, and according to whether the fate of the Hebrew people or the individual man was being considered. But both problems were thoroughly explored.

The most prevalent early view, the one expounded by the priestly writers when they considered the history of the people of Israel, was that in fact the people had not obeyed the Law and were rightly punished. The individual kings were also punished for leading Israel into sin.

According to the priestly tradition, then, the sins of the people of Israel and Judah were responsible for the destruction of these independent kingdoms; but Judah, because it was the home of David, to whom God had made special promises, would not be destroyed forever, because of God's mercy and because of his oath to David. God therefore was able to act unilaterally on behalf of his people out of his mercy, though the people had not in fact deserved it. The people sinned and deserved punishment; God sometimes spared and sometimes condemned them.

The great prophets, deeper thinkers than the priests, gradually moved away from the strict tradition of the Law as comprising the sum total of human duties, and would not accept the traditional answer. Some of them came to the thought that the sufferings of the people were not the result of sin, but a preparation, a testing, for an even higher destiny. At the time of the fall of Jerusalem to Babylon, and during the Exile, this thought alone seemed to fit the circumstances. It was not only because of God's mercy that the remnant was saved; it was because God had need of them. Not all of them, but those who had continued to worship him in spite of all their disasters. Instead of the idea of suffering as the due recompense of sin was developed the concept of suffering as a discipline, a purification by fire, so that those who survived were fitted for this great destiny. And so ultimately, fully in accord with this thought, followed the idea of a messiah who should redeem the world, sometimes conceived of as an earthly king who would inaugurate the rule of righteousness on earth, and sometimes as a suffering servant, "the man of sorrows and acquainted with grief," who would take upon himself the sorrows of the world. In both cases the mission of the whole Hebrew people was seen as preparing themselves to be ready to receive the Messiah, forming an elect body of righteous men to leaven the great masses of wicked humanity in the new age.

It did not, however, need a prophet to give the answer to the other parallel problem, the sufferings of the individual. To the logical mind, if the man who keeps the Law suffers, there must be some reason. Conversely, if the man who fails to keep the Law is not punished, why not? Here there are more possibilities, and the Hebrews explored all but one—the possibility of a future life of rewards and punishments—very thoroughly. This last possibility, indeed, was abandoned as soon as it was suggested by all the thinkers included in the canonical books of the Old Testament. Moreover, even when it was accepted by some Jews, it did not attain the dignity of a revelation, and was still not accepted by the priestly party at the time of Christ.

We see a suggestion of the problem very early; and already in the Law there is a typically primitive answer. The sins of the fathers are visited upon the children, an answer scornfully rejected by the prophets Ezekiel and Jeremiah: "The fathers have eaten sour grapes, and the children's teeth are set on edge." It is posed frequently in the Psalms: "Why do the ungodly flourish like a green bay tree?" Look to the end of their life, suggests one answer. Their good fortune will change. But manifestly this is not always true. The fullest answer is offered by the book of Job, which is entirely devoted to the problem. Job is presented as a righteous man, afflicted without any known reason. His friends carry on an extensive dialogue with him, trying to persuade him to admit that he has sinned, but in vain. Finally Job appeals to God himself to give him an answer, but the only answer he receives is that man cannot understand the ways of God. This, indeed, is the final answer of the ancient Hebrews. It is beyond the capacity of man to fathom the wisdom of God, and it is purposeless to question his judgments. He must, like the Psalmist, rely on faith in God's justice, and seek the only answer in the sanctuary of God.

The canonization of the Law   It should be emphasized that the bulk of Hebrew thought on the relationship between man and God was achieved by prophets and independent thinkers rather than by the priests. But in the last days of the kingdom of Judah a book of the Law was "found" in the temple and became the basis of a thoroughgoing religious reform carried out by King Josiah and the priests. This book is almost certainly the one called Deuteronomy, and from it we can see that as yet there has been no great change in the concept of sin and punishment held in earlier times, no emphasis on righteousness beyond the dictates of the Law. God will prosper the people if they keep his Law. "If you will but heed the commands that I am giving you today, to love the Lord your God, and serve him with all your mind and heart, he will give you rain for your land in due season . . . and he will produce grass in your fields for your cattle, and you will eat your fill."[3] This is the tone of the whole book, as was indeed to be

expected in a religious reform carried out by the aid of the priesthood. The emphasis was on the tribulations that had come upon the people because they had not kept the Law, and the material rewards that would be their lot if they returned to it.

A short time afterward the kingdom was conquered by the Chaldeans, and some of the leading Jews were taken captive and brought to Babylon. There, in spite of leaders who laid little emphasis on the Law, they were held together as a people by the Law, and on their return to Palestine under Persian auspices it was the priests who supervised the return and rebuilt the temple. As can be clearly seen, especially from the apocryphal book called Ecclesiasticus, or the Wisdom of Sirach, the Law had become the cement binding together both the Hebrew religion and the Jewish nation. The Law in its now definitive form was sufficient for all human purposes. The Torah or Pentateuch (the first five books of the Old Testament) was canonized as the revealed word of God. It was not earthly but divine; and it was unchangeable. It remained for Jesus Christ and his followers to return the emphasis to the *spirit* of the Law, as suggested by Jeremiah, and allow scope for human ethics beyond it.

The influence and importance of the Hebrew religion   The importance of the whole Hebrew religion to the world is incalculable. Once the problems of man's relationship with God and the resultant ethics had been wrestled with and certain conclusions reached, the world would never be the same again. One may deny the original premises[4] and ask for the evidence for the existence of any God at all; one may say that the Hebrews projected their own highest aspirations into their imagination of a supreme ruler of the universe. But one cannot deny the aspirations nor that the conclusions, as far as they go, follow from the premises. Not only did Christianity, the predominant religion in the West, base itself upon Hebrew thinking, but Islam also adopted the idea of the single transcendent God and much of Hebrew social

---

[3] Deuteronomy 11:13–15.

[4] The author of Ecclesiastes, a canonical book, even presents this point of view himself!

thought. The teachings of the Old Testament became the standard of conduct and even provided some of the law for the Protestant reformers in the sixteenth century, especially for those who followed the teachings of Calvin. And the Jews themselves have preserved their heritage and their belief in the Promised Land even thirty centuries after the death of Moses, and over nineteen hundred years after they ceased to exist as a separate nation. But more important than all this may have been their belief that man is answerable to God for his deeds on earth, that there is a divine sanction over man's activity. Whether we forget this, or believe with Aristotle that man cannot be happy unless he is good and that, since man must seek for happiness, no divine sanction is necessary, we cannot deny that the concept has profoundly influenced all subsequent civilization. Few men in the West have not at some time in their lives been forced to consider the possibility of its truth.

Suggestions for further reading

PAPER-BOUND BOOKS

Albright, William F. *The Biblical Period From Abraham to Ezra: A Historical Survey*. Torchbooks. The most recent and up-to-date of this author's books on the subject; precise, clear, and specific.

Albright, William F. *From the Stone Age to Christianity*. Anchor. A thought-provoking study of early religions in the light of archaeological investigation.

Breasted, James Henry. *Development of Religion and Thought in Ancient Egypt*. Torchbooks. Unlike Breasted's other books on Egypt, this one is largely free from the tendency to interpret ancient religious thought in the light of modern Christian concepts. Much of the book is quotation, on the whole well translated, but again with Christian overtones.

Breasted, James Henry. *A History of Egypt*. Bantam. Still the best general history of Egypt in English, though in several respects out-of-date and not in accord with more recent interpretations.

Chiera, Edward. *They Wrote on Clay*. Phoenix. An older work (1938) by one of the pioneer cuneiform scholars. Well-written general account, brief but good introduction to the subject.

Driver, Samuel R. *An Introduction to the Literature of the Old Testament*. Meridian. Though the last edition of this famous pioneer work dates from 1914, it is still worth reading. Most of the interpretations have been incorporated into all later writings on the subject.

Frankfort, Henri. *Ancient Egyptian Religion: An Interpretation*. Torchbooks. Many stimulating and original insights, though several are disputed by other students of ancient Egypt.

Frankfort, Henri, *et al. Before Philosophy*. Penguin. This symposium by scholars of the Oriental Institute of Chicago contains an article by John A. Wilson which he enlarged in his *Culture of Ancient Egypt*. The book is available in hard cover as *The Intellectual Adventure of Ancient Man* (Chicago: University of Chicago Press, 1946); the paper-bound edition omits the article by W. A. Irwin on the Hebrews.

Frankfort, Henri. *Birth of Civilization in the Near East*. Anchor. Useful introduction to the subject by a distinguished archaeologist.

Gurney, O. R. *The Hittites*. Penguin. Reliable survey of all phases of Hittite culture, with illustrations.

Kramer, Samuel N. *History Begins at Sumer*. Anchor. A list of the contributions of the Sumerians to history and the various fields in which they were the pioneers, written by one of the few living Sumerologists who was himself the first to read many of the documents analyzed here.

Kramer, Samuel N. *Sumerian Mythology*. Torchbooks. An earlier book (1944) than the author's *History Begins at Sumer;* the myths and legends are more fully described.

Neugebauer, Otto. *The Exact Sciences in Antiquity*. Torchbooks. Re-evaluation of Babylonian contributions to science. Somewhat difficult and technical, but well worthwhile for students with a knowledge of modern science.

Oesterley, W. O. E., and Robinson, T. H. *An Introduction to the Books of the Old Testament*. Meridian. Largely an abbreviated version of the authors' *A History of Israel*, old (1934), but still useful.

Olmstead, Albert T. *History of the Persian Empire*. Phoenix. Well-written work, best on history and political organization; somewhat weak on Zoroastrianism.

Orlinsky, Harry M. *Ancient Israel*, 2d ed. Cornell University Press. Short, clear, up-to-date account of Hebrew history by a Jewish scholar, taking good advantage of archaeological and recent biblical criticism.

Steindorff, G. and Steele, K. C. *When Egypt Ruled the East*. Phoenix. Attempts to bring Breasted's pioneer history of Egypt up to date, especially on the period of the Egyptian Empire.

Wilson, John A. *The Culture of Ancient Egypt*. Phoenix. This interpretation of ancient Egyptian culture and the relation between Egyptian religion and politics has been used extensively in this chapter. A uniquely valuable work published also as a hard-cover book under the title of *The Burden of Egypt* (Chicago: University of Chicago Press, 1951).

HARD-COVER BOOKS

Frankfort, Henri. *Kingship and the Gods*. Chicago: University of Chicago Press, 1948. Another valuable work from the Oriental Institute in Chicago. The first half is concerned with Egypt and should be read in conjunction with Wilson, mentioned above. Concentrates on concepts of kingship in Egypt. By a practicing archaeologist who devoted many of his last years to pondering the significance of the material he and others had uncovered.

Gordon, Cyrus H. *Before the Bible*. New York: Harper & Row, Publishers, 1962. Many stimulating ideas on the Sumerians and the early Semitic peoples. Puts forward, with many examples, the notion that the Greek heroic literature and mythology rest on a Semitic and Sumerian base.

Gordon, Cyrus H. *World of the Old Testament*. New York: Doubleday & Company, Inc., 1958. Uses effectively recent archaeological material, with stimulating suggestions. See also Gordon's *Introduction to Old Testament History* (Ventnor, N.J.: Ventnor Publishers, Inc., 1953) which covers partly the same ground.

Graham, W. C. *The Prophets and Israel's Culture*. Chicago: University of Chicago Press, 1934. Brief but stimulating study of the prophets, primarily as social reformers.

Heckel, Frederick. *A Tale of Ancient Egypt*. New York: Philosophical Library, Inc., 1963. Imaginative picture of life in Old Kingdom Egypt, couched in the form of a novel concerning a modern man who returned to Ancient Egypt in a time-machine. The Egyptian scenes, unlike those in almost all modern novels on the subject, are true to our knowledge of that age. The contrast between our age and the Old Kingdom is thought provoking. The novel is especially successful in depicting through a presentation of one Pharaoh the role of the king-god in ancient Egypt.

Oesterley, W. O. E., and Robinson, T. H. *A History of Israel*. 2 vols. Oxford, England: Clarendon Press, 1932. Carefully planned, judicious, and readable study, using all the material available at the time of writing. Probably the best general history of the subject.

Pritchard, James B. *Ancient Near Eastern Texts Relating to the Old Testament*, rev. ed. Princeton, N.J.: Princeton University Press, 1955. Excellent selection of readings from the ancient world, including all the most important ones from Egypt. The editor has interpreted his mandate liberally and not tried to confine his selections to those with immediate bearings on the Old Testament. Translated by leading scholars in each area, with valuable notes.

Smith, J. M. P. and Goodspeed, E. J., eds. *The Complete Bible: An American Translation*. Chicago: University of Chicago Press, 1939. This excellent translation of the Old Testament from several hands was used by the author for his biblical quotations. Any modern version is preferable to the King James version if understanding is desired, though none equals it for poetry. The King James version, however, occasionally contains quite serious errors in translation.

Zaehner, Robert C. *The Dawn and Twilight of Zoroastrianism*. New York: G. P. Putnam's Sons, 1961. By far the best available work in English on the subject, careful and thorough, though most of the book is concerned with the later history of the religion.

FOUR

The Heritage of Greek Civilization

❖ The Aegean civilization

One important civilization, contemporary with ancient Egypt and Mesopotamia, has not hitherto been mentioned. As early as 3000 B.C. a maritime civilization had been founded on the island of Crete. As we have seen, the Egyptians tended to be self-sufficient, and did not care to venture beyond the borders of their country in early times. This left open possibilities for any enterprising people who wished to do so to bring foreign products to Egypt, accepting Egyptian goods in exchange. For almost two millenniums the Cretans provided this service for the Egyptians, and in the process colonized many islands of the Aegean Sea and a few important centers on the mainland. Almost all our knowledge of this Aegean civilization comes from archaeology. Only within the last few years has the Cretan language yielded most of its secrets. But it now appears that we shall learn little of Cretan civilization from its writings as the vast majority are merely lists of household objects, names of gods, and other unhelpful data. Literature seems to be altogether missing.

Even the history of the island civilization is not yet fully agreed upon. It seems probable that the Cretans first brought some of the benefits of civilization to the native peoples of Greece. Then, somewhere in the second millennium B.C., much of Greece was conquered by a people called the Achaeans, who presumably moved into Greece from the north, perhaps from Central Europe. These Achaeans learned from the Cretans. They also gave better attention to their military forces, centered in particular around the city of Mycenae, of which Agamemnon was king in the time of the Trojan War. Somewhere around 1400 B.C. the Achaeans attacked Crete and conquered it, perhaps because the Cretans had allowed themselves to become unwarlike in the course of their always successful trading. They ruled Crete for the next two hundred years until they, in turn, were overwhelmed by a new wave of barbarians. These were the Dorians, who had already penetrated into southern Greece and settled there. The success of the Dorian expedition to Crete marked the end of Cretan (Minoan) civilization, which never recovered from this final blow.

Such knowledge as we have of Cretan civilization is, for the most part, derived from the remains of Cretan art and architecture, though there are also helpful references in later Greek writings and in some contemporary Egyptian documents and inscriptions. We therefore know about such things as the Cretan love of sports and life in the open air. We know also of their taste for luxury, and something about their home life. There is also enough information available for us to be able to say with some confidence that the Cretans should be regarded as precursors of the Greeks rather than as legatees of the Egyptians, in spite of the fact that there is a visible Egyptian influence in some of the Cretan works of art. There can be little doubt that the Cretans prepared the way for the later civilization of Greece by giving the Aegean world its first acquaintance with foreign civilization by way of maritime trade. Like the

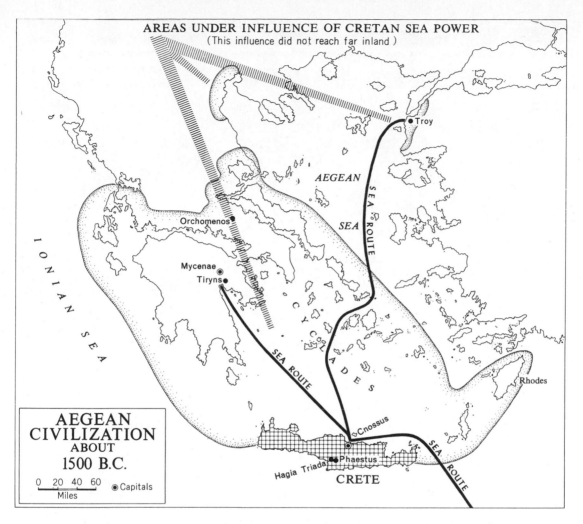

AREAS UNDER INFLUENCE OF CRETAN SEA POWER
(This influence did not reach far inland)

AEGEAN
CIVILIZATION
ABOUT
1500 B.C.

0 20 40 60 ⊚ Capitals
Miles

Etruscans who gave so much to the Romans, and who are also known only from legends and their material remains, the Cretans will almost surely never be assigned the place due to them in the history of civilization.

❖ The Homeric Age in Greece

From the middle of the second millennium, as has been said, barbarians began to penetrate into Greece from the north. Apart from the Achaeans, the leading groups were the Ionians (who may have been in Greece even before the Achaeans), the Aeolians, and the last group of invaders, the Dorians. The Dorians used iron, and this may in part account for their easy conquest of the bronze-using Achaeans and Cretans, since bronze was an expensive metal

and its use was necessarily confined to a small group of warriors. Much of the history of Greece from the beginning of these conquests is obscure, illuminated only by the Homeric epics, the *Iliad* and the *Odyssey*. These poems, still considered by many to be the greatest works of Western literature, are surrounded by mysteries which will probably never be solved. It is not known who wrote them, when they were written, whether they were both written by the same poet, or whether they are not merely traditional poems edited by a man whom later ages have called Homer.

These problems need not concern us here. All that needs to be said is that these epics purport to tell the history of a part of the war between a group of allies from the mainland of Greece and the city of Troy (the *Iliad*), and

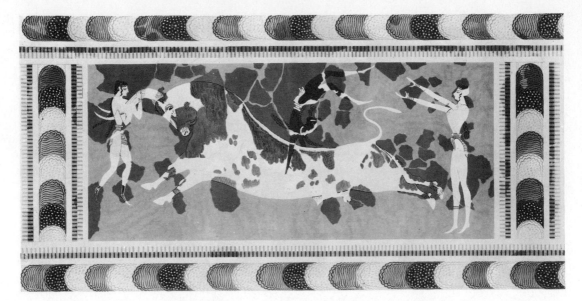

Reproduction of a Cretan fresco from the palace at Cnossus, showing the sport of bull leaping. Evidently the man uses the bull's horns as an aid in leaping over the bull, to be caught by his female partner on the other side. (COURTESY THE METROPOLITAN MUSEUM OF ART)

Reproduction of a fragment of a wall fresco from Hagia Triada in Crete. This famous fresco, showing a cat hunting a pheasant, is the earliest of the frescoes shown in this chapter. (COURTESY THE METROPOLITAN MUSEUM OF ART)

the story of the wanderings of Odysseus after the fall of Troy. It is probable that the *Iliad* and the *Odyssey* took their final shape about 800 B.C. The conditions described by Homer are therefore likely to have been similar to those prevailing in the early part of the first millennium B.C., when the invaders were settling in Greece. Society was aristocratic, but the freemen obviously were allowed their say in the council and assemblies; the kings and chiefs held their position by heredity, but they were far from absolute. There is no trace whatever of anything resembling the divine monarchy of Egypt. Agamemnon, leader of the Trojan expedition, holds some special prerogatives by virtue of his position, and, though he is a lesser warrior than Achilles, he is nevertheless strong enough to force Achilles to give up his captive slave-girl after the god Apollo has forced him to give up his own prize. Yet Agamemnon can use no sanctions against Achilles when the latter refuses to fight any longer in the war. For the rest, it is clear that Greece was not yet overpopulated; and there are numerous descriptions of feasts which would have been unthinkable in a later age, when Greece was too poor to support her population save on the most meager of diets. The chieftains themselves knew how to plow and did not regard agriculture as menial work; indeed, farming and sheepherding were clearly the main occupations of the era. It would seem also that the Greeks were not yet skilled in the making of industrial products, and the chief method of distribution of surplus goods was barter.

Not long after the Homeric Age and perhaps even during the lifetime of the poet, all the peoples of Greece, with a few notable exceptions, took part in a considerable movement of colonization. The movement was probably the result of land hunger and pressure of population on the scant resources of the country. The Greek colonies, unlike those of earlier peoples such as the Phoenicians, were not mainly for the purposes of trade. They were rather settlements of citizens, who were expected to make permanent homes for themselves in their adopted countries. The mother state usually organized the colonizing expeditions, and gave them its blessing. In return the colonists, it was hoped, would eventually produce a surplus of agricultural products which could be exchanged for the goods of the mother country. No jurisdiction over these colonies was asserted by the mother country. The colonies were free to set up their own form of government. It was regarded as an offense against common decency to wage war against the mother country. But if the colonies did turn against her, the latter could do nothing to prevent it. In later times several important colonies did in fact side against their founders in a general war.

In the course of two or three centuries colonies were founded on the borders of the Black Sea, in the coastal areas of Africa bordering on Egypt, and as far away from the homeland as eastern Spain; in addition, the coastal areas of Asia Minor and much of southern Italy were largely peopled by Greeks. It was not unusual for such colonies to be more powerful and prosperous than the often small city-states from which they had sprung.

❖ The Greek city-states

THE POLIS—CHARACTERISTIC GREEK POLITICAL AND SOCIAL UNIT

The very word "political," used in the heading above, comes from the Greek word *polis*, the characteristic Greek unit of government. If the achievements of Greek culture are to be understood, it is necessary to consider briefly what this unit consisted of, and how it may be said to have favored the special development of man as a political being. Historically, the polis probably derives from the period of the invasions, when a strong point was necessary to hold off marauding enemies. This strong point was the *acropolis*, and around it were the cultivated fields and the centers of trading necessary to keep the fortress supplied. The developed polis included not only the central strong point, the nucleus of the city, but all the territory around until the boundaries of the neighboring polis were reached. Thus the polis is a city-*state* in the true sense of the word, a city plus its environment, over which the gov-

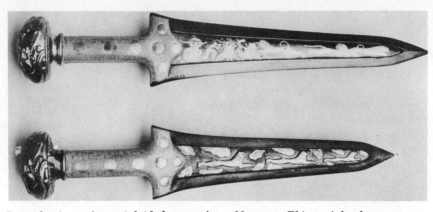

Reproductions of two inlaid daggers from Mycenae. This mainland center was especially noted for the fine bronze weapons it produced. (COURTESY THE METROPOLITAN MUSEUM OF ART)

ernment of the city exercised jurisdiction. The military leaders in early times necessarily administered the government, but when the invasions ceased to present such a pressing problem, the peaceful farmers and traders naturally expected to be consulted and perhaps to take some responsible part in the government. Each polis, however, had its own interests and liked to exercise its own self-government. Another polis might be absorbed in war, and no doubt in early times many budding *poleis* (plural of polis) were incorporated into the territory of larger neighbors; but such mergers could, as a rule, be accomplished only by war. Each polis strove fiercely to maintain its complete independence and autonomy, and all the citizenry were prepared to defend their polis at a moment's notice against any attempted encroachment.

The number of citizens in a polis naturally varied according to its size. In the smaller polis doubtless everyone knew everyone else, and in a sense this was always the ideal. The polis was at least as much an enlarged family as it was an official governmental unit. Aristotle once remarked that a man who could live without a polis "must be either a beast or a god," that is, he must be either subhuman or superhuman. In his view it was the ideal field of development for man. Man is a creature, he says elsewhere, "whose nature it is to live in a polis." It gave him a sense of belonging and a secure status. If he emigrated to another polis he would be ac-

corded only the status of a *metic*, or resident alien. He did not possess full political rights since he could not be expected to know enough of the aims and ideals of his new polis to participate effectively in its political life.

THE LEADING CITIES—ATHENS AND SPARTA

A study in extremes　In the study of Greek political life—a study which has been considered worth while for only about a century, in contradistinction to the study of the Roman Republic, which, even in the Middle Ages, has never failed to find interested scholars—it is fascinating to observe how extreme the two leading cities are as examples of a particular kind of society. Sparta was the perfect type of what the philosopher Henri Bergson called the "closed society," whereas Athens was the almost perfect type of the "open society." Athens was ruined by her democratic excesses, her too extreme freedom, whereas Sparta became a classic case of arrested development, all her forms so rigid that there was no possibility of a peaceful evolution in a necessarily changing world. The student can therefore study these two societies with profit not only for their inherent interest, but for the lessons they have to teach of the danger of excess—a danger which the Greeks themselves fully appreciated. The leading ideal of Greek thinkers was *sophrosyne*, or moderation; but from all that we can discover from their history, they may have continued to seek but did not find it.

Chronological Chart

Early Bronze Age in Crete	before 3000 B.C.
Minoan civilizations in Crete	3000–1400
Mycenaean civilization on mainland	before 1600
Conquest of Crete by Achaeans (?)	*ca.* 1400
Conquest of Crete by Dorians	*ca.* 1200
Fall of Troy to Achaeans and others	*ca.* 1184
Dorian invasions	1200–1000
Settlements in Asia Minor (Aeolians, Ionians, Dorians)	1000–900
Homeric poems	*ca.* 850
Hesiod	*ca.* 700
Greek colonization of Sicily and southern Italy	760–700
Great age of Miletus	750–550
First Messenian War (first enslavement of Messenians by Spartans)	736–716
Rule of Areopagus and archons in Athens	*ca.* 683
Second Messenian War	650–630
Draconian Code (Athens)	621
"Lycurgan" reforms in Sparta	610?
Solonian reforms (Athens)	594
Regime of Pisistratus	561–527
Constitution of Cleisthenes	508
First Persian invasion—Battle of Marathon	490
Second Persian invasion—Salamis and Plataea	480–479
Organization of Confederation of Delos	477
Ascendancy of Pericles	457–429
Treasury of the Confederation removed to Athens	454
Peloponnesian War	431–404
Knights of Aristophanes—Ascendancy of Cleon	425
Athenian expedition to Syracuse	415–413
Battle of Aegospotami—Defeat of Athenians	404
Spartan hegemony of Greece	404–371
Regime of Thirty and Ten "tyrants" (Athens)	404–403
Restoration of the democracy	403
Trial and execution of Socrates	399
Battle of Leuctra—Defeat of Spartans by Thebans	371
Hegemony of Thebes	371–362
Philip II becomes king of Macedon (Macedonia)	359
Battle of Chaeronea	338
Congress of Corinth and foundation of Hellenic League	338–337
Reign of Alexander	336–323
Ptolemy I Soter seizes Egypt	321
Civil War between the generals	322–301
Seleucus I founder of Seleucid dynasty in Asia	305–280
Battle of Ipsus—Final division of Alexander's kingdom	301
Foundation of Museum of Alexandria	286
Eumenes I founds independent kingdom of Pergamum	263
Attalus III of Pergamum bequeaths kingdom to Rome	133
Syria made a Roman province by Pompey	64
Cleopatra (VII) on Egyptian throne	51

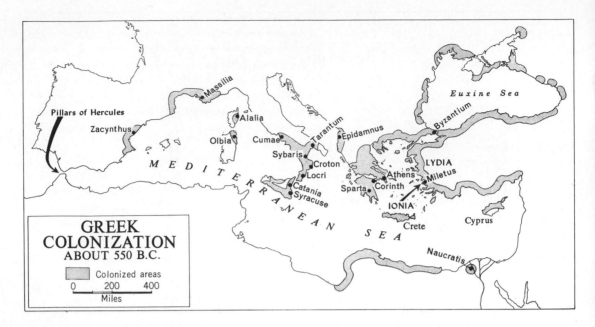

GREEK
COLONIZATION
ABOUT 550 B.C.

Colonized areas
0   200   400
Miles

Political and social development of Sparta
Lest we be astonished that the Spartans should
have developed a society and institutions that
seem to demand so much of human nature and
go so contrary to what we think of as natural
human impulses and instincts, it should be explained at once that there were sound historical
reasons for the development of a militarized
state. The Spartan nobles, evidently hungry for
land, committed an aggression upon their neighbors, the equally Dorian Messenians. After winning the First Messenian War and imposing
severe terms on their enemies, the Spartans soon
had to defend themselves against an attempt by
the Messenians to recover their position. During
this war the Spartan homeland was in very
grave danger, and only a providential death of
the general of the leading ally of the Messenians
saved the Spartans from conquest. Recovering
from their early defeats, they succeeded once
more in conquering Messenia. Then, instead of
being content with territorial changes of a
minor nature, they decided to enslave the whole
Messenian population. This meant that the Spartans were now in the sorry position of having
to keep down a considerable population, possibly
one outnumbering their own, and forcing them
to work for their new masters. And these people
were not alien barbarians but Dorian Greeks,
in every respect the equal of their masters save

that they had been defeated in battle. Thus, the
Spartans, in order to force their victims, who
were called *helots*, or state slaves, to work, had
themselves to be prepared constantly to put
down a revolt; and such revolts were not uncommon, although conditions in the country
prevented easy coordination between the scattered helots.

Although nothing is known for certain of
the famous lawgiver of Sparta who has passed
down to history as Lycurgus, and we know
neither if nor when he lived, the laws are authentic enough. They probably considerably
antedate the Messenian Wars, since long before
these culminating wars the Dorians of Laconia
(whose chief city was Sparta) had had to fight
hard to conquer their territory, and the system
of state slavery had already been established.
Now, however, it was more thoroughly systematized, and the Spartan constitution in effect in
the fifth century B.C. was already in operation
by the end of the seventh century.

There were three classes of people in Sparta
at this time, the free-born, who were called
Spartiates, the *perioeci*, and the helots. The
perioeci were not Spartan citizens; they could
not become professional soldiers nor intermarry
with Spartans; they possessed no political rights.
Their task was to handle all the economic affairs
of the Spartans, especially dealings with for-

eigners. Sometimes, in case of war, they could serve with the Spartan infantry. The helots, as the property of the state, possessed certain elementary rights. They could not be put to death save by the authority of the state, and they possessed a certain amount of personal freedom as long as they farmed well and provided their particular master with enough for his subsistence. In times of grave danger they could serve in the Spartan army, though they were naturally regarded as untrustworthy. It was, however, possible to earn their freedom from helotry by such means. The helot, therefore, was in a sense lent by the Spartan state to the free citizens as a source of permanent labor, relieving them from menial work and leaving them free for a totally military life.

The professional military class devoted itself to nothing but war and preparations for war. This class was rigidly selected. Children who were weak and puny at birth were simply exposed to die. Education for boys consisted of all forms of athletics, military instruction, and physical exercise. Boys were made to go barefoot and ill-clad in winter, to sleep without coverings, and to prepare all their own meals. Girls fit to be mothers of Spartans had to undergo a similar regime of athletics and games, and were taught courage, endurance, and patriotism. Boys lived at home with their mothers till they were seven years old. Then they went into military training in groups under the charge of older boys, and lived in barracks. At the age of twenty marriage was compulsory, but the husband continued to live in barracks, and could visit his wife only on rare occasions. According to Plutarch, it was hoped that this continence would serve to procreate more healthy children, and in any case it would protect the Spartiate from a possible weakening caused by contact with home comforts. From the labor of his helots each adult had to supply his share of the food eaten at the public mess. If a Spartiate for any reason could not supply his share, he lost status and became an inferior citizen, with reduced political and social rights.

The temple of Poseidon at Paestum, one of the Greek colonies in Italy. In spite of being located in Italy, this temple is older than the Parthenon, and is the best-preserved Greek temple in the world. These Greek colonies were conquered by the Romans and absorbed into the Confederation of Italy at the close of the wars with Pyrrhus. (PHOTO BY MRS. JOSEPH E. WISAN)

Two views of a Spartan kylix (terracotta). The painted interior depicts the apotheosis of Heracles. This piece shows that by 580 B.C., the date of the kylix, the Spartans were still able to produce works of craftsmanship comparable to that of the other Greeks. (COURTESY THE METROPOLITAN MUSEUM OF ART)

To prevent contamination with foreign ideas and people, aliens were rarely admitted to the city; and those who received permits were periodically expelled. To prevent the accumulation of wealth the Spartans maintained a heavy iron currency which was not exchangeable anywhere else.

This logical "Lycurgan" system fulfilled its purpose. The helots were kept under control for more than two hundred years, and Sparta possessed an army which was able to play a noble part in defeating the Persians. Its heavy infantry was unbeaten by any Greek city in battle until the rise of Thebes in the fourth century, and was the most highly disciplined and efficient body of troops in Greece. However, it should be understood that the main purpose of this army was internal control, and not foreign imperialist adventures. Spartan heroism, however, was proverbial, and undoubtedly real. The

social sanctions ensured it, for no Spartan dared go home in disgrace; he dared not even leave the battlefield to take news home.

The other Greeks, with their high ideal of civic virtue and duty, recognized that on this score the Spartans were their superiors. Civic duty was accepted freely by the Spartans as a requirement that the polis might reasonably impose on its citizens. Obedience to the laws of the city was as binding an obligation for the citizen as obedience to divine laws was obligatory for the individual. The other Greeks did not think the Spartans lived under a tyranny, but under a regime chosen for them by Lycurgus and accepted by them. The Athenian would not have accepted such laws for a moment, nor would he have put up with the Spartan food and frugality, which were the object of frequent jests among citizens of other states, frugal as they were themselves by our standards.

It was the privilege of the Spartans to choose their laws and to obey them; and to all appearances they did obey them. We do not hear of Spartans leaving their city to enjoy the delights of Athens or Corinth until after the Spartan victory in the Peloponnesian War (404 B.C.). It was perhaps the heroic nature of their extreme and narrow ideal and the heroic way in which they lived up to it that excited the admiration of their neighbors; whereas the philosophers admired the way they used their laws to form character and the logical nature of the laws themselves. The vulgarity, boasting, and propaganda of modern fascist states distinguish them effectively from Sparta. It was the Spartan's pride that he was a man of few words; and the word "laconic" has passed into our language. And a "Spartan" regime means, not an imperialist, fascist, communist, or oligarchic state, but a regime of simplicity and abstinence.

Athens—Political evolution As soon as we come to study Athens we are at once made aware of a marked difference between the two peoples. The Athenians themselves, of course, were fully aware of it, and on the whole they tended to attribute it to the fact that they were Ionians while the Spartans were Dorians. The Athenians were experimental; they were willing to take a chance that change might mean improvement; and their ruling classes at a crucial moment in Athenian history did not fight to stave off change and maintain their privileged position, but preferred to allow the political forms of their state to evolve. Once this initial step had been taken they may well have been sorry, since the Athenians went forward to the most complete democracy the world has yet seen. In the process the aristocrats lost all their privileges and had to submit to rule by the majority, which did not mean themselves. It is worth devoting some attention to this process, since it tells us much about the Athenian people and why to this day we remember their civilization as one of the greatest in world history.

The land of Attica, which comprised the polis of Athens, was not a territory rich in resources. Yet it was large in comparison with

This model of the Agora shows Athens in the second century A.D. rather than in the period covered by the text. Many changes were made during the period of domination by the wealthy Hellenistic monarchs; however, the model will serve to give some idea of the layout of the Agora. Although the buildings of the fifth century B.C. were less sumptuous and costly and the arrangement was less orderly, the style of architecture was not greatly different. (COURTESY AMERICAN SCHOOL OF CLASSICAL STUDIES AT ATHENS)

most of the Greek city-states, and Athens had taken but little share in the great colonizing movement of the eighth and seventh centuries. But the Athenians were trying to grow wheat and be self-sufficient on land that was for the most part totally unsuited for it. The result was that the peasants who made up the bulk of the population by the middle of the seventh century were having a great deal of difficulty in making a living. Moreover, the majority probably did not own their own land and had to supply a considerable proportion of their crop to their landlords, who also controlled the effective machinery of the state. The result was that they fell into debt, borrowed money for their new crops, and ultimately had no security to offer but their own persons. They were then sold into slavery abroad. This state of affairs caused the agitation that might have been expected, and there were no doubt murders and much ravaging of property. It should be added that the

landowners used wheat, which was readily salable everywhere, as payment for their industrial imports, in spite of the fact that there was too little wheat at home to fill the needs of the people, even with fair distribution. So the peasants, who produced the wheat, went hungry.

Probably because trade was seriously affected by the disturbances, the peasants found an ally in the traders, who put pressure upon the landowners for reforms. The first effort at reform was merely to produce a code of law so that the peasants could be properly tried before being punished (the code of Draco, 621 B.C.). But in the early part of the sixth century the aristocrats at last agreed to allow one of the wise men of Greece, Solon, to try his hand at a political and economic reform, which he was peculiarly well fitted to do since he had both landowning and trading interests. Solon realized that the basic difficulty in Athens was the unsuitability of its main crop and the lack of

Each of these three amphorae is from a different century. The one on the left is from the seventh century B.C. and is a product of inferior technique; also, note that the decoration still shows some Oriental influence. The center amphora is from the great age of Pisistratus when Athens was striving hard against severe competition in the export market. The amphora on the right is from the age of Pericles when Athens was secure and prosperous and these amphorae were often used for the home market; note the ornateness of this amphora. (COURTESY THE METROPOLITAN MUSEUM OF ART)

Farewell scene from a gravestone. Note the way in which the artist has tried to emphasize the common grief of the family, a theme certainly underemphasized in Greek literature. (COURTESY THE METROPOLITAN MUSEUM OF ART)

industry in the city. To solve this twofold problem he forbade the export of wheat, encouraged the growing of vines and olives instead of wheat, and invited skilled artisans into Athens with the promise of full citizenship. Thus it would become possible for dispossessed peasants to make an alternative living in the city. It meant also that Athens thereafter would be dependent upon imports of grain to make up the deficiency in production, and that therefore, like some modern economies, she would have to export manufactured goods to pay for them. Solon also inaugurated a far-reaching reform of the law courts and instituted an assembly and council made up of propertied classes, but with far wider representation than the old exclusive aristocratic council of the Areopagus.

Solon's reforms were evidently too drastic to be carried out without some degree of com-

pulsion. This was supplied by an enlightened autocrat named Pisistratus, who managed to rule Athens by political manipulation for upward of thirty years and nevertheless die peacefully in his bed. By the time of his death most of the economic problems had been solved; the most recalcitrant of the aristocrats were in exile in Sparta; Athens was a leading exporter of pottery and specialized agricultural products; and she was the possessor of a fine navy. She was now ready for a further dose of democracy.

The occasion for political reform was provided by the autocratic behavior of Hippias, son of Pisistratus, who never recognized that his father had been able to rule only because his rule was accepted by the majority of the citizens. During the regime of Pisistratus the aristocratic exiles could expect to find little support in Athens. But when Hippias began to behave like a real tyrant the aristocrats saw their opportunity. Led by Cleisthenes, they invaded Athens with the help of a Spartan army; but once they had won a military victory the aristocrats fell out among themselves. Faced with this situation, Cleisthenes suddenly decided to join the democratic forces, who accepted him as their leader and instructed him to draw up a new democratic constitution. He fulfilled his mandate loyally. By a piece of skilled gerrymandering, he prevented the rise of another dictator like Pisistratus while giving the Athenians their first real democracy.

The pivot of the Athenian constitution was the Assembly of all male citizens, without property qualification, which had to be called into session at least ten times a year and was absolutely sovereign except for certain safeguards which need not be entered into here. In addition to the Assembly, which decided on all important questions, a Council of 500 was elected, soon afterward if not in the time of Cleisthenes, by lot from a list of eligible citizens who had not sat in the Council in at least the ten previous years. This Council, divided into committees of 50, each the chief committee for a tenth of the year, acted as the executive of the state, looking after all the details of administration. Later there was instituted a board of 10 generals who had further executive duties to perform. From their number the Assembly chose the actual war

This gold bow case was found in Scythia (South Russia). It was evidently an Athenian export item of special interest to the barbarian princes in this area on whom the Athenians were dependent for imports of grain. (COURTESY THE METROPOLITAN MUSEUM OF ART)

leaders in case of hostilities. The government therefore was a full democracy of a town-meeting type not unlike that of the early American Colonies. It was based on the theory that government by amateurs is best, that each citizen was as qualified as the next one in the somewhat elementary duties of government, and that full participation and interest in the affairs of the state can alone make a democratic government work. The only representative principle in this government is to be found in the board of generals. A general could be elected and re-elected as long as the people had confidence in him. It was customary for each general to represent one of the ten tribes, but it was also possible for some noted citizens, such as Pericles in later years, to be elected at large by all the citizens. It was generally understood who was the leading citizen at any given time, and such a man would usually have the privilege of addressing the Assembly first and putting forward his suggestions. The Council was expected to prepare other legislation for the Assembly and to give it a preliminary discussion.

For a century this government worked on the whole very effectively, probably because the people during this period were still willing to choose as leaders men of ability from the old aristocracy. The government deteriorated badly during the Peloponnesian War, when the ruling majority too often forgot the interests of the state and showed themselves excessively docile in the hands of warmongering demagogues. Nevertheless, even after its comparative failure at this time, the people restored it as soon as they were able after their defeat and occupation by Sparta, and a form of government quite recognizable as a descendant of that of Cleisthenes remained in Athens until its conquest by Macedonia in the late fourth century B.C.

❖ Intercity relations

THE PERSIAN WARS

Only a few years after Cleisthenes had established the new Athenian constitution all the peoples of Greece were to be put to a severe test. The expanding empire of Persia took over the Greek city-states in Asia Minor, which appealed to their friends on the mainland for help. Athens sent a small expedition, which soon returned after some successes. The Persian king, Darius I, was furious with this interference, however, and sent an expedition of his own against Athens and such other states as would not submit and send earth and water as a token of submission to the great monarch. The result was the campaign of Marathon (490 B.C.), in which the Athenians almost alone defeated the great expedition. The Persians were ignorant of the country, and had evidently hoped that some influential Athenians would give them aid against their own compatriots. Although the traitors did their best, their aid came too late to help the Persians. Darius' son Xerxes prepared a much larger expedition, which was to proceed by both land and sea. The Greeks knew of the preparations but found it extremely difficult to concert any policy. Athens was obviously best fitted for leadership by sea, and Sparta by land. Matters were further complicated because some of the northern cities submitted rather than defend themselves.

The outcome was the heroic defeat of the Spartans at Thermopylae, followed by the capture and sack of Athens, mitigated by the great Athenian sea victory of Salamis (480 B.C.). In spite of the loss of their city, the Athenians fought on, and the following year a grand alliance led by Sparta was able to defeat the Persian land forces at the battle of Plataea, while the Athenian and allied navy defeated the Persian navy at Mycale (479 B.C.). Thereafter Greece was free from attack by Persia, though from the end of the fifth century through the fourth until the conquest of Persia by Alexander, Persian influence was strong in Greece, and Persian money played a not inconspicuous part in the final defeat of the Athenians in the Peloponnesian War.

THE CONFEDERATION OF DELOS— ATHENIAN IMPERIALISM

After the war was over the Athenians decided that the only way to prevent a renewed attack was to form a league of defense, composed of Athens herself and as many of the

Ostraka, or ballots, used for ostracism in Athens in the fifth century B.C. Note the names of prominent Athenian statesmen written on them: Kimon, Themistokles, (A)risteid(es), Perikles, Miltiades. (COURTESY AMERICAN SCHOOL OF CLASSICAL STUDIES AT ATHENS)

Aegean islands as she could persuade to join her. Sparta was also invited into the league (called the Confederation of Delos), but firmly and politely inclined. Originally it was a free league, although obviously Athens was the leading partner. Some of the islands provided money, and a few of the larger ones provided ships. The money was used by the Athenians to build ships, but the sailors were trained in Athens and the commanders were Athenian. It is therefore not surprising that the instrument thus forged proved to be too tempting for the Athenians, and under the leadership of Pericles it began to be used for purposes for which it had not been intended. After a defeat had been sustained in the eastern Mediterranean, where the navy had no business to be, Pericles turned the debacle to good account by having the treasury, hitherto located in Delos, one of the smaller islands sacred to Apollo, transferred to Athens. When Athens decided not to permit anyone to leave it, the free league had clearly become an Athenian empire.

THE PELOPONNESIAN WAR

In addition to using the fleet as he saw fit, and using the surplus of the treasury for beautifying Athens, Pericles began to interfere in the internal affairs of the islands, encouraging the setting up of democratic governments favorable to Athens in place of the older oligarchies which had been traditional. For a time also he carried on some minor wars on the mainland of Greece until a few setbacks decided him to pursue his ends by the more diplomatic means of trying to bring over states allied to Sparta into his league. Ultimately the fear induced in Sparta and in the leading Peloponnesian trading state of Corinth caused them to launch a preventive war, to be known henceforth as the Peloponnesian War, since the historians of the war were Athenian. Honors in this war were fairly equally divided for the first half, which was concluded by a temporary peace. The Spartans could not be seriously defeated by land (though they did suffer some severe losses in minor Athenian expeditions), nor could the Athenians be defeated by sea; and as long as they held command of the sea they could not be starved. However,

when the peace was broken and the war renewed, the Athenians overreached themselves and, through bad judgment in the campaign, lost the whole of a great expedition sent to Syracuse in Sicily. Thereafter the Athenians were on the defensive. They had lost more than they could recover, a number of the islands revolted, and the Persians saw their chance to finish off their ancient enemy by giving aid and comfort to Sparta. The last Athenian fleet was destroyed at Aegospotami in 405 B.C., and Athens was forced to surrender for lack of supplies, now cut off by the victorious Spartans. Though the Athenians made a partial recovery in the fourth century, they were forever afterward plagued by poverty and never built up a first-class state again.

Throughout the great fifth century, Athens had been able to maintain her position as a first-class power in the Greek world only because of the tribute money that she had at her disposal from the islands in the league. She was always faced with a large visible unfavorable balance of trade due to her overpopulation and general underemployment. But the carrying trade and the balance of money from the islands not actually used for the allied navy were able to make up this deficit. To the use of this money we undoubtedly owe the incomparable artistic achievements of the fifth century.

Both Sparta and Athens, and indeed all Greece, suffered severely from the internecine struggle of the Peloponnesian War. Not only had many thousands of men been killed, but a great deal of the territory had been ravaged, and, perhaps worst of all, the custom had arisen of looking to Persia for support in the fratricidal struggles between the city-states. Persia, however, had no interest in them except to keep as many states as possible weak and disunited. No great thing was achieved by the war, party struggles and bitterness were exacerbated, and the necessary unity of Greece was postponed until the city-states were conquered by the outsider Philip of Macedon in the second half of the fourth century. If Athens, Sparta, and Corinth had learned to live together, or if Athens had been willing to let her league be really free and perhaps ultimately federal, then the work of Philip of Macedon would have been

431 B.C.
GREECE AT THE
BEGINNING OF THE
PELOPONNESIAN WAR
ATHENS AND ALLIES
SPARTA AND ALLIES
NEUTRAL

impossible. It was the Peloponnesian War that made his ultimate rise, or the rise of another like him, inevitable.

❖ Daily life in Athens

The whole social life of Athens, and indeed that of all other Greek cities, reflects, above all, the extraordinary poverty of material resources, which was not only accepted philosophically by the Greeks but regarded as the natural and even desirable order of things. The ordinary man remained a frugal liver, both in

imperial times and in the fourth century. Even what he considered luxuries would be to the imperial Roman very little indeed. Everything must be judged by Greek standards. When Pericles boasts that luxuries from the whole world stream into Athens we must set this against the background of the known national income, and the known social life as shown by the inscriptions, by the artistic remains as well as by the literature. All Greeks wore clothes of the utmost simplicity at all times, an undergarment fastened with a safety pin, and an outer garment draped about their person. The same garment served as a blanket. Beds were usually planks, without springs. The average house, un-like the temples, was made of sun-dried brick, and houses were built close together. The walls were not decorated, the furniture was crude and utilitarian. When Pericles insisted that Athenian homes were beautiful and elegant, he may have been speaking the truth, because the artistic decorations that the Greeks knew so well how to make may have been in use. If so, we know nothing of such decorations; but the furniture in the house of the most fashionable young man of Athens in his day, a list of which we do possess, is singularly unimpressive. The houses themselves were adequate for living in, but bear no comparison at all with those of pre-Greek Minoan Crete.

The reason for this utter lack of luxury in the private homes of the Athenians is simple enough. The Greek lived primarily in the open air. More hours of the day were spent in the gymnasium, the agora, or the streets than in his house. When it was dark he went to bed, and at dawn he usually rose and went into the street, without breakfast. We hear nothing from any source of any great mansions of the Roman type in classical times, nor of palatial private gardens and pleasure grounds. Rich men con-tributed their wealth to the polis, and did not use it so much for their own pleasure; but even their riches were small enough by Roman or Cretan standards. There were no gargantuan feasts; food was scarce and lacked variety. Meat was rarely eaten.

The truth seems to be, hard as it may be for us to believe, that the Greek really did not care for luxury, or not enough to give up his leisure to gain it; and it was frowned upon by public opinion. A contrast sometimes made be-tween Athenian luxury and Spartan simplicity is extremely relative. Both lived simply; but the Spartan cultivated simplicity, wearing only one garment in winter and going barefoot, whereas the Athenian had sandals. The Athenian was able to decorate his city superbly because he cared for it rather than for his home; and to the service of his gods and his city he devoted all his unparalleled artistic talents.

The kind of freedom that resulted from this doing without is one that is unique in history, and can never be repeated. But if one delights in free talk, assemblies, festivals, plays, the de-velopment of the mind and the body, self-government, and civic glory, the logical thing to do is to avoid cluttering oneself up with posses-sions useless to this kind of life. The Athenian was never afraid that he would lose his posses-sions. Even if his city were to be destroyed it could always be rebuilt—as Athens was rebuilt after its sack by the Persians. But freedom, once it had been lost, might never be restored; and such a loss could destroy the whole basis for life in the polis. In the rest of this chapter we shall see how the Athenians used this freedom.

❖ **The searching mind of the Greek**

GENERAL CHARACTERISTICS OF
GREEK THOUGHT

All knowledge, said the Greeks, begins in wonder—wonder about the world, and wonder about man. The Hebrews asked only one ques-tion about man: his relation to his God. The Greeks asked not only this question but all other questions. They were the greatest people for questioning that the world has yet seen, or at all events until our own time. When Aristotle came to write his *Politics* he felt obliged to ask a great many fundamental questions before he dared to generalize. He had amassed material on 158 constitutions, constitutions evolved by generations of men struggling with the problem of how men could best be governed. None of the constitutions was perfect; all had failed in some respects. But the people themselves had discovered the defects, and by asking why and considering the alternatives they had tried to remedy them. So Aristotle conceived it to be his task to classify these constitutions, to see whether he could evolve a system that would have the most merits and the fewest weaknesses even if it would not be ideal. Plato, on the other hand, was looking in his *Republic* for an ideal state. So it was necessary for him to inquire first on what principles an ideal state could be built, and then to find institutions through which it could be expressed. This took him a long way. For, having discovered that it must be based on justice, he then had to find out what justice was. Neither Plato nor Aristotle ever thought for a moment that it was not the duty of man to improve his institutions, as the ancient Egyptians had thought. And it is this willingness to seek new knowledge and to stake their lives on the result of continuous experiment based on the best thinking of which they were capable that distinguishes the Greeks from their predecessors.

The Greeks wondered about the physical world. What was the underlying stable substratum in a world where everything appeared to be in flux—was it water, air, fire, or atoms? Clearly, everything changed in appearance; but they did not doubt that this change was only an apparent change. Underneath was a unity. When Thales saw the Egyptian notebooks which told of the measurements of the angles and sides of a triangle, his mind leaped ahead to the universal idea underlying all these particulars. And he is credited with the famous pons asinorum theorem—in *all* triangles, the angles subtending equal sides are equal to one another.

The Greeks wondered about man—his nature, the seen body, and the unseen soul that gave life to it. They assumed the existence of the soul, but they tried to find the relationship between soul and body. How does man acquire knowledge? What is the nature of the mind that knows it? What are the laws of thinking? How does one idea connect with another? What is an idea? What are the activities proper to man? What is morality?

In all these questions except the last, the Greeks were pioneers in human thinking; and even in the last they were different from the Hebrews in that at least the later Greeks accepted nothing, not even the gods, as final arbiters. While they might admit that the fear of the Lord was the beginning of wisdom, this to them would only be one more reminder that they were men and not gods. The last thing a classical Greek would do would be to enter the sanctuary and there receive a comfort which would save him the necessity of questioning further.

WONDER ABOUT THE WORLD—COSMOLOGY

The first thinkers to speculate about the nature of the world and the universe were not

Athenians, nor indeed did the Athenians show much interest at any time in physical speculation. Their almost exclusive interest was in man. The early cosmologists hailed from Ionia, and the problem they set themselves was the fundamental problem, which, expressed literally, was: Out of what does everything come? What is the primal substance underlying all visible physical phenomena, however much the form or appearance of objects changes? The Ionians assumed that there was such a substance. Thales suggested water; Anaximenes, air; Heraclitus, fire. Naturally they could not prove which, if any, of these substances was the primary one, although no doubt they had observed such phenomena as the three visible stages of water.

The Eleatic school of thinkers in southern Italy gave consideration to the same problem. Parmenides came to the conclusion, on theoretical grounds, that there could be no such thing as nothing. The whole idea, for him, was inconceivable. Thus there could be no such thing as a real change, since this would involve the appearance of something new that had not been in existence before. Essentially all phenomena must be the same, with the consequence that all visible change must be illusory. This criticism having been accepted by all later thinkers, the question was shifted, and now became a quest for what caused the visible changes in phenomena. Out of all this speculation ultimately arose the Greek atomic theory, explained in detail by Democritus of Abdera. All things, said he, are made up of filled space and empty space, atoms and the void. The atoms were not infinitely small but simply very small (like our molecules). Each atom had its own characteristics, a characteristic shape and a characteristic movement, which gave rise to the qualities observed in objects by men: sweet and sour, hard and soft, and all the infinite variety that we perceive.

The importance of all this speculation was not, of course, in its results, but in the fact that it is altogether new in its objectives and in the kinds of explanation that it offers. The gods are not brought in to explain phenomena; it is assumed that the basis of all things is material. Man had, in his mind, removed himself from his universe and stopped to look at it. He had taken the first steps along a road the ending of which is not yet in sight, but which, along the way, has led to modern science and a transformed world.

WONDER ABOUT MAN AND HIS PLACE IN THE UNIVERSE—THE ATHENIAN CONTRIBUTION

The relationship between man and gods— Greek tragedy It has become customary to call the cosmologists whose work we have been considering the "pre-Socratic" philosophers. Philosophers or not—and we prefer to think of them as early theoretical scientists—the term pre-Socratic suggests an important truth, that Socrates, though he never wrote a line, is the key figure in the history of Greek thought. The philosophers who follow him build upon his work, while the thinkers before him, notably the great Athenian tragic dramatists, Aeschylus and Sophocles, seem to live in an altogether different world, with different assumptions and different insights. Yet it was not Socrates himself whose thought was crucial. He was the first thinker who tried to repair the damage done to traditional thinking by the Sophists, but the intellectual revolution itself was the achievement of the Sophists. Thus in this chapter we shall deal with the pre-Sophists and their framework of ideas first, show how the Sophists destroyed this framework with their criticism, and finally how the great thinkers—Socrates, Plato, and Aristotle—repaired the damage as far as it could be repaired, and set the world on a new path of thinking that has persisted since their time. Because this intellectual revolution can lay claim to being the most important such revolution in the history of mankind, and is the most distinctive contribution of the Greeks to the intellectual heritage of mankind, most of the rest of this chapter will be devoted to it.

The great question, for the Greeks as for the Hebrews, was, What is the relation between the earthly and the spiritual man—what is the relation between man and the gods? This may well be the question we in our Western civilization should be asking ourselves, but too often we have forgotten it, still under the spell of the Sophists who claimed that it was unanswerable. The central thought of early Greek civilization was that man lives within a framework of destiny, which the Greeks called Moira. This idea suffuses the work of Homer; it is implicit in the *Odyssey* and extremely explicit in parts of the *Iliad*. In Homer it is made clear that man's deeds on earth, however pleasing they may have been to the gods, will not avail to save him from his destined destruction. Hector, it is explicitly stated, has always fulfilled his religious obligations toward Zeus and the other gods; his moral character has been impeccable; and yet he must fall a victim to the spear of Achilles, who is on all counts his moral inferior. Zeus himself is ruled by the superior power of Moira. He weighs the lot of Hector and the lot of Achilles in the balance; when it is shown by this test that Hector is the one who must die in the duel between the two heroes, then Zeus has to forbid further divine help to him and turns him over to his godly and earthly enemies. Hector himself, elsewhere in the poem, recognizes that he is no match for Achilles and that he will die. Andromache, his wife, cannot persuade him to escape the duel, not with all the love she bears him and he bears her. It is his duty as a man to engage in the conflict, a duty toward himself, or what the Greeks called *arete*. Man can therefore, in the view of Homer, not escape his fate. There is a realm of necessity which is the framework within which his deeds must be performed, and his only task within this framework is to bear himself nobly and with dignity as befits a true man.

This thought is the core also of early Greek tragedy. The tragedian's task was not to entertain but to teach the people. The tragedy was performed at the Dionysiac festival; it was a part therefore of Greek religion. Aristotle, in a famous definition of the purposes of tragedy, explains that it must be "of some magnitude" (concerning matters of moment), must present "an imitation of life," and must, by inspiring compassion and awe, lead to a "catharsis" of these and other emotions. The process of taking part in the performance of tragedy was therefore a cleansing one. For this purpose Aeschylus and Sophocles always showed noble actions performed by heroes who were not fully realistic but were to some degree idealized. In every tragic hero there was some nobility, even though he may have erred greatly (all Greek "sin" is error; there is no other word in the Greek language for sin but error). Prometheus, in Aeschylus' play, *Prometheus Bound,* has disobeyed the gods in pursuit of a higher task for mankind, so he is punished though it was ultimately within the needs of destiny that man should receive the Promethean gift. The whole house of Agamemnon has been pursued by a cruel destiny that was not of Agamemnon's original making. In the Oedipus trilogy of Sophocles it is expressly shown that Oedipus has been destined to kill his father and marry his mother, and all the puny human efforts to avoid this fate succeed only in deepening the tragedy. Both Aeschylus and Sophocles thought profoundly on these problems. Sophocles in his last play, *Oedipus at Colonus,* suggests as a solution that the sufferings of Oedipus ultimately have been worth while because the land in which he is buried is to be blessed. But, in the thought of these dramatists, as in that of Homer, there is no explanation of why men suffer that can be universally applicable. Human suffering is the work of Moira or the gods, and man has but a limited freedom. It is right for the people to be instructed in these things, to admire and revere the nobility of man in the face of his suffering, and to accept the decrees of the gods and learn humility and fortitude. As Sophocles says in the last words of the *Antigone,* only in old age can man learn wisdom and acceptance.

This was the world of the Athenians before the age of Pericles. In Aristophanes, the great comic poet, who was a younger contemporary of Pericles, we can find a nostalgic yearning for the past. His "old men who fought at Marathon" were to him the repository of all the ancient virtues, virtues no more to be seen in his own decadent era. This charge of decadence has been a time-honored complaint of conservatives. But in looking back with the perspective of more than two thousand years we can see that there was something in the substance of Aristophanes' complaints, that indeed there had been an overturning of the old thoughts and the old values, and that these would never reappear. The criticism of the Sophists was fatal; the world would never be the same again.

Criticism of traditional beliefs—The Sophists The central thought of the Sophists was stated powerfully and succinctly by one of the earliest of them. Protagoras' dictum, "Man is the measure of all things, of things that are, that they are; of things that are not, that they are not," when taken as seriously and as comprehensively as his successors took it, proved to be the lever which lifted Greek traditional thought off its hinges. Everything hereafter must be looked at from the point of view of man. The gods may exist but they do not reveal themselves to us; therefore they may be disregarded. Laws were made by men and for men; the gods do not sanction laws and do not punish those who offend against them. The individual is more important than the community; he has only one life, let him make the most of it and not lose it stupidly. There is no "natural" difference between the slave and the free; it is just an unfortunate but temporary condition due to historical circumstances.

Such thoughts fell upon fertile ground during the days of the Athenian Empire and the Peloponnesian War. Who can really refute the saying of Thrasymachus the Sophist that "justice is the interest of the stronger," or that might makes right? "Of men we know, and of gods we can be fairly sure, that they take power whenever they can," say the Athenian ambassadors to the Melians who try to opt for neutrality in the war. In essence they say, "We are stronger than you, so you may as well submit, and don't believe that the gods will save you. We have as good reason as you to believe they are on our side, not yours." Plato himself, in the *Laws,* has an Athenian stranger remark that the troubles of Athens all stem from their acquired belief that man, not God, is the measure of all things. Alcibiades defends his action in betraying the Athenians to the Spartans by saying that it is only "natural" for an exile to look after his own self and to do everything he can to get back to his old city, even by betraying it to the enemy and returning in the wake of the conquerors.

Euripides, pupil of the Sophists, cannot accept altogether the thought that there are no gods. He is too well aware of the inexplicable fate of man; he is too sympathetic with human suffering; and he cannot, like the Hellenistic individualists of a later era, merely attribute suffering or success to chance. But for him the gods are unjust, man is not noble and does not often suffer in well-trained resignation and fortitude. So he does not care to show his heroes as heroes in the old sense; he presents them as fallible human beings. His study of Agamemnon in the *Iphigenia in Aulis*, his best and most mature tragedy, is a psychological masterpiece; but Agamemnon is no hero. He is a weak and unfortunate man, ruled by ambition, caught in an impossibly difficult dilemma. So Euripides puts real men and women on the stage; tragic destiny and heroic human acceptance disappear; and all possibility of catharsis is lost. Faith had been a casualty in the warfare, and it was never to be replaced during the rest of Greek civilization.

Reconstruction of religious thought—Search for ethical standards—Socrates It was left for Socrates, himself a Sophist in many ways, to try to show that the Sophists had neglected an important part of human experience—the inner self. Accepting, in the main, the Sophistic criticism that man has always relied upon traditional thought rather than the best thought of which he is capable, Socrates set out to discover what it is that man really does know and how he comes to know it. Plato tells us how the oracle at Delphi made the categorical statement that Socrates was the wisest man in Greece, and how Socrates, trying to confirm or disprove this statement, searched Greece looking for a wiser man than himself. Finding none, he came to the conclusion that he alone was wise because he alone knew that he knew nothing. This profound paradox is the heart of Socratean thought. It is, of course, already implied in the dictum of Protagoras; and in so far as Socrates stresses the ignorance of those who profess to know, and the unproved nature of all traditional thinking, he is one with the Sophists. But he goes further than they; and this marks his constructiveness as a thinker. We must not indeed take received opinion on trust; but man *can* know through self-examination.

In order to discover this truth, which every man knows inwardly, it is necessary to bring knowledge to birth. For this purpose Socrates developed a method of question and answer, ever since associated with his name, by which it is gradually discovered first what is *not* true; and thereafter the truth is built up stage by stage, allowing no definition to stand until it has been examined, and no questionable statement to pass without criticism. When the process has finished, the questioner will find that he really knows something, however little, that he was not aware of knowing before. Socrates thus calls himself the "midwife" of knowledge in that he has brought knowledge to birth through the labor of the dialectic (the technical term given to the Socratic method).

Clearly this method is above all applicable to the realm of ethics; and the greater part of the Platonic dialogues in which Socrates seems to be himself and not the mere mouthpiece of his pupil is devoted to inquiry into the nature of the good, and how it can be pursued by man. Furthermore, can virtue (*arete*) or moral excellence be taught? If the code of right behavior is not to be dictated by tradition, received opinion, and the supposed will of the gods, then it must emanate from man. An individual ethic based on man's own best knowledge must replace the traditional one. It is Socrates' belief that if we rid ourselves of all prejudice and previous thinking on the subject, then by constant criticism followed by constructive thought we can obtain an idea of the good which will be the same for all; because the human being is so constituted that he *can* know the good. And, knowing it, he can follow it; for no one who truly knows the good would deliberately choose to follow the evil. This is a typically Greek notion, and is attractive to all rationalists. The greatest medieval rationalist, Thomas Aquinas, goes with Socrates as far as *knowledge* of the good is concerned; but, being a Christian, he also stresses the infirmity of the human *will*, which, being evil as the result of original sin, cannot carry out without divine grace what the intellect indicates as the good. Most medieval Christians would not even allow a true knowledge of the good without grace. But Socrates concludes that virtue is knowledge and ignorance is the root of moral evil; from this conclusion he and his pupil Plato drew out the full consequences.

In dealing with the Sophists, Socrates deliberately points out the inadequacy of their aim of teaching "useful knowledge." He asks pertinently, "Useful for what?" and has no difficulty in showing that the only truly human aim is the pursuit of the good, to which all else is subordinate. He denies their premise that knowledge is relative; but he admits that it must be tentative. No one knows, or can know, the final truth about anything (Plato excepts mathematics); and the frequency with which Plato shows him as dissatisfied with his preliminary destructive criticism, and the tentative conclusions that fill the vacuum he has created by it, suggests the real humility before knowledge which entitled him to the accolade of Apollo of Delphi, god of wisdom.

In spite of his apparently individualistic ethics, Socrates was a profoundly social being and lover of his polis. He had a high opinion of the truth that lay behind the religious traditions of Greece, though he always interpreted them in his own way, as spiritual rather than physical truths. It was not his task to destroy the law and government of his polis, even though they were based on tradition; he fully accepted the right of the democracy to put him to death under its laws. These laws provided the whole framework of his social life; they were not unchangeable and their ethical content might no doubt be improved. But if it happened that he was the victim of the laws in their present state, then it still behooved him as a citizen to abide by them.

Within himself he only answered to the call of his own inner knowledge. He understood very fully that others might be moved by tradition and prejudice; but this was no excuse for him to follow their example. Very gravely and accurately he describes the activity of the human conscience which never tells him what to do but only what not to do. And he calls this his "daimonion," his little god—as indeed for him it was, since it took the place of the sanctions of the gods and the traditional piety associated with them.

The teachings of Socrates may have been too heady for many who were not of the highest moral fiber. Alcibiades, traitor and loose liver, was one of his pupils; so was Critias, oligarchic leader of the Thirty Tyrants, who instituted and carried out a bloody proscription of the democratic leaders—though it is not altogether reasonable to blame the master for the human frailties of his pupils. We can see in the Platonic dialogues how easily Socrates' method lends itself to misconstruction, and how quickly an enemy could take his gently objective criticism as personal disbelief. In the *Meno*, for instance, Socrates has been showing that no virtuous man has been able to teach virtue to his son. Anytus, one of the accusers at his trial, at once jumps to the conclusion that Socrates is maligning these men instead of using them to prove his philosophical point. In the political conditions of the restoration of the democracy after the oligarchic revolution, it was difficult to believe that any man could be searching for philosophical truth. Yet Socrates continued in the only activity that for him made life worth living.

In 399 B.C. his enemies brought him to trial before the people's jury on a charge of atheism and corrupting the youth. It was a clever charge, for it was, in appearance, true. Socrates took part in all the festivals and performed all his religious observances, but he did speak of his daimonion, a strange god, and he did teach—indeed, the whole of his teaching led inevitably to the conclusion—that a new dispensation had come when man was to be free, to rule himself, not be ruled by the gods. And in so far as this was his instruction to his pupils, then he "corrupted the youth."

The account of his trial in Plato's *Apology* shows his moral courage and his confidence that his own path was right. He defends himself against the charges only by affirming them. Convicted by a small majority and asked for a suggestion as to what punishment he deserves, with the same serene confidence he tells them that he ought to have a pension and be supported at the city's expense for the rest of his life. This irony is too much for human endurance, and by a larger vote the jury condemns him to death. Instead of going into exile as his friends urge, an exile which would undoubtedly have been winked at, he accepts his sentence, not in stoical resignation but with dignity, tenderness for his friends, and good humor. While he awaits the fatal hemlock he discourses on immortality, still with the same calm reason that he had shown during his life. There is, he believes, an inner self in man, his divine part; this, being of the same nature as the divine, cannot die, and will dwell forever with the gods. But he will soon know. He shows no fear and no regrets. So he drinks the hemlock; and by the manner of his dying he truly ensured his immortality on earth. For it was a turning point in the life of his pupil Plato, then a young man of about twenty-eight years of age.

Constructive philosophy—Idealism of Plato
The heart of Plato's teaching stems from the original conception of Socrates that the human being can know the good; and that, knowing it, he can do it. What Plato seeks to discover is *how* he can know it, and *what* it is exactly that he knows. By using the dialogue form he shows us the whole process by which he arrived at his conclusions; hence the endless stimulation that Plato has afforded to all subsequent mankind. All that we must do is hitch up to his thought at one place, and either follow him to the same conclusions, or, by casting aside some of his thoughts as based on assumptions which we will not accept, move on to different conclusions.

Assuming, then, that man can know the good, with what faculty does he know it, and what is the object of this faculty? To this Plato answers that man is possessed of the power of thinking (*Nous*), and that this spiritual element in man can recognize the spiritual element akin to it—the Idea. This Idea, however, is not in the physical world but in the spiritual world, forever hidden from every faculty in man save the Nous. Following this thought further, he concludes that everything we see in front of us is a *particular*, a single example of something, the Idea or archetype of which is really spiritual, and not to be found on earth. We see, for instance, a single plant; but the Idea of the plant is in the spiritual world. From this it is but a short step to the value judgment that the earthly example is necessarily an inferior copy of the ideal plant—that the spiritual reality is more beautiful, more worthy of contemplation than anything on earth.

The next step is to consider how we can recognize this earthly copy as indeed a copy of an Idea. And to this Plato's answer is that the soul, with its active faculty, the Nous, existed before incarnation on earth in a human body. Before it descended to earth it glimpsed these Ideas, which were implanted forever in the soul. Thus knowledge of the universal behind the particular appearance on earth is simply *recognition*. This, it will be seen, completely accounts for man's possession of innate knowledge, which Socrates had shown man did possess.

It is clear that this "idealist" philosophy gives an enormous scope to the philosopher. He is not compelled to examine the phenomena in front of him but may reason a priori; indeed, since it is only human thinking that can perceive the Ideas, there is no other method of reasoning than a priori. Thus by reasoning, the moral and political philosopher must try to discover for himself the ideal good, and not the practicable good.

The *Republic* is the Platonic masterpiece of this kind of reasoning. But from this it should not be thought that Plato had no practical ends in view. He tells us specifically that he has. No political state of which he has knowledge has been *thought* out; all are defective. But in his view these defects need not be inevitable. For if men know the good they will not deliberately prefer the evil unless they have been warped beyond cure. Since "virtue" may be taught, men can be educated to admire the best, and not choose a second-best polity to live in.

His method, then, is to discover what is the bond which holds society together (justice), and then try to arrive at a definition of justice. He comes to the conclusion that justice in the citizen and in the state is identical. If each man is given a position in the social order which enables him to do that for which he is best fitted, and he performs this task properly, then the ends of both the citizen and the state will be fully served, and the society will be a just one. Plato then proceeds to inquire into how human potentialities can best be realized in a social framework, and what will be the nature of the social institutions required.

Given his premises, the whole work, built up on these lines, is logically impeccable. Its value in all ages has been its suggestiveness, and the joy of following the thought of a truly creative mind, willing to pursue the argument wherever it will lead, without deference to conventional Greek notions—as, for instance, on the inequality of women. It is not native conservatism or a preference for oligarchy—though these may have been present, they are irrelevant—that forces him to the conclusion that the enlightened despotism of a board of professional guardians (philosopher kings and queens) is the only possible "best" government. These alone have been able to discover the good, and they must be dedicated utterly to its pursuit, without the warping of judgment which would arise from the possession of either material goods or family. With such a body of truly scientific professionals there would be no need for laws or for the exercise of power; for at all grades in the society each man would have received the education, and hold the position, for which he was best fitted.

It has often been pointed out, justly, that Plato makes a number of assumptions which are extremely questionable—for instance, that public and private virtue are identical, and that a state made up of good individuals will be able to function harmoniously as a state. But it will usually be found that these assumptions are the result of his fundamental belief that no one, knowing the good, would deliberately choose to do evil. If the state is a just one, its duties will be just and good; the individual, if he is good, will desire to do this duty. Duty and inclination must coincide. If they do not, then either the state needs to be corrected or the individual needs to be improved—by development and adjustment, not by repression and force.

Plato may also be accused of neglecting the psychology of man, as it *must* have been known to him from experience. What was the use of theorizing about an ideal state when he knew of its impossibility in real life? Again the answer must be that by showing men the ideal good—which was, for him, not impossible of realization but only extremely difficult—he was pointing out a direction for the aspirations and endeavors of man. That it was not his last thought on the subject is shown by his later works, the *Statesman* and *Laws*, in which he outlines the "second-best state," the state ruled by laws. Laws are directed to the ethical improvement of man, but

cannot be as scientifically impeccable as the personal guidance of the philosopher kings. Elsewhere he shows that he is not unaware of human psychology. He recognizes the irrational part of man, but does not consider it incurable. The desires are controlled by reason, which, in the light of its knowledge of the good, will give man the power of evaluating his desires at their true worth.

As with the state, so with man. The harmonious functioning of all the parts that go to make up the full man, this is self-realization under the guiding power of the Nous. It is a psychology the truth of which would be vehemently denied by both Christians and Freudians, who both deny the power of the mind to control the will unaided. Perhaps to these the psychology of Plato would seem naïve; but it was the fullest and most complete expression of the Greek ideal of harmony and sophrosyne, and of the Greek belief in the efficacy of human thinking. If it is a glorification of the one specifically human power, this to the Greeks would have been a recommendation. Oedipus to the Greeks was not a complex but a human being, proud and erring but undefeated; and they were glad to be considered of his company.

Philosophy becomes science—Aristotle

Aristotle was the son of a Chalcidian physician in the service of Philip of Macedon. He studied at the Academy of Plato and was unquestionably his most brilliant pupil. He was tutor of Alexander, son of Philip, for several years, returning to Athens and opening a school himself (the Lyceum), where he taught for twelve years. Forced into exile on the death of Alexander, he died a year later in 322 B.C. at the age of sixty-two.

Thus Aristotle stands at the end of the Classical Age of Greece before the great emigration to Asia that followed the conquests of Alexander; and in a very real sense he completed it. Though he left one or two things undone which were repaired by Theophrastus, his pupil and successor (for instance, a work on plants and another on human character), and though he contributed nothing to Greek mathematics, which followed an independent course, in other respects he took all the varied speculations of his Greek predecessors, brilliant and disorganized as they were, and by the giant force of his capacity for system, order, and classification, discharged them from his hands as sciences—a body of work that could be communicated to others in comprehensible form. Once he had laid down the principles of scientific inquiry, the work would not have to be done again. He was the first true scientist in the history of mankind; and few who have really studied his work would dispute his title to be the greatest the world has yet known. And now that we have passed beyond recovery into a world of specialists, there never will be anyone again who will be able to lay claim to the universality of his learning. Any one of half a dozen of his mental achievements would have entitled him to an undying fame. The sum is almost beyond belief.

If this seem excessive praise, let us consider for a moment a few of Aristotle's achievements. Basing his observations upon Plato's theory of ideas, he formulated the laws of thinking, the relation between the universal and the particular, the formal procedure required for arriving at conclusions and correct reasoning, giving in passing a different solution to the problem of the origin of the universal. Disturbed by the way in which objects were described without including all their features, he formulated a method for describing them inclusively (the "categories of being"). Stimulated perhaps by Socrates' remark that he himself knew that his will prevented him from going into exile and not "his bones and sinews," as Anaxagoras would have claimed, he formulated a system for dealing accurately with causation and had to invent a new vocabulary for the purpose. Faced with a mass of biological data, he evolved a system of classification into genus and species which has been followed with modifications ever since.

Aristotle is usually praised in these days rather patronizingly for his excellent and careful observation and description of the animal world, and for his early recognition of facts which modern science, with its greater knowledge and improved instruments, has shown to be true—as if anyone with the time and the patience could not observe correctly! He has been criticized for premature guesses on the basis of insufficient information, for his doctrines of purpose, for his denial of the atomic theory, and in general for having held back medieval scientists from more correct theories while they elaborated on his incorrect ones instead. But insufficient attention has been paid to the gigantic mental effort required to create order out of chaos, and to make the world *intelligible*, which was his primary purpose. No one before his time had seen the need for a method of inquiry or a classification of knowledge. Philosophers had speculated, and looked for universal principles, every now and then carrying out a few desultory experiments but always jumping to theoretical conclusions of little value beyond their aesthetic appeal. To watch Aristotle at work trying to determine how to deal with zoology with no previous guide, as in the first book of his *Parts of Animals*, is to see the enormous difficulties that faced him in the struggle to put the material in order; and to read any part of the *Metaphysics* is to realize his extraordinary ability to handle the most difficult abstractions of thought with the utmost delicacy and sureness—in which again he had no predecessor. Plato charms us because of his artistry and imagination, and because there is no word that we cannot understand, no thought that we cannot follow. He flatters our ignorance, making us believe we are not as ignorant as we are; in reading Plato we all imagine ourselves philosophers. But Aristotle is hard work, and he makes no concessions to us; even when we think we have grasped one of his thoughts it quickly eludes us again. Then suddenly it becomes clear and fruitful and applicable in a hundred other ways, and we possess a tool for understanding the world.

In following the Aristotelian method, as we have all followed it since his time without acknowledgments, our work has been made easy. But it was not easy for him. He had first to invent the tools of analysis, and then with these to set to work on all the phenomena of knowledge available to the Greek world. Both parts of this work he largely accomplished. His nephew went with Alexander on his expedition, and Alexander himself sent back data that he thought would be of interest to his old tutor. His students collected material for him, and he analyzed and classified it, no doubt with their assistance. For his *Politics* he analyzed and digested the constitutions of 158 different states, this analysis enabling him to classify the different kinds of states on the basis of evidence. He viewed the plays of his own age and the tragic drama of the great era, and in his *Poetics* classified the results, together with his findings in general terms of the requirements of tragedy. He did the same thing for the animal world in his three great works in zoology, the *History of Animals, Parts of Animals*, and *Generation of Animals*; and so on. Certainly in some cases he generalized and theorized too soon; but only very rarely did he fail to offer good reasons for the theories and for his acute criticisms of his predecessors. And never did his analysis fail. His successors could have built always upon his foundations, and revised his theories when necessary.

It was a tragedy that Aristotle, of all men, should have been regarded as an authority and the last word on any subject—he who was the most ready of all the ancient investigators to base his theories on the observed facts. But it is now the prevalent opinion that when at last the late medieval scholars did begin to work on his findings at the University of Padua without accepting him as infallible, they only had to revise his groundwork, and criticize some of his conclusions on the basis of their improved knowledge of the facts. Their work made it possible for Galileo, who studied at Padua, to lay the basis for modern science. Aristotle was not abandoned, save by the ignorant; but adapted, improved upon, and commented upon until at last he emerged as the great pioneer he was, but no longer "the master of those who know," which he was not.

If we examine the conclusions reached by Aristotle in all the numerous fields of inquiry to which he gave his attention, we shall find that they were almost always inspired by common sense. Common sense has not been regarded as a useful tool in modern exact science, with its powerful mathematics and instruments of research. Almost none of the findings of modern science, from the electron to the Copernican theory, from the physics of Einstein to the corpuscular-wave theory of light, is validated by common sense or direct sense observation. For this reason Aristotle's conclusions in the physical sciences have to be interpreted very spaciously and charitably if they are to be in any way acceptable, while his conclusions in the social sciences may be as valid as in the days they were written.

Both Plato and Aristotle had an advantage over later thinkers in that the known world was small. Because the whole range of knowledge was not very great, it was still possible for one man to try to encompass it. Frequently, throughout the work of Aristotle, we find him making the statement that any science or art ought to cover the whole of a subject; and it is true that he makes the attempt. But not only this; he tries also to cover the whole of *all* subjects, using his key of logical analysis and systematic organization. This no successor has ever been able to do, and few have tried. Friar Roger Bacon was to make the effort in the thirteenth century, but even he did not find it necessary to go over a subject again once Aristotle had "completed" it; though toward the end of his life Bacon suggested that a corps of specialists should be organized for the purpose of producing the necessary compendium. It is certain that no single person will ever try again.

This work of Aristotle was therefore unique, a last and most nearly complete expression of the Greek desire for an orderly and harmonious whole, one of the greatest intellectual monuments in the history of mankind. If the highest praise is to be given, let us say that his work is worthy of the Greek genius.

❖ **Influence of Greek thought— Significance of Greek search for new truth**

The great thinkers dealt with so far have occupied so much of the space in this chapter because they were the men whose thoughts provided the substratum for all the thinking of later Western man. The revolution ushered in by the Sophists has never been completed and perhaps never will be. At times, especially in the Middle Ages, men have preferred to take the traditional religiously inspired picture of the world as true and have not questioned its validity. This attitude has seldom led to new knowledge. The attitude of resignation in the face of divine will has sometimes prevailed in Western civilization, but always to the detriment of scientific inquiry. It might be more comfortable and give greater security to the individual to live in a world in which everything is known, and knowledge is contemplated, not enlarged; but such a world would be static. The world of the Sophists, in which one idea is as good as another, is a difficult world to live in, and it cannot be long endured. But the answer may well be that we need another Socrates to help us seek out the good, rather than despairing of finding it and resigning ourselves to the ethical nihilism which too often appears to present the only alternative to the acceptance of the teachings of tradition. The Greeks were the first to escape from the bonds imposed by their ancestors and strike out on a new path, the end of which could not and cannot now be seen. It is this above all that is meant by the Greek spirit. Greek art, perfect in its way as it is, has only been imitated by the West, copied but not equaled. For though we have inherited the Greek view of life and carried it on with our own genius to new realms unsuspected by the Greeks, the Greek feeling for man as a union of soul and body in equilibrium was peculiar to themselves. We of the West can only dimly sense this view when we touch the few authentic masterpieces that have been preserved to us, and wonder at their perfection.

❖ **Greek art**

ART AS EXPRESSION OF THE GREEK SPIRIT

We have remarked earlier that the Greek ideal was sophrosyne, or moderation, although as a people the Greeks markedly lacked this virtue. In the realm of art, however, their search was not doomed to the same failure as in the necessarily imperfect world in which they had to live, and their volatile passions could not be involved in this ideal world as deeply as in the political world of live men and women. In art man is a creator. His materials are at hand but as yet without form. It is for the artist to give form to them. The soul, in Greek thought, is the *form* of the body; it shapes the inchoate mass, the mere raw physical material which decays at death into its original primal matter. So, for the Greek artist, the task is to give form to matter, to give it a soul which makes it live. And it is a curious feature of Greek above all other art that this illusion of life is indeed given to the dead material, marble. This feature can be perceived best in Greek sculpture, but even the Greek temple does not seem to be altogether dead. We can analyze these temples and see by what technical means certain illusions were created, but the miracle remains. Even with our greatly advanced technical ingenuity, we have not been able to achieve the same results.

Two slabs from the Parthenon frieze known as the Elgin marbles after the English lord who carried them off to England. Note the mastery of the riders in the Panathenaic procession, and the absence of any sense of the strain which is noticeable in some of the realistic sculpture of the Hellenistic Age. The riders are caught in a moment of eternity rather than individualized as riders taking part in one particular procession at one particular moment. The frieze was designed by Phidias and carried out at his direction though by different craftsmen. (COURTESY BRITISH MUSEUM)

The Greeks of the Classical Age did not think of art as useful, nor did they set out to create self-consciously something "artistic." Indeed they did not possess a word for what we speak of as "artistic." Their only word for art was *techne*, which means craft. Every product of the Classical Age in Greece is, by our standards, artistic; form and substance are united in a harmony that can be recognized at once. Form is given to the material in accordance with the nature of the material and the purpose for which the object is to be used. This quality seems to have been an almost instinctive achievement of the Greek craftsman; and though it is very possible that the barbarian princes and Persian nobles who often bought these works did not appreciate what they had acquired, it would have been impossible, working in the Greek artistic tradition, for the craftsman to have made a shoddy and inferior product, even for barbarians.

The same honesty is observed when we consider the temples. The most famous of Greek temples, the Parthenon at Athens, was filled with sculptures that could never be seen by mortal eye, high up in the part of the temple where the statue of the goddess Athena was housed. Yet this sculpture was as honestly and truly wrought as anything in the visible parts of the temple. The building of a temple was the highlight in the life of the Athenian craftsman. We know that Greek artisans all received the same low wage each day they were at work for the city, just enough to maintain their wives and families for that one day. It was considered the highest honor to work for the polis; even those who scorned private employment as unworthy of free men welcomed the opportunity. The temple was a home for the god to whom it was dedicated and whose statue inhabited it. The god thus honored gave protection to the city. The great temple of the Erechtheum at Athens was completed in the darkest days of the Peloponnesian War, with resources which the city could ill spare. Thus the Greek craftsmen, like the medieval craftsmen who built the Gothic cathedrals as an expression both of civic pride and of their devotion to God, gave of their best with complete honesty. The result is what no man would deny as being true art.

The famous Hermes of Praxiteles, the only almost complete statue extant from the fourth century B.C. Note how the god is given truly human features, which should be contrasted with the less differentiated features of the participants in the Panathenaic procession shown in the Parthenon frieze (Elgin marbles).

ARCHITECTURE AND SCULPTURE

The Greek temple is not an imposing building from the point of view of size, and it makes use of the simplest structural forms known to man. Essentially it was composed of the *cella*, a rectangular chamber, the dwelling place of the statue of the god; the columns surrounding the cella and forming a porch; the lintel which rested on the columns and supported the roof; the gabled roof itself; and the pediment, the triangular section under the roof. The style of the temple is determined by the column. Three types were used by the Greek architects: Doric, Ionic, and Corinthian, though the last named was too ornate for classical Greek taste and came into use only after the expansion of Greece into the Oriental world. In the sculpture of the age of Pericles, the era of the Parthenon, the

Greek ideal of man as a harmony of body and soul was brought to perfection. The figures in the Parthenon friezes were ideal figures, perfectly proportioned. There is no striving after effect; each muscle is perfectly rendered, whether in tension or repose. The effect is one of dignity and restrained movement. The horses are prancing, the young riders are in perfect control; a moment appears to have been captured in stone—not an event but a moment of eternity, as if the riders will go on prancing and the young riders will sit their horses forever.

Yet a word of warning should be given. All Greek sculptures were painted, and what we now see in the whiteness of marble must have looked utterly different in classical times, so that it is hard for us to imagine either the Parthenon or the city of Athens as they appeared to the Greeks who lived there, with statues on every corner gleaming and shining in full color in the Greek sunlight. We may think it crude of the Greeks to disguise and embellish their lovely masterpieces, which needed no such adornment. But this is the way the Greeks were, and who are we to criticize them? Can we be so sure that we have learned sophrosyne?

Head of a young athlete (fourth century B.C.). This is a fragment of a statue contemporary with the Hermes of Praxiteles, and shows the trend toward increasing realism. (COURTESY THE METROPOLITAN MUSEUM OF ART)

❖ The expansion of Greece— The Hellenistic Age

RISE OF PHILIP OF MACEDON

We have briefly alluded earlier in this chapter to the Greek loss of independence to Philip of Macedon. This remarkable monarch came to the throne of his semibarbaric country in 359 B.C. He built himself a small but powerful army, which he trained in new military tactics; he financed his operations by the acquisition of some gold mines through a piece of cunning manipulation; and then he set out to use these assets to conquer all Greece. He never fought a battle if he could win what he needed by diplomatic means, but he was not hesitant to use his army when it appeared to be the best means of achieving his goals. He recognized the venality and poverty of the Greek poleis

of his day and their ruling politicians. He did not scruple to buy their support and sow as much discord as he could among the cities. Demosthenes, the Athenian statesman, was aware of the danger to Greek liberties early in Philip's career, and did his best to rouse the Athenians from their fatal torpor. But he was only partially successful. The aid given to threatened cities that should have been Athenian allies was always too inconsequential to save them. Thebes, the leading power of Greece, always thought that Philip was her friend until the last moment, when it was too late. So, by piecemeal conquest, Philip made himself the master of Greece and achieved a final decisive victory on the battlefield of Chaeronea in 338 B.C. His terms, except for Thebes, were light. He aimed at conquest of Asia; Greece was to be for him only the first step. He desired to go to Asia as the chosen leader of the Greek people, whether they supported him with arms or not.

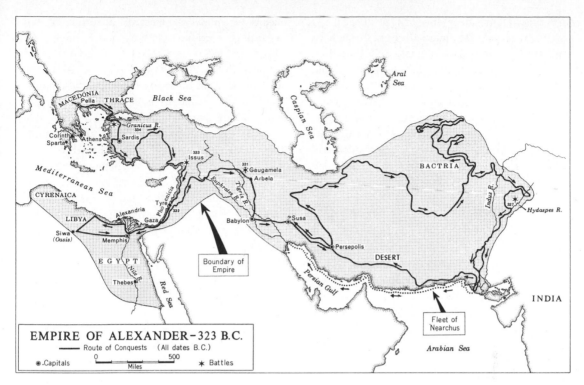

EMPIRE OF ALEXANDER - 323 B.C.

—— Route of Conquests (All dates B.C.)

●.Capitals   0   500   ★ Battles

Miles

But before he could organize the Asiatic expedition Philip was murdered. He was succeeded by his son, known to history as Alexander the Great.

THE CONQUESTS OF ALEXANDER THE GREAT (336–323 B.C.)

The military career of Alexander is the most astonishing in all history. He rapidly quelled a revolt in Greece which marked the beginning of his reign, then organized for himself the expedition that his father had planned. Meagerly financed, and hardly supported at all by the Greek cities, which hoped for his speedy defeat and their own liberation from Macedonian rule, he nevertheless succeeded in destroying the huge Persian Empire and succeeding to its rule. He added Egypt to his possessions without more than token fighting. He advanced into India and defeated an army that included elephants, which he had never seen before. Improvising tactics and policy as he went along, never at a loss for an expedient, possessed of a personality that overawed the toughest of generals and quelled incipient revolt among his

followers when they objected to his policy of fraternization with Persians after their defeat, and yet singularly lacking in sophrosyne in spite of a personal education at the hands of Aristotle, Alexander and his life and works became legendary soon after his early death. Even now books about him pour from the press, and movies celebrate his deeds. For the purposes of this history it is enough to say that the world was altogether changed by his work. Of no other man can it be said with equal justice that he laid his mark upon all the civilizations that followed him in the lands where he had fought, and upon all those civilizations to the West which in turn took over from them.

Alexander's original purpose was to avenge the expedition of Xerxes. This duly accomplished by the defeat and death of the Persian monarch, he then proceeded to invite immigration from Greece and to become himself the Great King of Persia. As Persian king it was his duty to care for his Persian subjects as for his Macedonians. He thus took Persian nobles into his service, and encouraged intermarriage between Greeks and Persians. Though he roused opposition amongst his Macedonians, who felt they should have been specially privileged, his policy prevailed. He founded cities throughout the newly conquered lands, and imported Greek institutions suitable for the polis, which, as he had no doubt been instructed by Aristotle, was the most perfect form of social entity. Once the initial distrust had worn off, the immigrants from poor overpopulated Greece began to pour into the country, giving the rather outclassed Persians a dose of Greek efficiency which galvanized the ancient Orient into unaccustomed life.

THE SUCCESSORS OF ALEXANDER

Alexander died at the early age of thirty-three, and his generals struggled for the succession. After thirty years of civil war the territory was finally divided amongst the survivors. Ptolemy Soter took Egypt, the prize of the empire, though not the largest section; Seleucus took most of the Asiatic mainland, leaving a small but prosperous kingdom in Asia Minor for Attalus; while Greece and Macedonia fell to a general named Antigonus. The mainland of Greece, from having been overpopulated, now was denuded of its most enterprising sons, and its history need concern us no further. Egypt

became a model of efficient government and expanding economic activity under monarchs who fully appreciated and exploited the old fiction that the Pharaoh of Egypt owned all the land and that all his subjects were royal tenants. The Seleucid monarchs in Asia were faced with many minor wars, but on the whole were able to make of their empire a fairly efficient unit, and pursued a cultural policy based directly upon the original plans of Alexander. Pergamum in northern Asia Minor became a prosperous commercial state noted for the fine buildings, palaces, and temples paid for by royal bounty and the enterprise of individual merchants.

THE HELLENISTIC AGE—MINGLING OF GREEK AND ORIENTAL

The age that followed the death of Alexander is called the Hellenistic Age, as distinct from the earlier Hellenic Age when the center of culture was on the mainland. The Hellenistic period is marked especially by a mingling for the first time of Greek and Oriental culture. To this the Orientals contributed primarily their religions, while the Greeks contributed their philosophy. Within the new cities, populated for

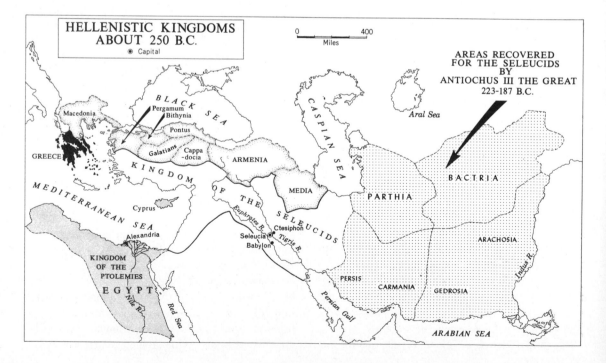

Ruins of the temple of Zeus at Pergamum as they appear at the present time. The size of the ruins will give some indication of the scale of the work of the Hellenistic monarchs of this commercial state. (COURTESY TURKISH INFORMATION OFFICE)

the most part by immigrant Greeks, some of the forms of the old polis were maintained. The governments were made up of assemblies and councils as in Athens; but full self-government and freedom to act could not be granted to them since foreign policy necessarily remained in the hands of the monarchs. Thus to a large extent the forms were a façade. But not altogether; for the most part the cities possessed at least a kind of municipal self-government, a tradition which was of great value to the Romans when they incorporated this part of the world into their own empire. Persians in the Seleucid Empire were able to participate in the new culture and contributed to it. The Greek language prevailed, though no longer so pure as in the days of Pericles. All the educated classes could speak the *koine*, as it was called—the common tongue of the wider *koinon*, or community of the Hellenes, which composed the whole Hellenistic world.

On the whole it was a prosperous world. The Greeks on the mainland had always been fertile in inventions and expedients. They had invented many financial tools which could now be put to use in a land where there was wide scope for them. But there was far more slavery than in the Hellenic Age, and while there were

more rich men there were also far more poor ones. Moreover, the ancient security of the polis had been entirely lost. Socrates would have felt completely out of place in a Hellenistic city. No one would have known him, no one would have had time to talk. Each man had to look after his business or be defeated by a competitor; no age of the ancient world so much resembles ours as the Hellenistic Age. The result was that a great many of the immigrant Greeks felt they had lost their roots. No imitation polis in Asia could take the place of the old, secure polis, where everyone had status as a citizen and everyone participated in government and held all the responsibilities of the active participator with his full share of responsibility. Cosmopolitanism (the world-polis) could exercise no hold upon his heart and mind. So all men had to become individualists, and seek to make what they could for themselves. The Sophist teaching at last came to full fruition. Each man was an individual; he had to look after his own interests first, and leave the government to Ptolemy or Seleucus.

Hellenistic philosophies—Individualism In a world where not all men could succeed, it was not surprising that there should be a marked growth of religions. Since these will be dealt with at the beginning of Chapter 6, nothing need be said of them here save that they no doubt performed the important function of giving hope in a better world to those who could not succeed in this. A similar function was performed by the new individualistic philosophies that are characteristic of the Hellenistic Age. Stoicism, Epicurism, even Cynicism, all stem from the desire to attain what the Greeks called *ataraxia*, or a state of "being unmoved," an inner tranquillity of soul. The Cynics scoffed at worldly wealth and tried to acquire wisdom, this wisdom to consist primarily in the understanding of the uselessness of possessions. The typical early Cynic was Diogenes, who lived in a tub and cultivated rudeness and self-sufficiency. The movement, obviously not designed to attract a numerous following, was largely absorbed in the long-lasting and extremely important philosophy of Stoicism, which grew in scope as the centuries passed, much of it being woven into Christian ethics and much into Roman law. The purpose of the Stoic is to become indifferent to all earthly joys and pleasures, not to care whether success is attained or not, and to rest secure in the consciousness of one's own rectitude and obey only one's conscience. There is a Divine Reason which rules in the world, and man also shares in this reason. All men are equal in their ability to discover and obey the dictates of reason; there is no natural inequality, but all men are equally doomed to suffering and all are equally able to rise above it by cultivating the life of the soul and reason. Stoics therefore were the first Greeks to speak out against slavery; and it is an interesting fact that the two best-known Stoic writers, who were both born long after the Hellenistic world had been replaced by the Roman Empire, are Marcus Aurelius the Roman emperor, and Epictetus, born a crippled slave.

Epicurism was likewise an attempt to deal with the conditions of the Hellenistic world. Do not strive for success, said the Epicureans, for it is unlikely to be attained, and desiring what cannot be attained leads to unhappiness. The goal of the Epicurean was happiness, but happiness attained by simple pleasures and curtailment of the desire for more. Epicurus himself lived a simple life, eating frugally and discours-

ing gently on philosophy with his disciples. He believed in the atomic theory of Democritus and that the gods, if they exist, play no part in the affairs of men but dwell peacefully at ease in some remote part of the universe. Free will is possible for man because some of the atoms make an unpredictable swerve (*clinamen*). The affairs of men are ruled by chance and the fact might as well be accepted. The conclusion was that one should make the most of life as it is and not seek to change it by excessive (and unsuccessful) activity. It is ironical that the philosophy of Epicurus, who himself taught a gentle asceticism, should have been so transformed by the Romans that the word Epicurean, in Roman as in our own time, should have been associated primarily with gluttony—although it must be admitted that a purely hedonistic philosophy is

Hellenistic realism. This statue of an old market woman, discovered at Rome, dates from the second century B.C. and was perhaps looted from Greece by the Romans. (COURTESY THE METROPOLITAN MUSEUM OF ART)

Opinion has varied remarkably at different times on the merits of the Laocoön, a late Hellenistic group showing the priest Laocoön and his two sons grappling with snakes. The impression of strain and power has appealed to many as one of the finest expressions of Hellenistic realism, while others have found the whole composition theatrical and forced and, from the Greek point of view, "bad art."

capable of this transformation. Epicurus may have said "eat, drink, and be merry, for tomorrow we die"; but it was always possible to forget the last four words and leave the first five naked.

Hellenistic science The Hellenistic world is noted for its science, the first really practical science attained by the Greeks. The opportunity for study was provided above all by the Museum of Alexandria, a great research center founded by the Ptolemies and maintained by them with funds gained through the successful management of the estate of Egypt. Here scholars of all kinds were subsidized. Their work did not have to be useful so long as it redounded to the prestige of their master. Here the works of the great literary masters of the mainland were edited and their manuscripts multiplied. Here the Greek astronomers met with the vast records of astronomical data collected in previous centuries by the Babylonian priests and astrologers. Faced with such data the Greek theorists soon began to explain, whereas the Babylonians had been con-

tent to record and use for astrological purposes. Hipparchus discovered (or possibly restated the Chaldean theory of) the precession of the equinoxes, and was able to explain satisfactorily all the known data on the supposed movement of the sun around the earth and to predict correctly on the basis of his theories. Here Aristarchus propounded the opposite theory that the earth moved around the sun but was unable to convince his contemporaries. Here Euclid and Archimedes worked as mathematicians, and Eratosthenes calculated the diameter of the earth. Finally, Hero explained the vacuum and invented a machine using the principles later incorporated in the modern steam engine. Medicine was not neglected, the theories of the earlier Hippocrates, father of secular medicine, being studied and carried further. The great library of Alexandria, containing more than half a million books, was unique in that age and for more than fifteen hundred years afterward.

Hellenistic art—New realism Finally, a word should be said on Hellenistic art. The tendency in Hellenistic architecture was away from classical simplicity. The buildings were larger and the columns more ornate, with the Corinthian coming into fashion toward the end of the epoch. Hellenistic sculpture tended toward realism. There was no loss of technical ability, but there is sometimes, as in the "Laocoön," a rather marked straining after effect. A dying Gaul with blood flowing, and a market woman straining under her heavy burden, are well-known works of this age. But so also is the perfect "Aphrodite" of Melos, and the "Winged Victory" of Samothrace, suggestive of movement in every line, and far removed indeed from the rather static splendor of the Parthenon friezes. There was a great growth of portrait sculpture, for it is clear that art had now, like everything else, become a business, and Greek artists had to find their patrons apart from the polis.

❖ **Summary—Greek influence on subsequent Roman civilization**

When the Hellenistic world was conquered by the Romans, in a very real sense it may be

The Aphrodite of Melos (so called because the statue was discovered on the island of Melos) is widely regarded as the finest statue of a woman ever made. The artist is unknown, but the figure probably dates from the second century B.C. No photograph can do justice to this masterpiece. Located in the Louvre, it is displayed to perfection —especially at night, when it is most effectively lighted. (COURTESY THE LOUVRE)

peace. So when the unified Romans, with their distinctive gifts in the fields of government and law, were forced into contact with the Greeks of the Hellenistic world through the never-ending internecine squabbles of their rulers, their policy of divide and rule was made to order. They conquered this world by force and diplomacy. But they did not Latinize it. It remained Greek, and became Greek in government again with the fall of Rome. Not until the Muslims took over the Near East in the seventh century A.D. was Greek influence ousted. And even then the Muslims took over much of Greek thought, ultimately transmitting it to a revived Western civilization. But this story will be told in a later chapter.

The Nike (Victory) of Samothrace, a statue (now in the Louvre) in the form of the prow of a ship. Note how the Nike suggests speed and movement, unlike the static figures of the Parthenon. (COURTESY THE LOUVRE)

said that the Greeks made a cultural conquest of Rome at the same time. It was contact with the Greek cities of southern Italy that inspired the first Roman poetry and the first Roman art; and the Near East was always both the most prosperous and the most highly cultured part of the Roman Empire. The second language of every cultivated Roman was Greek, and Greek rather than Latin was spoken in all the eastern domains of Rome. But the Hellenistic world did not and could not supply good government to the peoples of the East, and it did not enforce

Suggestions for further reading

NOTE ON LITERATURE OF THE PERIOD: No recommendations can be given here for the numerous translations from the individual Greek writers now available in paper-bound books. Among the most useful selections are W. H. Auden, ed., *The Portable Greek Reader* (Vintage); T. F. Higham and C. M. Bowra, eds., *The Oxford Book of Greek Verse in Translation* (New York: Oxford University Press, 1938); and an invaluable selection with commentary from the works of the pre-Socratic philosopher-scientists, M. C. Nahm, *Selections from Early Greek Philosophy* (New York: Appleton-Century-Crofts, Inc., 1947). Books of criticism, sometimes with extensive selections, are listed below with the other suggestions.

PAPER-BOUND BOOKS

Barker, Ernest. *The Political Thought of Plato and Aristotle*. Dover. A fundamental study by a student of ancient and modern politics. Better on Aristotle than on Plato.

Bowra, C. M. *The Greek Experience*. Mentor. Excellent modern synthesis of the Greek cultural achievements to 404 B.C. Thoughtful and analytical, and very readable. Especially good on the role of religion in Greek life and the development of religious ideas in the fifth century.

Burn, A. R. *Alexander the Great and the Hellenistic Empire*. Collier. Popular short presentation.

Cornford, Francis M. *From Religion to Philosophy: A Study in the Origins of Western Speculation*. Torchbooks. Short but suggestive and stimulating study throwing much light on the Greek beginnings of philosophy.

Coulanges, Fustel de. *The Ancient City*. Anchor. In spite of the age of this book (published in 1864), modern scholarship has added little to our understanding of its theme—the relation of religion to the life of the ancient city.

Dickinson, G. Lowes. *The Greek View of Life*. Ann Arbor. A classic, written at the turn of the twentieth century, still unequaled as a presentation of all that we think admirable about the Greeks.

Dodd, E. R. *The Greeks and the Irrational*. Beacon. Explodes the point of view, still too frequently held in spite of the evidence to the contrary, that the Greeks were a calm and restrained people.

Ehrenburg, Victor. *The People of Aristophanes: a Sociology of Old Attic Comedy*. Schocken. Modern investigation of Athenian social life with information derived from all sources to throw light on conditions described by Aristophanes.

Farrington, Benjamin, *Greek Science*. Penguin. This book, first published in 1949, was long the only available work on Hellenistic science. Still useful, but explanations often simplified too much. Supplement with less technical parts of Sarton and Neugebauer.

Graves, Robert. *The Greek Myths*. 2 vols. Penguin. By a learned English poet, profoundly interested in mythology and religion. Interpretations often farfetched, but argued with such overwhelming erudition and determination that they are often difficult to refute by those less learned than Graves. To be treated, like all this author's works, with caution.

Guthrie, W. K. C. *The Greeks and Their Gods*. Beacon. Good discussion for serious students.

Hadas, Moses. *Ancilla to Classical Reading*. Columbia University Press. An informative and helpful guide. Also by the same author, *A History of Greek Literature* (Columbia).

Hamilton, Edith. *The Greek Way to Western Civilization*. Mentor. A popular account, beautifully written and enriched by many quotations; but not a book to be read by itself. Its catching enthusiasm sometimes blinds the judgment of the reader.

Harrison, Jane. *Prolegomena to the Study of Greek Religion*. Meridian. Very thorough study, not recommended for beginners, but rewarding for serious students.

Kitto, H. D. F. *The Greeks*. Penguin. Valuable short study.

Lucas, F. L. *Greek Poetry for Everyman*. Beacon. By a noted English literary critic.

Neugebauer, Otto. *The Exact Sciences in Antiquity*, 2d ed. Torchbooks. This is excellent on Hellenistic science, made still more useful by careful study of its debt to Mesopotamia.

Nietzsche, Friedrich. *The Birth of Tragedy and the Genealogy of Morals*. Anchor. This youthful work of Nietzsche not only is the key to the later work of the nineteenth-century German philosopher but also contains profound insights into the distinction in kind between early and late Greek tragedy. Nietzsche sees Socrates and Euripides as the promoters of the intellectual revolution that destroyed the religious basis of Athenian society.

Robinson, Cyril E. *Hellas: A Short History of Ancient Greece*. Beacon. One of the best introductions available. Clear, up-to-date, and well organized.

Rose, H. S. *Gods and Heroes of the Greeks*. Meridian. By a noted scholar of Greek mythology and religion.

Sarton, George. *Ancient Science and Modern Civilization*. Torchbooks. Brief treatment by a leading historian of science.

Smith, Morton. *The Ancient Greeks*. Cornell University Press. A useful introduction.

Tarn, W. W. *Alexander the Great*. Beacon. One of the best biographies of the great conqueror.

Tarn, W. W. *Hellenistic Civilization*, rev. by G. T. Griffith. Meridian. Comprehensive study of all phases of the civilization, the best single-volume treatment.

Taylor, A. E. *Socrates* (Anchor), *Plato* (Meridian), *Aristotle* (Dover). Three separate studies by a renowned classical scholar, all well written and interesting, all controversial. Taylor's estimate of the influence of Socrates on Platonic thought, however, is widely accepted, especially by those who have read little but Taylor.

Weil, Simone. *The Iliad or the Poem of Force*. Pendle Hill. Looks at Homer as anti-war poet, stressing his compassion for human suffering. Original and interesting, by important modern religious thinker.

Zeller, Eduard. *Outlines of the History of Greek Philosophy*. Meridian. A good introduction by one of the best of the earlier historians of philosophy.

Zimmern, Alfred. *The Greek Commonwealth*. Galaxy. Also Modern Library, Inc., hard-cover edition. This book, though written as long ago as 1911 and revised only slightly until its last edition in 1931, is still indispensable as the only relatively brief presentation of ancient Greece in a topical manner, giving full weight to economic and social as well as political data.

HARD-COVER BOOKS

Jaeger, Werner. *Paedeia*. 3 vols., trans. by Gilbert Highet. New York: Oxford University Press, 1943–1945. The most complete study of Greek intellectual and cultural development available. Rather difficult for the beginning student but worth the attempt.

Jones, W. T. *A History of Western Philosophy*, vol. I. New York: Harcourt, Brace & World, Inc., 1952. Well-organized modern history of philosophy with very fair summaries of the Greek thinkers.

Jouguet, P. *Macedonian Imperialism and the Hellenization of the East*. New York. Alfred A. Knopf, Inc., 1928. Thoughtful and analytical study.

Rostovtzeff, M. I. *Social and Economic History of the Hellenistic World*, vols. I and II. Oxford, England: The Clarendon Press, 1941. Not as formidable as it looks. Packed with information and well written.

Sarton, George. *A History of Science*, vol. I. Cambridge, Mass.: Harvard University Press, 1952. A very thorough study by the dean of American historians of science.

Warbeke, J. M. *The Searching Mind of Greece*. New York: Appleton-Century-Crofts, Inc., 1930. In my opinion, one of the best introductions to Greek thought, especially good on the nature of the problems Greek writers were trying to solve.

FIVE

From Republic to Empire—
The Evolution of Roman Civilization

❖ Republic and empire—a contrast

The study of Rome within the compass of a single chapter presents a peculiarly difficult problem. The history of Rome falls into two distinct parts: the first, ending in 31 B.C., is the history of the republic, governed under forms which can be considered democratic, but which permitted an oligarchy to rule for almost the whole period; the second is the history of the empire, under a monarch, with the forms of the monarchy at first disguised and then obvious to all. Most of the territory acquired by the Roman people and later called the Roman Empire was won during the republic; in the imperial period this territory was thoroughly reorganized and converted into the efficient institution which so much impressed the Christians and which affected so profoundly the whole civilization of the Western world.

The republic is a classic instance of the inability of institutions which grew up to take care of one set of conditions to function effectively when these conditions have altogether changed. The Roman Republic was utterly unable to administer its empire either efficiently or for the benefit of the governed; it collapsed in a civil war amid a welter of blood. Yet the gradual progress toward empire, the policies by which the numerically few Roman people won such a large expanse of territory, the way in which the democratic forms were attained, the manner in which these forms worked and were ultimately lost, are subjects of perennial interest to all students of history and government. The story of the republic therefore is far more interesting than that of the rather static Empire, which was evolving toward nothing, though it provided a framework for the gradual civilizing of peoples who until then had known little of the blessings of civilization. To understand the republic a considerable amount of intricate detail has to be mastered, as always when a complex governmental system is studied. This detail is out of place in a single chapter devoted to Rome and cannot therefore be given. All that will be attempted is a brief account of the evolution of republican institutions and a description of the government as it functioned at the height of the republic. All detailed explanations of why this should have come about will have to be studied in a larger work.

❖ From kingship to democracy— the evolution of the republic to 287 B.C.

STRUGGLE OF PLEBEIANS FOR EQUAL RIGHTS

The traditional date of the founding of Rome was 753 B.C. This date, however, is not accepted by historians, who are well aware that there was a settlement on the site of Rome at

Chronological Chart

ROME—THE EARLY MONARCHY

Traditional date of founding of Rome	753 B.C.	Etruscan domination	616–509
Traditional first four kings of Rome	753–616		

THE REPUBLIC

Internal history		*External history*	
First secession of plebs—Election of tribunes and establishment of Concilium plebis (plebiscites binding on plebs)	494 B.C.	Battle of Lake Regillus—Roman victory over Latin League	496 B.C.
		Treaty with Latin League— Promulgation of Latin rights	493
Establishment of Comitia tributa (Assembly of Tribes)	ca. 460	Rome leader of Latin League— Gradual expansion	490–430
Twelve Tables	450–449	Conquest of Veii (southern Etruria)	396
Valerio-Horatian Laws (legislation by plebs binding on state if accepted by Senate)	448	Invasion of Italy by Gauls— Sack of Rome	387–386
Intermarriage permitted between plebeians and patricians	445	War with Latin League	340–338
Suspension of consulship, substituted by military tribunes, open to plebeians	444–367	Defeat of Latin League— Roman Confederation	338
		Samnite Wars	327–290
Licinian-Sextian Laws—Consulship opened to plebeians	367	War with Pyrrhus and Magna Graecia	281–272
Censors to give preference to ex-magistrates in drawing up list of senators	310	First Punic War	264–241
		Sicily becomes first Roman province	227
Loss of senatorial veto on all legislation (Hortensian Law)	287	Second Punic War	218–201
Tiberius Gracchus elected tribune	133	Wars with Macedonia	200–197; 171–168
Tribunate of Gaius Gracchus	123–122	Defeat of Antiochus III (king of Syria) at Magnesia	190
Death of Gaius Gracchus	121	Third Punic War	149–146
Marius first elected consul	107	Destruction of Carthage and sack of Corinth	146
Reorganization of army on volunteer basis by Marius	106	Macedonia becomes Roman province	146
Sullan Constitution	83–80	Jugurthine War	112–106
Pompey given extended command against Mithridates	66	Marius defeats Cimbri and Teutones	102–101
Return of Pompey to Rome	62	Social War in Italy	90–88
First Triumvirate	60	Sulla undertakes war with Mithridates	87
Caesar appointed to command in Gaul	58		

THE REPUBLIC

Internal history		*External history*	
Return of Caesar to Italy	49	Wars with Mithridates (Lucullus)	75–66
Caesar as dictator	46–44	Slave War in Italy	74–71
Murder of Caesar	44	Conquest and reorganization of Asia by Pompey	66–62
		Caesar conquers Gaul	58–51
		Crassus defeated and killed in Parthia	53

THE PRINCIPATE

Second Triumvirate—Proscriptions and death of Cicero	43 B.C.	Reign of Caligula (Gaius)	37–41
		Reign of Claudius	41–54
Battle of Philippi—Death of Brutus and Cassius	42	Reign of Nero	54–68
Antony goes to the East	42	Year of the Four Emperors	69
Battle of Actium	31	Vespasian and the Flavian dynasty	69–96
Death of Antony and Cleopatra	30	Final conquest of Britain under Domitian	84
Augustus given *proconsulare imperium* and *tribunicia potestas* for life	23	Nerva chosen emperor by Senate	96
Danube frontier established for empire	15	The "Good Emperors"—Nerva, Trajan, Hadrian, Antoninus Pius, Marcus Aurelius	96–180
Rhine frontier accepted after defeat of Varus	A.D. 9	Conquest of Dacia by Trajan	107
Death of Augustus	14	First barbarian invasions under Marcus Aurelius (Marcomanni and Sarmatians)	166–175
Reign of Tiberius	14–37		

least as early as 1000 B.C. Traditionally the first king was Romulus, a person of whom nothing is known beyond what later and unreliable legend tells us. However, it is certain that during the seventh and sixth centuries B.C. Rome was ruled by a monarchy, and the last of these monarchs was an Etruscan named Tarquin the Proud. It is also certain that the Etruscans, a people whose origins are still obscure but who probably came from Asia Minor, dominated Rome for the last period of the kingship, and Roman legend always speaks of the expulsion of the kings as the beginning of Roman independence under republican forms (about 509 B.C.). All through the period of the republic the name of king was detested by the Romans

in memory of this famous expulsion of men presumed to be tyrants.

The position of the king was taken by two consuls, each holding office for a year, chosen exclusively from the noble or patrician class. In early Rome there was a formal and definite class distinction between patricians and non-patricians, who were called plebeians. Patricians held their position by birth, and it was not possible to rise into the patrician class, since intermarriage between the two classes was prohibited. Thus, traders, small farmers, artisans, and all other free men who did not belong to the noble families were lumped together into the plebeian order. In the class struggles that followed the establishment of the republic, it is natural that the wealthier and better-placed members of the plebeian order should have taken the lead in fighting for reforms, and it should not be thought that the ordinary peasant or small farmer was likely to be especially interested in breaking down the class distinction or repealing the laws against intermarriage. His daughter was unlikely to marry into the aristocracy, whatever the laws might permit.

Since early Rome was engaged in constant wars, the plebeians who took their share in the fighting had a potent weapon at their disposal for extracting concessions from the patricians. As the result of a strike (about 494 B.C.) of the army when it had been called out for campaign duty, the first concessions were granted. The plebeians were allowed to have two officers of state, called tribunes, with power to veto any acts of the consuls. These men were to be elected by the plebeians themselves, assembled into a council for the purpose. About 449 B.C., probably also as the result of another strike or threatened strike, the law was codified in such a manner that plebeians could expect due process in case of being brought to trial, and they could only be punished for infractions of these definite laws (Twelve Tables). A few years afterward plebeians were permitted to intermarry with patricians. Some time during the years between the first and the second strikes the Assembly of the plebs, which chose the tribunes, was permitted to pass legislation binding on the plebs alone, and the Assembly itself was reorganized to permit the entry of patricians. In 448 B.C. this reorganized Assembly, most of whose members were, of course, plebeians, was permitted to pass laws which were then submitted to the patrician body, the Senate. If accepted by the latter, the laws were considered binding on the whole people. Apart from legislation, however, the Senate continued to dominate the state, and the veto that the senators exercised prevented the plebeians from having any real say in the government. It was, however, a good beginning, and the struggle continued, with ever-increasing victories for the plebeians.

The most important disadvantage now suffered by the plebeians was their exclusion from the highest office in the state, the consulship.

The patricians were reluctant to give way on this, and for a time, rather than admit plebeians to an office of such prestige, they abolished the office altogether. However, in 367 B.C. they gave way, relying upon the fact that they controlled the electoral machinery and could thus ensure that no plebeians would in fact be elected. The attempt to hold up plebeian election by such means was, however, a failure. The plebeians who controlled the legislature so often forced the bill on the Senate that one of the consuls *must* be a plebeian that the Senate at last withdrew its veto, and thereafter one of the consuls always was a plebeian. Gradually, by the same means, all the offices of state were opened to plebeians, until at last all that the Senate had remaining was the veto on legislation. A third general strike in 287 B.C. forced the removal of the veto, and thereafter all legislation passed by the Assembly (*Comitia tributa*) was binding on the state, whether or not the Senate approved it.

CONTINUED STRENGTH OF ARISTOCRATS IN DEMOCRATIC FRAMEWORK

Thus by 287 B.C. there was formal equality within the state, and all offices were open to all citizens. Yet the people did not in fact rule. The august Senate, now made up not only of patricians but of all those citizens who had held important office in the state, managed to rule indirectly for almost 150 years after it lost its veto. This feat was achieved by the effective process of disarming all likely opposition through admitting tribunes (of whom there were now ten, each with a veto) to the Senate and allowing them to call it into session. The tribunes therefore became accustomed to consulting the Senate before they proposed legislation to the Assembly. Since the latter body could only vote yes or no, whereas the Senate could debate for as long as it liked, it was natural for a tribune to go to the Senate for advice and to listen to and take part in its debates. Able tribunes, now welcomed into the homes, and sometimes the families, of the aristocrats, were tempted to adopt the attitudes of their new relatives. Thus the Senate came to have almost a monopoly of talent within its ranks, and it controlled directly both foreign policy and the treasury.

Finally, as if this were not enough, various senatorial factions controlled political machines which ensured that the urban masses of Rome could at all times be outnumbered in voting by senatorial clients and landowners—unless the farmers themselves came into Rome in person to vote on some issue that was of special interest to them, as happened in 133 B.C. at the time of the Gracchan Revolution.

❖ External history to 272 B.C.— The unification of Italy

SYSTEM OF DEALING WITH CONQUERED ITALIANS—ALLIED RIGHTS

As has already been noted, the Romans were engaged in constant wars, originally for survival against their neighbors and then for the control of the whole peninsula of Italy. In the early years of their independence they were greatly helped by the Latin League, a league of smaller city-states to the south of Rome. Although the league at times resented and feared Roman domination and fought against the Romans, the latter were never left altogether without allies, even though a great deal of prestige was lost on one occasion when the Celtic people called the Gauls descended from the north and were able to sack Rome itself (387–86 B.C.). The secret of the Roman success probably lies in the fact that they never agreed that they had been beaten in all their history. They never were forced to conclude a loser's peace. When they made treaties without winning a war, it was only to resume the war as soon as opportunity permitted. For centuries there was

Ruins of the temple of Mars in the Roman Forum. (COURTESY ITALIAN STATE TOURIST OFFICE)

nothing in Rome worth plundering. A foreign invader could take nothing worth his while. And without exterminating the whole Roman people, there was no way of concluding a war or making a peace settlement that could be expected to endure.

But, perhaps more important than their stubbornness and refusal to admit final defeat, the treaty system invented by the Romans was a crucial element in their success. If any enemy surrendered to the Romans he could usually expect good terms. The Romans seldom destroyed their enemies, but preferred to make it possible for themselves to live at peace with them afterward. Although treaties existed long prior to the Romans (the most famous early treaty known to us was between Rameses II of Egypt and the Hittites), it was the Romans amongst the ancient peoples who developed the art of treaty-making in the most systematic manner. Already early in the period of the republic they showed their talent for law and government that was their most conspicuous gift as a people, compensating thereby to a large extent for their lack of almost all the cultural graces which we associate with the Greeks.

The ability to make effective treaties rested on the Roman concept of citizenship. Citizenship, to a Roman, was vested in a person, and did not depend on his place of residence. Thus citizenship could be granted as well as inherited. Moreover, Roman citizenship included certain specific and definite rights. So it was possible to grant an enemy recently defeated in battle either full citizenship, or some of the rights of citizens. The main rights of citizens were three: the right to trade, the right to intermarry, and the right to vote. The last-named right included many other subsidiary rights, and was reserved for the full Roman citizen. When the Italians who possessed for centuries only Latin rights, or half citizenship, felt at the beginning of the first century B.C. that they needed the right to vote, with all its appurtenances, for their own protection, the Romans resisted the claim, and a severe war had to be fought before it was granted. But in the earlier centuries the Latin allies were content with rights other than the right to vote, and it was customary for the Romans to grant these, thus associating the allies

with the success of the Romans and giving them some share in the proceeds of their victories. When the Romans began to expand beyond Latium into the southern part of Italy they invented a new right, the right of an ally, which entitled the possessor to protection by Rome against external enemies. By the use of this right the Romans took over, in effect, the foreign policy of the ally, who could no longer make war on his own account and was bound to come to the aid of the Romans if they engaged in a war. Since the Romans were seldom at peace, it is clear that they stood to gain more than their allies from such an arrangement. However, as will be seen, the treaty could work the other way also and drag the Romans into a war which they would have preferred to avoid.

SAMNITE AND PYRRHIC WARS

From the latter part of the fourth century B.C. the Romans engaged in hostilities with a people originally more powerful than themselves and their Latin allies together. These people, the Samnites, proved very dangerous to them, especially since some of the Latin allies deserted to the Samnites in the course of the wars, feeling that Rome was becoming too powerful and ought to be restrained. Several times the Romans were severely defeated, but their persistence paid off in the end, and by 290 B.C. the Samnites, who found themselves in the course of the war compelled to set up a confederation of their own comparable to that of the Romans, submitted. This war, however, brought the Romans into direct contact with the Greeks in southern Italy, a people with a far superior culture, who made their living largely by maritime trade. Like most Greek cities they were constantly quarreling with one another, and the presence of such a strong power as Rome in central Italy exercised an overwhelming influence in a quarrel between any two of them. It was not long before Rome was called in when one of the smaller Greek cities found itself at war with a bigger one. In turn the larger city, Tarentum, called in the aid of a Greek king from the mainland. This new entry brought Carthage, the north African maritime power which controlled most of Sicily at the time, to the aid of the Romans,

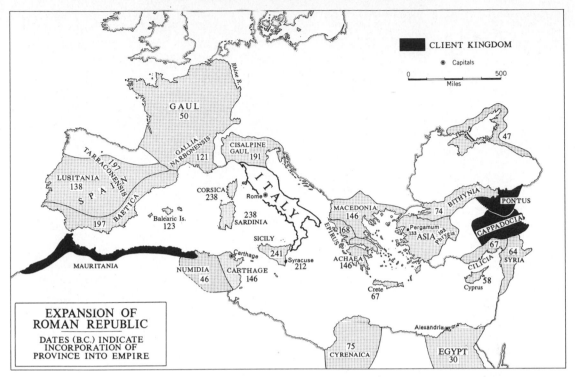

EXPANSION OF
ROMAN REPUBLIC

DATES (B.C.) INDICATE
INCORPORATION OF
PROVINCE INTO EMPIRE

For details on Italy, see front endpaper.

since Pyrrhus, the Greek king, had his eye on Sicily and had been interfering there prior to his being summoned by Tarentum. There ensued a war in which Pyrrhus, in spite of being aided by elephants, found himself unable to undertake succcessfully a two-front war. He was finally expelled from both Italy and Sicily, and the Romans added the Greek cities to their confederation as allies, with allied rights.

❖ The expansion of Rome beyond Italy

THE PUNIC WARS

It was not long before war broke out again, this time between Rome and Carthage. This was altogether natural, and could have been predicted. Prior to the conquest of the Greek cities in Italy the Romans had not been interested in maritime trade. But these cities had been carrying on a running fight with the Carthaginians, who jealously guarded their empire and permitted only very restricted trading rights to others. It was too tempting an opportunity for the Greek cities to resist, knowing that the Ro-

mans were compelled to aid them if they should get into open hostilities. The expected incident soon occurred, and though the Roman Senate did not desire to honor its obligations, pressure by the wealthy classes and the consuls who wished for military commands succeeded in overcoming its opposition, and the first Punic War followed. Again the Romans had the greatest difficulty in winning this war. They were unaccustomed to the sea and they did not trust the newly conquered Greek cities in spite of their alliance with them. More men in this war were drowned at sea than were ever killed in battle. But, as always, sheer persistence won the day; Carthage was defeated and forced to concede that part of Sicily that had been under its control. The island of Sardinia followed soon afterward.

But Carthage was far from subdued, and under a gifted general named Hannibal decided to pursue the Romans in their own stronghold of Italy. Roman leadership at first was completely unable to cope with the well-trained Carthaginian army which crossed the Alps (218 B.C.) and annihilated two Roman armies sent against it. Hannibal did not, however, succeed in taking Rome, and made no serious attempt to do so. His fine army, marooned in southern Italy and cut off from sources of reinforcement, wasted away while the Romans adopted harassing tactics. At last the Romans found a first-rate general too, and sent an expedition to Africa to take the Carthaginian homeland. Hannibal was forced to return, and was decisively defeated. Once again the Romans had won the last battle.

EXPANSION OF ROMANS INTO GREECE AND THE NEAR EAST

Meanwhile the Romans had found it necessary to protect their allies in eastern Italy, which meant policing the Adriatic Sea. Finding it impossible to do this effectively without a base on the Greek mainland, they proceeded to take such a base, thereby involving themselves with Macedonia, which resented the presence of an alien power on Greek soil. The Macedonians allied themselves with the Seleucid monarch of Asia, and the Romans were forced to deal with him too. Several times they defeated the Macedonians, and apparently tried not to incorporate either Macedonia or southern Greece into their expanding empire. Once a Roman consul theatrically proclaimed the liberation of all Greece, to the accompaniment of ecstatic cheers. But none of these countries could remain free permanently. One faction would quarrel with another and invite Rome in to settle the question. In the end the Romans stayed, and by the middle of the second century B.C. there were enough Romans with a vested interest in the empire, which by this time extended into the Near East, to be able to persuade the Senate and people to engage in new wars even when there was little excuse for them. This effect of the empire upon the government and people of Rome will be considered in a later section.

❖ The provincial system

PROBLEM OF ADMINISTERING LANDS OUTSIDE ITALY

When the Romans were ceded territory beyond Italy it was necessary to decide what kind of administration the new lands should be given. It did not seem feasible to extend the system of allied rights that had been so successful in Italy itself. Rome did not need or desire the help of these territories in her wars, nor would Roman rights at that time have meant anything to their peoples. What was needed was that the provinces, as they came to be called, should contribute financially to the well-being of Rome, and that their governments should not give Rome any trouble and should not have any independent policy of their own. Manifestly, too, many of these lands were incapable of governing themselves to Roman satisfaction—as we have seen, the Romans tried to let the Greeks and Macedonians continue to govern themselves even after they had been defeated in battle by the Romans. Where, however, there was an effective government in the hands of a respectable monarch, the Romans were content to leave him in charge provided he fulfilled certain necessary obligations. This system of client kings was maintained in parts of the Roman Empire till after the time of Augustus and the end of the republic. Herod the Great of Judea was a client king, as was Herod Agrippa later.

GOVERNMENT AND ADMINISTRATION IN THE PROVINCES

For territories where there was no king available the Romans devised the provincial system. Each province had its rights and duties clearly defined in a provincial law, dictated by the Romans but accepted by the provincials, sometimes with some difficulty—as in the case of Sardinia, where no legal-minded leaders could be discovered amongst the barbarian inhabitants. Under this system there was a Roman governor, appointed by the Senate from the ranks of men who had recently held high office in the state. His term of office was one year. He was assisted by a moderately large body of troops charged with the task of keeping order and preventing rebellion. A stated tax had to be paid into the Roman treasury each year, but, unfortunately, except in rare cases where there had been efficient government before the advent of the Romans, there was no suitable body of bureaucrats available for the collection of the tax. Thus the system grew up of farming out the taxes to private enterprise. In some of the provinces, including Sicily at the beginning, the tax contract was let to local bankers, who were restrained by local patriotism from fleecing the taxpayers too mercilessly. In other provinces, however—and they formed the large majority by the end of the second century B.C.—the tax contracts were let to Roman bankers, who were restrained by no such gentle feelings. The only safeguard the provincials had was the honesty of the governor, whose good offices were necessary if the tax collectors (*publicani*) were not to collect more than their due—a fixed percentage was stated in the law governing the province—and the possibility of prosecuting the collectors and perhaps the governor in Roman law courts.

FAILURE OF PROVINCIAL SYSTEM UNDER THE REPUBLIC

The two safeguards were not likely to be, and were not in fact, very effective. The governor, who held office for only a year and who expected at most two years as governor during his official career, was not allowed by law to take part in any trade or commerce himself. With living expenses, including the expense of election, rising every year, and with no regular source of income beyond what he could squeeze out of his lands, he was thus subject to extraordinary temptation, which, as far as we can ascertain, he did not often resist. Thus the governor and the tax collector flourished, while the provincials could look only to the courts for redress. And, unfortunately for them, the courts were manned by senators who were unlikely to be so austere as to betray their class by a conviction—especially not when there was a chance that they too might be placed within the reach of the same temptation and wish to succumb to it. Toward the end of the second century B.C. the courts were transferred to the equestrian order, a new order in the Roman state made up primarily of businessmen and the middle class. This, from the provincial point of view, could hardly be considered an improvement. The most notable conviction for extortion in the early first century was that of one Rutilius Rufus,

who had in fact himself scrupulously avoided any extortion, and had indeed clamped down upon the businessmen who had attempted it during his regime. The courts, interested only in discouraging honesty in governors, handed down a conviction in spite of the lack of reliable evidence. Rutilius was thereupon invited to take up his residence and live free for the rest of his life in the province he was supposed to have so mercilessly exploited!

Although the provincial system demonstrated the unfitness of the republic to rule an empire without drastic changes, it was not in itself an important factor in the collapse of republican institutions, as has sometimes been claimed. The governors in charge of provinces possessed insufficient military might to present a threat to the republic. As we shall see, it was the long-term commands of proconsuls, with jurisdiction over far more than a mere province, in command of less meager forces than a governor had at his disposal, that finally put an end to the Republic and ensured one-man rule.

❖ **Consequences of Roman expansion**

ENRICHMENT OF GENERALS, LANDOWNERS, AND BANKERS

In order to explain the many-sided effect of the expansion upon Rome, some preliminary explanations are necessary. The Roman army had originally been made up of both patricians and plebeians, but no man who was entirely without property could serve. The whole army was conscripted for particular campaigns, and the soldiers expected to return to civilian life as soon as the campaign was over. This system worked well enough for some centuries, but when the campaigns took the soldiers ever farther afield, many of those who returned found that their property had been taken over by local landowners, who could not be easily dislodged. Moreover, after the wars with Carthage, and especially after the Second Punic War, when Hannibal occupied a considerable section of Italy, the small farmer found that he had too little capital available to bring his land back into cultivation. The result was that the large landowner, with access to capital, continually increased his holdings at the expense of the small farmer, who often lost his land with very little compensation. So, when the farmer was conscripted into the army, he began to look upon his land as likely to be lost in any case. He was therefore willing to stay in the army for a longer period, provided he could compensate himself with war booty. Thus he began to gain a vested interest in continued warfare, especially warfare against countries which possessed sufficient movable property for his needs. The commanders of these armies likewise felt that they should make some material gains from the war. Commands were short-lived and the commanders had expenses as high as provincial governors; indeed, they looked forward to being provincial governors after their term of command in the army. Thus they too began to gain a vested interest in profitable warfare.

The middle classes, especially the bankers and contractors, found that tax collecting, and the purchase of provincial tax contracts, was a profitable business. The more provinces fell to the Roman sword, the richer the pickings for them. The populace of Rome, on the other hand, saw little good in warfare. The city was thronged with dispossessed farmers, and Rome never was able to provide much work, save in small industry such as shield-making and the manufacture of goods for local consumption. Imported goods were better and cheaper, and many imports had been merely taken as campaign booty. There were no taxes, to be sure; but it is doubtful whether most of the poor would have paid taxes in any case, since they possessed so little property or income. Their only gain was a subsidized price for grain, a very small consideration to be set against the low wages earned in competition with skilled imported slaves. But these men still had the vote, and the full consequences of their latent political power were not to be exploited until the Gracchan Revolution, when at last two leaders were found who were willing to stand up against the senatorial monopoly of power.

POLITICAL EFFECTS IN ROME

The Gracchan Revolution Tiberius Gracchus became tribune of the plebs in 133 B.C.,

pledged to a program of land redistribution that would break up the large estates and give them to the illegally dispossessed farmers. As soon as he introduced his legislation, he was faced with a veto from one of his nine colleagues. This was one of the traditional safeguards of the senatorial party (called the Optimates); hitherto it had always been possible to bribe at least one tribune. But Tiberius did not take this lying down, as no doubt his predecessors had done. He called upon the people to depose the tribune. This they did, though it was illegal. The legislation duly passed, there came the question of putting it into force, and this needed money. Providentially, just at this moment a Hellenistic king, dying without heirs, bequeathed his kingdom to the Roman people. Tiberius and his Assembly gratefully accepted the gift, while the Senate, the traditional repository of all monies, had to accept the situation with the best grace possible. Tiberius' action was not illegal. He was the representative of the Roman people, as the Senate was not, and the legacy had been made to the Roman people. But the control of finances had long been a cherished senatorial monopoly, so that the action of the tribune was certainly inflammatory. Finally, Tiberius, fearful that any successor would sabotage his program, decided that he himself must be re-elected; but such a re-election was certainly illegal. The Optimates, who controlled the armed forces, were quite capable of using them against such illegality. A band of supporters of the constitution, led by the high priest, murdered Tiberius on election day, and with him three hundred of his supporters. The land law, however, was put into effect, and much of the Italian land was indeed redistributed.

Ten years later Gaius, the younger brother of Tiberius Gracchus, was elected tribune. In the meantime re-election of a tribune had been made legal. Gaius therefore could look forward to several years of leadership in the Assembly if he could hold the confidence of the people. This time the Optimates had a better card to play. They had one of themselves elected tribune as one of the colleagues of Gaius. This man proceeded systematically to outbid his colleague, having no intention of carrying out his promises. His task was made easier by the fact that

Gaius was studiously moderate and not all of his proposals were equally popular with the people. The third year that he stood for office, with only half of his legislative program enacted into law, he was defeated. Fearing for his life, he surrounded himself with a bodyguard, whereupon the Senate, after a few inflammatory incidents had been provoked, called upon the consul to restore order, in effect declaring martial law. Gaius either was murdered or committed suicide, and more than three thousand of his followers were killed. The popular revolution had failed, but the Senate had declared its bankruptcy.

The rise of the soldier of fortune—Preparation for one-man rule The senatorial oligarchy supported by the monied interests had successfully curbed the possible establishment of a popular democracy in Rome; but it was unable to defend itself against the military. Only if the army was loyal and civilian rule was unthreatened could the Senate, which had few armed forces at its disposal, hope to rule Rome. It had been highly dangerous, as well as ruinous to its prestige, to use military force to suppress the Gracchan attempt at revolutionary reforms, however much provocation it had been given. Power was soon to pass from its hands into the hands of the soldier of fortune with an effective political machine.

Probably few could have foreseen the result of an important but necessary reform of the method of recruiting the army, which was put into effect about 108 B.C. A minor war had been in progress in Africa for some years, which had been going unfavorably for Rome. It was rumored that the generals had been bribed by the enemy, a not altogether unlikely possibility, indeed boasted of by the young African prince who led the enemy. An officer named Marius began to attack his superiors and boast that he could finish off the war if given the command. Instead of being court-martialed, as he would have been in our own day, he was permitted to go back to Rome to stand for election as consul. An efficient political machine assured his election, and when the Senate hesitated to give him the African command, the Assembly conferred it upon him by law. In order to win the war

he reorganized the army, making it into a volunteer army, recruited from any who wished to join. Naturally, the Roman proletariat regarded this as an opportunity to win booty and perhaps pensions at the end of their military service. Instead of being made up of the propertied classes, with a stake, however small, in the Roman state, the army was now made up of propertyless men to whom Rome had been a poor mistress, and to whom they felt they owed little. Their loyalty lay with the general who had trained them and led them to victory and booty, and whose influence could force the Senate to grant them pensions and property when they were too old to fight. From this time onward power was to lie with those generals who had held commands long enough for them to win the loyalty of their troops.

❖ **Collapse of the Roman Republic**

LAST ATTEMPT AT RECONSTRUCTION
BY SULLA

The full results of this policy were not visible for many years to come. Marius himself was a very feeble politician, and he still stood in some awe of the Senate. Not until his last years did he recognize the chance he had missed, when he saw his junior officer in the African campaign, a general named Sulla, dictate to the Roman Senate and people just how they were to behave while he was away on campaign in Greece. It is true that as soon as Sulla had left, Marius recaptured Rome with a rabble army; but he lived for only one month afterward. When Sulla returned triumphant from Greece, the supporters of Marius were given short shrift, while Sulla himself became dictator. If he had wished, he could have become the first emperor of Rome.

But Sulla did not so wish. Instead, he preferred to make an effort to reform the constitution. He deprived the people and their Assembly of much of their power, weakened the office of tribune, which had been so much abused, in such a manner that no ambitious man would wish to hold it, and reorganized the Senate into what should have been a really effective body.

Then he retired quietly to his estates, dying soon afterward. His constitution failed because no one, not even the Senate itself, apparently really wished to try to make it work. As soon as the next crisis arose, the Senate was willing to abdicate its responsibility and give extended powers to the nearest capable military man. At this time a continuous war was being waged in Asia against the most formidable enemy the republic ever had to face, King Mithridates VI of Pontus, so that short-term commands were obviously unfeasible.

POMPEY—THE POPULAR GENERAL

Pompey was the beneficiary of this situation. First elected by the Assembly to a long-term command against pirates in the Mediterranean Sea, and having made short work of these, he was given a further long-term command in the East. There he replaced a senatorial general whose tight-fisted treatment of his troops had caused them to go on strike, to the detriment of the campaign against Mithridates. Pompey, who cared nothing for money, soon settled this situation and proceeded to conquer not only Pontus but also several other countries ripe to be added to the ever-expanding empire. This conquest took several years, but during the period he kept his political machine at home well oiled. Everyone in Rome knew that when he returned home, he would assume whatever power he wished. There was no power in Italy or elsewhere that could possibly withstand his victorious army.

RISE OF CAESAR—THE FIRST TRIUMVIRATE (60 B.C.)

When, however, he did at length return home, he showed no signs of desiring anything but pensions for his troops and the ratification of his acts in the East. The Senate, taking this for a sign of weakness, refused these moderate demands. Pompey, nonplussed, looked around for some political help, as he now held no office himself. He discovered it in the person of Julius Caesar, a rising military man who had just returned from a campaign in Spain and was the consul-elect, and also in the person of a banker named Crassus, who had financed Caesar's career. Caesar's price was a long-term command in Gaul, Crassus remaining content with financial concessions. Pompey accepted the terms. Caesar accordingly introduced a resolution in the Senate giving Pompey the pensions and ratifications that he needed. When these requests were turned down, Pompey called upon a few troops who were still waiting patiently for their pensions and so could be relied upon, whereupon the Senate thought better of its refusal. For the next ten years the triumvirate of Pompey, Caesar, and Crassus did as it liked. Crassus, though aging, thought he would like a command in the East before he died, and was given it. He was killed in a stunning defeat by the Parthians. Caesar made a thorough job of conquering Gaul, although when he began his career there seemed to be no special necessity to add this province to the empire. Pompey, aging also, stayed close to Rome, taking no active command. Secure in the laurels he had won, he did not realize until too late that Caesar was building up precisely the same kind of loyal military following that he had once possessed himself.

CIVIL WAR AND THE DICTATORSHIP OF CAESAR

The showdown came when Caesar prepared to return to Rome. The Senate had decided that Pompey was less dangerous to the republic than the ambitious Caesar, and had succeeded at last in enlisting his support. But when Caesar crossed the Rubicon and illegally entered Italy with his army, there were no troops in Italy capable of withstanding him, in spite of all the commands that Pompey in theory still held. Pompey and his senatorial supporters therefore crossed over into Greece, where Pompey still had a considerable reputation. But bad management of their campaign played into Caesar's hands, and Pompey was decisively defeated at the battle of Pharsalia in 48 B.C. He fled to Egypt and was murdered shortly afterward. Caesar followed him, making the acquaintance of Cleopatra, Queen of Egypt, in the process. Having settled the affairs of Egypt to his satisfaction, he proceeded to mop up various pockets of resistance in North Africa and Spain, and returned to Italy to celebrate a magnificent triumph. He began to prepare a campaign against Parthia to avenge Crassus and recover the lost Roman eagles, while setting in motion numerous administrative reforms to take care of the most pressing problems. He had barely started on this work when he was murdered by a group of senators and disgruntled officers in 44 B.C.

None of the reforms initiated by Julius Caesar really touched the heart of the problem, which was in its essence political rather than administrative. Above all, the position of the ruler had to be regularized, and some substitute found for the rule by Senate and people which had so conspicuously failed. Caesar could think of nothing better than to make himself permanent dictator, a title which in Rome always referred to a temporary position held only in times of extreme danger. He thought of becoming king, but realized after a few trial balloons had been sent up that the people would not tolerate such a title. Kings had been execrated too long in Rome for a king to be acceptable now. Caesar was able to put into effect some much-needed reforms in the provinces before his murder, and he set up an important public-works program to give some occupation to the proletariat. He improved the tax system and took steps to ensure a regular supply of officials for public service in the free municipalities of the empire.

It was a good beginning and a considerable achievement for two years of absolute power. But it seems that Caesar could understand only the tangible needs of the empire, and he lacked that sense for the intangibles that characterized his successor and made the latter's work so much more fruitful and lasting. Caesar's attempt to "reform" the Senate consisted in packing it with military men and even provincials, which succeeded only in degrading it in its own eyes. The move might have been a wise one if he had really been interested in making this august and ancient body work. After all, it had ruled Rome for almost five hundred years, and though at the end it had fallen on evil times, it was surely not an institution that could be treated with disdain and given nothing to do but debate and

confer titles on its master. There can be little doubt that the tactlessness with which Caesar treated the Senate was the chief reason for the conspiracy against his life. So, for lack of the art of a true statesman, Caesar must remain as a first-class military man and an administrator of genius (Pompey, in this field, incidentally, must be counted as his equal), but not as the real founder of the empire—though without his preliminary work, the empire could hardly have been founded by his successor and heir.

❖ **The foundation of the Roman Empire**

THE SECOND TRIUMVIRATE AND THE TRIUMPH OF AUGUSTUS

The conspirators who murdered Caesar had no idea of what steps to take next. They appear to have assumed that the government would revert to the Senate and people as heretofore.

Bust of Augustus at the prime of his manhood. (COURTESY BRITISH MUSEUM)

But the republic was dead beyond any possibility of revival. Caesar's army had, for the most part, been disbanded, but it was still a potent political and military force. And Caesar, through his will, continued to exercise an influence even after his death. Mark Antony as consul commanded an army of Caesar's veterans, and Lepidus, Caesar's official second in command, had a legion at his disposal. Moreover, in his will Caesar, in addition to bequeathing large sums to his troops, had made his great-nephew, Octavian, a young man of little public experience, his heir, with the potent title of Caesar, which he was to exploit to its full value. Antony might have been murdered by the conspirators, but was spared. As soon as he had ridden out the immediate storm, he was able to rouse Rome against them, and they were forced to flee abroad. But Antony made a serious mistake in not giving the troops their donative promised by Caesar. This enabled the young Octavian to gain credit and support from the legions in southern Italy, with which he entered Rome, to be given the command against Antony by the Senate. Antony, faced with one of the conspirators in southern Gaul and with Octavian and the consuls in central Italy, was defeated by the latter and retired to the north, allowing Octavian to return to Rome in triumph. Again the Senate repeated its earlier mistake against Pompey and slighted the young man, refusing him high office in the state on technical grounds.

It was the Senate's last chance. Octavian with his legions proceeded to join Antony, and with Lepidus they formed the Second Triumvirate. All the triumvirs took vengeance on their political enemies with wholesale proscriptions. In part this helped them raise enough money from confiscated estates to put an army in the field sufficient to defeat the remnants of the conspirators, who were arrayed against them in Greece. When they had been disposed of at the battle of Philippi (42 B.C.), Antony and Octavian were supreme. Lepidus could safely be disregarded, and it only remained to come to an agreement about the respective roles that each should play. Antony, as the senior partner, was given the command against the East, while Octavian stayed behind in Italy with a number of minor campaigns to settle.

The uneasy alliance continued for more than ten years. But Antony played into Octavian's hands by acting like an Oriental monarch, and especially by his relations with Cleopatra, regarded by everyone in Rome as a dangerous Oriental princess who had fascinated Antony and charmed him away from his loyalty to Rome. Octavian fostered this point of view by an unexampled use of propaganda, gradually undermining Antony's position so effectively that when the break came, little actual fighting had to be done. Octavian had built up an important political party of his own, and had chosen at least one highly efficient general. So the battle of Actium in 31 B.C. was a foregone conclusion. Most of Antony's troops deserted when Cleopatra insisted on going into battle with him. Thereafter there was no power left in the Roman world to challenge Octavian. Four years later the Senate conferred upon him the title of Augustus, by which he was henceforth to be known.

THE SCOPE OF THE PROBLEMS

The magnitude and scope of the problems facing the young ruler (he had been born in 63 B.C. and was thus thirty-two at the time of the battle of Actium) can hardly be overestimated. The old Roman Republic had clearly failed to live up to the responsibilities of empire, and had collapsed from its own weaknesses. Yet some form of government must replace it which was capable of enduring. This government, whatever it might be, must also be able to keep under control the vast territories which had fallen to Roman arms during the previous three centuries. Rome had a responsibility to them also. It was impossible simply to decree their freedom and independence, even if the idea had ever occurred to Augustus. Their earlier forms of government had been destroyed beyond recall and could not be restored by a mere imperial fiat. In the last century of the republic the governors of the provinces had been political appointees of the Senate, anxious only to make their fortunes and return to Rome. By corruption and extortion they had advanced themselves; moreover, they were in league with the equestrian class of Rome, which had milked the

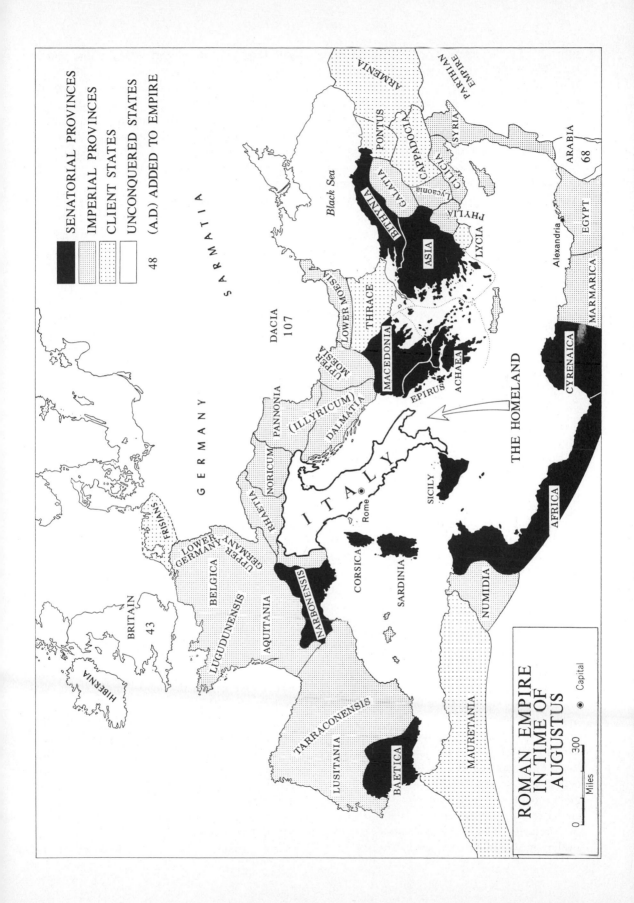

ROMAN EMPIRE
IN TIME OF
AUGUSTUS

● Capital

0   300
Miles

SENATORIAL PROVINCES
IMPERIAL PROVINCES
CLIENT STATES
UNCONQUERED STATES

48 (A.D.) ADDED TO EMPIRE

HIBERNIA

BRITAIN
43

FRISIANS

GERMANY

S A R M A T I A

LOWER
GERMANY
UPPER
GERMANY

BELGICA

LUGUDUNENSIS

AQUITANIA

NARBONENSIS

RHAETIA

NORICUM

PANNONIA

(ILLYRICUM)

DALMATIA

UPPER
MOESIA

DACIA
107

LOWER MOESIA

Black Sea

THRACE

ARMENIA

PARTHIAN
EMPIRE

BITHYNIA

PONTUS

GALATIA

CAPPADOCIA

CILICIA

Lycaonia

SYRIA

ASIA

PHYLIA

LYCIA

ARABIA
68

TARRACONENSIS

LUSITANIA

BAETICA

CORSICA

SARDINIA

I T A L Y

Rome

SICILY

MACEDONIA

EPIRUS

ACHAEA

THE HOMELAND

MAURETANIA

NUMIDIA

AFRICA

CYRENAICA

MARMARICA

Alexandria

EGYPT

provinces for the sake of its own financial interests. The provinces had suffered abominably from this regular regime, and in many cases had been driven into bankruptcy by the more recent civil wars and irregular extortions by would-be rulers of Rome. There was little encouragement to honesty or efficiency, qualities rarely found in the governors. Was it possible for Augustus to reward these qualities and so improve the provincial system that they would become the rule rather than the exception?

We have seen that the enrollment of volunteer armies by Marius had led directly to the fall of the republic, since the troops relied upon their generals for pay and pensions, and their loyalty was given to these generals rather than to Rome. Moreover, the various armies had swollen to such an extent in the civil wars that there were probably at least half a million men under arms at the time of the battle of Actium. Augustus had to consider what the real purpose of an army was in the Roman Empire, where the various legions should be stationed, how they were to occupy themselves during peacetime, how they could be persuaded to be loyal to Rome rather than to generals. At the same time, the armies must continue to have those professional military virtues whose absence in the earlier armies had compelled Marius to introduce long-term volunteer service.

Behind the great political and administrative problems was the ever-present social and economic background. Rome was not a great manufacturing city, not even a trading center of importance comparable to its size and population. There were far too many people in Rome unable to make a living and requiring public support. Yet these men were citizens and possessed the right to vote. In the last century of the republic the votes of this urban proletariat had always been for sale to the highest bidder. Could they be made into a self-respecting citizenry by any means available to a capable administrator? How could the numerous slaves live side by side with a free citizenry without depressing wages? In spite of the fertility of much of the soil, Italy had never really recovered from the depredations of Hannibal nearly two centuries earlier. The small estates had been swallowed by senators and capitalists and made into large specialized agricultural units, usually worked by slaves under overseers. Moreover, the small landholders who survived suffered from chronic insecurity of tenure, their properties often being sequestered for the benefit of veterans. And throughout the length and breadth of Italy, especially near Rome, rich men built their villas, too often neglecting the land itself and its cultivation.

The cleavage between rich and poor had undermined the old Roman traditional virtues, and the search for ever-increasing luxury among the upper classes had replaced the stern frugality of the earlier republic. Family life in the upper classes had almost disappeared, with divorce to be had for the asking and marriage used for political and financial advancement. The birth rate among the free Romans had naturally been declining. Was it possible to arrest this process, at least the decay of public morality, even if the ancient virtues had disappeared forever?

These were a few of the problems with which Augustus had to contend. If he did not solve them all, at least he perceived their existence and made an attempt to solve them. And the organization of an empire which endured for many centuries, the most enduring indeed that the Western world has yet seen, is almost entirely his work. The essential administrative structure was built by him, though the conquests themselves were bequeathed to him by the Roman conquerors of the republic.

THE WORK OF AUGUSTUS

The establishment of a legitimate government The most difficult problem of all was undoubtedly the reorganization of the government; and it was the most fundamental. Not even a provincial reorganization, the establishment of an equitable system of taxation, nor the enlargement of the conception of Roman citizenship, would have been of any permanent value without a governmental system which was capable of controlling the empire and which was at the same time acceptable to the people. Any dictatorship or arbitrary military rule can be cut short by assassination, as Caesar's own career had shown. It was a measure of the genius of Augustus that he made his government both acceptable and legitimate. Though he did not solve permanently the problem of succession, this may be only because, as will be discussed later, the problem may well be insoluble within the framework of absolute monarchy.

According to the tradition believed by the Romans, Rome had existed as a city for more than seven hundred years. For almost five hundred it had been free and self-governing. Though occasionally defeated in individual battles, it had never lost a war and had never been compelled to sign a peace with an undefeated enemy. For five hundred years magistrates had been elected and the noblest of the citizens had sat in the Senate and given their advice to the magistrates. The Senate was a body of incomparable prestige, even though in the last century, often through its own incompetence, it had been forced to bow to arbitrary military men with armies at their backs. The people of Rome had accepted its supremacy and shared in the glories won by their armies under its leadership. Though Rome was not a state, the Romans were truly a people, and Roman citizenship was prized by everyone who possessed it; those who did not possess it valued it and sought to win it for themselves. During all these years the name of *rex* or king had been detested. The Romans no less than the Greeks regarded it as an office fit only for barbarians.

Yet Augustus realized that he must be king in fact, even though he did not hold the title. It would never have occurred to him—nor indeed would it have been possible—to have ruled the empire, with its many different peoples of varying degrees of culture, through any kind of representative government. The empire was too vast and heterogeneous for any such experiment. But if the government had been returned to Senate and people as under the republic, the same weaknesses would have led to the same breakdown of government. Only a monarch could hope to hold it together.

Augustus solved his dilemma by one of the great creative compromises of history, a species of legal fiction which bridged the gulf between the fallen republic and the monarchy which had to come. In time the republic was forgotten, the monarchy supplanted it, and the necessity for the fiction disappeared. But in the competent hands of Augustus—who understood it, the reasons for it, and the behavior required of him to maintain it—the fiction worked. Though thinking Romans of course knew that he was the sole ruler and that his power was ultimately based on the army and the treasury, nevertheless, to the mass of the people, the republic still survived. They felt at home in the new Roman state. The magistrates were still elected by the same procedure as before, though no candidate would even have run for office without the approval of Augustus; the Senate and the Assemblies still met for debate and legislation; and though there was now a princeps, or first citizen, a title and office unknown to the republic, he was not obtrusive, he scrupulously respected all the old republican forms, and his public and private life were beyond reproach in the best tradition of the early days of the Roman Republic.

Augustus confined the offices held by himself personally to the minimum required for his possession of the reality of power. He had a permanent proconsular military power (*proconsulare imperium*) conferred upon him, giving him supreme command of the army; he was granted a permanent civil power as previously exercised by the tribunes (*tribunicia potestas*), which gave him the power to introduce legislation and veto it. He became chief priest (*Pontifex Maximus*), giving him authority in religious matters; but, characteristically, he did not assume this office until the death of Lepidus, who had been ousted from his position as triumvir in 36 B.C. and consoled for his loss of power by appointment to this honored position. Occasionally, in the early years of his rule, Augustus allowed himself to be elected consul, feeling that he needed the civil as well as the military power inherent in this office. But consuls, praetors, aediles, and even tribunes were elected as before to perform the specific duties of these offices under the guidance of the princeps.

Augustus tried his best to maintain the dignity of the Senate. He encouraged it to give him advice, and he presided over it personally as *Princeps Senatus*. The judicial functions of the Senate were maintained and even increased

under his rule. By setting aside certain provinces to be ruled by ex-magistrates under the
direct control of the Senate and not of himself,
he made it worth while to move through the full
sequence of offices (*cursus honorum*) to the exalted position of consul. The Senate also had its
own treasury. From the equestrian order, Augustus recruited a body of public officials, paid
out of the imperial treasury (*fiscus*), but with
the same duties as tax gatherers and tax
assessors that they had performed in their own
interests under the republic. Under later emperors these men became part of the imperial
civil service.

When it was proposed that he should be
worshiped as a god (his adoptive father had
already been deified), he refused the honor,
but permitted his Genius to be worshiped instead. According to old Roman belief every man
had a guiding Genius, and the Genius of the
head of a family guided the fortunes of that
family. In allowing a cult to be set up to his
Genius, Augustus was therefore directing Roman worship toward the state of which he was
now the controlling Genius. Later this indeed
became the worship of the living emperor as
god, a state cult to which all had to subscribe
or be condemned for treason. But Augustus in
his lifetime never claimed to be a god except in
the Hellenistic world, which had for centuries
been accustomed to a divine monarchy.

Unsolved problem of the succession   The
greatest difficulty inherent in his position as
sole ruler, the difficulty of the succession, Augustus never solved. Perhaps the problem is
incapable of solution and is one of the inherent
defects of absolute monarchy. The possibilities
are strictly limited. The Roman ruler had to
be an exceptionally capable man. If hereditary
succession were to be used, the chances of any
ruler's having a son capable enough are not
especially good. If such a son possesses good
natural talents, the experience of being brought
up in the household of an absolute ruler is likely
to damage his character, as was so often true
in the history of the Roman Empire. If the
choice were to pass into the hands of a civilian
body such as the Senate, then political considerations might become predominant. The army

might not accept the choice; and it was certain
that there would be disgruntled candidates
ready to make trouble for the new incumbent.
Moreover, there would be a period of transition
between the death of the old monarch and the
election of the new which could be dangerous
for the empire.

It was necessary for all to know who the
new ruler was to be before the old one died.
One possibility was to designate the old ruler's
son as the heir. The other possibility was for
the ruler to choose his successor and transfer
enough power to him in his own lifetime to ensure that there would be no competitor in the
empire strong enough to prevent his succession.
In fact, this is what usually happened in the
empire unless the incumbent came to an un-
timely death before he had made arrangements.
But Augustus, who had no surviving male heirs
in the direct line, preferred to use the principle
of adoption. Tiberius, who was his stepson, was
also adopted as his son and forced to marry his
daughter, after divorcing a previous wife. Later
a number of childless emperors adopted their
successors, choosing the most effective men they
could find. During this period (A.D. 96–180),
known as the age of the "Good Emperors," the
empire reached its greatest heights of prosperity
and good government. But the last of these,
Marcus Aurelius, had a son Commodus, whom
he did not wish to pass over. Thus the claims
of paternity and the claims of good government
came into conflict. Commodus was one of the
worst of the emperors, as it turned out, and his
reign was a disaster from which Rome never
really recovered.

The reorganization of the provinces   The
reorganization of the provinces was a further
example of Augustus' efficient use of such opportunities as existed. He saw at once that it
was not necessary to keep armies in every province, as had been the custom in the later years
of the republic. Those that had long been
pacified and had no frontiers to be defended
against barbarians needed no more than enough
troops to ensure local discipline. Such provinces
(see the map for details) he entrusted to the
Senate, which was given the power of appointing governors and administering the tax monies.

These provinces, as under the republic, were reserved for ex-magistrates, and constituted a reward for those who had progressed through the sequence of offices. In addition, the arrangement gave the Senate some real work to do and served to maintain its prestige. And though Augustus exercised a final supervisory jurisdiction over these provinces, he left them largely to themselves. Those provinces, however, which needed legions of trained troops, and whose frontiers had continually to be defended against enemies, were under his direct control, which he exercised through the appointment of salaried legates, personally responsible to him, who could hold their positions as long as they proved efficient. This arrangement gave them the opportunity to gain a real knowledge of their provinces and to win the loyalty of their troops, but in later times it proved a serious danger to the state in the event of a disputed succession to the throne. Egypt, as the richest province and the primary source of the grain supply for Rome and Italy, was given a special status, in keeping with its history as well as its present importance. As in the past, the ruler was divine and the owner of all the land. Augustus, therefore, was a Pharaoh in Egypt, with all the privileges of this office. He did not perform his duties as king-god there himself, but entrusted them to a prefect of equestrian rank, responsible to himself. The country, however, was farmed as an imperial estate rather than as a province with a certain degree of self-government, and its revenues accrued directly to the ruler. No one of senatorial rank was permitted within the territory without the permission of the princeps. Finally, a number of kingdoms on the outskirts of the empire were permitted self-government under their kings, who became clients or vassals of Rome.

The provinces of the Roman Empire had always been made up of more or less self-governing municipalities, city-states on the Greek model, together with a number of other communities whose position had been defined by treaty, usually without full self-government. Augustus encouraged as much local administration as was compatible with the imperial relationship, thus saving the burden of direct administration. The corrupt tax system of the republican period was not abolished by Augustus, probably for lack of any alternative method of collection. His successors, especially Claudius and Hadrian, developed a regular civil service which gradually supplanted the tax companies. Meanwhile, the abuses of the system were checked through more efficient supervision by the princeps, even in the senatorial provinces. Penalties for extortion were severe, and even senatorial governors were far too much under control to be able to lend the efficient aid to the tax farmers that had been the custom under the republic in its last years. The nucleus of the later civil service was formed with the inclusion of treasury officials in the staff of the governors.

The entire system of provinces was reorganized thoroughly by Augustus. New boundaries were set, chosen for the sake of efficient administration and defense (see map). In the process, a number of minor conquests had to be undertaken to round out territories acquired haphazardly by the republic. Augustus always hoped to make the northern boundary the Elbe rather than the Rhine, as shorter and more easily defensible. Such a boundary, however, would have necessitated the conquest of a large part of Germany. Though progress with this conquest was made in the earlier years of his reign, his armies suffered a severe defeat toward the end of his life, and the project was abandoned. The Rhine became the northwestern frontier, while Augustus maintained the Danube in the East, refusing to move into Dacia (the modern Rumania) to the north of the Danube on the grounds that it was indefensible. This policy was maintained until the reign of Trajan (A.D. 98–117), who not only took Dacia but engaged in extensive wars in the East, the spoils of which had to be abandoned by his successors, as Augustus had predicted. The empire was held together by the great Roman roads, which were constantly extended throughout the imperial period and over which the imperial post traveled, bringing news to the emperor and his instructions in return.

The provincial system proved to be the most enduring of the reforms of Augustus. Whatever happened at Rome, the life of the provinces went on much as usual, under good rulers and bad alike. Only when the burden of taxation was heavily increased, and prosperity declined as a result of the continuous civil and foreign wars in the third century A.D., was the strength of the provinces slowly sapped. But while the Roman peace (*Pax Romana*) gave them a respite from war they had never previously enjoyed, their prosperity increased, and with it the ability to pay the taxes which ensured the continuance of Roman rule.

Augustus himself was an Italian rather than a Roman, and always regarded Italy as the center of his dominions, the homeland with special privileges, with Rome as first the capital of Italy and then of the empire. The inhabitants of Rome, however, were no longer exempt from all taxation, as Roman citizens had been under the republic. But their taxes always remained lighter than those of the provinces. Every native freeborn Italian was a Roman citizen, with all the privileges attached to the position. The provincials could achieve Roman citizenship, but Augustus regarded it as a privilege to be earned and not a right to which they were entitled by birth. This policy was gradually abandoned by his successors, until in A.D. 212 citizenship was granted to every free inhabitant of the empire.

The reform of the army By virtue of his proconsular power, the princeps was naturally commander in chief of the army. Augustus, drawing upon the experience of his predecessors, and especially of his adoptive father, laid down a permanent basis for recruitment and for the composition of the army, which survived in its essentials throughout the whole empire. The regular troops, or legionaries, were drawn from Italians and the most Romanized provincials, who received citizenship on enlistment if they did not already possess it. They served for twenty years, receiving a regular salary and a pension on retirement. In addition to these were auxiliary troops who received citizenship only on retirement. These were also salaried men, but drawn from the less Romanized provinces, and served primarily within these provinces. Their officers were originally drawn from the same territory, but later, after it had been shown that these troops were capable of rebellion in the interests of their own provinces,

Italian officers were substituted. The armies were by no means always engaged in active warfare, although the legions might at any time be transferred to a danger spot on a distant frontier. During the first two centuries, however, the general practice was for the legionaries to live in camps, behind permanent fortifications built by themselves. There were strategic roads to be built, ditches and moats to be dug, walls to be erected; and many of the troops necessarily became skilled artisans as well as soldiers, not unlike the modern corps of army engineers. These men—holding Roman citizenship, speaking Latin, imbued with Roman tradition, enjoying even on the frontiers the comforts of Roman civilization, such as warm baths—naturally mingled with the peoples among whom they were stationed, and served therefore as an important instrument for the Romanization of the empire. The army, however, in its own estimation, was rarely paid enough in proportion to its value to the state. Its chronic dissatisfaction and its sporadic insistence on bonuses gave ambitious generals the opportunity to make lavish promises in exchange for support of their candidacies to the throne.

Social and economic policy Rome had never been an important industrial center, and even as a commercial city its usefulness was impaired by its lack of a good harbor. The muddy Tiber had constantly to be dredged to keep the harbor of Ostia at its mouth open for commerce at all. Puteoli, where Paul landed on his journey to Rome, became the regular seaport for Roman trade. It developed into a great city, peopled largely by Greeks and other foreigners, who remained the leaders in maritime commerce as under the republic. But in spite of the absence of large-scale industry, there were innumerable small manufacturing shops in Rome and throughout Italy. For centuries Italy was the chief manufacturer for the Western world, though its products were far surpassed in quality by those of Alexandria and the East. Nevertheless, if Rome is included with Italy, the Italian balance of trade was always unfavorable, since Rome remained a parasite on the economy.

Augustus did not take any active interest

in the economy as such. Except for Egypt, industry in the Roman Empire was overwhelmingly in private hands. There was no state industry, nor monopolies of the kind that later developed in the Eastern Roman Empire of Constantinople. But, indirectly, the establishment of the Pax Romana, with its network of roads and safe transportation, increased prosperity for all classes throughout the empire. Augustus used the tax money that came from the provinces to pay for an enormous program of public works, chiefly temples and other public buildings, gardens, and baths; and in this the majority of those emperors who had the money available and were not too heavily engaged in unproductive warfare followed his example. These public works provided a market for numerous products made by small industry throughout the empire, and direct work for the large army of unemployed in Rome itself. The provincial municipalities engaged in similar programs, and it became a matter of civic pride for wealthy citizens to improve their cities with gifts of parks, gardens, temples, and other public buildings.

The unemployment problem For the poor of the city of Rome, who were grossly underemployed, Augustus found no remedy beyond his public works programs and a continuance of the republican practice of providing them with cheap or free food. In addition he, and more particularly the later emperors, provided lavish public spectacles to keep them amused. This program was called by the later satirist Juvenal "bread and circuses." Since the elections were arranged and laws were now really made indirectly by the princeps, the Roman people, so powerful in the last century of the republic, when their votes were necessary for the election of magistrates and army officers, lost their power. Riots could be dangerous on occasion, but they could now be easily suppressed. On the other hand, all the rulers were anxious to keep the people as contented as possible, and tried to provide for their needs. Augustus, recognizing the irresponsibility that went with their unemployment and dependence on imperial handouts, tried to give them some status in the community and in their own eyes

by incorporating them formally into an order, the plebeian as distinct from the equestrian and senatorial orders. But since they had no real duties in addition to their privileges, it is probable that the gesture remained an empty formality. We are not told what the plebeians themselves thought about it.

The city, in the time of Augustus, was efficiently policed, and a fire brigade was established, first under elected officials and then under appointees of the princeps.

In agriculture, Augustus strove to increase the number of small farmers. He gave security of tenure to those who had farms already, and he made an effort to instill a real love of the Italian countryside into the free peasantry. In this effort he was ably assisted by the poet-farmer Vergil, whose *Georgics* are a long paean of praise of the rural life. But the tendencies of the time were against Augustus. It was difficult to arrest the growth of large farms and estates which could be worked more economically than the small unit. The exodus of farmers to the cities, which had been such an important feature of the last years of the republic, continued. Not all the praise of rural life could prevail against the hard necessities of making a living. Though there was, as has been seen, chronic underemployment in Rome, at least the citizen could scrape a living somehow, and free bread and circuses were available, as nowhere else. Not until the Industrial Revolution in modern times did it become possible to work farms efficiently with a small labor force, and at the same time keep millions employed in the large cities through the production of machine-made goods and the provision of multifarious services. The problem of Rome itself was almost certainly insoluble by Augustus, however great his power and intelligence.

Estimate of the achievement of Augustus
It is difficult to find in the records of all history a greater political and administrative genius than the first princeps of Rome, the "architect of empire," Augustus Caesar, and there are few who have approached him. He has suffered in comparison with his great-uncle, who was undoubtedly a more impressive personality, with more spectacular and captivating qualities. He

has also suffered from his biographers in ancient times, who could not appreciate at their true worth his farsightedness and understanding of the real problems involved in the transition from republic to monarchy, and who paid too much attention to minor failures.

He was conservative, cherishing the old virtues and the old institutions, and appreciating their value; and he devised means to continue what seemed good in them. He did not try to set back the clock in his governmental reforms, nor yet leap forward rashly into impossible experiments forbidden by the nature of the times. The most difficult and rare art of the statesman is to see the limits of the possible and pursue only the possible. And his monument was the Roman peace and the Roman Empire, which endured for hundreds of years in the framework which he had invented. The empire did not collapse after his death, as did Charlemagne's, nor fall to pieces because of military overextension, as did Napoleon's.

Augustus faced a tremendous job, in which all his predecessors had failed; yet once he had achieved supreme power he substituted, almost without friction, a legitimate and acceptable civil government for civil warfare and domestic anarchy. There is a tale that a man was brought before him who had attempted a conspiracy against him. Augustus reasoned with the man, asking him how he proposed to replace him, and succeeded in convincing him of the impossibility of any alternative. Thereupon he forgave the would-be murderer and even promoted him in the public service. The tale may well be apocryphal, but it is surely significant that Augustus evidently did not discourage belief in it. Perhaps Augustus was fortunate in being a young man with many years of life ahead to make full use of the opportunity with which he had been presented. But he was never a healthy man, and it is one of his titles to greatness that he was able to overcome the handicap. He lived without ostentation, and never let anyone believe that he had any other ambition than to be first citizen in a restored and transformed republic. He is the most eminent disproof in history of the famous dictum of Lord Acton that "all power corrupts, and absolute power corrupts absolutely."

❖ The successors of Augustus

TIBERIUS AND THE DECLINE OF THE SENATE

It is not necessary in a book of this compass to go into detail on the achievements of the successors of Augustus. The reign of Tiberius (A.D. 14–37) was marked by excellent provincial administration but a growing disharmony between the princeps and the Senate. Tiberius most certainly lacked his stepfather's tact, and he was already a morose and disillusioned elderly man when he became princeps. It was not surprising that the senators for the first time realized the potentialities for an *imperial* tyranny that had been masked under the principate of Augustus. Many of them began to look back nostalgically to the lost republic, viewing it through rose-colored glasses since few of them had actually experienced it. Brutus and Cassius, the tyrannicides, became their heroes, for they had defended with their lives the dignity of senators. Throughout the reign of Tiberius there were constant intrigues over the succession, even while his son, later poisoned by the orders of his favorite, the praetorian prefect Sejanus, was still alive. Betrayed by the one man he had trusted, Tiberius countered the opposition to him with new laws against treason and new rewards for informers, setting a precedent followed by too many of his successors. There were many real conspiracies against him, but, more than anyone else, Sejanus, master of Rome when Tiberius retired to Capri for a little peace in his old age, betrayed him; and though Tiberius was strong enough to crush this conspiracy, the aftermath of treason trials and executions was always remembered against him by later historians and posterity.

The position of the Senate was indeed unenviable. It had a long tradition of power under the republic, and its position, even at its worst, was always one of dignity. Augustus had given the senators work to do, but there was no doubt that all real power had been taken from them, and they were deeply offended. Tiberius would preside over the Senate; and though even the anti-imperial historian Tacitus admits that, at least in the early part of his reign, he encouraged the senators to speak freely, most of them were careful to catch every sign of approval or disapproval, so that they would not be found in opposition to the princeps. This subservience wounded them in their dignity. They were forced out of fear to agree, and their true opinions were not valued. As long as any republican tradition remained, as it did at least until the death of Nero, A.D. 68, they were bound to regret their lost freedom, human dignity, and respect. Not all the outward dignity of a special toga could compensate them. In the reigns to come only the Stoics, since they had a philosophy to sustain them and, at the last, a sword to fall upon, provided any real resistance to the rulers; and it was no accident that the tyrannous emperors especially singled out the Stoics as their enemies and treated them accordingly.

THE JULIANS, FLAVIANS, AND THE "GOOD EMPERORS"—RECURRING PROBLEM OF THE SUCCESSION

At last Tiberius died, and was succeeded by Caligula (A.D. 37–41), a young man of no ability and no experience who soon became insane, his insanity revealing itself in an undisguised tyranny and sadistic cruelty. When he was murdered in a praetorian conspiracy, he was succeeded by Claudius (A.D. 41–54), an able administrator and student of history who effected many valuable reforms in the provincial administration but was unable to keep order in his own house, being ruled by his successive wives. He was murdered by his last wife, who thus succeeded in securing the succession for her son Nero (A.D. 54–68), who was the stepson of Claudius. Nero lost no time in getting rid of his stepbrother, who was a real son of Claudius, but for five years he allowed his praetorian prefect Burrus and his tutor Seneca to exercise the actual rule of the empire. Thus the first five years of Nero's administration became proverbial for excellent administration at home and abroad. Then Nero began to show himself as the misfit he was on the throne—a second-rate artist, anxious only for the plaudits of the crowds for his theatrical performances, and careless of his administration. The people loved him for his spectacular games and gladiatorial shows, but he degraded the imperial dignity, emptied the treasury, and won only contempt and enmity from the upper classes—contempt which culminated in conspiracies against his life. Thereafter no one in Rome was safe from his vengeance, and especially not his former friends. His tyranny in his last years equaled that of the madman Caligula. When he was overthrown by an open revolt, perishing at the hands of a freedman because he lacked courage to take his own life, no provision had been made for the succession and no direct heir remained of the Julian house (called Julian after Julius Caesar). First the commander of the Spanish legions took the throne, then the praetorian prefect, then the commander of the German legions, none surviving the year (A.D. 69). Finally the commander of the Eastern legions, a plebeian general of rural ancestry, gained the throne and restored order.

Vespasian (69–79) ruled sensibly and restored some of its earlier dignity to the principate. He was succeeded by his two sons (the Flavian dynasty), one of whom died after two years, while Domitian, the second son (81–96), a suspicious tyrant but a good administrator, fell victim to a conspiracy. This ended the hereditary principle for nearly a century. For the first time no obvious candidate was available for the throne, and the choice fell into the hands of the Senate, which selected Nerva (96–98), a mild, elderly man whose most important act was the adoption of the best general in the empire as his son. Thus the adoptive principle superseded the hereditary, and the result was the period known as the era of the "Good Emperors." Each of the four emperors who reigned between 98 and 180 was a good administrator, and Trajan (98–117) was a great general, though it is not certain that his policy of enlarging the empire was altogether a wise one. The province of Dacia, north of the Danube, acquired by him in addition to territories in Asia, had to be abandoned before most of the rest of the empire, but not before it had been civilized by the Romans. The old Roman province of Dacia, the present-day Rumania, still has a language based upon Latin. Hadrian (117–138) was one of the ablest of the Roman emperors as an administrator. He it was who systematized the civil service, the most competent body of bureaucrats outside China in the ancient world, recruiting its members almost exclusively from the equestrian order, which was now entirely dependent upon himself. Hadrian also gave impetus to the study and codification of the Roman law by abolishing the edicts of the annually elected praetors (see the next section). By Hadrian's time it was recognized that the will of the emperor was the true source of law for the empire, and it may be said that with Hadrian disappeared the remnants of the old republican tradition. Antoninus Pius (138–161) further improved the law and provided a long reign of almost unbroken peace. Marcus Aurelius (161–180), the Stoic writer of the *Meditations*, was compelled to spend most of his reign defending the empire against barbarian tribes who were threatening the frontiers, but maintained the record of his predecessors in the administration of the empire.

All these emperors were chosen by their predecessors and adopted as their sons. The Augustan title of princeps, though still formally used, no longer seems appropriate for these absolute rulers. Unfortunately, as has already been mentioned, Marcus Aurelius was not, like the others, childless, and chose as his successor his worthless son Commodus (180–193), whose reign marked the beginning of the serious decline of the empire. But, whatever the principle of succession used, there was no thought now of restoring the republic. The monarchy as an institution had proved itself; the republic was a subject fit only for historical study.

❖ **The provinces in the first
two centuries**

The empire in its first two centuries consisted of a great many city-states with limited self-government, each controlling a rural area around it. This had been the system in the Near East during the Hellenistic age, and it was taken over intact by Rome. When the Romans organized Western Europe, which had never come under Greek influence, they created municipalities on the Italian model. The Roman Empire itself may therefore be thought of as a gigantic federation of city-states under the authority of the capital city of Rome.

For the first two centuries of the empire little was changed. The cities all had their assemblies, councils, and elected magistrates, but office holding and voting were confined to property holders. Moreover the magistrates were unpaid, and when elected were expected to make a special money donation to the city or provide it with some new public building or monument. Cities competed with one another in erecting such edifices, and for well over a century there was no difficulty in obtaining wealthy candidates for office, willing to spend their money for this purpose. Some opportunities for exploiting their position existed, but most of the emperors, especially the Antonines, kept a sharp eye out for irregularities. The lower classes, ruled by a local oligarchy, often suffered from their helpless position and we know of appeals sent by them to the emperors. Nevertheless, all classes gained from the complete freedom of movement within the empire and the almost unbroken internal peace. The only power in the first two centuries that presented any danger was the Parthian Empire in the Near East. Trajan inflicted several severe defeats on this declining empire and altered the Augustan settlement in this region by annexing some new provinces, which were returned to client kings by his successor Hadrian.

Life in the provinces was rarely affected by the disturbances in the capital. The chief annoyance undoubtedly was the arbitrary increases in taxation necessitated by the spendthrift habits of some of the early emperors, especially Caligula and Nero. Imperial governors usually remained from one regime to another, and senatorial governors continued to be appointed as before unless the emperor was especially interested in the appointment. The first two centuries of the empire were characterized by an increasing centralization of the government, above all through the growth of the bureaucracy, or imperial civil service. Hadrian brought every official, including those in Italy, under direct imperial control, even in some cases nominating the governors of senatorial provinces, who were in any case by now the prisoners of the bureaucracy provided for them by the emperor. The municipalities also lost some of their responsibilities. Though the "Good Emperors," including Hadrian, were not personally tyrants, and indeed kept on very good terms with the Senate, being themselves drawn from the senatorial class, their policies tended toward an increasing absolutism which was ultimately recognized by the formal changes in the nature of the monarchy brought about by Diocletian at the end of the third century A.D. It should be added, however, that the Senate no longer provided any opposition to the absolutist tendency, for it had itself been chosen by previous emperors, and the old qualification of nobility of birth alone had long ago disappeared. The tyrants Caligula, Nero, and Domitian had paid careful attention to see that it should.

By the end of the second century the Romanized provinces had become the real heart of the empire, though Rome, of course, remained the capital. The rank and file of the legions was made up exclusively of provincials, and the officers now came as often from the Romanized provinces as from Italy. One of the reasons why Trajan's wars in the East were ultimately so dangerous to Rome was that the most thoroughly Romanized provinces, Gaul and the two Spanish provinces, provided so many of his troops. These men too often did not return to their homelands; if they were not killed in the East, they were likely to settle there. All the emperors after Nero had had long experience in the provinces and recognized their importance; Trajan and Hadrian were both Spaniards. The Italian patriotism of Augustus was therefore slowly replaced by the wider patriotism of the citizen of the Roman Empire itself. This reality was ultimately recognized in the famous edict of the Emperor Caracalla in 212, which granted Roman citizenship to every freeman of the empire.

❖ Influence of the Roman imperial idea

The Roman Empire, then, by the end of the second century, had become fully established and accepted as the natural order of things. Internal opposition had disappeared, and the idea of the Roman Empire had such a hold on the hearts and heads of men as no empire in the past had ever achieved, with the possible exception of the Chinese Empire under the Hans. There was some excuse for the belief that it was eternal, that it had even been willed by the gods. It was in this atmosphere of eternity and impregnability that the foundations of the Christian Church were laid, and this Church, the spiritual successor of the Roman Empire, was deeply influenced by it.

The achievements of the empire had already been enormous. Rome had always given tolerable and often excellent administration and an equitable law to a vast area, and it had given this area a peace it neither knew before nor has known since. If liberty was missing, this was a lack not felt by the people of the time. No one alive had known it from experience. It survived, at most, as a philosophical ideal. In the remainder of this chapter we shall see the other contributions to the cultural heritage of the world made by this hard-headed, efficient, practical, but hardly inspired people who first unified and ruled the Western world.

❖ General characteristics of Roman culture

CONTRAST WITH CREATIVENESS OF THE GREEKS

It is one of the ironies of history that, in spite of our admiration for the Greeks, Western civilization has always been nourished far more by Roman ideas and institutions than by Greek. With the recovery of Greek literature in recent centuries and the opportunity to study some of the masterpieces of Greek art in the original, we have been able to make a comparative estimate of Greek and Roman contributions; and few would today claim the Romans to have been qualitatively superior in any single field of cultural endeavor to which the Greeks turned their attention. Roman architecture made use of far more forms than the Greeks had found necessary for their simpler needs, Roman engineering solved practical problems that were outside Greek experience. But though we are impressed by the grandeur of the Pantheon in Rome and admire the excellence of Roman roads, bridges, and aqueducts, it is to the Athenian Parthenon that we go for an ideal of architectural beauty. Yet our own public buildings are copied from the Romans, we are inclined to use the Corinthian rather than Doric or Ionic capitals, and our columns, like Roman columns, too often support nothing and are merely superfluous decorations. Remove a Greek column and the building will collapse. To us the Greek world is remote, to be admired but not imitated, whereas the Romans are close to us. We feel we understand them. They are people like ourselves. To enter the Greek world requires an effort of the imagination; but the Romans, nearly as far away from us in time, can be understood, it seems, without any such rare and difficult mental activity.

It would appear that even to the Romans themselves the Greeks were a people apart. They admitted that in every branch of cultural activity the Greeks were their teachers and masters, and they did their best to imitate them. But they never seriously tried to think in the way the Greeks had thought. It is impossible to conceive of any Roman with whom we are acquainted taking time out to consider the fundamental problem of the early cosmologist: What is it that is stable in a world of changing appearances? No Roman could speculate like Plato or reason like Aristotle. The simpler ideas of these masters they could understand, at least in part. But whenever they tried to explain what they had read—and many Romans, notably Cicero and Seneca, made a real effort to cope with the problems of philosophy—the result always appears as oversimplification, not touching the root of the matter, in some way debased. The truth seems to be, however it may be explained, that the Roman mind simply *could* not think in the Greek manner. Yet such thinking did not die out in the Roman period. The Greeks, Claudius Ptolemy the astronomer and Galen the physician, both lived in the second century of the Roman Empire. Recognizably Greek in their thinking, they were worthy intellectual descendants of the classical Greeks.

PRACTICAL NATURE OF THE ROMAN GENIUS

The great Roman contribution to world culture therefore lies not in the field of thought but in the application of thought in the ordinary world of men. In this way they served as a complement to the Greeks. They reaped the harvest of whatever had been thought before them, putting it to practical use. Where the Greeks had been concerned with ethical speculations, the Romans translated these into practical, everyday morality; where Democritus had speculated on the constitution of matter, and Epicurus had drawn the conclusion that in such a cosmology there was no need of gods, the Roman Lucretius makes a passionate attack on religion and superstition as the prime causes of human suffering; where human morality is conspicuously missing from the adventures of Odysseus as told by Homer, the Roman Vergil, in his *Aeneid,* emphasizes the filial devotion of his hero, and the glorification of Rome and its destiny—the purpose of the voyage of Aeneas— breathes in every line of the poem.

❖ Roman law

GENERAL CHARACTERISTICS

The Romans, then, were the greatest transmitters of culture the world has yet seen, though to a lesser degree the Arabs later performed the same function. But the Roman spirit is nevertheless imprinted on every line the Romans wrote, every idea they took up and put to use. They should not be regarded as mere copiers. Moreover, when the Greeks left no model, the Romans showed themselves quite capable of developing new forms of their own, as in satire, epigram, letter writing and perhaps even fiction. If anyone had ever had the temerity to translate a Roman work into Greek, it would at once have been recognized as Roman handiwork. So, though we can recognize the merits of these minor achievements, it seems best in a brief chapter to devote ourselves to a fuller study of the really great achievement of the Romans, their law. Owing to the extant writings of so many great jurists, and to the firsthand description of the working of republican courts derived from such men as the practicing lawyer Cicero, we are fortunately able to trace its development almost from earliest times.

As was seen earlier, the first codified law of Rome was the Twelve Tables, drawn up by a committee of ten in 449 B.C. under the stimulus of the second secession of the plebs. Primitive as this law was, it remained the basic statute law of the Romans. In addition, statute law was made from time to time by the Assembly. These laws, however, covered primarily constitutional and criminal matters, which have only limited importance. They were applicable only to Rome herself and her citizens. Since no principles were involved, they were incapable of wider application.

THE RIGHTS OF THE ROMAN CITIZEN— JUS CIVILE

But the Romans did have a new and quite original conception of citizenship, which covered certain well-defined rights, discussed earlier. The rights belonged to the man who was a citizen; they were inherent in his person, wherever he might happen to be. This is the first time these particular rights, which in earlier times accrued to a man only by birth, were believed to be vested in a *person*. In Athens the city gave certain privileges to its citizens, but there was no kind of contract between them and the city, and naturally they possessed no privileges unless they were living in the particular city which gave them. But Rome guaranteed certain definite rights to its citizens, and these they retained even when abroad. These rights collectively were known as *jus*, and a Roman citizen was entitled to have any case tried under the *jus civile*, or civil law.

Now this law was rarely affected by statutes (*leges*) passed by the Assembly. It was built up ordinarily in early times by the priests, who stated on authority what the law was. This task then passed to a special official called the *praetor urbanus* (city praetor). The praetor, however, was an elected official, probably a would-be general rather than a jurist. It was hardly possible for him to state what the law was, or to decide all cases personally, and it was not his duty to do so. He had as assistants judges who came from noble families, and who were in charge of the actual trial. But even these judges were not as a rule trained lawyers, though they had more experience than the annually elected praetor.

When, therefore, a civil case was brought to trial, it was necessary for the parties to the case to have some knowledge of what the law was likely to be in their case. So it gradually came about that the praetor every year, on assuming office, made a public statement of the law that he would use while in office. This was called the *edictum*, and it was made up largely of the instructions that he proposed to give to the judges. These instructions were called *formulae*. The edict was made up, for the most part, of decisions that had been made by his predecessors in office.

It will be seen, then, that in this way a collection of decisions was built up which really had the force of law, even though no statutes had been made on the subject. Statute law was of course taken into consideration by the praetor, but even this he could interpret, as our judges and higher courts interpret law today. And this interpretation would probably be incorporated in the edict of the next praetor and so be binding for the future, unless a praetor for good reasons decided to depart from it—as our judges may also on occasion depart from interpretations of their predecessors.

THE RIGHTS OF FOREIGNERS—JUS GENTIUM

This, then, was the system of public and private law for Roman citizens, and it lasted for a considerable length of time. But cases also arose where one party to a lawsuit was a Roman citizen and one was not, or where two resident noncitizens might engage in litigation with each other in the Roman courts. If the case concerned a foreigner's personal status, it would clearly be impossible to settle it through the *jus civile*, applicable only to citizens. So in 242 B.C. a *praetor peregrinus*, or foreign praetor, whose task was to look after such cases, was elected for the first time. Thus the idea arose that foreigners also had rights, and the new law under which they were judged was called the *jus gentium*, or law of peoples. Both praetors now issued annual edicts covering the cases for which they were responsible.

INTERPRETATION OF THE LAW—BEGINNINGS OF JURISPRUDENCE

As the Roman state grew in importance and undertook more and more responsibilities, and as legal decisions of wide significance had to be made by unqualified persons, an innovation was made which proved to be the real foundation of Roman jurisprudence. It became the custom for certain skilled lawyers, who had also held high office in the state, to assist the praetors in drawing up their edicts and in answering questions put by judges. They could also give advice to litigants. These men were not paid, nor did they hold any official position, but undertook the work from a sense of duty and for the prestige involved. Since these *juris prudentes* (men skilled in the law, hence our word "jurisprudence") were appealed to for advice, especially in cases where the law was doubtful, they became specialists in interpretation, and theirs was now the chief responsibility in the building up of new law for the future. It was among these men that the conception of equity (*aequitas*) grew up as a principle which could override a strict interpretation of the law. In time, especially under the empire, certain individuals among them became known for the excellence of their opinions, as certain Supreme Court Justices of the past may still be quoted and accepted in the United States even though they have been long dead.

INFLUENCE OF PHILOSOPHY—JUS NATURALE

Many of these *juris prudentes* were strongly influenced by Stoicism, with its conception of the natural law of divine reason (*jus naturale*), which became a commonly accepted ideal, a kind of ideal law in accordance with which all statute law should be made and all legal decisions rendered. The strongly humanitarian viewpoint of the Stoics thus became incorporated into Roman law.

Under the early principate the same system was maintained. But naturally the edict of the praetor and the opinions of the *juris prudentes* had to take account of the new influence of the princeps; and with the increasing absolutism of the emperors the decisions in public law tended to reflect the increasing importance of the state. There was also far more statute law in the empire than under the republic. The Assembly declined as a lawmaking body after Augustus, but the Senate now became for the first time since 448 B.C. a real legislative body, though its laws were naturally in accordance with the emperor's wishes. The emperors after Augustus also issued decrees which had all the force of law. Under Hadrian the praetors' edicts were codified into a perpetual edict, and the *juris prudentes* and their interpretations assumed still greater importance than before. After Hadrian many of them began to hold official positions in the imperial service, often serving as advisers to the emperor, who now felt in need of skilled legal assistance. The law continued to develop, often in accordance with newer Greek and Oriental philosophical ideas.

By this time there was virtually no distinction between the *jus civile* and the *jus gentium*. The vast majority of the inhabitants of the empire by the time of Hadrian, and all by A.D. 212, were Roman citizens; and it was the principles of the *jus gentium*, which had always been more nearly universal and thus more in accordance with philosophical principles as well as contemporary requirements, which prevailed. In the last stage of the empire, the great codification of the law began. Creativeness declined under the absolutist emperors. The opinions of the great *juris prudentes* of the past were taken as actual law, and a number of dead jurists were named whose opinions must prevail. In the event of a conflict, the opinion of the supposed greatest, Papinian, was to be decisive.

THE GREAT CODIFICATION OF THE LAW AND ITS INFLUENCE

The Theodosian Code of A.D. 438 was a collection of imperial edicts binding in the Eastern and Western Empires. This code was followed in the sixth century by the great definitive code of Justinian, drawn up by Trebonian and a group of distinguished jurists in Constantinople. The latter code, known as the

Corpus Juris Civilis, had four parts: the Code, which consisted of the imperial edicts of all the emperors (*constitutiones*); the Digest, which contained the decisions of the great *juris prudentes;* the Institutes, primarily a manual on legal principles for use in schools; and the Novels, a series of new laws which Justinian found necessary to complete the whole structure. Naturally the Digest was the most important part of the code for posterity, since these opinions, based on the best thought of the greatest jurists in accordance with their conceptions of the natural law, were to a large extent free from limitations of time and place. This law code, however, differed from earlier ones in that Christian influence had now been admitted to it. Religious crimes, such as heresy, were included, but on the whole the Christian influence made for the humanization of the law. Christian disapproval of slavery, in particular, was reflected in the Justinian *Corpus.*

The influence of Roman law is almost incalculable. It is not so much that codes of law in many modern countries are still largely Roman, nor that the canon law of the Church is almost exclusively Roman; but that this civilizing work was done by the Romans once and for all, and there was no need ever to do it again. The primitive laws of the barbarian invaders of the empire were so far behind Roman law in principles and sheer intellectual grasp of the problems involved that all took freely from the Romans, and no code in the Western world has not been influenced by it. It was used as a political tool to help the development of the national state by medieval monarchs. It was so patently superior to feudal law that when the king's justice was modified Roman, and the local law was feudal, every litigant, if he had the choice, would prefer the king's justice. When Napoleon needed a new law code for France in the early nineteenth century, it was to Roman law that he went for a model.

In the Middle Ages the great tradition of the *juris prudentes* was carried on by the jurists of the University of Bologna. Indeed, the university itself only came into existence as a law school with the rediscovery of the *Corpus Juris Civilis* of Justinian, which had been lost in the ages of barbarian domination of Europe.

❖ **Roman art**

ARCHITECTURE—CULT OF THE GRANDIOSE

Since far more Roman remains than Greek exist in Europe today, a few words should be devoted to Roman art, architecture, sculpture, and engineering, which owed much to the Greeks during the period of the republic, but became to a large degree emancipated during the empire.

After the Punic Wars, Greek influence became predominant in Rome, and during this period Roman buildings, public and private, were usually copies of those in Hellenistic cities. But even in this copying the Romans knew what they liked, which was invariably the ornate and the grandiose. The Corinthian column was preferred to the more severe Ionic and Doric, and in large buildings the post and lintel construction was abandoned in favor of the dome, vault, and arch. Gradually the Greek forms which the Romans, like ourselves, felt to be "artistic" became merely decorative on Roman buildings. They solemnly inserted useless columns, supporting nothing; they carefully fluted their columns, although the fluting now served no practical purpose. The volutes at the top of the columns became more and more luxuriant and decorative, the Corinthian and Ionic capitals now being welded into a new composite.

When the spoils of war began to flow into Rome during the last century of the republic, private houses, often built by successful bankers and generals, became larger and more ostentatious. For the most part they were still constructed by Greek architects, and often furnished with Greek works of art looted during the successful campaigns. Pompey built the first permanent Roman theater out of his spoils; Julius Caesar, from his Gallic booty, built a new Forum and repaved the old. Roman taste at this time, as usual with the new rich, ran to the extravagant and splendid, with elaborate ornamentation and statuary (copied from the Greek, of course) in wild profusion.

With the advent of Augustus, Roman architecture came into its own, and we begin to hear of Roman architects and engineers, even though Greek influence was still strong and perhaps

A Roman theater at Arles, in southern France, as it appears today.

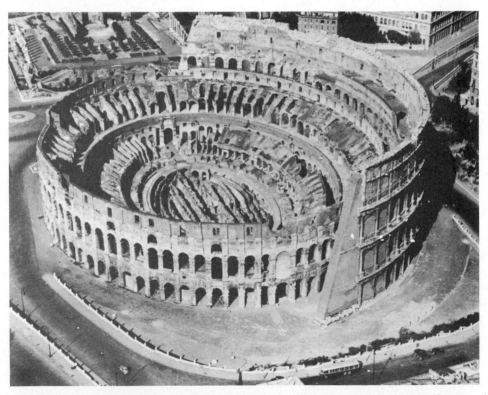

Aerial view of the Colosseum at Rome, built by the Flavian emperors for the display of such public entertainment as gladiatorial fights. (COURTESY ITALIAN STATE TOURIST OFFICE)

predominant. The rebuilding of Rome by Augustus, and the construction of vast new temples in accordance with his religious policy of trying to restore the old gods to honor, influenced provincial cities also to take advantage of the new prosperity and rebuild their cities. In the imperial period every city of any importance had its baths, and even the smaller cities were able to build theaters, amphitheaters, and basilicas, which were used for public business and to house the law courts. The best known of the Roman amphitheaters is the Colosseum, constructed by the first two Flavian emperors. Much of it is still standing today—a huge round structure with a great arena for the spectacle. Underneath the arena is a network of passages, enabling performers—beasts and men—to reach any part of the arena as required. The basilica is a typical Roman structure, the plan of which, with nave, aisles, and clerestory windows, was adapted by the Christians for their early churches. The cross-vaulting of the Romanesque

cathedrals seems to have been a Roman invention, and allowed far greater size to the buildings.

SCULPTURE—REALISM

Like architecture, Roman sculpture was first influenced by the Etruscans and then by the Greeks. Indeed, the Romans had such a high opinion of Greek (almost exclusively Hellenistic) sculpture that to the end of the empire many sculptors were employed simply at making copies of Greek statuary for the Roman market. But aside from these copies there is a pronounced difference between Roman and even Hellenistic sculpture, a difference which is in full keeping with the Roman character as we know it. The Romans liked their sculpture to be realistic, thus completing what was only a tendency in the Hellenistic world. In this preference they followed the Etruscan tradition also. The Romans therefore developed the art of realistic portraiture far more than the Greeks.

Left, a Roman of the third century B.C. (portrait bust in bronze). Right, a Roman of the first century B.C. Note how the Roman sculptors strove to express character in their subjects' faces. It would appear from their literature that the Romans indeed believed character showed in a man's face. This may perhaps account in part for the relative frequency of the bust in comparison with the full-size statue. (COURTESY THE METROPOLITAN MUSEUM OF ART)

When the Greeks, even Hellenistic Greeks, carved a portrait, they were always conscious of the harmony between body and mind or soul, between life itself and the material it informed. So the Greeks preferred to carve the whole body, of which the head and face were only a part. When, at the request of the Romans, who usually desired merely a portrait bust, Greek artists took to portrait sculpture, they remained aware of the mind which lay behind the mere features, and thus strove to reveal character through the features and the harmony of the whole composition. The details thus fitted into place as part of the whole, but were not insisted upon, and perhaps the Greek sculptor did not really care whether or not he caught the actual features of the model. This tendency is what is usually meant when we speak of the idealism of Greek sculpture.

The Romans, on the other hand, were as always preoccupied by the outer appearance, which they carved exactly as they saw it, including lines of anxiety and unruly hair. For a period in the early empire the two tendencies fully harmonized, the realistic detail being combined with the psychological penetration of the Greek. Then the Roman tendency again disappeared, late imperial and other portraits often being only suggestive of the subject rather than realistic likenesses. In noting the insistence of the Romans on detail, one is reminded of the way in which Tacitus describes the senators watching the emperor Tiberius for any change of facial expression, trying to discover what he was thinking from the outward appearance. It is clear that the Romans believed the outward face to be the true expression of a man's individuality, and they probably did not wish any detail, however apparently unimportant, to escape them. Hence their emphasis on what we call realism.

In technology the Romans made progress

This famous Roman aqueduct, the Pont du Gard in France, gives some idea of Roman engineering skill and the gigantic size of Roman public works of the imperial period. Such construction is even more impressive when one realizes it was carried on with only the most primitive machinery.

beyond their masters. Even in early republican days they developed a new technique for making roads, paving the best ones with stone and surfacing secondary roads with gravel. They built their roads up carefully from a depth of several feet below the surface of the surrounding country, using small stones and even concrete. It seems to have been by accident rather than through any scientific knowledge that the Romans discovered how to make a real concrete, composed of lime and a volcanic ash which happens to contain the necessary ingredients. This discovery enabled the Romans to construct their public buildings out of a readily available material. The always expensive marble was freed for use as a veneer.

The Romans knew how to construct strong bridges through the extensive use of the arch; they made tunnels through difficult mountain terrain; and they understood, but rarely used, the principle of the siphon for their baths and aqueducts. The many Roman remains, not only in Italy but throughout Europe, are ample testimony to the strength of the materials used and the effectiveness of the Romans as engineers.

❖ **The empire at the close of the second century**

In this chapter we have traced briefly the history of Rome from the establishment of the republic to the reign of Commodus. There can be no doubt that for the peoples of the empire the rule by emperors and bureaucracy was a great improvement over anything they had known when they were ruled by Senate and people. The empire had given them peace and the opportunity for prosperity. Roman officials, as yet, were for the most part honest and uncorrupted. A considerable amount of self-government was permitted, and the Romans tried to interfere as little as possible. The English eighteenth-century historian Gibbon asserted that this was probably the period in world history when more people were contented and secure than at any other time, and there may well be some truth in his remark. It is true that the emperor Marcus Aurelius had to spend a large part of his reign in unwelcome campaigns against German barbarians. But probably few Romans or provincials recognized the permanent and ever-growing danger of these barbarians to the security of the empire, still less that in the fullness of time they would destroy it.

In the next chapter Christianity, which in so many ways succeeded to the Roman heritage, will be considered, and in the following chapter the fall of the empire will receive attention. But it would have been a singularly inspired prophet who could have predicted either the fall or the legatee at the close of the second century.

Suggestions for further reading

NOTE ON LITERATURE OF THE PERIOD: Roman literature in translation is available in many paperbound and hard-cover editions, the most complete offering being that of the Loeb Classical Library (Harvard). Among my favorite translations are those of Juvenal's *The Satires* by Rolfe Humphries (Indiana); Lucretius' *Of the Nature of Things* by Charles E. Bennett (Classics Club); Tacitus' *The Annals of Imperial Rome* by Michael Grant (Penguin); and Vergil's *The Aeneid* by Kevin Guinagh (Holt, Rinehart and Winston). Particularly useful collections are Caesar's *War Commentaries* (Everyman); Horace's *Satires and Epistles* (Phoenix); *The Portable Roman Reader* edited by Basil Davenport (Viking); *Latin Literature in Translation* edited by Guinagh and Dorjahn (Longmans, Green); and *Roman Civilization* edited by Lewis and Reinhold (Columbia).

PAPER-BOUND BOOKS

Adcock, F. E. *Roman Political Ideas and Practice.* Ann Arbor. Useful short summary.

Barrow, R. H. *The Romans.* Penguin. A good first chapter on the Roman character and an excellent summary of Roman law and jurisprudence. Otherwise not especially distinguished.

Carcopino, J. *Daily Life in Ancient Rome*, trans. by E. O. Lorimer. Yale University Press. Lively and detailed picture of Roman life in the time of the emperor Trajan.

Cowell, F. R. *Cicero and the Roman Republic.* Penguin. The book, far from exclusively concerned with Cicero, presents a vivid and factual picture of the last century of the Republic.

Dill, Samuel. *Roman Society from Nero to Marcus Aurelius.* Meridian. An old classic (1904), still in many respects the best on the subject.

Duff, J. W. *A Literary History of Rome to the Close of the Golden Age* and *A Literary History of Rome in the Silver Age from Tiberius to Hadrian*. Barnes and Noble. Though old, these two volumes remain the best literary histories of Rome.

Grant, Michael. *The World of Rome*. Mentor. Topical treatment of Rome during the early Empire, preceded by a short historical survey. Illustrations in the original version (Cleveland, Ohio: The World Publishing Company, 1960) are superbly chosen and excellently reproduced.

Graves, Robert. *I, Claudius*. Vintage. This novel and its sequel *Claudius, the God*, now out of print (New York: H. Smith, 1935) present a colorful and accurate picture of the early principate. A more recent Roman novel by the same author is *Lost Eagles* (Pocket Books).

Hamilton, Edith. *The Roman Way to Western Civilization*. Mentor. Similar to her more famous *The Greek Way*.

Highet, Gilbert. *Juvenal the Satirist*. Galaxy. Excellent study, well written and often very entertaining. By the same author, a fine classical scholar, *The Classical Tradition* (Galaxy) is another good study of what we owe to both the Greek and Roman worlds.

Mackail, J. W. *Latin Literature*, rev. by Harry C. Schnur. Collier. An old but still valuable survey.

Mattingly, Harold. *Roman Imperial Civilization*. Anchor. Up-to-date study using much new material, including evidence from coins.

Mommsen, Theodore. *History of Rome*. Wisdom and Meridian. This classic history of the Republic remains the finest single work in its field.

Rostovtzeff, Mikhail. *Rome*. Galaxy. By one of the greatest authorities, covering both the Republic and the Empire in a relatively short survey.

Starr, Chester G. *The Emergence of Rome as Ruler of the Western World*. Cornell University Press. Valuable short survey on the period of expansion.

Syme, Ronald. *The Roman Revolution*. Oxford University Press. Argumentative and opinionated (but extremely valuable) work on the last century of the Republic.

HARD-COVER BOOKS

Anderson, W. J., and Spiers, R. P. *The Architecture of Greece and Rome*, vol. 2. New York: Charles Scribner's Sons, 1927. A very substantial account of the Roman feats in building and engineering. See also Showerman, *Eternal Rome*.

Buchan, John. *Augustus*. Boston: Houghton Mifflin Company, 1937. Masterly biography, very favorable to Augustus, written from the point of view of a British imperial administrator who recognized the difficulties experienced by Augustus in establishing the legitimacy of his rule.

Charlesworth, M. P. *The Roman Empire*. Home University Library. New York: Oxford University Press, 1951. Brief but valuable summary of the Empire, with cultural achievements.

Clarke, M. L. *Studies in the History of Thought from Cicero to Marcus Aurelius*. Cambridge, Mass.: Harvard University Press, 1956. Gives a fairly full picture of the modest efforts of the Romans in this field.

Greene, W. C. *The Achievement of Rome*. Cambridge, Mass.: Harvard University Press, 1933. Useful general survey.

Grenier, C. *The Roman Spirit in Religion, Thought, and Art*, trans. by M. R. Dobie. New York: Alfred A. Knopf, Inc., 1926. Interesting attempt to isolate the "Roman Spirit" and distinguish it from the "Greek Spirit."

Homo, Leon. *Roman Political Institutions*. New York: Alfred A. Knopf, Inc., 1929. Lucid account.

Jones, A. H. M. *Studies in Roman Government and Law*. New York: Frederick A. Praeger, Inc., 1960. Specialized study, partly on the Republic.

Marsh, F. B. *The Founding of the Roman Empire*. New York: Barnes & Noble, Inc., 1960 (originally published in 1927). Should be read in conjunction with Syme's *The Roman Revolution*. Covers the fall of the Republic as well as the beginning of the Empire under Augustus.

Mommsen, Theodore. *The Provinces of the Roman Empire*, 2d ed. New York: Charles Scribner's Sons, 1909. An old classic, still not superseded.

Rostovtzeff, M. L. *Social and Economic History of the Roman Empire*, 2d ed. Rev. by P. M. Fraser. New York: Oxford University Press, 1957. Standard work, though judgments often controversial. Excellent illustrations.

Showerman, G. *Eternal Rome*, vol. I. New Haven, Conn.: Yale University Press, 1924. Well-written and well-illustrated history of the city of Rome.

Smith, R. E. *The Failure of the Roman Republic*. New York: Cambridge University Press, 1955. Interpretative study tracing the failure to the work of the Gracchi.

III · THE CENTURIES OF TRANSITION

Main façade of the Byzantine Church of St. Marks' in Venice

Chronological Chart

THE CENTURIES OF TRANSITION

Roman Empire	Christianity	Century
Reign of Augustus (31 B.C.–A.D. 14)	Birth of Jesus (probably 4 B.C.)	0 B.C.
Reign of Tiberius (14–37)	Crucifixion of Jesus Christ (probably 30)	A.D. 0
Reign of Nero (54–68)	Neronian persecution of Christians (64)	
The Good Emperors (96–180)		100
Barrack Emperors (255–284)	Decian persecution (249–251)	200
Reign of Diocletian (284–305)	Diocletian persecutions (303–313)	300
Reign of Constantine (312–337)	"Edict of Milan" (313)	
Foundation of Constantinople (330)	Council of Nicaea (325)	
Theodosius the Great, last Emperor of East and West (379–395)	Conversion of Goths to Arian Christianity (340–348)	

Western Roman Empire		Islam	Century
Honorius moves capital to Ravenna (*ca.* 400)		Pope Leo I (440–461)	400
Sack of Rome by Alaric (410)		Negotiations of Leo with Attila (452) and Vandals (455)	
Invasion of Huns (452)			
"Fall of Rome" (476)			

Barbarian Kingdoms	Eastern Roman Empire	Christianity	Islam	Century
Clovis, King of the Franks (481–511)	Reign of Justinian (527–565)	Pope Gregory I (590–604)	Birth of Mahomet (570)	
Theodoric, ruler of Italy (493–526)	Loss of Italian possessions (568–571)		"Flight" of Mahomet from Mecca (622)	600
Byzantine conquest of Italy (535–554)			Military expansion of Islam (635–733)	700
Lombard invasion of Italy (568)	Reign of Heraclius (610–641)		Defeat of Muslims at Tours (732)	
Charles Martel, Mayor of the Palace (714–741)	Reign of Leo III (717–740)	Donation of Pepin (756)	End of Ommeyad Caliphate (750)	
Victory of Charles at Battle of Tours (732)	Iconoclastic controversy (726–843)		Abbassid Caliphate (750–1258)	
Pepin, King of the Franks (752–768)			Independent Ommeyad dynasty in Spain (755)	
Charles becomes King of Lombards (774)	Peace between Byzantines and Charlemagne (803)	Coronation of Charlemagne (800)	Caliphate of Harun-al-Rashid (785–809)	800
Reign of Charlemagne (768–814)				

SIX

The Rise of Christianity

❖ **Religious conditions in the Roman empire at the beginning of the Christian era**

THE GREEK BACKGROUND

In order to understand the setting for the new faith that is to be considered in this chapter, a faith that was destined to supersede the numerous religions current in the Roman Empire, it is first necessary to consider the religious conditions in the Augustan Age, especially in the Hellenistic world in which Christianity arose. We have already noticed briefly the political changes that occurred in Greece after the conquests of Alexander. When the Greek city-states lost their independence, the old civic pride, and with it civic religion, declined; but the Greeks did not lose their vitality and creativeness, nor their intellectual curiosity. The whole Hellenistic world became the field for their activities, and under their stimulus a momentous change came over the native Oriental peoples. No people in the whole Near East remained untouched by the Greek spirit, and Greek restlessness communicated itself to the others. After the Roman conquest, the Greeks absorbed the Romans into their culture, which continued to expand ever further westward as the Romans provided the means.

Deprived of what had been the joy of his life in earlier times, the restless Greek engaged in commercial activity, transforming the economy of the Near East; he introduced his language, his art, his literature, his philosophy, his sports, and his whole way of life wherever he went. But still he was not satisfied. Something essential had gone from his life, and for all the great show of activity, too often he felt that his existence was empty. The gods were pleasant myths to be explained away, and Chance ruled now; but though she could be wooed, she could hardly be loved or worshiped. Nor could philosophies hold the allegiance of the Greeks. The Skeptics were busy showing that all philosophies were based on untenable assumptions and that the truth could not be known. The vacuum could be filled only by a religion which appealed to the heart, giving meaning to the aimless life of the now cosmopolitan and rootless Greeks.

First came a revival of the native Greek mysteries of Eleusis and Samothrace, which, as Plutarch tells us, left the initiate feeling as if he had indeed had an experience of divinity. These mysteries had always demanded much of their devotees, but in return had assured them of immortality, through the undergoing of certain trials which purified the soul. Throughout the Hellenistic world the Oriental religions all experienced a revival. The cults of Cybele and Isis and of Mithra offered impressive ceremonial, festivals, ritual, and initiation, as well as purification and redemption of the soul with the aid of a mediator who sacrificed himself for the salvation of men. At last the Orient ceased to accept from the Greeks without giving in return. Now the culture became truly Greco-Oriental, with the Romans, as outside conquerors, resisting or succumbing to the allurements of this culture, but always alien in the Hellenistic world.

THE JEWISH BACKGROUND

But there was one Oriental people which held itself aloof, for the Jews had already received their separate promises. The Jewish religion had absorbed elements from the other Oriental teachings, and the more orthodox Jews now believed in the future life, in the Satan and demons of Persian Zoroastrianism and Mithraism; but they also held fast to their more ancient law and ritual which, with the ascendancy of their priesthood, had become ever more strict and rigid. They remained monotheists, believing that all other gods than Yahweh were either demons, idols, or nonexistent. Above all they were looking for a messiah who would come to redeem the faithful people of Israel; for him they must remain apart, a chosen people, the only righteous ones on earth, the only ones ready to greet him when he came.

The center of the Jewish religion was the holy city of Jerusalem, which had retained a precarious independence under the Maccabees only to fall to the arms of Pompey, and thereafter submit, first to a client king, Herod of Idumaea, and then to the direct government of Rome under an equestrian procurator. The Romans had never been able to understand the Jews. From sad experience they knew that they could not drive them into making any compromises with polytheism, not even the formal acknowledgment of the divinity of the emperor. So at last they accepted the fact and let them alone, giving them religious privileges withheld from any other subjects of Rome, for the Romans felt that the Jewish faith did not constitute any real danger. It seemed impossible that such a small and exclusive sect could expand so far that it could undermine the loyalty of the vast population of the empire.

But the Jews in Jerusalem were by no means the only Jews in the Hellenistic world. Elsewhere, in every city of importance, there was a Jewish colony which sent representatives to the great festivals at Jerusalem, willingly acknowledged the temple there as the headquarters of their religion, and from their greater wealth often sent donations for the poorer Jews of the religious capital. The widely scattered Jews of the Diaspora (Dispersion) lived in Greek cities, and were subject to the all pervading influence of Greek culture. They could not all be so strict in their religious observances as their brethren of Jerusalem. Though they studied and loved the Hebrew Law, they also studied Greek philosophy at Greek schools; they were familiar with all the intellectual currents of the Greek world. Such a one was Saul of Tarsus, who was to become the first great Christian missionary.

Even in Jerusalem itself not all the Jews had kept themselves free from Greek influence. As some had been ready to collaborate with the Greeks, so some also collaborated with the Romans. It was necessary for these Hellenized Jews (Sadducees) to play a very careful game with the Romans, for the ultimate benefit, as they no doubt felt, of the whole Jewish people. These men provided the High Priest at the time of the Crucifixion, and probably also a majority of the Jewish Council (Sanhedrin or Synedrion), which was entrusted by the Romans with local government, subject only to the general supervision of the Roman procurator. The Sadducees, however, differed in one important respect from their fellow Jews, the Pharisees. They did not believe in the resurrection of the body or in immortality.

With many fervent men and women looking for a messiah, and with no certainty of when he would come or how he would reveal himself, it was natural that there were many who claimed to be the Messiah. These men gathered around themselves fanatical bands of disciples, who were too often determined that their Messiah should prevail, if necessary by force. But all failed, and by the time of the birth of Jesus there was none who had been able to command the faith and allegiance of all the Jews. The Sadducees had found it necessary to suppress these would-be messiahs, for they were held responsible by their masters for all riots. Some Jews, like the Essenes, had gone into the desert, purifying themselves by ascetic practices, but they too were waiting for the Messiah to reveal himself. Others, like the Pharisee Hillel, had begun to teach the people that the true religion was a religion of the heart, one that emphasized love for one's neighbor, rather than only an affair of religious observances and ritual.

Such, then, was the atmosphere in Judaea and Palestine when Jesus was born.

❖ The life and death of Jesus Christ

We do not know as much as we should like about the early history of Christianity or the actual life and work of its founder, for reasons not unlike those already discussed in connection with the Hebrews. Almost all that we know is gathered from the four Gospels (the Greek word is *evangelion,* meaning "good news," hence the writers were called Evangelists). But the Evan-

gelists were highly selective, choosing only those parts of the story which each felt to be essential. They were not systematic historians or biographers. Their purpose was to "preach the good news." Thus, to a later historian, there appear to be contradictions and even discrepancies, as, for instance, in the differing accounts of the birth of Jesus and the events immediately following the birth which are recorded by Matthew and Luke. Yet these Gospels are all that we possess in the way of external record, and from them must be constructed such consecutive history as is possible. The personality of Jesus Christ shines out so clearly from all four narratives that there has never been any real question of their general truth and authenticity.

The story that follows will therefore necessarily be drawn from the Gospels and the other

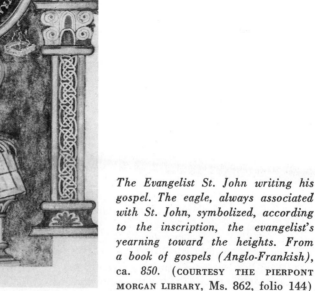

The Evangelist St. John writing his gospel. The eagle, always associated with St. John, symbolized, according to the inscription, the evangelist's yearning toward the heights. From a book of gospels (Anglo-Frankish), ca. 850. (COURTESY THE PIERPONT MORGAN LIBRARY, Ms. 862, folio 144)

books of the New Testament, with the reminder that it may not be fully accurate and cannot be independently verified by any means now available to us.

Jesus was born in Bethlehem of Judaea, as prophesied by the Hebrew prophet Micah. His mother was Mary, whose husband was Joseph of the lineage of King David. Mary had been informed by an angel that the child was to be born and was to be a "son of the Most High." Thereafter, according to the account in Matthew, the infant Jesus was visited by three wise men or kings, an event which excited the suspicion of King Herod, who commanded that all newly born children should be put to death. Joseph and Mary, warned in a dream, took the child to Egypt, returning to Nazareth to live after all danger was over. In the Luke account the child was visited by shepherds and adored by them, but thereafter returned peacefully to Nazareth, the home town of his parents. Only one further incident of the childhood of Jesus is recorded in the Gospels: a visit to the Temple in Jerusalem at the age of twelve, when he escaped from his parents and was later found by them disputing with the Rabbis, both hearing them and asking them questions.

Thereafter there is a break in the narrative until all four Evangelists record a visit to an Essene prophet, John the Baptist, who had been preaching the imminent coming of the Messiah and urging the people to change their way of thinking in preparation for this event.[1] John had already declared that he himself was not the Messiah. When he saw Jesus coming, he immediately recognized him as the one who should come, "the latchet of whose shoes I am unworthy to unloose," and baptized him in the river. A voice was heard from heaven saying, "This is my beloved son in whom I am well pleased," and the Holy Spirit was seen descending from heaven in the form of a dove.

This is the beginning of the Messianic mission of Christ (the word *Christus* means the "anointed one"). For the next three years he preached to the people and healed the sick, giving many signs of his Messiahship.[2] Sometimes he taught straightforwardly, attacking above all the strict Pharisees, whose religion was mere outward show. At other times he hid his true message within parables, sometimes adding, even as he gave one interpretation, the words, "Let him hear who has ears to hear." He chose twelve men to be his special aides, and these were called apostles; around him gathered many more who came to listen to him. Those who decided to follow him were called disciples.

Throughout Christ's teaching there is always the emphasis that true religion comes from the heart, and that "the Law and the prophets" are comprised in two commandments, the love of God and the love of one's neighbor. Though these teachings, with their evident wealth of hidden meanings, have inspired Christians ever since, nevertheless it is not the teachings of Christ so much as his life and death and whole personality, as revealed by the Gospels, that have been taken by the Christian Church and Christian believers as the truest evidence for the divine origin of his mission and for the divinity of his person. The Gospels thus gave Christianity some of its human appeal over such competing religions as Mithraism and the Egyptian mystery religions. The central figure of Christianity was a man who had actually lived on earth, and had been seen and could be remembered by his followers. The teachings have been expressed by others almost equally well, and there is nothing profoundly *new* in them. But the inspiration of the death and resurrection has been constantly renewed in countless Christian hearts in all the centuries since.

The Gospel accounts are in substantial agreement with each other on the death and resurrection of Jesus Christ. After three years of preaching and healing he had aroused the resentment of many Jews, who had not been convinced by his signs or his teachings. But it was one of Christ's own apostles, Judas Iscariot,

---

[1] The Greek word *metanoeite* means literally "change your outlook" or "change your way of thinking." This conveys a different sense from the word *repent*, by which it is usually translated.

[2] The Greek word *semaion* or "sign" was translated into Latin in the authoritative Latin Bible of St. Jerome as *miraculum*; hence our word *miracle*, which probably gives the wrong impression of these symbolic acts.

Chronological Chart

Birth of Jesus	(probably)	4 B.C.
Mission of Jesus Christ	(probably) A.D.	26–30
Crucifixion of Jesus Christ	(probably)	30
Missionary journeys of Paul	*ca.*	34–60
Paul appeals to Roman emperor		60
Fire of Rome—First Martyrdom of Christians		64
Pliny's correspondence with Trajan about Christians		111–112
Rescript by Marcus Aurelius against Christians		169
General persecution of Christians by Emperor Decius		249–51
Diocletian "persecution"		303–13
Constantine succeeds to throne		312
"Edict of Milan"		313
Council of Nicaea		325
Conversion of Goths to Arianism (Bishop Ulfilas)		340–348
Rule of St. Basil	*ca.*	360
Julian the Apostate		361–363
Theodosius I forced to do penance for massacre at Thessalonica		390
Proscription of pagan religions by Theodosius		392
Death of Augustine (*City of God, ca.* 425–430)		430
St. Patrick's mission to Ireland		432
Invasion of Italy by Attila the Hun		452
Western bishops subjected to Pope Leo I by Emperor Valentinian III		455
Rule of St. Benedict		529
Irish monasticism of St. Columba		533–597
Columba founds monastery of Iona and Scottish Church		563
Missionary work of St. Columban in Europe		590–615
Pope Gregory I the Great		590–604
Conversion of England to Catholic Christianity		597
Synod of Whitby—Submission of Irish Church		664

who betrayed him to the leading Jews, who thereupon sent a guard to take him prisoner. Christ made no attempt to defend himself, and indeed forbade his disciples to use any violence against the guard. He had already warned them that he would be put to death and raised from the dead after three days, but they had not understood him. When they saw that he was captured and would not defend himself, they deserted him. The leading apostle, Peter, even went so far as to deny publicly that he had ever known Christ, thus again fulfilling a prophecy of his master.

Christ was then examined by the High Priest, and admitted that he was the Son of God. The High Priest and Council, declaring that this admission was a blasphemy, wished to put him to death in accordance with Jewish law, but to do so they needed confirmation of the sentence from the Roman procurator, Pontius Pilate. Pilate then questioned him, but finding that his offense seemed to be only a religious one, was anxious to release him. However, when the Jews insisted that Christ wished to make himself "King of the Jews," Pilate became afraid, no doubt remembering that Tiberius was on the throne, and had recently passed severe laws against treason. He therefore confirmed the sentence and Christ was crucified. A rich follower claimed the body, and buried it in the tomb prepared for himself.

At this point it must have seemed to anyone alive at the time that Christ's mission had failed. The new Messiah had been put to death, and his followers, mostly men and women of the lower classes and of no influence, had deserted him. Like other Jewish messiahs, of whom there had been many, he would be forgotten.

❖ **The early Christian Church**

THE CONVERSION OF ST. PAUL AND THE NEW
MISSIONARY IMPULSE

This time, however, there was a strikingly
different outcome. On the third day after his
death Peter, John, and a woman follower of
Jesus named Mary Magdalene went to the
tomb and found it empty. Then they saw their
master once more alive in the body, and he
showed himself to his disciples several times.
This experience gave them new hope and energy,
and after they had seen the resurrected Christ
received into heaven, they all awaited the last
fulfillment of his promise—the coming of the
Helper or Holy Spirit who, according to the
promise, could come to them only after Christ
had died and been resurrected. One day, when
the apostles had gathered together in an upper
room and after they had chosen by lot a twelfth
apostle to replace Judas Iscariot, who had, in
remorse, hanged himself, there was suddenly
"the sound of a rushing mighty wind." They
were all filled with the Holy Spirit, and began
to prophesy, and speak each in the tongue of
the land of his origin. The onlookers thought
them drunk, but with new inspiration they began to preach the resurrection of Christ and to
make converts. One of the disciples, Stephen,
addressed an assembly of Jews, accusing them
of always having maltreated, rejected, and put
to death their prophets. The Jews, goaded beyond their endurance, stoned him to death,
making him the first Christian martyr (Greek
for "witness"). Apparently the Roman officials
looked the other way and did not interfere.

Present at the stoning was Saul of Tarsus, a
Roman citizen, an orthodox Hellenized Jew of
the sect of the Pharisees, who at once saw the
danger from these new fanatical believers in a
messiah who had failed and died without fulfilling the mission expected of him. Saul therefore, with a band of determined helpers,
proceeded to lead an expedition of extermination
against the Christians, presumably with the aid,
or at least the connivance, of the authorities.
Having done his best in Jerusalem, he set out
on a journey to Damascus in Syria to continue
the persecution of converts in the north. On the
road to Damascus he had an experience in
which the crucified Christ appeared to him in
a vision. This experience gave him an absolute
conviction from which he never afterward
wavered, leading him to regard and speak of
himself as an apostle called out of due time. At
first, however, he was paralyzed and struck
blind; his servants brought him to Damascus,
where his faculties were restored by a Christian.
From this moment Saul, whom the records
thereafter call Paul, was as strongly for the
Christians as he had previously been against
them. After a period of retirement during which
he was apparently coming to an understanding
of his experience on the road to Damascus and
the realization of his mission, he went to Jerusalem, where he was naturally received with some
distrust by his late enemies. But, even without
any real authorization from the body of Jewish
Christians who had now formed a church in
Jerusalem as headquarters of the new religion,
he set out on a missionary journey. During the
course of this journey he took the epoch-making
decision to baptize Greeks and other non-Jews
as Christians without making them become
Jews first, sparing them the Jewish rites and
ritual which Peter had been insisting on in
Palestine.

Returning to Jerusalem, Paul reached a
compromise with Peter that Gentiles outside
Palestine need not become Jews, while the
church in Jerusalem would continue with the
requirement. Then Paul set out again, making
converts everywhere, especially among the
Greeks to whom he, with his Greek education,
was able to speak in their own language and in
their own terms. At Athens itself, finding an
altar dedicated "To the unknown God," he
showed the Athenians who this God was, and
why he hitherto had been unknown to them.
With rare organizing ability and drive, he
founded churches in all the places he visited,
and kept in touch with them afterward by correspondence. His letters, the earliest authentic
Christian documents, expounded the new Christian theology, which seems to have been almost
entirely his own work, and answered the numerous questions put to him. In all the cities Paul
visited in Asia Minor and Greece, his most determined opponents were always the Jews.

OPPOSITION OF THE JEWS TO CHRISTIANITY

It cannot be stated categorically why the Jews were so determinedly hostile as a body to the Christians, although individual Jews were of course converted, especially in the Hellenistic cities. The Jewish leaders, Pharisees and Sadducees alike, had instigated the proceedings which led to the Crucifixion, but only a few took an active part in this event. The usual explanation is that the Jews were looking for a messiah of an entirely different kind from Jesus Christ, one who would give them temporal power and not merely redeem them through suffering. Their prophet Isaiah had devoted his matchless eloquence to a description of a "suffering servant," a "man of sorrows and acquainted with grief"—but it was not certain that this prophecy referred to an actual man, a messiah. It might only refer to the people of Israel as a whole. Moreover, by no means all Jews had yet accepted the idea of a future life. If there was no such future life and no heavenly kingdom, then clearly such a messiah as Christ was worse than useless, since his religion tended to create a schism within Jewry which could not be tolerated. All through Hebrew history there had been such schisms, and in Jewish belief these had been punished by Yahweh. They had, indeed, been responsible in part for Yahweh's continual postponement of the fulfillment of his promises. The temptation offered by Christianity, therefore, was just one more test of their faith. Even those Jews who took account of political rather than religious realities could see that Christianity represented a grave danger to the privileged status of their religion in the Roman Empire. They realized that the Romans would look upon Christianity as a Jewish sect—but potentially dangerous not only because of its exclusive monotheism but also because of its zeal for conversion, from which the Jews themselves had usually been free.

Christ had been a Jew, thoroughly grounded in the Law and the prophets. But he had claimed that the Law itself had to be newly interpreted, not in the manner of the rabbis, but through breathing a new spirit into it. Many were impressed by the authority with which he spoke, even daring to criticize Moses—"Moses said to you, but *I* say." Now Paul, claiming a similar authority as an apostle, was even more explicit. The Law, he wrote in a letter, is a schoolmaster to bring us to Christ. The Law had been given to the Hebrews because at that time they did not know right from wrong, nor did they know how God was to be worshiped and what he required of them. Now, however, under the new dispensation of Jesus Christ, they were no longer children, needing to be kept under discipline, but "sons," with their knowledge of right and wrong coming from within, through faith and love. Therefore, although Hebrew thought, formerly an exclusive possession of the Jews, was spread throughout the whole Western world by Christianity, the orthodox Jews took no pride in this dissemination of their heritage, for if this heritage was to be a possession of the world, then their mission as a chosen people was over.

ST. PAUL AS THE FOUNDER OF CHRISTIAN THEOLOGY

On the whole Paul met with little opposition from Greeks and Romans unless, as at Ephesus, he offended the priesthood of a powerful Greco-Oriental mystery cult. But regularly the local Jewish community tried to prevent him from preaching. Several times he was thrown into prison by the Roman authorities for causing riots, but in general it was the Romans who protected him. When at last he returned to Jerusalem, opposition to him was so strong that he was first taken into protective custody by the Romans. Then, when he was about to be punished for his part in the riots, he used his right as a Roman citizen and appealed to Caesar (Nero). The local governor was thus forced to send him to Rome, where he was allowed a limited freedom even before his trial came up. We know nothing further of his life for certain, but tradition has it that he was beheaded during the first organized persecution of Christians in Rome about A.D. 65.

Paul was the real founder of Christianity as a universal religion. If the other apostles, who wished to confine Christianity to the Jews, had been successful, it hardly seems possible that it could have survived. Paul also deserves to be considered as one of the most influential thinkers of history. It was no mean feat to transform what was, after all, to external eyes nothing beyond the life and death of a great prophet, into a system of theology—logical, clear, and compelling—which has stood the test of time, and is still the fundamental theological doctrine of all Christian churches, Catholic and Protestant alike.

Christ, according to Paul, had been the Son of God—a God-man—though he was also fully a man by virtue of his incarnation into a human body. Every man born into the world suffers from the sin of Adam. ("As in Adam all die, so in Christ shall all be made alive.") Man would have been doomed to hell if it had not been for the voluntary sacrifice of Christ upon the cross, which redeemed mankind through his blood, and made possible man's salvation and reception into a blessed immortality in heaven. For Paul the necessity for man was to believe in Christ—a faith effecting an inner transformation of his whole being, freeing him from the bonds of original sin and enabling him to be good also on earth. Thus man was not saved through good works, but the good works were the fruit of his faith. The symbol of the washing away of the original sin of Adam was baptism, by which a man of his own free will declared his faith in Christ, and was received into the Church.

It should be added that, although Paul founded churches as communities of Christians who had all accepted Christ and been baptized, it was not the reception into the Church which was decisive for salvation, but the inner act of "putting on the whole armor of Christ," allowing Christ to live within the inner self—the symbol for which was the baptism in water, which symbolically washed away the sins of the convert. Only in later days, with the growth of the Church, did the belief come to be accepted that the Eucharist and the other sacraments were necessary to salvation, and that the transubstantiation, the miracle of the turning of the bread and wine into the body and blood of Christ, was the supreme need of all human beings. The baptism then became a rite to be performed in infancy, and not an affirmation of faith by a believer; from childhood a Christian

was cleansed from original sin and was thus eligible for heaven even though he never lived to participate in the other sacraments.[3]

THE APPEAL OF CHRISTIANITY IN THE ROMAN WORLD

Christianity, as it emerged from the mind and heart of St. Paul, was eminently fitted to make the deepest appeal to religious men and women throughout the world. It promised salvation in the hereafter to all who would accept Christ, and this acceptance was simply an act of faith. Thus, in spite of its complex theology, perhaps never understood by more than a small minority of its adherents, it was basically simple. It was no respecter of persons. The meanest slave was eligible for salvation, and to him it also offered the fullest compensation for his hard life on earth—which was merely a testing ground for the hereafter. No distinction was made between men and women, and there were no difficult trials or initiation ceremonies to be undergone by the convert. And in early days there was a belief in the imminent second coming of Christ to judge the world, so that the faithful Christians might not even see death. No religion in the world of the time, not even the mystery religions, could offer as much to its converts—community fellowship, a sense of mission and urgency, a promise of a blessed immortality, and a systematic theology and philosophy which could satisfy even the Greek mind when later it set to work on it. If at first Christianity lacked gorgeous ceremonial, this was later added in full measure by the Church. And in the recorded sayings of Christ it had a fund of ethical and moral teachings which could satisfy even the Roman feeling for active morality.

Yet it did not appeal in early times to the upper classes among either the Romans or the Greeks; indeed, for centuries it was primarily a religion of Greeks and Orientals, with com-

---

[3] It may be noted that there are varying interpretations of the teachings of St. Paul, and that what has been said here is still in dispute among theologians.

Very early sculptured figure of Christ at Santillana del Mar (Spain).

paratively few Roman converts, no Roman pope for two centuries, and hardly a single Roman martyr. The Romans, even when they were correctly informed about it, regarded it as a religion for slaves and foreigners, and it was difficult for men who considered themselves morally superior to the rest of the world and destined to rule, to accept as a redeemer a man who had belonged to a despised people and had suffered a slave's death in a remote part of the empire. His origin and manner of dying offended their class consciousness and pride of race, while the Greek intellectuals considered his teachings at first as philosophically negligible. In time, however, as the Greeks learned more

about the religion, many of them began to take an active role in the formulation of Christian theology, and, especially in the early days of the Byzantine Empire, they entered passionately into theological controversy.

Physical conditions in the Roman Empire, however, were ideally suited for the spread of Christianity. The establishment of the Pax Romana made it possible for missionaries to travel in perfect safety from one end of the empire to the other, and the strategic Roman roads provided an ideal means of communication. The common languages of Greek and Latin could be understood everywhere. Roman protection was extended to all without discrimination, at least until the new religion was proscribed as a subversive organization. And, as we have seen, any missionary like Paul who happened also to be a Roman citizen had special privileges in addition to the general protection extended by the Roman Empire to all its subjects.

The Romans, in general, were hospitable to all religions. But the religion of emperor-worship, which was the official cult of the empire, was both more and less than a religion. On the one hand, it was not expected to command the religious devotion of the people, but on the other hand no one, save only the Jews, whose uncompromising monotheism was well known to the Romans, was exempted from paying at least formal tribute to the emperor as a god. This allegiance the true Christian was unwilling to give, since he regarded worship as the prerogative of God alone. Roman attention was first officially drawn to the Christians when they were accused in the reign of Nero of having set fire to Rome (A.D. 64). At that time Christianity became a proscribed religion, and the first Christians were put to death by the Roman authorities. The steadfastness of the martyrs, whose number traditionally includes Peter and Paul, probably aided the Christians more than the laws against them harmed them. The religiously indifferent Romans had never been treated to such a display before; and even while the majority ridiculed, it is certain that a minority was impressed. When the immediate persecution died down, the laws against Christianity remained on the statute book, presenting a difficulty to Roman officials who regarded them with distaste. An interesting correspondence between Pliny, a Roman writer and official, and the emperor Trajan is extant, in which Pliny asked for advice about enforcing the laws. The emperor instructed him to take action only when Christians were denounced to him and refused to pay the required worship to the emperor.

This indifference remained the official Roman policy until the middle of the third century A.D., by which time Christianity had become a powerful organized religion, whose leaders commanded more respect from their followers than the often shadowy emperors of that epoch from their titular subjects. Several emperors revived and strengthened the laws against Christians, but they were not effectively enforced until the reign of Diocletian, who, as we shall see in Chapter 7, was able to secure his own position and rule as an absolute monarch. A part of his program for the re-establishment of imperial authority was the revival of emperor-worship. In this aim he naturally came into conflict with Christian beliefs. The persecution, however, in spite of creating many martyrs, ultimately failed, and a few years later (312) Constantine, opposed by a sun-worshiper who was competing with him for the throne, called upon the Christian God for support in his struggle. When the victory was won, he and his co-emperor in the East authorized the toleration of Christianity, and during the course of his reign he himself became converted. Thereafter all the emperors but one (Julian the Apostate) acknowledged themselves as Christians, until the emperor Theodosius in A.D. 392 proscribed all other religions, thus making Christianity the official religion of the empire.

❖ **The organization of the Church**

IN THE PROVINCES

As the Church grew, so naturally did the complexity of its organization. St. Paul himself, as we have seen, kept in touch with all the congregations he had founded, giving them advice and visiting them when he could. As yet there were no priests or Church officials of any kind, and the simple ceremonies and meetings did not require the services of men set aside for purely religious duties. The affairs of the churches were managed by elders, active men in the congregation who took the initiative in matters of religion. But as ever more congregations were organized and it was realized that they might drift apart both in doctrine and in practices if left to themselves, it became clear to the leaders that some kind of more elaborate organization was necessary to keep them united. Living, as they did, within the Roman Empire, there was obviously one particular pattern of organization that could best be imitated, the organization of the empire itself. Within the congregations three hierarchies differentiated themselves in the process of time: deacons, whose task was to give help to Christians in their ordinary daily affairs and especially to take care of the administration of charity; presbyters, who looked after religious affairs of the church; and then an individual leader, called an overseer or episcopus, from which comes our word *bishop*.

In early times neither presbyters nor bishops were in any way superior to the ordinary layman, nor did they go through any special ceremony when they were elected to their position. But by the end of the second century, with the elaboration of the ceremonial of the Church, and the growth of the belief that its services were needed for salvation, these clergy became set apart as a class of real priests who were *ordained* by the bishops. Ordination, like baptism and the Eucharist, had now become a *sacrament*, while the ceremony of ordination became a ritual conferring special sanctity upon the holder. For several centuries more it was the congregations who chose their bishops; but once chosen, these men had full monarchical power within their churches. As time went on, it became necessary to have archbishops, whose seats were usually in the Roman capitals, or chief cities, of the provinces, and who were in charge of all the churches in their respective provinces. These men were called metropolitans. The bishops in the whole empire met from time to time in ecumenical (universal) councils, presided over by the metropolitans or by the bishop of

Rome (later called pope[4]), to consider doctrinal problems and to discuss matters which concerned the Church as a whole.

IN ROME—THE BISHOP OF ROME— PETRINE SUPREMACY

The bishop of Rome had a peculiar position as the head of the church in the capital city of the empire. Probably as early as the second century A.D. the Roman congregation was the largest in the empire. The church in Rome, according to tradition, had been founded by the apostle Peter, who had become its first bishop and been martyred and buried there.

But it was a long time before St. Peter's position was supposed to confer any supreme authority upon his successors. Other bishops claimed to be the equal of the bishops of Rome, and it was usually the reputation and personality of individual bishops which gave them whatever authority they might possess in spiritual matters. Ambrose, bishop of Milan in the fourth century, was clearly the most influential bishop of his day, and was able to force the emperor himself to do penance for a massacre he had committed. But in the course of time it gradually became accepted doctrine that Peter, who had been entrusted by Christ with the task of founding the Church, had delegated his authority to his successor, and the latter to his successor, right down to the present time. This theory of the Petrine (or Apostolic) succession, is still the basis for the authority claimed by the Catholic Church.

As long as an emperor ruled in Rome, the bishop's authority was naturally limited to his spiritual domain. But when Honorius, Emperor of the West, removed his court to Ravenna at the end of the fourth century, the bishop was left as the chief dignitary in Rome, and at times he performed the functions of a Roman ruler in the city. One great pope, Leo I, negotiated with Attila the Hun, and succeeded in diverting him

---

[4] The Latin word *papa* merely means "father," a title given by courtesy to other priests than the pope. It is not known for certain when the word *pope* was first applied exclusively to the bishop of Rome.

from the city; and the same pope negotiated for the safety of its inhabitants during the sack of Rome by the Vandals. As the Roman provincial administration gradually collapsed in the fifth century, under the impact of the barbarian invaders, the bishops in many of the provinces took over from the helpless Roman governors and tried to protect the interests of the people as best they could. They now started to look to the pope (as we may now call the bishop of Rome) for guidance in political policy as well as for spiritual leadership. Pope Leo I was given official recognition by Emperor Valentinian III of Ravenna, who conferred upon him full authority over all the bishops in the empire. He did not hesitate to use this authority, demanding implicit obedience from them and pronouncing final decisions in matters of doctrine.

❖ The establishment of Christian doctrine

THE QUESTIONS NOT ANSWERED BY ST. PAUL

St. Paul, as already mentioned, was the founder of Christian theology; but his teachings, usually given in response to definite questions put to him by his churches, were very far from satisfying inquiring minds, especially those of his Greek audience. Early in the history of the Christian Church his authority was accepted as that of an apostle chosen by the resurrected Christ to explain the nature of his relationship to God the Father and other mysteries of the religion; and by A.D. 170 his letters, together with letters of the other apostles, the four Gospels, the Acts of the Apostles, and most of the present books of the New Testament were accepted as canonical or inspired books. These are the basic books of Christianity, and nothing else written by any later Christians has quite the same authority. Other men might add to this theology, but these men were not apostles; they had never known Christ personally on earth, and there was no inherent reason why one man's ideas on the subject should be better than any other man's. Yet clearly all the questions that could be asked had not been answered by Christ, Paul, or the other apostles. And it was equally clear that some questions really did need answering. Moreover, many men came into Christianity after earlier experience in the mystery religions, and they were not all ready to abandon what they had been taught before conversion.

There were questions of doctrine, in particular concerning the relation of the Son of God to the Father and the relation of both to the Holy Spirit, a question which was to exercise theologians for many centuries; and there were practical questions, such as the respective roles of faith and good deeds in the achievement of salvation, and the effect of God's infinite foreknowledge and omnipotence upon man's free will. Many differing opinions on these matters had been stated publicly by the time of the conversion of Constantine, and there was no evident way of establishing the truth. Yet the truth must be established if Christianity were not to divide into many competing sects, each holding its own beliefs as established truths.

THE ESTABLISHMENT OF ORTHODOX DOCTRINE

The question of heresy   Constantine himself in 325 summoned a council at Nicaea, over which he presided in person. Here the bishops of the empire assembled and a statement of beliefs, or a creed, was agreed upon. The teachings of a certain Bishop Arius, who claimed that Christ was sent from God, possessed divine substance, but was in no sense co-equal with God the Father, were condemned. The teachings had been making considerable headway, especially among the barbarians who were in the process of being converted to Christianity. Indeed, this simpler belief appealed to some of the emperors subsequent to Constantine, and they continued to permit Arianism to be preached by the missionaries in their domains. The consequence was that all the Germanic barbarian peoples who later penetrated into the empire, with the single exception of the Franks, had already accepted Arianism before the fall of Rome. They were thus hostile to the papacy, which adhered to the teachings of Athanasius, another bishop, whose teachings were pronounced by the papacy to be "orthodox" (the

"right opinion"). Arianism was termed a "heresy" (Greek word for "choice"), and true Christians were forbidden to hold it.

Arianism, however, was far from the only heresy of the early centuries of Christianity. Especially in Constantinople there were numerous heresies, sometimes supported by the emperor and his nominee, the patriarch who was the chief Church official in the East. In the eleventh century the Eastern and Western Churches were finally split over a doctrinal difference. But in the West, as the doctrine of the Petrine supremacy gained acceptance, it was agreed also that the pope, by virtue of his authority as the successor of St. Peter, could declare the true doctrines of the Church which must be held by all believers. He could also state which of the early Christian writings were authoritative, and contained truths inspired by the Holy Spirit. Thus grew up the authority of the Fathers of the Church, whose teachings were to be regarded as orthodox. Indeed, the Catholic Church today teaches many dogmas that are not to be found in the Bible, but have been derived from the inspired writings of the Greek and Latin Fathers.

The teachings of St. Augustine   Most influential among these Fathers was St. Augustine (354–430), bishop of Hippo in North Africa (to be distinguished from the later St. Augustine of Canterbury, who was sent by Pope Gregory I to convert the English), who criticized severely the teachings of one Pelagius, who had claimed that man could be saved by his own good deeds. Augustine argued in reply that the human will is too weak to perform good deeds unaided; indeed, the human mind cannot even know the good without God's grace. Christ's sacrifice had made possible the receiving of grace by mankind, even though it remained God's choice whether man would receive grace or would remain forever ignorant and evil. The Church was the medium chosen by God to administer the sacraments, which were the *means* of grace. Not all who partook of the sacraments would receive grace; but without them there could be no grace and no salvation. Thus St. Augustine made clear the necessary role of the Church in the winning of salvation, and this part of his teaching became the orthodox teaching of the Church. The simple performance of good deeds according to whatever light may be in us, as advocated by Pelagius, was stigmatized as heretical teaching,

Augustine was also a pioneer in another field of thought at least as influential as his theology. An earlier Christian Father, Eusebius, had written an *Ecclesiastical History* which interpreted all the events of his own and earlier times in the light of the Old Testament, and especially of Hebrew prophecy. But Augustine went much further, and in his *City of God* wrote a history designed to show that with the coming of Christ an entirely new phase had opened. Attacking the pagans who claimed that the sack of Rome by Alaric was due to the desertion of the old gods by their worshipers, Augustine declared that this was part of God's scheme. Rome belonged to the "City of Man," which was only temporary and must pass away, to give place to the "City of God" on earth, which would endure forever. The beginnings had already been made under the Hebrew theocracy, and now from the coming of Christ must be continued by the Christian Church. Augustine with great passion and power described God's whole plan for the world, the creation and fall of man and the old dispensation, followed by man's redemption in the new age and the building of the City of God. It need hardly be pointed out how much this conception owes to the Hebrew interpretation of history, already discussed in an earlier chapter.

In Augustine's own thought it is clear that the perfect City of God can never exist on earth; but it is the ideal to which all Christians should aspire, and the beginnings of the building can be made in the here and now. Christians in subsequent ages, however, took it to be the ideal of Christendom, a working plan for all Christians to follow, justifying the extirpation of heresy as treason to the City of God, and later justifying also the extermination of infidels as a fulfillment of God's plan for the unity of all men on earth in the Christian religion. The *City of God* was perhaps, after the Bible, the most influential book in the medieval world.

❖ The persistent ideal of holiness and poverty—Monasticism

Over the first Christian centuries Western men thus gradually came to accept the new religion, and Christianity became a part of their lives. The Church was omnipresent, and penetrated to a greater or lesser degree into every aspect of the life of a Christian. Representatives of the Church baptized the newborn child, and prayed for his soul as his end approached. The Church became a great organization. It held lands and administered property. It became rich and influential, and, as we shall see in later chapters, it too often became embroiled in secular affairs, sometimes to the detriment of its spiritual mission. But in spite of its position as a great organized institution, it was also able to take care of the needs of those who felt that the true purpose of religion was to occupy oneself with deeds of personal piety.

Very early there appeared men and women who wished to take little or no part in the affairs of the world. They wished to follow personally the teachings of Christ, who had told a young man that he should sell all his goods and follow him. In the East such people became ascetics, and were regarded as holy men by their contemporaries. Some became hermits; others lived in small communities with like-minded men, holding all goods in common. The Church at first had difficulty in maintaining any kind of discipline among them, but ultimately was able to some degree to institutionalize their practices, adopting in the fourth century the moderate Rule of St. Basil, which prescribed an orderly, regular life for these monks, as they came to be called. This Rule required the monks to live in a communal dwelling house or monastery, in which each did a share of the work required for his subsistence.

In the West asceticism of the kind practiced in the East was not feasible. But there were many who wished to devote themselves to prayer and worship. For these, the leading Rule among many that were sanctioned by the Church was the Rule of St. Benedict, who founded the great monastery of Monte Cassino. Those who lived by the Rule of St. Benedict had to cut off all

The monastery of Monte Cassino, in southern Italy, as it was before it was destroyed during World War II. It is now being rebuilt.

ties with their family and their previous life before entering the monastery. They took vows of obedience to the abbot, the head of the community. Periods were set aside each day for prayer and worship; the rest of the day was to be spent in manual labor, either in the fields, which were cultivated with great care and made to yield all the food required by the community, or in the monastery itself. No monk was permitted to own anything at all; all property was to be administered by the abbot, whose word was law within the monastery. Monks slept in a common dormitory and ate in a common dining room.

By the eighth century the Benedictine Rule was adopted by the vast majority of monasteries in the West except the Irish. For centuries it was the model life for the religious, and faithfully observed by those who had chosen it. Even when abuses began to creep in, all those who undertook reforms returned to the Benedictine Rule, or some modification of it, as the ideal Rule for a religious community. There was no doubt that in spite of its initial reservations the Church was wise to permit and ultimately take the lead in organizing these communities of monks. For if it was necessary to institutionalize the Church, and the papacy had no doubt of this necessity, then it was also necessary to take care of those deeply earnest men and women

who wished to devote all their lives to their religion, and to live a communal life of poverty that seemed to them in accordance with the teachings of Christ. As long as the monks continued to live holy lives, they were a standing example of the virtues of Christianity; they troubled no one, and at the same time they absorbed into their communities all those who might have attacked the Church for its institutionalism and worldliness.

The Irish monasteries alone did not conform to the Benedictine Rule. Remaining for centuries unconnected with the Church in Rome, they were unaware even of many of the newer teachings of the Church. The result was that they developed a Christianity that was never institutionalized in the Roman manner, and they retained a fervor, especially in missionary activity, that had begun to disappear from Europe. St. Columba converted some Celtic tribes in Britain before they had yet been visited by official emissaries of the Church; St. Columban penetrated into Gaul, making converts in places where Christianity had as yet no foothold and founding monasteries there; another Irishman founded the great monastery of St. Gall in what is now Switzerland. Moreover, once the first monks had gained a knowledge of Greek, it continued to be taught in the monasteries, and was never allowed to die out in Ireland. The only

THE RISE OF CHRISTIANITY

great philosopher of the Dark Ages in Europe, John Scotus Erigena, was an Irishman.

But this progress of the Irish monks was rudely checked in Britain. Pope Gregory I (the fourth and last of the officially recognized Latin Fathers of the Church), at the end of the sixth century sent a missionary to Britain named Augustine, who succeeded in converting the South. As this Catholic Christianity progressed northward it came into contact with the communities converted from Ireland, which had quite unknowingly adopted a different form of ecclesiastical usage. Both sides agreed to accept the decision of a synod at Whitby (664), presided over by the king of Northumbria. The question hinged upon the Petrine supremacy. The Irish could point to no such authority as that of the pope, descended from St. Peter. Their failure was decisive. The Roman Church received the award, the new English Church was organized after the Roman manner. The monasteries accepted the Benedictine Rule; in time even the Irish themselves accepted the inevitable, and adopted the discipline and organization of the central Church in Rome.

❖ Summary

With the acceptance of Christianity and its gradual diffusion over all Europe, Western civilization had acquired its own religion, which is indeed a peculiar possession of this civilization. Whenever Christianity has spread outside the borders of Europe, it has been carried by Western peoples; non-Western peoples have accepted it, with rare exceptions, only when they have also accepted Western civilization.

Christianity itself owes much to its predecessors. The religion of the Hebrews gave Christianity its idea of God, its concept of sin and punishment, and its fundamental ethics; Christianity of course inherited its Old Testament from the Hebrews. From the Greeks Christianity took much of its theology and almost all its philosophy. The hierarchical organization of the Christian Church was adapted from the contemporary Roman practice of government, and Church (canon) law was solidly based upon Roman law.

The barbarians who were later converted to Christianity were made most aware of the organization and ritual of the Church, and for centuries only a few understood anything of its theology. But Christianity showed itself capable of adapting itself to many pagan practices that survived from pre-Christian days; and in turn the pagans were often able to accommodate themselves to the new religion by adding certain elements from Christianity without totally abandoning their former beliefs. Thus resistance to Christianity was rarely prolonged. When missionaries faltered, the State felt it to be its duty to compel at least an outward conversion; while the monopoly enjoyed by the Church made an alternative religion hard to come by. Christianity became the accepted and universal religion of the West, a position it still holds today, even though the Catholic Church itself has no longer a monopoly of Christianity.

Suggestions for further reading

The New Testament is available in paper-bound books in several modern translations, including *The New English Bible: New Testament* (Oxford; Cambridge), *The New Testament in Modern English* trans. by J. B. Phillips (Macmillan), *New Testament, Revised Standard Version* (Bantam), Official Catholic Versions (Guild and Image). A hard-cover edition is Edgar J. Goodspeed's translation, *The New Testament: an American Translation* (University of Chicago Press).

PAPER-BOUND BOOKS

Asch, Sholem. *The Apostle.* Pocket Books. A fine attempt by a non-Christian to evoke in historical fiction the life, work, and times of St. Paul.

Augustine, Saint. *City of God.* Tedious and rambling but extremely influential book, available in an abridged Image edition. Also selections in an Ungar edition.

Augustine, Saint. *Confessions.* A moving account by the great churchman of how he came to Christianity via Neoplatonism and Manichaeism, a masterpiece of autobiography. Available in several different modern translations. Old translation by Edward B. Pusey (Collier) is, in my view, to be avoided. The best translation is by F. J. Sheed (New York: Sheed and Ward,

Inc., 1943). A useful selection of St. Augustine's writings, edited by Roger Hazelton, is available from Meridian.

Bainton, Roland H. *Early Christianity*. Anvil. Short informative history with relevant documents.

Burckhardt, Jacob. *The Age of Constantine the Great*. Anchor. Interesting study by the nineteenth-century Swiss historian, who gives little credit for sincerity to the first Christian emperor. A useful corrective is to be found in a hard-cover book by K. Setton and H. Winkler, eds., *Great Problems in European Civilization* (Englewood Cliffs, N.J.: Prentice-Hall, Inc., 1954), in which Setton excerpts a number of pertinent passages from ancient and modern authors, including Burckhardt. See also Jones.

Bultmann, Rudolf. *Primitive Christianity in Its Contemporary Setting*. Meridian. Brief but scholarly and up-to-date work (1956).

Deissmann, Adolf. *Paul: a Study in Social and Religious History*. Torchbooks. Scholarly estimate of St. Paul and his influence, using all available sources, including papyri.

Duckett, Eleanor S. *Gateway to the Middle Ages: Monasticism*. Ann Arbor. Extracts from a larger book on the early Middle Ages. One of the few books available on the subject, shows the author's usual familiarity with the material available and her customary good judgment.

Goodspeed, Edgar J. *Paul*. Apex. By a distinguished scholar who also translated the New Testament.

Grant, Frederick D., ed. *Hellenistic Religions: The Age of Syncretism*. Liberal Arts Press. Documents bearing on the religious background of Christianity in the Near East.

Harnack, Adolf. *The Mission and Expansion of Christianity in the First Three Centuries*. Torchbooks. By a distinguished Protestant historian of the turn of the century, full and thorough. The same author's masterpiece *History of Dogma* (4 vols., Dover) might be attempted by serious students.

Jones, A. H. M. *Constantine and the Conversion of Rome*. Collier.

Lebreton, Jules, and Zeiller, Jacques. *History of the Early Church*. 4 vols. Collier. Comprehensive and scholarly. Covers to the end of the third century.

Loisy, Alfred. *Origins of the New Testament*. Collier.

Marrou, Henri. *St. Augustine and His Influence through the Ages*. Men of Wisdom Series, Harper & Row. Small but valuable book dealing briefly with the life and thought of St. Augustine, and more fully with how his thought was retained and transformed in the Middle Ages.

McCann, Justin. *Saint Benedict*. Image. The Benedictine Rule with commentary by a present-day Benedictine monk.

Waddell, Helen. *The Desert Fathers*. Ann Arbor. A classic account of the Greek Fathers of the Church who escaped from organized Christianity into lives of solitude.

Weiss, Johannes. *Earliest Christianity, A History of the Period* A.D. *30–150*. 2 vols. Torchbooks. Very thorough and interesting work making use of all available sources and written with great insight.

HARD-COVER BOOKS

Bettenson, H. S., ed. *Documents of the Christian Church*. New York: Oxford University Press, 1947. Valuable collection of primary documents.

Duchesne, Louis. *Early History of the Christian Church*. 3 vols. New York: David McKay Company, Inc., 1922–1947. Standard; very full history, including all the early heresies.

Fisher, G. P. *A History of Christian Doctrine*. New York: Charles Scribner's Sons, 1923. Very full and thorough, without noticeable bias, but not easy.

Goodenough, E. R. *The Church in the Roman Empire*. New York: Holt, Rinehart and Winston, Inc., 1931. Short, readable account without much attention to doctrine.

Latourette, Kenneth S. *A History of Christianity*. New York: Harper & Row, Publishers, 1953. One of the standard histories and in many ways the best. Good on early Christianity.

Pegis, Anton C., ed. *The Wisdom of Catholicism*. New York: The Modern Library, Inc., 1949. Contains important selections from the writings of the Church Fathers and others.

Shotwell, J. T., and Loomis, L. R. *The See of Peter*. New York: Columbia University Press, 1927. Documents on the growth of the papacy and gradual acceptance of the bishop of Rome as head of the Church.

SEVEN

The Fall of Rome and the Establishment of Successor States in the West

---

❖ The beginning of the end

The murder of Commodus in 192 was the signal for the opening of a period of outright domination of the Roman emperor by the army, a condition which was to last till the fall of the empire. The first half of this period, up to the accession of Diocletian, was characterized by the increasing disintegration of the civil government under a series of military usurpers whose chief, and sometimes only, ability lay in the military sphere. The empire itself was, on the whole, successfully defended against external pressure on the boundaries, but at tremendous cost to its internal stability. The second half of the period was characterized by the development of a totalitarian state under a civil administration backed by a usually obedient professional mercenary army, directed by an absolute emperor.

The economic and military policies of the emperor who succeeded Commodus, a general named Septimius Severus (193–211), may with justice be debited with the semi-anarchy that persisted, except for short intervals, until the accession of Diocletian in 284. Severus evidently had little knowledge of the political and economic basis of the empire; still less was he aware of the delicate basis of consent combined with effective military supremacy that underlay the position of the princeps. A soldier himself, and only a soldier, Severus was primarily interested in providing for the needs of his army, and he ruled as a military despot rather than a civilian magistrate. The army was dissident as long as its pay was uncertain. Only the still fairly prosperous cities could find its pay, and the surplus produce of the peasants had to provide for its subsistence. Meanwhile, the relatively unproductive proletariat had to be kept contented, and prevented from undermining the emperor's position while he was away on campaign. These elementary needs were taken care of in a rough-and-ready manner by the policies of the emperor, quite certainly without an awareness of what they would come to mean for the future of the empire.

To ensure that his treasury was kept full, Severus initiated the policy of making municipal magistrates personally responsible for the collection of the taxes due to the emperor from the cities they nominally ruled. If they were not paid in full, the magistrates themselves had to make up the difference. To see that all sources of income were tapped and that all officials were kept to their duty, Severus inaugurated a secret police to report directly to himself on any failure to fulfill obligations and to warn him of any tendencies toward treason. On the other hand, he won the approval of the proletariat by increasing its dole from the state, and passed other special legislation which protected its interests.

THE ASCENDANCY OF THE PEASANT ARMY

But the real danger of the policy of Severus was in the favoritism he showed to his legions. Their pay was considerably raised, and many concessions were made to them which had the effect of impairing their usefulness to the state, while incidentally lowering their efficiency. Married soldiers were allowed to live with their wives in towns behind the lines; auxiliary divisions were given permanent lands; and social clubs in the army were encouraged. This policy made the troops relatively immobile and unfit for service on an endangered frontier. It also made them less willing to fight and less amenable to discipline. Time after time in the third century we hear of mutinies and of the assassination of military leaders when they called upon the troops to fight in defense of the frontiers or tried to instill some discipline into them. Moreover, Severus now made it possible for all provincial soldiers to rise to the position of centurion, which carried with it equestrian rank. Since this was the class favored both by Severus and by his successors for all posts in the imperial bureaucracy, the result was that a military career became the best means of entry to the highest positions in the state, and civilian rule was gradually replaced by military. The very highest offices in the imperial service brought their holders within the senatorial aristocracy, which carried special privileges. Thus the senatorial order became increasingly filled with successful soldiers who acquired large tracts of land and settled down, unencumbered by taxation, having in their progress from the ranks avoided any payment of taxes whatever, and having acquired a vast contempt for those more productive members of society upon whom fell the whole burden of their upkeep. Thus the army became a privileged career, and the military caste, pampered and favored by Severus and all the third-century emperors, became a state within the state, entirely irresponsible, and giving its support only to those rulers who perpetuated its position and catered to its demands.

By opening to soldiers from the ranks the way even to the crown itself, the emperors might have attracted into the army men from the upper and middle classes. But, though Italians and provincials of equestrian rank did continue to provide some of the officers, the bulk of the army was recruited, by design, from the peasantry. It has even been suggested that this was a deliberate policy to increase the class struggle between the peasantry and the urban middle classes. It would seem more probable, however, that the conscript army could find recruits in sufficient number only from the peasantry, and that the concessions made were of the kind more likely to appeal to a largely illiterate and semi-civilized peasantry, which had always found it difficult to make a living from the land. The result of the whole policy, as doubtless intended, was to undermine the position of the upper classes and infiltrate them with uncouth but able soldiers; but it was probably not foreseen that the army itself would become progressively barbarized, nor that it would prefer its privileged life behind the lines to defending the state. The soldiers preferred to follow only those leaders who promised them the most at the least cost to themselves in military activity. So many emperors were assassinated by rebellious troops during fifty years of the third century that only one of eighteen such "emperors" died peacefully in his bed.

FIFTY YEARS OF ANARCHY—THE "BARRACK EMPERORS" (235–284)

There is no need to dwell on the lives, activities, and sudden deaths of these "barrack" emperors. No real rule of succession was observed, though on a few occasions fathers were in fact succeeded by sons who had made appropriate donatives to the legions; frequently there were several competing emperors supported by their own troops but not accepted by any others. On several occasions the Germans penetrated into Gaul, once even passing the Alps and only meeting ultimate defeat in northern Italy. For ten years there was a separate and completely independent kingdom of Gaul. Without effective central administration, tax collecting was by the rough-and-ready method of requisition of supplies and forced levies of money. Almost the whole of Roman Asia acquired virtual independence for a time (267–273) under the leadership of a desert city

Chronological Chart

Murder of Roman Emperor Commodus	192	Puppet rulers in Rome	455–476
Reign of Septimius Severus	193–211	Visigothic kingdom of Spain	466–711
Edict of Caracalla—Extension of Roman citizenship to virtually all free inhabitants of the empire	212	Odoacer deposes last emperor ("Fall of Rome")	476
"Barrack Emperors"	235–284	Clovis consolidates Franks into kingdom	481–511
Reign of Diocletian	284–305	Merovingian kingdom	481–754
Constantine emperor of West, Licinius of East	312	Conversion of Clovis and Franks to Roman Catholicism	486
"Edict of Milan"	313	Invasions of England by Angles, Saxons, and Jutes	5th and 6th centuries
Constantine sole emperor	324–337	Invasion of Italy by Theodoric the Ostrogoth	488
Council of Nicaea	325		
Foundation of Constantinople	330	Murder of Odoacer—Theodoric king of Italy	493
Conversion of Goths to Arian Christianity	340–348	Theodoric the Ostrogoth king of Italy	493–526
Advance of Huns into Europe, defeating Goths	372	Execution of Boethius	524
Goths permitted across Danube by Emperor Valens	376	Vandal kingdom of Africa reconquered by Justinian	533–548
Battle of Adrianople—Gothic victory—Death of Valens	378	Reconquest of Italy by Justinian	535–554
Honorius moves Roman capital to Ravenna	ca. 400	Southeastern Spain conquered from Visigoths by Justinian, but lost soon afterward	554
Vandals advance into Gaul	406	Invasion of Italy by Lombards	568
Roman legions leave England	407–442	Gradual conquest of northern and central Italy by Lombards	568–605
Sack of Rome by Alaric and Visigoths	410	Conversion of Visigoths in Spain to Roman Catholicism	587
Visigoths move into Spain	415	Pope Gregory I, the Great	590–604
Vandals move into Africa	429	Mission of St. Augustine of Canterbury to England	596–597
Vandal kingdom of Africa	429–534		
Aetius becomes master of the troops under Valentinian III	430	Conquests of Angles, Saxons, and Jutes completed by	615
Franks penetrate into Gaul	431 onward	Influx of Celtic Christianity into England from Iona	633 onward
Rise of Attila to power among Huns, moves west	445	Conversion of Lombard ruler to Roman Catholicism	ca. 650
Battle of Chalons—Partial victory of Aetius over Attila	451	Synod of Whitby—Triumph of Roman Catholicism over Celtic Christianity	664
Attila invades Italy	452		
Death of Attila	453	Charles Martel "mayor of the palace" in France	714–741
Murder of Aetius by Valentinian III	454	Pepin crowned king of the Franks (Pepin the Short)	754
Sack of Rome by Vandals under Gaeseric	455		

named Palmyra, and its queen, Zenobia. The middle classes and active peasants were progressively impoverished; it hardly seemed worth while to plant crops or to engage in any commercial activity when so little could be kept from the insatiable maw of the army. Near the frontiers the Germanic barbarians at times were able to enter the empire and plunder at will.

But at last a succession of emperors from Illyria was able to re-establish discipline in the armies. And though the greatest of these, Aurelian, was himself murdered (275) after enjoying only five years of supreme power, it was not before he had restored Asia to the empire, defeated the Parthians, brought Gaul back to her allegiance, and unified the old Roman Empire almost within her ancient boundaries, though the province of Dacia, added by Trajan, had been lost forever.

❖ Re-establishment of discipline— Totalitarianism

THE ESTABLISHMENT OF ABSOLUTE GOVERNMENT—DIOCLETIAN AND HIS ASSOCIATES

When Diocletian (285–305) became sole ruler of the empire in 285, having vanquished his only serious rival, he was faced with problems beyond the capacity of any ruler to solve. The years of anarchy had impoverished the middle classes to such an extent that desperate measures to ensure their continued service to the state and payment of taxes had already been put into effect; the industrial and agricultural workers were already being regimented in a similar manner. Trade had been meeting increasing difficulties, not only because of the insecurity of transport but because of constant depreciations of the currency. The Illyrian emperors had been driven to the expedient of inviting warlike barbarians to serve in the imperial armies for pay, and even in the ranks of the officers barbarians were rapidly becoming as frequent as Roman citizens. But at least these barbarians were usually willing to serve; and, being professional soldiers, they fought better than the peasantry of the earlier part of the

century and were better disciplined, not yet having grown to look upon the army as a privileged existence which entitled them to live indefinitely off the civilian economy without giving services in return. On the other hand, they owed no loyalty whatever to the empire. Serving for experience and pay alone, they were loyal to their paymaster the emperor, but to no one else.

Finally, there was no acceptable method of succession to the throne, and no apparent way of preventing usurpation by the strongest commander.

Diocletian, though in no sense an innovator, may justly be regarded as the refounder of the Roman Empire. The character of the empire he ruled was forever changed by the emphasis on strong, absolute government that was necessitated by the conditions of his age. But the empire itself survived as an institution in the West for almost two hundred years, while in the East its successor state, the Byzantine Empire, survived for more than a millennium, with institutions recognizably similar to those of Diocletian and Constantine I, the founder of Constantinople on the Bosporus.

Realizing that the administration of the empire and the defense of its boundaries against the increasingly dangerous barbarians were too much for one man, Diocletian invited Maximian, another Illyrian general, to act as his colleague in the empire, sharing the title of Augustus. Maximian and he then chose two seconds-in-command, with the title of Caesar. The two Augusti were to retire after twenty years in office, to be succeeded by the two Caesars, each then naming a Caesar who would in turn succeed him. Unfortunately, not all these potentates were as disinterested as Diocletian himself, nor were the sons of the Augusti willing to be discarded in favor of generals of greater experience, even under parental pressure. The scheme actually never worked at all except when Diocletian was able to compel the Augusti to keep to their agreement, and civil wars continued until Constantine (312–337) established for good the hereditary principle, in spite of the danger that the empire might fall into childish or incompetent hands.

The scheme of the two Augusti and the two

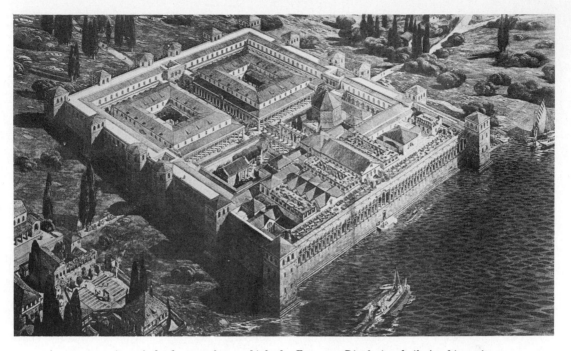

A reconstruction of the huge palace, which the Emperor Diocletian built for his retirement after he abdicated, at Split, Yugoslavia. (COURTESY YUGOSLAV STATE TOURIST OFFICE)

Caesars proved effective enough in Diocletian's own lifetime to enable him to put into effect the necessary administrative reforms that made the empire into what may reasonably be called a totalitarian state. The frontiers were guarded, a number of minor revolts were quelled, and the expanding Persian Empire was held in check.

Diocletian and Maximian as Augusti took divine titles, although they did not call themselves actual gods. They withdrew as much as possible from direct participation in public life, instituting an elaborate court ceremonial of an Oriental kind, including prostration and kissing the hem of the emperor's robe when the privilege of an audience was granted. The persecution of Christians which accompanied the elevation of the monarchy has been discussed in the last chapter. Many new temples were built to the old gods, while there was an insistence on greater observance of the imperial cult.

REORGANIZATION OF ARMY AND PROVINCES UNDER IMPERIAL CONTROL

Under Diocletian and Maximian the army was considerably enlarged; friendly barbarians were allowed to settle in frontier districts with an obligation to military service; companies of barbarians, sometimes even under their own chiefs, were welcomed. The more warlike sections of the empire provided further conscripted recruits; if not of high quality, their discipline and training were better than they had been for years. Diocletian also organized a force of picked men who could be moved from one part of the empire to another as danger threatened, helping to stiffen the resistance of the resident legions. The army was under the direct command of the emperor and his associates, who were all experienced generals, so that there was less opportunity for local armies to revolt and try to set up a new emperor.

The number of the provinces was increased by subdivision to 101, with every governor an appointee of one of the emperors. The governors were subject to control by vicars, who had about seven provinces (dioceses) each, and in their turn were responsible to four prefects, personal representatives of the four rulers. The vicars, however, had the right of direct appeal to Diocletian, as senior emperor, against decisions of the prefects. Thus was established a graded hierarchy responsible to the emperor and his associates alone.

It was clear at once that the expenses of the new administration could not be less than the old. The increased burden of the army and the building program could be met only by increased and more efficiently collected taxes. This necessarily entailed an increase in the unproductive army of imperial bureaucrats whose task it was to see that the taxes were paid. Diocletian's solution was simply to use his army and his bureaucrats, including secret police and paid informers, to ensure the collection, and hope to keep up the necessary agricultural and industrial production by all the legal weapons available to him.

REGIMENTATION OF PUBLIC AND PRIVATE LIFE

In all fields of activity Diocletian exercised compulsion when he deemed it necessary for the security of the state and the stabilization of production and finances. The free farmer was compelled to pay taxes based on the number of cultivators on his land and on the amount of land under cultivation, irrespective of its yield. By the time of Constantine he was forbidden to leave it. These *coloni*, as they were called, became virtual serfs, and in many cases sharecroppers, having lost their land to the privileged large landowners, many of whom became so powerful that they could avoid payment of taxes to the emperor. These men were the real beneficiaries of the imperial policy, and their large estates, or villas, survived the fall of the Roman Empire itself.

Since municipal magistrates had been made personally responsible for the collection of taxes in their areas, it was not unnatural that men who were eligible for the position should have attempted to escape the responsibility. Diocletian, however, compelled men of the necessary property qualifications to become magistrates, and to undertake the various financial obligations involved. Constantine laid the same obligation on all men belonging to the class eligible to hold magistracies. These *curiales*, as they were called, could not even escape by disposing of their property. Unable to escape from the im-

perial net, the class was gradually ground down until it virtually disappeared.

City workers were likewise organized into castes, each worker compelled to follow the trade of his father. Members of the *collegia* (guilds) were forbidden to change their occupation, and thus became a docile proletariat at the disposal of the emperor.

CONSTANTINE AND THE PERFECTING OF TOTALITARIANISM

Economic and military policy By the end of the reign of Constantine the totalitarian state was complete, and the hereditary caste system no longer had any loopholes in it. Each man was securely fixed in the position in which he had been born; and his obligation to fulfill his quota of work and provide a surplus for the ever more insatiable needs of the army was absolute. The police and the bureaucracy were ubiquitous in ferreting out any source of income, returning escapees to their duty, and requisitioning food and supplies when money was unavailable.

Constantine completed the barbarization of the army by carrying Diocletian's policies to their logical conclusion. The old frontier legions, which had been at least recruited from Roman citizens, even though they had been little enough influenced by Roman civilization, were now degraded to a local militia, and troops still drawn from the citizen body were made inferior in status to the German mercenaries. The real army was a mobile field army, recruited from the neighboring barbarians, chiefly the Germanic tribes in the West and the Sarmatians on the Danube. The elite corps of cavalry, the crack troops of the empire, were entirely composed of German mercenaries. It was possible for the foreign mercenaries to reach the highest position in the army and become *magistri militum*, or masters of the troops. From the time of Constantine onward, and especially in the fifth century, we find German masters of the troops far more powerful than their puppets who wore the purple and were still called emperors. As a rule, the barbarian leaders did not aspire to the throne themselves—a possible reason for their appointment to the supreme military position. This army, at least in the hands of Constantine, was the most efficient instrument the Romans had possessed in centuries for its two primary purposes—the defense against unauthorized barbarian immigration and armed attacks, and the enforcement of discipline upon the civilians who paid for its upkeep. Always increasing as defense needs grew more imperious, it devoured the substance of the civil population, laying its heavy, unproductive hand upon all enterprise until the Roman Empire collapsed from within under the impact of foreign peoples with a population almost certainly far short of its own. But the army at least served to introduce many of the most able barbarians to the civilization of the empire, which trained them and gave them military experience—an experience turned by many of them in later years against the empire itself.

New Rome on the Bosporus   The most significant act of the reign of Constantine was the founding of a new capital near the incomparable site of ancient Byzantium on the Bosporus at the entrance to the Black Sea. This city, called Constantinople, quickly grew to surpass Rome. The eastern provinces of the empire, though equally ground down by taxation, never sank to the level of the more agricultural West. Some cities still prospered and trade continued, if less luxuriantly than in the past. It was certainly for this reason that Constantine founded his new capital in the midst of this area. The western provinces hardly served to support themselves and their defense, whereas the defense needs in the East were not so vast. Moreover, the provinces provided some surplus for luxuries appreciated by the now entirely Orientalized court of the first Christian monarch.

Constantinople was also a port, which Rome had never been; it could be made impregnable by sea and it was strongly fortified by land. Not very far from the capital was the river Danube, more easily defended than the distant Rhine. Time and again the barbarians threatened the Danube, and on some occasions they crossed it and reached almost to Constantinople. But, faced with the formidable bastion of the city itself, they realized they could hardly conquer it with their crude weapons.

Constantine himself ruled over the united empire, and he ensured the succession of his sons to the throne. But he realized the empire was too vast for efficient rule by one man; since he had two sons, he divided it between them. Thereafter, though in theory they were co-emperors of the whole, the empire was in fact divided between two emperors, one resident in Constantinople, the other with an official residence in Rome, but more often living in Milan, Trier, or Ravenna.

❖   **External dangers to the empire— The barbarians**

Little has been said up to this point of the uncivilized peoples who lived beyond the boundaries of the empire. These peoples, known to the Romans as barbarians, had always been a threat to the empire. Some had penetrated into Italy and even defeated occasional Roman armies long before the fall of the republic. Others had pressed into the empire in the second century A.D. and compelled the Stoic emperor Marcus Aurelius to spend much of his reign in military operations which he detested. By the end of the fourth century most of these peoples were on the move—the Germans call the barbarian invasions simply *Völkerwanderung*, wanderings of the folk—sometimes pressed from behind by Asiatic peoples such as the Huns. Moving westward, they necessarily came up against the defended boundaries of the Roman Empire, and were compelled either to fight or make terms with the Romans. They certainly had no desire to conquer the Roman Empire. Indeed, all evidence suggests that they admired the empire and were attracted by its culture.

Most of the Romans, on the other hand, despised the barbarians as uncivilized, although Roman military men had a wholesome respect for their fighting abilities. They were therefore usually willing to admit limited numbers into their own armed forces, but wished to control the immigration of their wives and families, and above all maintain their frontiers intact and never allow wholesale immigration. As the empire became internally weaker, however, they found themselves unable to maintain the frontiers, especially in the West, and they had need of military aid wherever they could find it. A partly Romanized barbarian often was willing to defend his new masters even against the people to whom he had formerly belonged, and in time the Roman armies became composed predominantly of barbarians. On the other hand the Eastern, or Byzantine, Empire (after the old name of the capital, Byzantium), being internally stronger, was able to control barbarian infiltration better than the West, and on some occasions Byzantine emperors were able to persuade barbarian leaders to move westward, thus saving their own territories at the expense of the West.

As among all primitive peoples, the basic unit of the German invaders was the family, and a number of families composed a clan or tribe. The clan had a hereditary chieftain who was the leader in war and peace. There was also a tribal assembly of all free men, who met in council to discuss policies suggested by the chief. If they agreed, they showed their assent by clashing their shields. In later times many tribes would unite under a king; as a rule, when the Romans came in contact with them, it was with the king they had to negotiate.

The most distinctive organization among the German barbarians was the *comitatus*, or league of companions. In a fighting people it was to be expected that powerful warriors would sometimes arise who held no hereditary position. These men would attract around themselves others who looked to them for leadership. They fought together, and if necessary died together. The leader looked first to the needs of his men, and they in turn were bound to him by the strongest ties of loyalty. In this institution we evidently have the germ of the later feudal relationship between lords and the vassals who were tied to them by an oath of fealty, and who owed military service to them.

The men of the German tribes spent most of their lives fighting or looking after the animals. The women stayed home and looked after the household, while the slaves, who had some personal freedom though tied to the land, looked after such crops as the tribes possessed. Since they were not closely attached to any piece of land, it was not difficult for whole tribes or

nations to migrate, either in search of better pastures or cropland or from simple restlessness. None of the Germanic peoples had moved very far from the nomadic life; whereas other barbarian peoples who now began to endanger the empire were still truly nomads. Some of these, especially the Huns, pushed the more settled peoples before them and, as a result, set an even larger migration in motion.

The invasions themselves need not detain us long. Late in the fourth century the Asiatic Huns began to move westward into Europe, forcing the Germans to press ever more strongly against the Roman frontiers. One group of barbarians, the Ostrogoths (East Goths) were penned into an area close to the Black Sea; another, the Visigoths (West Goths) crossed the Danube and killed an emperor of Constantinople in battle. They were finally persuaded to move off toward the West, leaving a minority permanently ensconced within the Byzantine boundaries. This minority, however, was small enough to be "digested" by the Byzantines without ill effect. Another group of Visigoths, under Alaric, sacked Rome in the early fifth century, but when Alaric died soon afterward, the Goths retired without conquering Italy. During the fifth century the bulk of the Visigoths settled in Spain.

The Vandals, whose name became a byword for later generations because of the destruction they wrought in Gaul and their subsequent sack of Rome, passed through Spain and made a permanent settlement in North Africa. A few years later (451) Attila and his Huns invaded Gaul. Here he was turned back by a predominantly barbarian army led by a Roman general. The following year Attila invaded Italy, but did not take Rome. When he died soon afterward the Hunnish hosts disintegrated, leaving the Germanic groups masters of Europe and facing a greatly weakened Rome. The emperors had retired to Ravenna in northeastern Italy, leaving the pope in charge of their former capital. Barbarian generals were now in command of the armies still called Roman, but it was clearly only a matter of time before some general would decide to capture Rome and depose the shadowy emperor at Ravenna. This was accomplished in 476 by a Herulian named Odoacer, who did

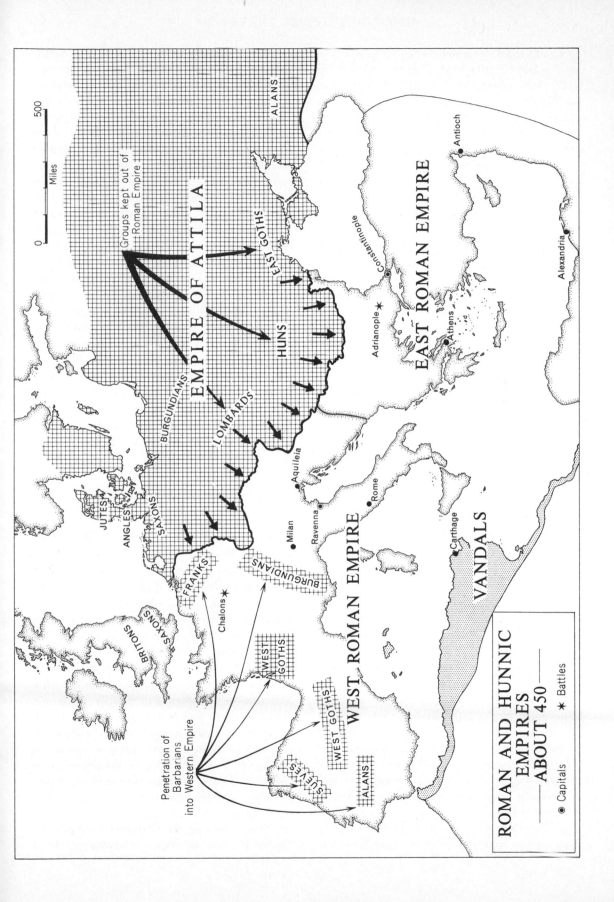

ROMAN AND HUNNIC
EMPIRES
—— ABOUT 450 ——

● Capitals   ★ Battles

WEST ROMAN EMPIRE

EAST ROMAN EMPIRE

EMPIRE OF ATTILA

VANDALS

Penetration of
Barbarians
into Western Empire

Groups kept out of
Roman Empire

ALANS

EAST GOTHS

HUNS

BURGUNDIANS

LOMBARDS

JUTES

ANGLES

SAXONS

BRITONS

SAXONS

FRANKS

BURGUNDIANS

Chalons ★

WEST
GOTHS

WEST GOTHS

SUEVES

ALANS

Antioch

Alexandria

Constantinople

Adrianople ★

Athens

Milan

Ravenna

Aquileia

Rome

Carthage

Miles

0   500

not long enjoy his conquest. In 493 the Ostrogoths, freed from the Hun menace, penetrated into Italy under the command of Theodoric, a Byzantine-trained general, and established a kingdom in Italy. Meanwhile the Franks had moved into Gaul, and under their king, Clovis, were engaged in consolidating their rule in that thoroughly Romanized province.

Thus, by the turn of the sixth century, the Vandals were ensconced in North Africa, the Visigoths in Spain, the Franks in Gaul, the Ostrogoths in Italy and Illyria, and the Angles and Saxons in much of England, which had been abandoned by the Romans at the beginning of the fifth century. Other groups, notably the Burgundians in southeastern Gaul, had smaller areas under their control, and were intermingled with the above-named barbarians in all the provinces of the former Roman Empire, as were the Romans themselves. The latter were now in a minority, save in Italy; and though, as we shall see, Roman institutions long survived the fall of the empire, the character of Western European government was for the future to be determined by the Germanic invaders rather than the Romans.

❖ The barbarian kingdoms—Italy

We have already noted that Theodoric established an Ostrogothic kingdom in Italy. During the reign of Theodoric (493–526), Italy knew a period of good government such as she had not known for centuries. The Roman administration of government and justice was maintained; the Senate remained, on the whole, loyal to the king; and taxes were drastically reduced, since there was no longer the need for them. Agriculture and commerce revived; even private enterprise began to reappear. Theodoric dredged the harbors, rebuilt aqueducts, and restored the cities as far as he could with his limited means. No longer having a vast empire to maintain, and with a greatly reduced population to support, Italy became the self-supporting territory she had always had it in her power to be.

The king was content to acknowledge the theoretical overlordship of the surviving emperor at Constantinople; and though he was in the eyes of the pope an Arian heretic, as were all his people, he maintained correct relations with the pontiff, and made no attempt to convert his orthodox Roman Catholic subjects to Arianism. There was even a brief revival of culture in his reign, with the two great scholars Boethius and Cassiodorus the chief ornaments. Boethius, foreseeing correctly the loss of all Greek culture in the West under the barbarian monarchies, spent much of his life translating the logical works of Aristotle into Latin. He also wrote textbooks based on the dying Greek knowledge, but suitable for the barbarians and barbarized Romans who alone would remain to study them. Unfortunately, he was suspected of treasonable designs against the throne and was cast into prison. There he wrote the *Consolations of Philosophy*, which has been read ever since, and was especially popular in the Middle Ages. Ultimately he was executed by order of Theodoric. Cassiodorus, however, long outlived the Gothic king, supervising the translating and copying of manuscripts in a monastery which he founded on his own estate. He also wrote a *History of the Goths*.

RECONQUEST OF ITALY BY THE BYZANTINE EMPIRE

Italian policy of Justinian Theodoric's kingdom, however, did not survive his death. It was evidently only his personality that held it together. Civil war disrupted the kingdom, the succession, as so often in the Germanic kingdoms, being disputed between several contestants; in 535, Justinian, the emperor of the East, decided that the time was ripe for the restoration of the old Roman Empire. Justinian was also a strong zealot for the orthodox faith, as long as he was allowed to interpret it himself. In the laudable aim of extinguishing Arianism, he had the moral support of the papacy in Rome, plus whatever more tangible support it could give him—at least until the popes recognized that Justinian's authoritarianism extended to the field of religion as well.

Destruction of the Ostrogothic kingdom— Economic and strategic consequences In a

EAST ROMAN EMPIRE AND
GERMANIC KINGDOMS
AT THE DEATH OF THEODORIC-526 A.D.

long-drawn-out and ruinously expensive war, Justinian's generals, Belisarius and Narses, reconquered Italy piecemeal. Behind them came the imperial bureaucracy and the tax collectors from whom the fortunate Italians had been free for a generation. The Ostrogothic nation resisted to the last, and was virtually destroyed. Italy was devastated. Twenty years of warfare, in which neither side showed any mercy, was the final crippling blow to a country which had been able to recover from so many in the past. From this latest invasion she did not recover for centuries.

Justinian, leaving an *exarch*, an imperial official, to rule Italy from Ravenna on his be-

half, and a pope grateful for his orthodoxy but disliking intensely his autocratic manner of dealing with spiritual matters, turned his attention to other affairs. He died soon afterward, having saddled his empire with a territory almost useless for exploitation, and incapable of self-defense against any barbarian horde that wished to enter.

INVASION OF ITALY BY LOMBARDS (568)—PARTITION OF ITALY

The Lombard conquests (568–605) A new invasion was not long in coming. Justinian had not been in his grave three years before the

Lombards, another Germanic people, but by far the least civilized of any that had hitherto penetrated into Southern Europe—nominally Arians but in fact nearer to heathenism—swept into Northern Italy, where there was no one left to oppose them. This time they made no compromises with the emperor, nor were they interested in Roman civilization. The Italians lost their estates, which were simply sequestrated by the Lombards. Northern Italy was consolidated under their rule in seven years, and they began to push southward. The exarch of Ravenna maintained his stronghold, still theoretically the ruler of Italy under the emperor; but neither he nor the rest of Italy could obtain any support from the various emperors of Constantinople, who were fully engaged elsewhere. Nor did the emperors give any aid to the other isolated areas in Italy under their nominal rule.

The Lombards had united only for conquest and plunder. They had no partially civilized king, such as Theodoric had been. Their leaders (dukes) took what Italian land they could, and kept it for themselves. By 605 all Italy except Ravenna, Naples, Rome, and parts of the extreme south were in their hands.

Remnants of Byzantine rule What remained to the empire from the warfare of Justinian was the isolated and relatively useless Ravenna, and the south. Rome acknowledged the overlordship of Constantinople on the principle that a distant overlord is better than a local one, especially if he is powerless to intervene. Since such acknowledgment carried with it no obligation to obedience, the popes were content to give it for centuries to come.

The pope of Rome was now at last in fact its temporal ruler. He was the spiritual lord of all Christendom, the owner of many scattered estates in Italy which had been given to the Church in the troubled times, and the defender of Rome against the barbarian Lombards, from whom he had managed to keep his city intact.

Position of the papacy—Gregory I *(590–604)* This achievement was the work of one man—one of the greatest of the popes, a Roman by descent, a saint, and a gifted administrator and diplomatist—Gregory I, the Great.

It is possible that the Lombards, vastly superior in numbers as they were, could have taken Rome by force if they had united against it. But they seem to have respected the person of the pope, and perhaps the sanctity of the city, in spite of the fact that they were only nominal Christians, and a heretical sect at that. At all events, they never made any serious effort to do so, perhaps in part because of their internal disunity. Thus for centuries the popes were able to exist, often isolated and always precariously, until they were rescued in the eighth century by the orthodox Frankish kings. Gregory, who had at an earlier stage in his life been an official agent of the papacy in Constantinople, knew how useless it was to look for help from this quarter. He therefore accepted the position, negotiating directly with the Lombards. The emperor continued to bid him resist, and for many years refused to accept his arrangements. Ultimately, the empire recognized the conquests; and Gregory, through the negotiations, was allowed to keep his city and the territory around it.

Perhaps the most important of Gregory's work was his insistence that all the clergy of Europe should obey the papacy and receive instructions from it. He was not very successful in France, where the appointment of the clergy was largely in the hands of the Merovingian kings, but the bishops nevertheless listened to him with respect, and later popes could quote Gregory as authority for their own claims. Newly converted Spain and England accepted the overlordship of the papacy from the first. Wherever there were orthodox clergy in Italy, they too accepted his supremacy. Though Gregory could not actually alter the domination of the Church by the state in Constantinople, he constantly repeated his claim that all the Eastern bishops and the patriarch of Constantinople were subordinate to the Holy See by virtue of the Petrine supremacy. In all these things he gave a lead to the popes who followed him. For, though the practice of appointing bishops by lay rulers was never abandoned in France and Germany, and discipline could hardly be enforced, the clergy nevertheless did look to the papacy for guidance in spiritual affairs when they felt the need for it. This dependence

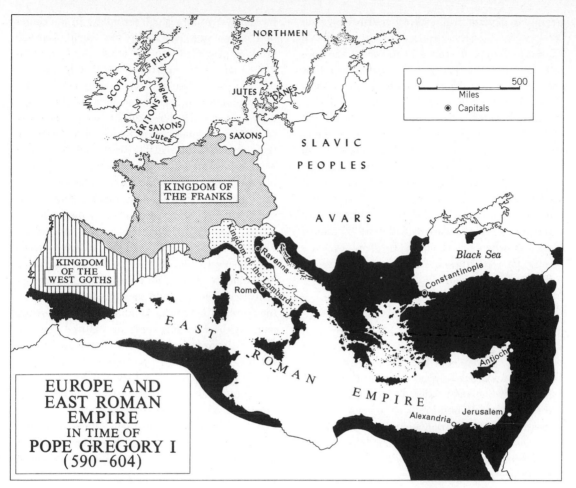

EUROPE AND
EAST ROMAN
EMPIRE
IN TIME OF
POPE GREGORY I
(590–604)

largely remained even when the papacy fell into weak hands, and when Constantinople and the Eastern Empire drifted entirely away from papal rule.

❖ **Conquest of Gaul by Clovis—
The Merovingian kingdom**

Like the other Germanic peoples who entered the Roman Empire in the fifth century, the Franks had no unified leadership. In 481, however, a young prince named Clovis became the ruler of one small kingdom clustered around the modern Tournai. Able and ambitious, he began to expand his kingdom to the south by judicious murders, treachery, and open warfare. France at the time was peopled by Visigoths, Burgundians, Alemanni, as well as the old Gallo-Romans, including a Gallic noble who called

himself king of Rome. Defeating this pretender first, Clovis then drove the Alemanni back across the Rhine into Germany (to which they gave their name, Allemagne in the French language) and incorporated their kingdom into his; then he turned south and drove the Visigothic remnants into Spain to join their fellow tribesmen; and at last, having disposed also of his fellow Frankish kings, he consolidated a kingdom not much smaller than present-day France (481–511).

CONVERSION OF CLOVIS TO ORTHODOX
CATHOLICISM

Clovis, as it happened, had a Christian wife, Clotilda, who was orthodox and not Arian. After his victories he allowed himself to be converted by her clerical adviser and with him his Franks, who thus became the first barbarian group to deviate from the otherwise universal Arianism. Publicly baptized at Reims by a Catholic bishop, by this act he gained the support of the entire clergy of France, who now rallied to his aid. This was no mean help, since they controlled what was left of the old Gallo-Roman administration, while the remainder of the old Gallo-Roman population, also orthodox Christians, offered Clovis at least their moral support. From this time onward the Frankish monarchy remained the papal favorite among secular powers, and it was to the Franks that the papacy looked for help and military aid when it became involved with the Lombard kings, or when its official overlord in Constantinople showed himself unable or unwilling to provide effective aid.

MEROVINGIAN KINGDOM

After the death of Clovis his kingdom, according to Germanic custom, was divided among his four sons, who spent most of their lives fighting against each other. They did, however, unite against all non-Frankish outsiders, consolidating their total dominions by the addition of almost all the remainder of modern France. The Merovingian kingdom (418–754, so called after Meroveus, grandfather of Clovis) was sometimes under the rule of one member of the family and sometimes subdivided. But until the eighth century at least one of Clovis' descendants occupied the throne, though in later years the authority of the kings was only nominal. The real power was in the hands of hereditary officials, chief stewards, who are usually, and incorrectly, called mayors of the palace (*major domus*). Ultimately, as we shall see, one of these officials deposed his titular master with papal approval and became king of the Franks himself.

It is difficult to generalize about the state of the country in Merovingian times. Some of Gaul had been thoroughly Romanized, and remained so, even under alien monarchs. On the whole, it can be said that the Latin element tended to prevail. The French language has barely four hundred words of Germanic origin, all the remainder being of Latin origin. Much of Roman law and even of the Roman govern-

mental system remained, especially in the center and the south, while in the north German customs prevailed. On the other hand, the barbaric habits of the kings, their addiction to murder—wholesale and retail, their lack of care for commerce and trade so long as they were able to have the Oriental luxuries, especially of dress and ornament, in which they delighted, their general propensity to treat their territories as if they were private estates to be exploited for their own gain, and their failure to control the rapacity of local, semi-independent chiefs called counts—all these tended to push the unhappy country further into barbarism, which historians have politely called a fusion between German and Gallo-Roman culture. This fusion undoubtedly existed, and the result, after many centuries, was the modern kingdom of France, far more Latin than Germanic—in this showing once again how the superior culture tends to absorb the inferior. The best that can be said for the Merovingian monarchy is that, by providing government of a sort and by not interfering too drastically with institutions they were incapable of understanding and with a culture that meant nothing to them, they preserved France for a brighter future when the Dark Ages which had fallen on all Europe should at last come to an end.

❖ England, Spain, North Africa

Finally, a few words should be said about the other barbarian kingdoms. When the Romans left England, they laid open the way for invasion by the Celts, who had been kept in check by Roman forces. But the Celts were not to become the Roman successors. Angles, Saxons, and Jutes soon entered England from Scandinavia and Germany, driving the various Celtic peoples back into Wales and Scotland, which are still largely peopled today by their descendants. England was converted by missionaries sent from Rome by Pope Gregory I, and by Irish missionaries who had lost contact with Rome and practiced a somewhat different form of Christianity. The Roman faith, however, ultimately triumphed, and England became one of the most loyal of Catholic countries. In the ninth century England had to submit to Danish rule for a period, but on the whole it was perhaps the most successful of the Germanic kingdoms, although not united into a single kingdom until the time of Alfred the Great in the ninth century. In the eleventh century the Danes again conquered the kingdom, but the crown reverted once more to an Englishman, Edward the Confessor (1054–1066). In spite of the Norman conquest that followed the latter's death, the predominantly Anglo-Saxon makeup of the people persisted, making England the most nearly Germanic of the countries peopled by the barbarian invaders.

The Visigothic kingdom of Spain remained under Gothic rule until the eighth century, when it was conquered by the Muslims. A small part in the south remained under Byzantine control for a short period, and some sections of the north never submitted to Muslim rule. The Vandal kingdom of North Africa was captured in the early sixth century by Justinian, who converted it into a Byzantine province which fell to the Muslims a century later.

❖ **The end of an era**

With the fall of the Roman Empire we reach the end of an era. Though the successor state in the East, the Byzantine Empire, survived for almost a thousand years longer, its civilization was so different from the old Roman Empire that it will be discussed separately in the next chapter.

The achievements of Greco-Roman civilization were far from lost, even in the West; but the destruction of its political system and the decline of its culture as a living creative force threw Europe into a condition of political, social, and cultural degradation which used to be called the Dark Ages. If these centuries are not believed by modern scholars to be as dark as earlier historians thought them, the term remains not altogether inappropriate. It was a period of fermentation which ultimately proved to have in it the potentiality for new life and creativity; but while the fermentation was in process life was dark indeed, and no one could have foretold what would arise from it.

The conditions which made possible the Greek and Roman achievements had disappeared—as it proved, forever. The Roman Empire had survived as long as it had because it was able to make use of the old city-state culture which was the distinctive achievement of the Greeks. The empire had succeeded in the one field in which the Greeks had failed; it had provided a political framework under which the ruinous intercity warfare was no longer possible. But the later empire had destroyed the basis for its own government when, by relentless pressure, it undermined the ability of the cities to survive as independent entities. It was not possible to force them to produce in the same way they had produced under their own impetus; and though the peasant has always been ready to work his land under the most tyrannous oppression, either by landlords or by monarchs, Europe was too vast to treat as if it were an Egypt. No emperor could be strong enough to keep every landlord in Europe directly subject to him and obedient to his orders. No basis therefore remained for absolute government; the army could not be maintained when the cities and peasants refused to work. The army was merely an instrument for compulsion; it could not itself produce.

With the destruction of the cities, land alone remained; and for the next few centuries the rule of Europe was in the hands of landlords, sometimes nominally subject to monarchs, but actually exercising almost independent control of comparatively small areas which were not beyond their capacity to rule. With the subsequent rise of cities, it again became possible for monarchs to use their aid to subject the landlords to control. But never in subsequent history have any European monarchs been able to exercise permanent rule over territories as extensive and diverse as those of the Roman Empire.

This is not to say that this fact was ever accepted by contemporaries. To the people who could remember, or whose institutions had been formed by the Roman Empire, it seemed that the natural form of government was a huge universal state ruled by an emperor who, at least according to Christian thought, was responsible to God, or perhaps to God's spiritual representative on earth, the pope. Many were the efforts made to restore it, both in the form of a revived empire and in the form of a spiritual rule of Christendom by the Roman pontiff. But all were destined to fail.

There was no restoration of the Roman Empire, either by secular or by religious powers. It had served its purpose in history. Its achievements had been many: It had given to the Western world its first long experience of peace; it had spread Greek culture, with its ability to deal with abstract thought, its thirst for experimentation and explanation, and its tendency to think of life in terms of this world; and it had itself introduced mankind to the idea that each human being has rights which should be embodied in a law which ought to be just, clear, and not arbitrary, and as far as possible in accordance with what man could discover about the Divine Reason. It had given hospitality to an Oriental religion which gave man hope of a blessed hereafter, and explained this life as a proving ground for a world to come; and it has been contended that it also laid the impress of its own thought on the ancient Hebrew idea of man's atonement for sin by making it into a contract between man and God, with salvation as the reward. It certainly gave the organization of the Church as a gift to this religion. It provided a language for the Church which could be understood throughout Europe, and which has remained its chosen language to this day.

If little that was authentically Roman survived outside the Church in the Dark Ages, Roman and Greek rationalism was not lost forever. When the human mind awakened again—when, with Anselm, it was first found necessary to *prove* the existence of God—the process was set in motion that led to modern Western civilization. And in this the work of the Greeks and Romans, gradually recovered and assimilated, had no mean share.

Suggestions for further reading

PAPER-BOUND BOOKS

Bede, The Venerable. *The History of the English Church and People*. Penguin. The finest historical work of the seventh century, by an English monk.

Boethius. *The Consolation of Philosophy*. Ungar and Liberal Arts Press. A dialogue concerning the merits and values of philosophy written when the author was in prison awaiting his execution by Theodoric.

Bury, J. B. *The Later Roman Empire*. 2 vols. Dover. The pioneer work in English on the period, also covers early Byzantium to the death of Justinian. Not all interpretations now acceptable, but the work should be known.

Dawson, Christopher. *The Making of Europe*. Meridian. This popular book by a Catholic historian is excellent on the heritage of the Roman Empire. In the later chapters he sees more light in the "Dark Ages" than is commonly acknowledged.

Dill, Samuel. *Roman Society in the Last Century of the Western Empire*. Meridian. A classic, especially valuable for its long quotations from contemporary writers who were ignorant of the impending fall of the Empire.

Duckett, Eleanor S. *Alfred the Great: the King and His England*. Phoenix. By a fine medieval scholar, very familiar with the few sources available for the period. By the same author, two volumes entitled *The Gateway to the Middle Ages* (Ann Arbor) deal with France and Britain, and Italy separately. Especially good for use of literary sources, showing interaction between Romans and barbarians.

Gibbon, Edward. *Barbarism and the Fall of Rome*. Vol. II of *The Decline and Fall of the Roman Empire*. Collier. The section of Gibbon's eighteenth-century rationalist masterpiece printed in this paper-bound edition may whet the student's appetite for more. To be treated cautiously as history. The interpretation is one-sided, but the book is still part of every man's literary education.

Kagan, Donald. *Decline and Fall of the Roman Empire; Why Did It Collapse?* Heath. Contains judicious extracts from several modern historians from Gibbon onward stating the various points of view on this most controversial of subjects.

Katz, Solomon. *The Decline of Rome and the Rise of Medieval Europe*. Cornell University Press. Brief treatment.

Lot, Ferdinand. *The End of the Ancient World and the Beginning of the Middle Ages*. Torchbooks. The most adequate analytical account in English of the fall of the Empire and the establishment of successor states.

Tacitus. *On Britain and Germany*, trans. by H.

Mattingly. Penguin. Contains the *Agricola* and *Germania*, the last named our only important literary source for early Germany.

Taylor, Henry Osborn. *The Emergence of Christian Culture in the West*. Torchbooks. By a sympathetic American cultural historian, author of the masterpiece *The Medieval Mind*, discussed under Chapter 12.

Whitelock, Dorothy. *The Beginnings of English Society*. Penguin. A competent survey of Anglo-Saxon England.

HARD-COVER BOOKS

Dill, Samuel. *Roman Society in Gaul in the Merovingian Age*. New York: The Macmillan Company, 1926. Exhaustive study of Merovingian society rather than an analysis of the remnants of Roman culture in Frankland.

Gregory of Tours. *History of the Franks*, trans. with an introd. by O. M. Dalton. New York: Oxford University Press, 1927. Colorful account by an observant Merovingian bishop on which all historians have had to rely for the social and political history of the time.

Moss, H. St. L. B. *The Birth of the Middle Ages, 395–814*. Oxford, England: The Clarendon Press, 1935. Good, brief general picture of the last period of the Empire, the barbarian invasions, and the new European states, written with admirable clarity.

Rostovtzeff, M. L. *Social and Economic History of the Roman Empire*. See suggestions for further reading at end of Chapter 5.

EIGHT

Successor States of the East— Byzantine and Muslim Empires

❖ **Constantine and his successors— The heritage of despotism**

When Constantine founded New Rome on the Bosporus in 330 A.D., he was certainly motivated by the desire to have a capital that was not simply an overgrown city-state like Rome, which had none of the requisites of an imperial capital except history and tradition. Constantinople, it is true, lacked both history and tradition; but it was capable of becoming a great seaport, it had an incomparable site, and communications by sea and land could be constructed which would unite it with all those provinces in the empire which were worth retaining. Though Constantine and his early successors were not yet ready to abandon the West to its fate, when the barbarians became too strong to be prevented from settling in the empire, the rulers in Constantinople contented themselves with preserving the Eastern provinces. This territory was far more manageable than the ramshackle Roman Empire. Although the Byzantine rulers continued to pretend that they ruled a "Roman" empire, and it pleased them to call themselves Romans (spelling the word in the Greek language), in fact it was a Greek empire that they ruled, Greek and not Roman in culture and language. The only distinctively Roman contribution was that of law and administration, which had proved itself superior to anything the Hellenistic rulers of the East had evolved for

themselves prior to the Roman conquest. Indeed, from the Byzantine point of view, the new empire based on Constantinople might well have been thought of as the revival of the Greek (Hellenistic) rule of the Near East, after an unfortunate interlude of a few centuries of submission to the barbarian Romans, who, through their superior military might, had kept control of land rightfully Greek ever since the time of Alexander.

There was in fact in Constantinople little that was derived from earlier Roman tradition, nothing from the days of the free Roman Republic, and almost nothing from the days of the principate. What was inherited by the Byzantines was the despotic rule of Diocletian and of Constantine—the control by the state of all phases of life and activity within the empire, the Oriental tradition of absolute obedience to, and worship of, the emperors, as systematized by Diocletian, and the late Roman notion that "the pleasure of the emperor has the force of law." The idea of the absolute supremacy of the emperor extended also into the relations between Church and State in the Byzantine Empire. The chief official of the Church in the empire was the patriarch of Constantinople, appointed by the emperor and deriving his power from him. Although at times in Byzantine history the patriarch after his appointment opposed his master, he was always subject to dismissal. He was not, like the popes in Rome, chosen, at least in theory, by the clergy, and after appointment responsible only to God. Thus the Byzantine emperor, through his patriarch, had much more authority in the realm of religion than any ruler in the West was accorded by the pope, even though Western rulers sometimes assumed it.

The Byzantine heritage of absolutism, which persisted as long as Constantinople remained independent, was taken over on the one side by the Ottoman Turks, who captured Constantinople in 1453, and on the other by the tsars of Russia, who acquired almost all their cultural and governmental traditions from Constantinople. Subsequent Russian history cannot be understood without reference to the Byzantine heritage, any more than the organization and history of the Roman Catholic Church can be understood without reference to the Roman imperial tradition which it inherited; and if the cultural and religious history of the Balkan peninsula is to be understood, it must always be remembered that the Slavic peoples of the peninsula were civilized by Constantinople, adhered to the Church that was centered in Constantinople, and maintained their religion and culture even through the long centuries during which it was ruled by the Muslims and Ottoman Turks.

STRENGTHS AND WEAKNESSES OF THE BYZANTINE EMPIRE

The Byzantine Empire survived for more than a thousand years, largely by reason of the strength of its economy. Despite being taxed heavily and saddled with an expensive bureaucracy, the empire was honeycombed with prosperous cities. Though there were many state monopolies, there was considerable scope for private enterprise. Constantinople was a center of industry, as Rome had never been. If one became rich, one paid heavy taxes; but, at least, with the surplus, life could be made more pleasant. There were luxuries to be bought, there were innumerable forms of entertainment, new and old, especially horse and chariot racing in the Hippodrome in Constantinople. The bureaucracy was not permitted to grow beyond reasonable bounds; and though at times it was

corrupt, it was usually efficient, and most of the emperors kept it in firm control. In spite of intrigues over the imperial succession, numerous foreign wars, rule by dissolute women and incompetent and irresponsible men, the state never went bankrupt in all its history; several times it was even able to produce an effective ruler from most unpromising sources, just when to an outsider it would have seemed that all was lost.

Although the state was in danger successively from the Persians, the early Muslims, and the Bulgars, and the territories of the empire were sometimes so contracted that the capital was almost the only great city left in Byzantine control, Constantinople nevertheless was not conquered until the Western crusaders took it by treachery in 1204. Even then the Greeks had sufficient strength to recapture it in 1261 and give it another lease on life until the final conquest by the Turks.

Perhaps the greatest source of Byzantine strength, in comparison with the Roman Empire, was the refusal of the Byzantine rulers to be tempted by imperial expansion. On the whole their wars were defensive in nature—attempts, largely successful, to hold on to what they had inherited from Rome. Although they lost Egypt and Palestine to the Muslims in the seventh century and never recovered them, they were able to push the Muslims back from Constantinople and recover Anatolia, which was far more important to them. The great exception to the rule of defensive wars was the effort to reconquer Italy, undertaken by Justinian (527–565)—an effort whose very success was to prove nearly disastrous in a later age. Justinian's generals succeeded in destroying the relatively civilized Ostrogothic kingdom of Italy, and in subjecting Italy for a brief period to Byzantine rule. They also destroyed the Vandal kingdom of North Africa, and acquired a toehold in Spain. But a few years after the death of Justinian the Lombards invaded Italy, leaving the Byzantines only a few remnants of their domains in the south, the exarchate of Ravenna, and the theoretical overlordship of Rome. Justinian's neglect of the northeastern frontiers of his state, and his payment of tribute to the growing Persian Empire to stave off invasion,

Chronological Chart

Foundation of Constantinople	330	Reign of Leo III (the Isaurian)	717–740
Theodosius the Great last emperor of East and West	379–395	Beginning of the iconoclastic controversy	726
Reign of Justinian	527–565	Conquest of Georgia by Muslims	727–733
Corpus juris civilis of Justinian	533	Battle of "Tours"	732
Conquest of North Africa	533–543	End of the Ommeyad caliphate	750
Conquest of Italy	535–554	Abbassid caliphate	750–1258
Great Persian War	540–562	Conquest of exarchate of Ravenna by Lombards	751
Fifty years' peace with Persia— Justinian to pay tribute	562	Defeat of Lombards by Pepin the Short, king of the Franks	754–756
Loss of Italian possessions to Lombards (except Rome, Ravenna, and Naples)	568–571	Independent Ommeyad dynasty under Abdu-r-Rahman in Spain	755
Birth of Mahomet	570	Ommeyad caliphate in Spain (Cordova)	756–1031
Reign of Heraclius	610–641	Donation of Pepin of Lombard (Byzantine) lands to pope	756
"Flight" of Mahomet from Mecca to Medina	622	Reign of Charlemagne in the West	768–814
Persian Wars of Heraclius	622–630	Caliphate of Harun-al-Rashid	785–809
Organization of the commonwealth of Islam in Medina	622–630	Peace between Byzantines and Charlemagne (Byzantines retaining southern Italy, Venice, and Dalmatia)	803
Return to Mecca of Mahomet	630		
Death of Mahomet	632	End of iconoclastic controversy; image worship restored	843
Caliphate of Abu Bekr	632–634	Fatimid dynasty of Egypt	968–1171
Caliphate of Omar	634–644	Bulgaria incorporated into Byzantine Empire	1018
Conquest of Syria by Muslims under Khalid	635–641	Final schism between Rome and Constantinople	1054
Conquest of Persia by Muslims	635–641	Capture of Bagdad by Seljuk Turks	1055
Conquest of Egypt by Muslims	639–655	Reign of Alexius Comnenus	1081–1118
Conquest and slow subjugation of North Africa	643–711	The First Crusade	1096–1097
Ommeyad caliphate founded by Moawiya	661	Latin Conquest of Constantinople (Fourth Crusade)	1204
Blockade of Constantinople by Muslims	673–678	Latin Kingdom of Constantinople	1204–1261
Thirty years' peace concluded between Byzantines and Muslims	678	Capture and sack of Bagdad by Mongols, execution of last Abbassid caliph	1258
Conquest of Carthage by Muslims	698	Reconquest of Constantinople by Michael VIII	1261
Conquest of Transoxania and part of Turkestan by Muslims	705–712	Rise of the Ottoman Turks in Asia Minor	1326
Conquest of Punjab by Muslims	708–715		
Conquest of Spain by Muslims	711–715	Serbs under Stephen Dushan at the gates of Constantinople	1355
Invasions of southern France	715 onward		
Second siege of Constantinople by Muslims	717–718		

Siege of Constantinople by Turks under Bayazid I	1391–1397	Siege and Capture of Constantinople by Ottoman Turks	1453
Defeat of Turks by Tamerlane at battle of Angora	1402	Marriage of Ivan III, Grand Duke of Moscow, to Zoë, niece of last emperor of Constantinople —Ivan takes title of Tsar, and	
Council of Florence—Agreement by Byzantine emperor to religious union with Rome	1439	adopts Byzantine court ceremonial	1472

stored up trouble for his successors; and though southern Italy and Sicily remained for long intervals under Byzantine control, such control, though costly, was seldom of much value to the empire.

RELATIONS WITH PAPACY

Suzerainty over Rome was of little practical value to the Byzantines. Rome on several occasions appealed to Constantinople, and until the ninth century acknowledged the Byzantine emperor as the only true emperor, inheritor of the mantle of the Roman emperors. From the papal point of view this acknowledgment meant that the Byzantine emperor had the duty of protecting Rome from encroaching barbarians and other secular powers. The Byzantine emperor, however, regarded the pope as in duty bound to protect his interests in Italy and render what aid he could to such material projects as the preservation of the exarchate of Ravenna. Furthermore, he expected the pope, as a good subordinate, to follow his religious dictates, if he issued them. Justinian himself, in particular, fancied himself as a theologian, giving much offense to the pope, who, in religious matters at least, acknowledged no superior. When the Byzantine emperor Leo III commanded that icons (holy pictures) should be destroyed, since in his opinion they were becoming an object of idolatry rather than an aid to worship, and his successors, with one exception, for more than a century adopted a similar policy, the Roman pontiffs refused to obey, thus embittering relations between Rome and Constantinople and ultimately causing the pope to look elsewhere for his protection (Iconoclastic Controversy). By the beginning of the ninth century a pope was willing to offend Constantinople by crown-

ing another emperor in the West. He also adopted a theological position concerning the procession of the Holy Spirit (that the Holy Spirit proceeded from the Father and the Son, rather than, as held in the East, from the Father *through* the Son) which finally divided the Eastern and Western Churches forever in the middle of the eleventh century. Thus the relation between the two powers that had been established by Justinian was seldom of value to either. The pope obtained no protection, and the emperor no control over papal policy. The pope in the end learned to look to the Franks for protection, and the Byzantines set up their own "Orthodox Church," whose spiritual head was the patriarch of Constantinople. The pope remained the head of Western Christendom, as the emperor was the head of the empire which still called itself Roman, and ruled Eastern Christendom through the patriarch.

CULTURAL AND RELIGIOUS IMPERIALISM OF THE BYZANTINE EMPIRE

If the long history of the Byzantine Empire is considered, it must be stated that its contribution to the cultural heritage of the world is relatively small. The great period of Greek history in the fifth and fourth centuries B.C. was incomparably more creative in all realms. Even the Hellenistic period was notable for its artistic and scientific achievements, and its philosophy was far from negligible. But the great creative genius of the Greeks was no longer in evidence in the Byzantine world. The Byzantines preserved the ancient Greek heritage—the works of the earlier Greeks were studied and commented upon, the language developed, and there were many literary craftsmen of the second rank. But Justinian closed the School of Athens and expelled the last of the pagan philosophers. Several of these took refuge in Persia, whose rulers encouraged their work. As a consequence, a great academy was founded with Persian aid at Gondisapur. Here the invading Muslims first came in contact with Greek philosophy, which they grew to admire. Through the medium of Gondisapur Greek philosophy became known throughout the Muslim world, and translations were made into Arabic. Many of these works, especially those of Aristotle, indeed came to the West through Arabic translations discovered in Spain by the Western conquerors in the twelfth century. But in Constantinople itself there was a greater interest in theology than in philosophy. The Greeks, even the illiterate classes, took a passionate interest in theological controversy. Many were the heresies which sprang up in Constantinople and made their way to the outposts of the empire, where even today they still have their adherents.

On the whole the Byzantines in literature and learning must be regarded as preservers rather than creators or innovators; but even this preservation was of great value to the world. When the West wished to recover its knowledge of Greek classical learning, it was to Constantinople that it went for teachers and for the manuscripts long unknown in the West. The Greek revival of the fifteenth and sixteenth centuries that forms part of what is customarily known as the Renaissance owed much to the Greeks of the day, and to the heritage which they had preserved and absorbed.

It was far otherwise with Byzantine art, which only in recent years has obtained any serious appreciation in Western Europe. Byzantine art is suffused with religious thought and feeling. To many, Byzantine art, like medieval art, seems alien and remote, comprehensible only with difficulty. It was art created with the express purpose of arousing religious feeling, not intended in itself to be beautiful. One meditates upon the painting or mosaic; it is not the aesthetic feelings that are aroused. To a Westerner the figures often appear distorted; yet the distortion is fully intended and is in no sense the result of inability to portray the human form. The mosaic was not a Byzantine invention, but developed to a high degree of per-

fection by Byzantine religious artists. The art essentially consists in using colored materials such as marble, glass, and even wood as an inlay in some other material to fashion a picture —geometrical figures, flowers, animals, or human beings. In the Byzantine churches mosaics were used with extraordinary sophistication; in the Hagia Sophia, in particular, the use of gold backgrounds and gold cubes was able to produce scintillating effects of great richness.

More influential than Byzantine painting, and even than mosaic, was Byzantine architec-

Church of the Holy Wisdom (Hagia Sophia, Sancta Sophia) at Constantinople, built by the Emperor Justinian. This building embodied altogether new principles of architecture. Especially difficult was the erection of the huge dome. The angle of this photograph sets off the commanding position of the church, which is often obscured from other directions by the modern Turkish buildings. The minarets close to the church are later additions dating from the period when the church was used by the Muslim Turks as a mosque. In the foreground is the Mosque of Sultan Ahmed, one of the minarets of which appears just in front of the camera. (COURTESY TURKISH INFORMATION OFFICE)

ture. The great majority of the edifices were influenced by the wonderful church of Hagia Sophia (Holy Wisdom), built by architects in the employ of Justinian. Except for its size, this huge church is unimpressive from without—again by intention. For its interior, before it was desecrated and altered by the Turkish Muslims, must have been the most beautiful and impressive in the world. In spite of the fact that the dome has to be supported on arches which rest themselves upon huge pillars, it appears to be supported by nothing and to float in space. This effect is created by numerous windows, which allow the light from outside to illuminate the dome. Byzantine church architecture was imitated widely in the West, especially in those areas influenced in other respects by Constantinople. At Ravenna there is a church only slightly subsequent to that of Hagia Sophia, which has mosaics almost the equal of those that must have decorated the older church. The much later church of St. Mark's in Venice, illustrated on page 123, remained Byzantine in conception, as do numerous churches in Russia.

The Byzantines also excelled in decoration, and Constantinople was full of skilled craftsmen

SLAVS IN EUROPE IN 814 AT DEATH OF CHARLEMAGNE

| | SLAV PEOPLES | 0 100 200 300 Miles | | BYZANTINE EMPIRE |

—jewelers, metal workers, weavers of fine materials, and others. The luxury goods thus manufactured were greatly sought after, not only within the lands of the Byzantine Empire and among foreign princes allied with Constantinople, but also in the West, where such articles for centuries had to be imported and could not be manufactured at home. The imperial purple, a royal monopoly, was allowed to be exported by the emperor only to princes who were in his favor.

CONVERSION OF SLAVS

From early times the Byzantines were active in missionary work. The Arian emperors of the fourth century were instrumental in converting the barbarian peoples to Arianism; all the barbarian peoples who later settled in the empire sooner or later came to accept the Christianity preached by Greek missionaries from Constantinople. In some cases the barbarian princes would have preferred the Roman rite, since acceptance of Roman Christianity would have saved them from even a nominal subservience to the head of the Eastern religion, the patriarch nominated by the emperor. The subservience in fact was far more than nominal; it brought them within the political as well as the cultural and religious orbit of Constantinople. But the peoples who formed part of the Byzantine cultural orbit never were able to escape indefinitely into the Roman sphere. The Roman clergy insisted on the Roman liturgy and the Latin language for Church services; and this could not be accepted by the Slavs or Bulgars, who were permitted by Constantinople to use a liturgy in their own tongue.

Perhaps the best known of Byzantine missionary efforts was the conversion of the Moravians to Christianity by two brothers, Cyril and Methodius, about 862 A.D. The prince of

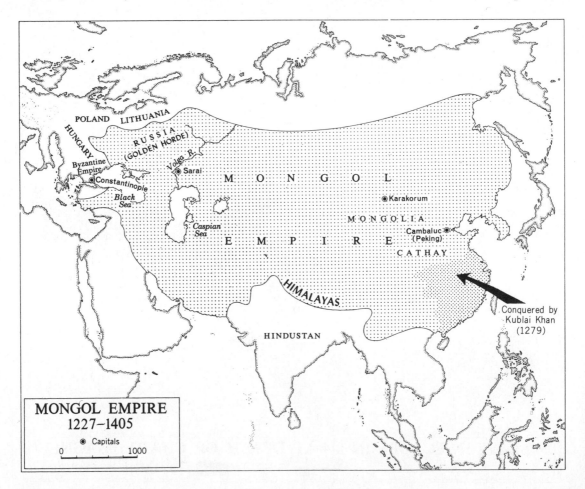

MONGOL EMPIRE
1227–1405
◉ Capitals
0   1000

Moravia, a Slavic territory in Central Europe, living in a land where Christianity was far from unknown and where German missionaries had already been active, sent to Constantinople for missionaries, probably in order to escape the influence of the German clergy. The emperor sent the two brothers, one of whom had invented, or perfected, a Slavic alphabet (Cyrillic). The missionaries were successful and introduced their alphabet and a liturgy in the Slavic tongue to their converts. By a strange quirk of fate, the Moravians and other western Slavs were ultimately brought into the Western Church by the papacy; but the alphabet and liturgy devised for them was made use of by the eastern Slavs, who remained within the fold of the Eastern (later to be called Orthodox) Church. Shortly afterward the Bulgars, after some hesitation, joined the Eastern Church. Russia remained pagan until the end of the tenth century, when the Grand Duke of Kiev, Vladimir I, married a Greek princess and per-

mitted Greek missionaries to convert his people, in spite of much opposition by them. The Russians thereafter became the most steadfast and faithful of Christians. Kiev and Novgorod became cities of churches. Orthodox Christianity in Russia survived the long Mongol occupation of the country (1240–1380) and the fall of Constantinople to the Ottoman Turks. Thereafter, Moscow became the center of Orthodox Christianity, though the Greek Orthodox Church was recognized by the Turks and survived their rule.

BYZANTINE INFLUENCE IN EASTERN EUROPE

The Byzantines had an incalculable influence on all the invading peoples whom they introduced to civilization. Among these should be numbered the Bulgars, the Serbs, and other Slavic groups. Although the Bulgars fought the Byzantines in several long and destructive wars, and at one time seemed within measurable dis-

Most Byzantine icons were destroyed during the iconoclastic controversy by order of the emperors. This picture shows a fifteenth-century Russian icon, with Christ enthroned. Painted in oil on wood, these pictures received a reverence from pious worshipers that the Byzantine emperors claimed was close to idolatry. (COURTESY THE METROPOLITAN MUSEUM OF ART)

tance of inheriting the Byzantine Empire, they were ultimately defeated and settled down in the empire. At a later date (fourteenth century) a great Serbian monarch (Stephen Dushan) died when marching on a Constantinople that was greatly weakened, and might well not have been able to resist the man who had created a Greater Serbia and subjected almost the entire Balkan peninsula to his rule. But his ambition and power died with him. Both Bulgars and Serbs fell victim to the Ottoman Turks.

Hungarians, Croats, and Slovenes for short periods came within the cultural radiation of Constantinople, but ultimately followed their religion into the Western sphere. They are Roman Catholics, and owe no adherence to the Eastern Orthodox Church. The Russians, however, were Orthodox Christians and took over the greater part of their cultural and political heritage from Constantinople. When Constantinople fell to the Turks, the Grand Duke of Moscow married the niece of the last Byzantine monarch, and proclaimed his realm as the center of the true faith. Ivan III called himself Caesar, or Tsar, thus using the name of the Roman emperors. He proclaimed his capital of Moscow to be the "third Rome." The Muscovite court was Byzantine, the architecture of the great Russian city was Byzantine, and the religion was Byzantine. As far as was possible in such a vast domain, the government and administration were Byzantine. When Ivan proclaimed himself sovereign of all Russia, he ruled the only territory in Eastern Europe comparable to that of the Turks. If the Ottoman Turks had inherited the body of Constantinople, Ivan III and his successors had surely inherited the soul. And if today the Russians still do not possess the body, it has not been for want of trying.

BYZANTINE EMPIRE AS BULWARK AGAINST EXPANDING ISLAM

Finally, to go back several centuries in time, a few words should be said of the role of the Byzantine Empire as a bulwark against the Muslims. Though Constantinople was ultimately to fall to the Ottoman Turks, it had been able to hold all their Muslim predecessors at bay. In the great expansion of Islam in the seventh century, the Byzantines were successful in driving the Arabs from the gates of Constantinople. Long wars with Persia had weakened the empire and made prolonged resistance to the drive of the Arabs through the more remote Byzantine possessions impossible. As we have seen, these were lost to the Muslims forever, and never recovered by the Byzantines. But after five years' resistance to a blockade by the Arabs (673–678), the Byzantines concluded a peace and recovered their immediate hinterland of Anatolia, their most valuable territory. Again the Muslims came up in force in 717–718, but were driven back by the Byzantine emperor Leo III. Thereafter Muslim dynamism and power waned, and they turned toward territories easier to conquer than the impregnable city on the Bosporus. The Seljuk Turks were turned back in the eleventh century with the aid of Crusaders from the West. But the Ottoman Turks could not be held. A brief respite was afforded at the end of the fourteenth century by the successes of an Asiatic conqueror, Timur Lenk (Tamerlane). who captured the Turkish monarch even as he was preparing to attack Constantinople. Timur himself made no attempt to conquer Constantinople, and died soon afterwards while trying to add China to his dominions. The Turks recovered, and at last captured the prize in 1453.

If Constantinople had fallen to the early Arab attack, the history of Europe would have been incalculably different. At that time there was no comparable Western power, and Eastern Europe might well have been overrun. The victories of the Byzantine emperors in 678 and 718 were far more fateful than the turning back of a Muslim advance guard at Poitiers in France in 732. Constantinople survived as a bastion of Christianity and Western culture into an age when the West had grown too strong to be defeated. Though the Ottoman rulers were able to besiege Vienna in the time of Charles V, they could not take it; though they ruled most of Hungary and the entire Balkan peninsula for many years, they could not convert it to Islam.

Thus, even if it cannot be credited with very many enduring achievements in the realm of thought and culture, the Byzantine empire may nevertheless be credited with the supreme success of preserving its Greek and Christian heritage for all the peoples of Eastern Europe. Insofar as Europe is today a cultural and religious whole, distinct from the continents of Asia and Africa that border her, much of the glory of this achievement must surely be given to the persistence and will-to-endure of the Byzantine Empire.

❖ Beginnings of Islam

If the Romans could have foreseen which people would enter into their inheritance in North Africa and much of the Mediterranean, they would surely have been astonished, for they were hardly aware of the existence of the Arabs. Parthians and Persians they knew and respected as dangerous enemies who sometimes defeated them in battle. But the Arabs, in the days of the empire, had remained in their desert peninsula. A small Roman province had been organized in the north, but the Bedouin tribesmen, always fiercely independent, had given the Romans no trouble, and in turn were left untroubled by the Romans. They spent their lives wandering from oasis to oasis with their flocks —warlike, hospitable, illiterate but with a remarkable natural shrewdness and understanding, fiercely loyal to their tribes, families, and chiefs (sheiks), but quick to take offense and as quick to avenge a slight as an injury. The sheiks were independent chieftains, owing homage to no man, and their country was without political organization of any kind; the few families who made up a tribe were part of no larger unit.

Along the coasts of Arabia, however, the land was more fertile, and a few cities had grown up. Jidda was the seaport; Mecca and Yathrib were trading cities, with their bazaars selling the products of the country—meat, dates, nuts, palm oil, and other foodstuffs, luxuries imported by sea and caravan or made by local industry. From these cities camel caravans set out to the north, south, and through the desert to the east, manned by shrewd Arab traders and Jewish merchants. The cities, like the Bedouin tribesmen, were dominated by local families. One of the greatest of these was the Kuraish, which dominated Mecca, the chief commercial

and religious center of the country. Though often warring among themselves, the Kuraish, with their many collateral branches, could be relied upon to unite when the family interests were threatened.

Probably such a people as this would never have been united by political means; no king had yet arisen among them. Loyalty from such a people could not be commanded or enforced. But what could and did unite them, and make of them one of the greatest fighting forces the world has yet seen, was a new and dynamic religion whose early successes, often against overwhelming odds, must have seemed to doubters proof indeed of its divine origin.

RELIGION BEFORE ISLAM

Before the days of Mahomet, Mecca was already a religious center. A stone, believed to have fallen from heaven (a meteorite?), around which a temple, the Kaaba, had been built, was the chief object of veneration. Arabs from distant lands came to pay homage at it, to the financial advantage of the trading community. Idols and other sacred objects were worshiped. Both in the holy city of Mecca and elsewhere there seem to have been many varieties of sacrifice offered both to deities and to deified forces of nature. But, as far as we can tell, no synthesis of beliefs or religious practices existed which would justify our calling it in any way a religion. This was surprising, since Judaism and even Christianity were known to the Arabs from traders and wandering missionaries. And yet, as we shall see, the religious spirit was there, quiescent, waiting for the words of inspiration that would kindle it. This task was the lifework of Mahomet.

Mahomet (the name is spelled in even more ways than Shakespeare's) was born in Mecca in 570 of one of the poorer and less influential branches of the leading Kuraish family. His childhood was apparently spent in the shadow of poverty. But when he was twenty-five he began to work for a widow Khadija, older than himself, a business woman of ability and in comfortable circumstances, whom he later married. By her he had his only child, Fatima. From this time on Mahomet prospered as a trader, and until the age of forty gave no indication that he would later preach a new religion. But it seems clear that he must have pondered long on what he knew of the other religions of the Near East and often have thought of the religious backwardness of his native land. It is said that for a month each year he went into the desert. There his thoughts became clearer, and he prepared himself so that at last, when the revelation came to him, he was ready. The revelation was that there was only one God, Allah, and that he, Mahomet, had been chosen to be God's prophet. Islam therefore stands firmly on the revelations to Mahomet, as Judaism stands upon the revelations to Moses. It is consequently a religion that calls for faith, with all the dynamism that such a religion entails. Although Islam contains much from the older religions, commingled with observances growing out of the customs of the desert tribes, it should not be regarded as a religion that was simply tailored by the keen intellect of Mahomet to fit the circumstances of his country. Students of history should avoid such an easy assumption, which is sometimes made when we speak of *syncretistic* religions, or those which draw their chief elements from several others of the day.

RELATION TO OTHER RELIGIONS

The fundamental belief in Islam (Arabic for "submission") is monotheism of the strict Judaic kind. For the Muslim,[1] there is no Trinity of Persons in God. Mahomet did not claim to be a god, but a prophet of God. There had been, in his belief, other prophets before him, among whom he numbered Moses and Jesus Christ; but he himself was to be the last, revealing the whole truth as it had been partially revealed to his predecessors. There was thus no reason for despising these earlier religions, or for denying their teachings; but they were not complete, and not fully understood. Islam therefore did not wish to exterminate the other religions. Those who converted to Islam showed

---

[1] The word *Muslim*, also Anglicized as "Moslem" or "Mussulman," means one who "surrenders himself to God."

that they were a chosen people, since they had been able to accept the higher revelation, and for this reason in a Muslim country were entitled to special privileges. Those who preferred to keep their second-class religions could do so, but they must then expect to be treated as second-class citizens in a religious state. As "people of the Book," believers in other religions were permitted to keep their Books. Only those who had no Book and no religion were to be converted by force. This attitude always remained the religious policy of Islam, and was reflected in its political policies. A holy war (*jehad*) could be proclaimed only against heathen, or when Islam was forced to defend itself against other religions which attacked it. A holy war, enjoined upon the faithful only in certain well-defined circumstances, could never be arbitrary, or for the sake of simple conquest; the true religion must first be endangered by the enemy.

THE KORAN—HADITH, ULEMA

Mahomet, from the time he began his mission, received many revelations from, as he proclaimed, the angel Gabriel. These were given to the people orally, but collected after his death in the sacred book of Islam—the Koran. Each revelation (or sura) is separate, and the compilers assembled them only in order of length. There is thus no logical, chronological, or other order in the Koran, and if read consecutively by an unsympathetic critic, it appears to be a medley of unrelated teachings, most of them concerned with everyday life and behavior. This appearance of confusion is the natural result of the fact that Mahomet did not trust to his own judgment to answer the innumerable questions put to him in his earlier years. When asked for an authoritative answer, he meditated in the desert until the answer came. This was then a new revelation, later to be incorporated in the Koran. It may be added that throughout the book the language is beautiful, the words are chosen with masterly care, and the whole betrays a poetic imagination which makes it not unworthy to stand beside the Hebrew Scriptures. It has never been difficult for any believing Muslim to accept it as inspired, in spite of occasional contradictions between various instructions to the faithful. These contradictions are explained as a progressive understanding of his mission by the Prophet—who, after all, was not divine, but partook of some of the frailties of mortals.

The Koran contained all the positive teaching given by Mahomet in his lifetime; but, as with Christianity, not all points of Islamic theology had been cleared up by the Prophet himself. Since the Koran was also a guide to ethics and ordinary worldly activity, it early became necessary to have authoritative rulings on knotty points of doctrine. Moreover, Mahomet had also given oral instructions to his disciples, which were not direct revelations like the suras in the Koran, but were almost equally authoritative. Thus were added to the teachings of the holy book itself the *Hadith,* or traditions, which derived directly from the Prophet; and a number of learned men, the *ulema,* became recognized as the interpreters of the sacred text and the Hadith. These ulema still exist today with the same tasks in orthodox Muslim communities, even though there is no priesthood.

ORGANIZATION AND DOCTRINES OF ISLAM— SIMPLICITY, APPEAL TO JEWS

In Islam there has never been any recognized priesthood. Each community may have an *imam,* who leads the prayers, and there is also a *muezzin,* who summons the faithful at sundown to turn toward Mecca and pray. The prayers are regularly prescribed, as are also fast days; and a whole month, Ramadan, is set aside during which no Muslim may break his fast between sunrise and sundown. In addition, there are moral duties to be performed, such as giving alms to the poor and showing hospitality to strangers. There are injunctions against pride and worldliness and taking advantage of the difficult position of one's neighbor. There are laws of ritual cleanliness to be observed, following the general pattern of the Jewish codes: the pig is unclean, and there are ritual washings to be performed. No wine or strong drink must be taken, and there must be no images or idols of any kind, since these will divert the faithful from the strictest monotheism, persuading them to believe that other beings beside Allah have

godlike attributes. The articles of belief are few and equally simple. There is a resurrection of the body and Paradise for the righteous, and an unending suffering in Gehenna for the wicked; both places are eloquently described in the Koran. There are also angels of God and evil beings, emissaries of the Devil.

Thus the religion is essentially simple. It does away with the complexity of Christianity, with its Trinity and doctrine of the redemption, and concentrates on the few essentials which proved acceptable to the simple people to whom these were preached. The simple elements of Jewish ritual were alone retained, while the whole of Jewish legalism was abandoned. The ancient desert morality at its best—such virtues as simplicity, straightforwardness, hospitality to friends and even enemies—was enshrined now as moral law, binding on the faithful, so that little change was needed from what was already practiced. The religion, there can be little doubt, was intended to appeal to Jews as well as to the heathen, and much of early Hebrew legend is incorporated in the Koran as fact. Although in the process of time many Jews within this culture were indeed converted, on the whole Islam did not succeed in weaning them from their law. In early times there were many wars against Jewish communities, but the communities were not destroyed; and within a Muslim state Judaism was tolerated in the same way as Christianity. Mahomet, who always regarded Jerusalem as a holy city, and indeed chose it himself as the place from which he ascended to Heaven, ultimately did not adopt it as the chief, but only the second, holy city in Islam, the place of supreme honor being reserved to his birthplace, Mecca.

❖ Expansion of Islam

The progress of Islam was at first very slow. Mahomet's family did not accept him. His uncompromising monotheism offended all those, including the Kuraish, who had a vested interest in the old religion. Most of his early followers were in Yathrib, rather than Mecca, and it was to Yathrib that he finally decided to go. The date of the "flight" from Mecca to Yathrib

(622 A.D.) marks the birthday of the religion of Islam, and 622 is therefore the year from which the Muslim era is counted. Yathrib was renamed Medina, the city of the Prophet.

Having organized Medina and gained many converts also among the Bedouin tribes, Mahomet was ready to take on Mecca and his own powerful family. The latter, threatened by a large army, decided to cast in their lot with the Prophet, and thereafter the peninsula of Arabia became, as it has always remained, a Muslim preserve. Two years after his return from Medina (632) Mahomet died, and the astonishing progress of Islam began.

Unfortunately the Prophet himself was unique, and no provision had been made for a successor as head of the religion. Mahomet had himself received all the revelations from Allah, including military instructions, and he was looked upon as the infallible leader. Should the leadership go to Ali, his son-in-law and cousin, or to his father-in-law Abu Bekr? Both had been faithful followers of Mahomet from the first. As it turned out, the choice fell upon Abu Bekr, and only later did Ali gain the title, after two intervening successors had been murdered. Ali himself was likewise murdered, whereupon the succession fell to the Ommeyad family, whose members were not descended from Mahomet. The events of this time caused a major schism in Islam which has persisted to this day, the Shiite sect, centered mainly in Persia, believing that the succession should have passed through Mahomet's own family, and the Sunni contending that the succession of the Ommeyads was legitimate, since they had been chosen by the faithful followers of the Prophet.

Meanwhile the caliphs, as they were called —both a political and a religious title (Arabic for "successor")—had been spreading the new religion into the countries bordering Arabia, and meeting with remarkable success. The long wars between Persia and Constantinople had greatly weakened both powers, and the Arabs were able to conquer both Persia and the eastern Mediterranean lands of the Byzantine Empire with comparative ease. The inhabitants of the countries had been ground down by heavy taxation to pay for the wars. Islam offered them special privileges if they converted, including freedom from formal taxation, which was replaced by the Koranic religious obligation of giving alms and undertaking charitable works for the benefit of the faithful. If, like the Christians and Jews, they were "peoples of the Book," then, as already noted, they were permitted to keep their religion, but were required to meet the burden of ordinary taxation. Only pagans were converted to Islam by the sword. Instructions for all these matters were contained in the Koran.

The Muslims did not feel it to be their duty to extirpate the cultures of the countries they conquered. On the contrary the Arabs, having only their primitive desert culture, often became actively interested in the cultures of the peoples they subjected to their rule. The result was that an advanced culture such as that of the Persians not only survived but gained from the dynamism of the Arabs. The religion of Islam replaced their own religion, which had long before fallen into decay. But Persian culture itself gained a new lease on life, especially under the Abbasid dynasty centered on Bagdad (750–1258). It was this quality of cultural tolerance which made the Muslims and the civilization they created the most influential transmitters of culture that the world has yet seen, superior to the Romans in that these new imperialists took also from the best that India and the Far East could give. Only when the Turks entered into the Muslim heritage, after it had been in decay for centuries, did Islam become fanatical, and, on the whole, destroy more than it created and preserved.

The Ommeyad dynasty, after the murder of Ali, chose as its capital the Syrian city of Damascus. There it ruled from 661 to 750. The period from the death of Mahomet in 632 to the end of the Ommeyad caliphate was the great period of expansion. During this time Constantinople, as noted earlier, was twice besieged but not captured. Palestine, Persia, North Africa, and ultimately Spain were won by Muslim arms. In the later stages the new converts, especially the Berbers of North Africa, carried the religion onward rather than the Arabs themselves, who were spread thinly through their empire. Beyond Persia Arab rule did not go; but the religion was carried further by Persian converts

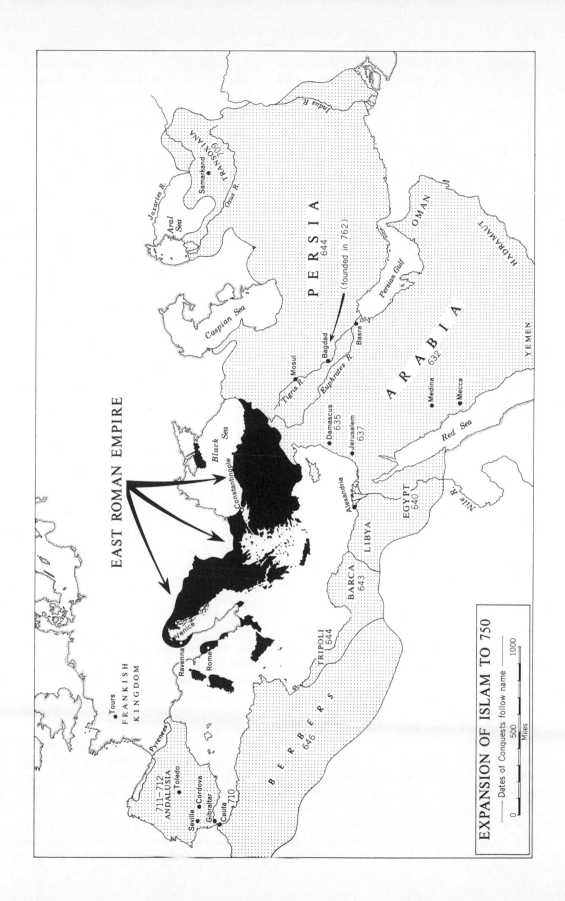

EXPANSION OF ISLAM TO 750

—— Dates of Conquests follow name

EAST ROMAN EMPIRE

TRANSOXIANA 709
Samarkand
Jaxartes R.
Aral Sea
Oxus R.
Caspian Sea

P E R S I A 644

Indus R.

(founded in 762)
Bagdad
Tigris R.
Mosul
Euphrates R.
Basra
Persian Gulf
O M A N
Damascus 635
Jerusalem 637
Medina 632
Mecca
A R A B I A
Red Sea
H A D R A M A U T
Y E M E N

Black Sea
Constantinople
Alexandria
EGYPT 640
Nile R.
LIBYA
BARCA 643
TRIPOLI 644

Venice
Ravenna
Rome
B E R B E R S 646

Tours
FRANKISH KINGDOM
Pyrenees
711–712 ANDALUSIA
Toledo
Seville
Cordova
Gibraltar
Ceuta 710

0   500   1000
Miles

and traders. In the course of the next centuries parts of India, the Malay peninsula, and most of Indonesia were converted to Islam. They remain Muslim to this day.

When the Ommeyad dynasty was overthrown by Abbas, a direct descendant of Mahomet, the Spanish conquests were retained by an Ommeyad who had managed to escape the systematic destruction of his family attempted by the Abbasids. There he set up a separate caliphate. Abbas himself founded a long-lived dynasty and changed the capital from Damascus to Bagdad. As caliph, he claimed allegiance from the whole Muslim world; but the Ommeyad ruler in Cordova, Spain did not acknowledge him. In the tenth century Egypt and North Africa escaped from Abbasid control and likewise set up their own caliphate. Thus Islam split into separate states, each with a caliph who was recognized only by his own subjects. In the early sixteenth century the Ottoman sultan of Constantinople, Selim I, proclaimed himself caliph, and as the only important remaining Muslim potentate his title was generally recognized by the Muslim faithful. But the title of successor to the Prophet, signified by the word *caliph*, was clearly no longer meaningful— though the secular ruler of an Islamic state has always remained head of its religion as well.

The governments of Syria and Bagdad were Oriental despotisms of a familiar kind, owing much to the example of Constantinople. Their courts were centers of luxury and culture; but both were, on the whole, more creative than Constantinople, which relied too exclusively on its ancient Greek heritage. The subjects of the caliphates of Syria and Bagdad were kept under central control as far as it was possible for the monarchs to establish such control. But the Bedouin tribes of Arabia, whose dynamism had been responsible for the upsurge of Islam in the first place, were unwilling to submit to any kind of central rule. Nor were the warlike tribes in Africa. So the despots made only sporadic efforts to enforce their authority over these tribes, which, for the most part, remained independent under local leadership, retaining to this day the religion of Islam but never more than nominal subjects of the Muslim political empires. Islam as a religion was congenial to them and did not interfere with their way of life; but the political system of the Muslim Empire interfered with their traditional independence, and it is not surprising that they rejected it.

❖ Muslim culture

Perhaps the greatest contribution of the Arabs that can be specifically credited to the Arabs themselves, rather than to their converts, is the incomparable Arabic language. The Koran may not be translated into any other language, according to the law of Islam. And the Koran must be read by all the faithful. Therefore it was necessary to learn Arabic, which became, as Greek had once been, the common language of the whole empire and of the whole area converted to the religion of Islam. It is true that the original language was greatly altered in its transmission through these lands. But it proved capable of meeting the demands made upon it. When necessary, words were imported from the Greek, and other words were invented to express concepts that had never before been needed in the lands of the desert. Arabic, with its delicate signs used so beautifully in decorative work designed in Muslim lands, has remained one of the great languages of the world, strengthened and enlarged through the centuries, but retaining still the marks of its Arab origin.

As has already been said, the Arabs, unlike the Romans, were genuinely interested in learning. As a practical people, the Arabs were chiefly interested in science. But there were also many learned philosophers in the new Muslim Empire, though their influence was probably not as great as the quality of their work would have justified. Philosophy never seems to have become a regular subject of instruction in their academies, perhaps because of the difficulties that always arise when philosophy and revealed religion must be reconciled. The Muslims took from the people in their empire what interested them, and neglected the remainder. They did not, for instance, show any interest in Greek literature or poetry, probably because there was already a long Arab tradition in these fields and the work in the ancient Hellenic tradition did not lend itself to translation into Arabic. Moreover, Greek religion, which suffused Greek literature, would not be acceptable to confirmed believers in the Koran. No Roman work except the law seems to have come into Arab hands at all, suggesting that, with the exception of Spain, Latin knowledge had died out in the territories which they controlled.

In every field they touched, the Muslims added something of their own. Though they regarded Aristotle as the real master of philosophy, calling him simply "The Philosopher," they nevertheless tried to understand him, and the great Muslim philosophers took his work as the starting point and added commentaries, trying to explain and enlarge his often brief and cryptic remarks. They took the great synthesis of Greek scientific knowledge written by Claudius Ptolemy in the second century A.D. as the point of departure for their own science, and then added numerous observations to it, especially in the fields of optics and astronomy. Since they were in contact with Hindu thought also, they added the mathematical knowledge of the Hindus to the work of Euclid and the great Greek geometricians, and they advanced trigonometry beyond the point that Ptolemy had reached in his fundamental work. These instances are only given here to suggest the kind of work that the Muslims performed; a later section will give more detail on their specific contributions. The Muslims were the heirs of all the ages up to their own time; and though little that is really new can be credited to them, they preserved the Greek and Persian heritages, added something of Hindu achievements, and even took a fundamental invention from China, paper. This heritage they handed on to Western civilization intact and improved. Though much in Western civilization owed little to the Muslims, and their influence should not be exaggerated, nevertheless in theoretical and applied science their influence was crucial. The large number of scientific words incorporated into Western languages—most of them words in daily use, such as *algebra, alcohol, zenith,* and *zero*—sufficiently demonstrates this fact. Muslim commercial invention and innovations made possible the voyages of discovery, the exploitation of which led directly to the modern world.

PHILOSOPHICAL AND SCIENTIFIC ACHIEVEMENTS

In a book of this scope it is unnecessary to do more than indicate the special fields of competence of the Muslims. In philosophy the great names are Avicenna and Averroës, the former an eleventh-century Persian, the latter a twelfth-century Spaniard. The philosophical work of both these men was read and appreciated far more by medieval Western scholastics than by their own people. Both were extremely competent as philosophers, Avicenna developing Neoplatonist thought and Averroës writing commentaries on Aristotle which became so widely known among medieval thinkers that he came to be called simply "The Commentator." Avicenna was better known in his own country for his great *Canon* of medical knowledge, which was not superseded in the Muslim world until very recent times.

The Western world knows the Arabs for their supposed invention of the "Arabic" numerals, which, however, were not invented by the Arabs at all, but adapted from similar signs used by the Hindus. Their importance does not lie in the particular signs used—any signs with a universally accepted meaning would have sufficed—but in their combination with the zero. The zero may have been of Muslim origin, but is usually regarded as also invented by the Hindus, whose work the Muslims, of course, knew well. The use of the Arabic numerals with the zero permits a positional system to be used instead of the cumbersome letter system of the Greeks and Romans. Such a positional system, based on the number 60, was already in use as early as the ancient Babylonian civilization. The so-called Arabic system is based on the number 10, requiring the use of nine numerals and the zero. The fundamental work on the subject was written about 810 by one Al-Khwarizmi (from whom comes our word *algorism*). His system was introduced to the Western world by Leonardo of Pisa at the beginning of the thirteenth century. The same Muslim mathematician wrote a basic textbook on algebra. Algebra itself appears to have been a genuine Muslim invention (as is the word itself), though based on the work of earlier Greek and Hindu mathematicians. The Muslims also were well acquainted with trigonometry, using the work of Claudius Ptolemy, the second-century Greek scientist, and developing it further. Another Muslim, Al-Farabi (died 950), was responsible for the elements of musical notation and the measurement of time values in music.

In the field of physics Al-Kindi, the only true Arab who gained eminence in science, invented a complex theory concerning lines of force, based on optical observations. Even more important work in optics was done by Al-Hazen or Al-Haitham (*ca.* 965–1038), who wrote extensively on the reflection and refraction of rays. This work was the foundation for the optical studies carried out in medieval times by such noted figures as Robert Grosseteste and Roger Bacon. The Muslims were naturally much interested in astronomy, as might be expected of a desert people, but they were for the most part content to rest their theoretical knowledge on the great second-century compilation of Ptolemy. They were also interested in astrology, and much of medieval astrology is indebted to the Muslim technique for casting and interpreting horoscopes. More important, perhaps, than anything else done by the Muslims in this field was the invention of the astrolabe (illustrated in the text), used to observe the movements of the heavenly bodies.

It has already been noted that certain exiles from Constantinople founded the academy of Gondisapur in Persia. When the Arabs conquered Persia, they inherited the academy, and soon persuaded the Hellenized Christians they found there to turn their accumulated learning into the Arabic language. Thus the Muslims had at their disposal, among other things, the whole corpus of Greek medical writings. For many centuries the Muslims were noted as doctors and observers of diseases. They were greatly sought after in the Middle Ages, since medieval medical knowledge was, for the most part, a terrifying compound of superstition and quackery.

Muslim chemistry is not always judged fairly, owing to the prevalent belief in the transmutation of elements, the search for a universal catalyst (the philosopher's stone), and the diversion of intellectual and practical effort to these unprofitable pursuits. In the practice of this science of alchemy there was much that

An Arabic astrolabe. This instrument, which was suspended by the ring at its top, was used to take bearings by the stars. The crosspiece, called the alidade, was directed toward a particular star, and the navigator or astronomer took his bearing by sighting along it. By the fourteenth century it was customary to use two alidades and thus take a double bearing and calculate exactly the position of the ship. (COURTESY THE OWNER, MR. BARNEY OF NEW YORK. PHOTO BY MORTON A. BERGER)

we should call excessively mystical, even in the hands of the Muslims. But if we have lost our wonder at the marvelous transformations possible in the world of chemistry, this is not because there is nothing wonderful in it but because we have been so accustomed to think of all scientific wonders as commonplace. The fact remains that in their experimentations the Muslims discovered how to isolate many important chemicals, including sal ammoniac, saltpeter, and a number of oxides, and learned how to prepare sulfuric and nitric acids. There can be no doubt at all that Muslim alchemy laid the basis for modern chemistry by performing this pioneer work, whatever the objectives of their experimentation may have been.

The Muslims made considerable progress in agriculture, especially in the science of irrigation. They improved the irrigation system in Egypt by carrying the Nile water further from the river and up slopes to higher ground; in Spain they brought water from the higher regions down to the plains, which had always been arid. It is possible that Spain was never so well cultivated in all her history as under the Ommeyads. Vineyards were planted, and scientific methods of terracing were used, perhaps learned from the Far East. Cordova was noted for its beautiful landscape gardening, made possible by irrigation.

Muslim voyages into areas previously unknown to the West and to the Near East made possible a great increase in geographical knowledge, and an improvement in map making. The best-known geographer, Al-Idrisi (1099–1154), was employed by the Normans in Sicily in the twelfth century, thus introducing the best geographical knowledge of the day into the West. The Muslims also introduced, if they did not invent, the crucial mariner's compass. The actual inventor is unknown.

ART

Architecture The most characteristic Muslim structure is the mosque, which differed essentially from the Christian church or the Greek temple in that no provision had to be made for the celebration of the mass, nor was there, of course, any god to be housed in it. The Muslims, keeping strictly to the law against "graven images," allowed no representation in

A Moorish temple in Tetuán, Spanish Morocco, features a horse-shoe arch typical of Moorish architecture. (COURTESY THE SPANISH STATE TOURIST DEPARTMENT)

their mosques of either human beings or animals, thus limiting sculpture to flowers and leaves, but above all to geometrical patterns which reached a high degree of intricacy and beauty (arabesques). On the other hand, since the Koran had to be read publicly, a pulpit was necessary; a place had to be provided for the ritual washing; and, from the mosque, the muezzin called to prayer. For the last-named function the Muslims added to their mosques the graceful minaret, so characteristic a feature of all Muslim ecclesiastical architecture—a feature which was, as usual, copied by other peoples who did not use it for any such purpose. In other hands the minaret became mere decoration, like the Roman and Renaissance columns which supported nothing. The campanile, or bell tower, of Christian churches, however, was often modeled on the Muslim minaret.

The Muslims used many different forms of the arch, especially the horseshoe arch, almost a signature of Muslim architecture. For decoration the Muslims, like the Byzantines, excelled in mosaic. This seems to have been a Persian invention taken over by both the Byzantines and the later Muslims. The dome, brought to perfection by the architects of Justinian, was almost universal in Muslim architecture.

Applied arts　Muslim craftsmen were noted throughout the world for the excellence of their handwork, their only competitor being the Byzantine Empire. The process known as damascening, the inlaying of gold and silver on cheaper metals, was called after the city of Damascus and was a Muslim invention. Persian carpets are still famous today. The tooling of leather was a specialty (morocco, cordova), and swords and rapiers of Toledo steel were valued by Christian knights as the finest weapons in the medieval world. The designing of silks, brocades, muslins, and other materials was brought to high perfection, and many of the materials used still keep their Arabic names (damask, muslin).

Literature　When we think of Arabic literature we think almost automatically of the *Rubáiyát* of Omar Khayyám and the *Arabian Nights*. The former, written by a Persian mathematician, gives expression to the refined hedonism and polite fatalism of late Muslim Persia, and is, of course, known to the West through its very free translation by Edward FitzGerald. The poem is, in fact, better known in English-speaking countries than in its native Persia, where Omar was only one of many great poets. The *Thousand and One Nights* reflects the society of Bagdad in the time of Harun-al-Rashid, who appears in many of the tales in person. Arabs had always been fond of storytelling, even in the days before Mahomet, and this is one of many collections which was to exercise a considerable influence upon medieval and even modern storytellers. Boccaccio especially was influenced by the mode; though as a rule he wrote on contemporary themes, nevertheless many of his stories made use of those of his Arabic predecessors. The minstrels of Spain had a decisive influence on Provençal medieval poetry associated with the troubadours, and for a long time the whole civilization of Provence, so ruthlessly destroyed in the Albigensian Crusade, was indebted to the Muslim culture of Spain.

Finally, a few words should be said of the man who was the greatest of Muslim historians, and one of the few philosophers of history from earlier times whose works may still be read with profit today. He took the history of the Arabs as a special example of the expansionist urge in a people and considered seriously and carefully the question of why they had been able to conquer sedentary peoples with so much ease. His conclusions led him further to speculate on the reasons for the rise and fall of all empires. Ibn Khaldun is one of the few historians whose generalizations are fit to be compared with those of the great Greek Thucydides, and it is by no means certain that, having regard to the material available to each, the Muslim historian would come off second best.

DECAY OF MUSLIM CIVILIZATION—SUMMARY AND CONCLUSION

Muslim civilization was unable to recover from the political disasters that overtook it from the eleventh century onward. The Seljuk Turks from Central Asia took over effective control of the Abbasid Empire in the middle of the eleventh century, though permitting the Abbasid rulers to retain nominal sovereignty. The Mongols captured Bagdad in 1258, forcing the last of the Abbasid family to flee to Egypt. Bagdad was captured by Mongols again in 1400, and later by Persians and Ottoman Turks. But by that time the distinctively Muslim civilization was over. Only in this century have there appeared signs of a cultural renascence in Islam, though now under the spur of nationalism as well as religion.

The achievements of Muslim civilization have sometimes been minimized and sometimes exaggerated, especially by scholars who have enjoyed contrasting medieval European backwardness, lack of science, and superstition with Muslim enlightenment. The Muslims were not, on the whole, great creators or innovators, but they were incomparable imitators and assimilators. For many centuries they acted as the sole bridge between East and West. They studied Greek science, neglected and almost unknown in the West of the day, and they studied and translated Greek philosophy. They did not add much to Plato and Aristotle beyond commentaries, but they added a great deal to Hellenistic science from their own thinking and observations. They were able to make use of Hindu speculation and discoveries hitherto unknown in Europe. Their medicine, both theoretical and practical, was renowned in Europe, and the first European medical school at Salerno was originally staffed by Muslims.

The Muslims were an extremely mobile people, and their traveling merchants carried more than news and gossip and geographical information over the thousands of miles of their trade routes. They carried Persian techniques and manufacturing processes into Spain and Sicily, and so ultimately into Christian Europe. They navigated the seas and brought the perfected astrolabe, quadrant, and mariner's compass to the West. Their storytellers provided the basis for much of medieval European literature. If the West had had to discover for itself all that the Muslims taught it, Western civilization might have been delayed for centuries.

But it is hardly fair to judge the Muslims by what they gave to the West, great though our debt is to them. Anyone who visits southern Spain today and sees the ruins of the great works of the Muslims, who looks at the arid lands which were made to blossom by Muslim genius and are now desolate, does not need to be reminded that this was a great civilization in its own right. The peoples who worshiped the one God Allah, whose prophet was Mahomet, do not need to fear comparison with the greatest there have been—even though their genius has been overshadowed in recent centuries by the expansionism and dynamism of the Christians and of Western civilization.

Suggestions for further reading

PAPER-BOUND BOOKS

Aladdin and Other Tales, trans. by N. J. Dawood. Penguin. Collection of Persian and Arabic stories from the *Thousand and One Nights*. There are several more complete hard-cover editions, including the famous translation by Sir Richard Burton, the nineteenth-century explorer, reprinted in the Modern Library.

Andrea, Tor. *Mohammed: the Man and His Faith*. Torchbooks. Sympathetic account of the founder of Islam.

Baynes, N. H. and Moss, H. St. L. B. *Byzantium*. Galaxy. Topical treatment of different aspects of the Byzantine Empire by different authors.

Creswell, K. A. C. *Short Account of Early Muslim Architecture*. Penguin.

Dermenghem, Emile. *Muhammad and the Islamic Tradition*. Men of Wisdom Series, Harper & Row. Illustrated.

Gibb, H. A. R. *Mohammedanism*. Galaxy. Very fair and objective brief study by a leading western scholar of Islam.

Grunebaum, G. E. von. *Medieval Islam*. Phoenix. Interesting interpretation of Islamic culture.

Guillaume, Alfred, *Islam*, 2d ed. Penguin. Good survey by a noted Arabist.

Hitti, Philip K. *The Arabs—a Short History*. Gateway. The earlier chapters of this popular but scholarly and factual work cover the period dealt with in this chapter. The same author has written a brief cultural survey with documents, *Islam and the West* (Anvil).

Hussey, J. M. *The Byzantine World*. Torchbooks. Short but interesting survey.

Jeffery, Arthur, ed. *Islam: Muhammad and His Religion*. Liberal Arts Press. Good source book for the religion of Islam.

Koran, The, trans. by N. J. Dawood. Penguin. Fundamental work of Islam.

Lewis, Bernard. *The Arabs in History*. Torchbooks. Valuable short account, useful as introduction.

Runciman, Steven. *Byzantine Civilization.* Meridian. Well-written and interesting survey by a leading English scholar.

Talbot-Rice, David. *Byzantine Art.* Penguin. Brief but useful manual.

Vasiliev, Alexander A. *History of the Byzantine Empire.* 2 vols. University of Wisconsin Press. Standard history, solid and well informed.

HARD-COVER BOOKS

Arnold, T. W., and Guillaume, A., eds. *The Legacy of Islam.* Oxford, England: The Clarendon Press, 1931. Especially good on geography, commerce, and the minor arts in which the Muslims excelled.

Artz, Frederick B. *The Mind of the Middle Ages,* 2d ed. New York: Alfred A. Knopf, Inc., 1954. Contains good chapters on Byzantium and Islam, and a useful bibliography.

Baynes, Norman H. *The Byzantine Empire.* Home University Library. New York: Oxford University Press, 1943. The best short survey covering Byzantine civilization topically. Large bibliography.

Cross, S. H. *Slavic Civilization.* Cambridge, Mass.: Harvard University, 1948. Excellent short essay, covering very well the influence of Byzantium on the Slavs.

Diehl, Charles. *Byzantium: Greatness and Decline.* New Brunswick, N.J.: Rutgers University Press, 1956. By the leading French scholar of Byzantium. One of the few of his books available in English. The same author's *Byzantine Portraits* (New York: Alfred A. Knopf, Inc., 1927) is an abridged version of an original French work, which was composed of a number of biographies and character sketches of some representative Byzantine men and women of different classes.

O'Leary, De Lacy. *Arabic Thought and Its Place in History* (1939) and *How Greek Science Passed to the Arabs* (1949). New York: Humanities Press, 1957. These two books, though not well organized and in some respects inadequate, are still useful introductions to the subject.

Ostrogorsky, George. *History of the Byzantine State.* New Brunswick, N.J.: Rutgers University Press, 1957. Most important recent book on the Byzantine Empire, with many new and interesting interpretations.

Sarton, George. *Introduction to the History of Science.* Baltimore: The Williams and Wilkins Company, 1931. Vols. I and II contain well-considered thumbnail sketches of various Muslim scientists.

Spuler, B. *The Muslim World.* 2 vols., trans. by F. R. Bagley. New York: Humanities Press, Inc., 1960. The fullest and most authoritative work on the period covered.

Thorndike, Lynn. *The History of Magic and Experimental Science,* vols. I and II. New York: The Macmillan Company, 1923. Contains an account of the work of several outstanding Muslim scientists.

IV ❖ THE MIDDLE AGES

Manorial tenant touching his cap to his lord. From a Book of Hours *(Flemish),* ca. *1515.* (COURTESY THE PIERPONT MORGAN LIBRARY. Ms. 399, folio 4)

Chronological Chart
THE MIDDLE AGES

Papacy	Empire	England	France	Spain and Portugal	Century (All dates A.D.)
Coronation of Charlemagne (800)	Reign of Charlemagne (768–814)	Alfred the Great (871–900)			800
	Otto the Great crowned (962)		Rollo becomes Duke of Normandy (911)	Conquest of León by Castile (1037)	900
Pontificate of Gregory VII (1073–1085)	Henry IV does penance at Canossa (1077)	Edward the Confessor (1042–1066)	Hugh Capet, king of France (987)	Christian advance into Muslim Spain (1072 onward)	1000
First Crusade called (1095)		William I of England (1066–1087)		Union of Catalonia and Aragon (1137)	1100
	Frederick Barbarossa (1154–1190)	Henry II (1154–1189)	Philip Augustus (1180–1223)	Earliest Cortes in Castile (1188)	
Pontificate of Innocent III (1198–1216)	Frederick II (1220–1250)	John (1199–1216) (Magna Carta–1215)			1200
	Last Hohenstaufen executed (1268)	Simon de Montfort's Parliament (1265)	Louis IX (1226–1270)	Capture of Cordova from Muslims (1236)	
Pontificate of Boniface VIII (1294–1303)	Rudolph of Hapsburg becomes emperor (1273)	Model Parliament of Edward I (1295)	Philip IV (1285–1314)		1300
Babylonian Captivity of the Church (1305–1376)		. . Hundred Years' War . . (1337–1453)		Portuguese independence assured by victory over Castile (1385)	
Great Schism (1378–1417)		Loss of all France except Calais (1453)	Death of Joan of Arc (1431)	Union of crowns of Castile and Aragon (Ferdinand and Isabella–1469)	1400
		Wars of the Roses (1455–1485)	Louis XI (1461–1483)		

Introduction

There are several ways of considering the Middle Ages, to which the next four chapters are devoted. They may be thought of as the "springtime" of Western civilization, during which the tendencies which came to fruition in later centuries first became visible. To those who regard the Middle Ages in this way, there is no marked break between the medieval and the modern periods. The Renaissance was in no sense a rebirth, but rather the natural cultural expression of the urban civilization of the later Middle Ages. Once the rise of the towns had made possible the growth of a small but influential leisure class, it was only to be expected that this leisure class should turn away from the predominantly religious interests of the "age of faith" that preceded it, when only the clergy had enough leisure to engage in serious cultural activity.

A second way of regarding the Middle Ages is to look upon them, as the men of the High Renaissance did, as a unique period sandwiched between the great age of antiquity and their own. They themselves were the moderns, and the men of Greece and Rome were the ancients. Both ancient and modern civilizations were dynamic and creative, whereas the civilization of the Middle Ages was static and culturally stagnant. It was, indeed, this latter concept of the Middle Ages that was responsible for the name that we still apply to them. The Middle Ages are in the middle between the civilizations of the ancient and of the modern world. The men of the Renaissance held that the civilization of the Middle Ages had been backward, dominated by clerics, possessed of a barbaric architecture (disparagingly called Gothic), interested in the next world rather than in this, uninterested in the search for new knowledge, and content with merely commenting on the Bible and the few works of antiquity known to it.

Although some truth may be conceded to this picture by twentieth-century historians, the whole would today be accepted by no one. For it is certain that almost everything in modern Western civilization can indeed be traced back to its roots in the Middle Ages, and the more knowledge is accumulated about the Middle Ages, the more it is possible to discern these roots. Yet the Middle Ages do also exhibit certain well-defined characteristics. An outlook clearly recognizable as medieval is visible, and it came to a rather abrupt end in the fourteenth and fifteenth centuries. A medieval voyager like Marco Polo appears to be almost different in kind from a conquistador like Hernando Cortes or an adventurer like Sir Francis Drake. The collapse of medieval civilization can be seen in the peculiar reaction to the Black Death, with its mass hysteria, the parades of flagellants, the violent attacks on the immorality of the clergy and the Avignon papacy, the almost universal belief that the plague was a punishment of God for the wickedness of the people, the interest in devil-worship and the dance of death. Such a reaction to social and physical catastrophes was distinctly medieval and never reappears in such a form in later centuries. The people of the time, at least in Europe outside Italy, indeed felt that a world was coming to an end, that the world they had known was passing away, perhaps even more clearly than the Romans had perceived the disintegration of their world in the fifth century under the hammer-blows of the barbarians.

With the passing of the Middle Ages, there passed away also the concept of a Europe coterminous with Christendom, whose natural form of government was a universal state, inspired by a universal Church. The universal state—an idea inherited from the Romans, who actually ruled such an empire—became split up into many national states, and the universal Church ceased to be universal under the impact of the Protestant Reformation. Even in states whose national religion remained Catholicism, the Church was no longer a truly universal Church. The pope, though recognized as head of the Church, was no longer all-powerful in matters of religion. The French Gallican Church, for example, though Catholic in doctrine, was nevertheless dominated by French clerics and by the French king, rather than by the pope.

If one considers the period of the Middle Ages from the point of view of its political and religious theory and, to some extent, its practice, it may be distinguished with considerable sharpness from the period that succeeded it— but less sharply from the Roman era that preceded it and was also dominated by the notion of universality. The Germanic barbarians accepted the Roman framework they had inherited and changed it as little as they could. Charlemagne added to his empire some countries that had never been in the Roman Empire. But the means that he used to incorporate them within his polity were provided for him by the Church; and he himself was as interested in the conversion of the heathen as he was in merely subjecting them to his political jurisdiction. He regarded himself as the ruler of Christendom rather than as the ruler of a united Europe. The philosophy and theology of the Middle Ages were solidly based upon the work of the Greeks, Plato and Aristotle. Medieval philosophy struck out along no new paths. The problem of knowledge (epistemology), which has dominated modern philosophy since at least the time of Descartes—How does the subjective mind know the objective world?—was not felt to be such a crucially important question in the Middle Ages. The Middle Ages were interested rather in the question of universals—whether the Idea, or abstraction, is real, or whether the particular alone has reality—a problem inherited from Plato. Interest in this problem simply appears to evaporate in modern times, and now is usually regarded as a tiresome splitting of hairs indulged in by medieval thinkers.

Thus the Middle Ages can also, in a sense, be regarded as the culmination of the ancient world, its last dying thrashings before the opening of a new era. If this is the correct way to view the Middle Ages, then the seeds of the new era that are undoubtedly visible in the period should be taken for what they are, seeds planted then that bore fruit in later times. The historian should search for such seeds and identify them. The age looked both backward and forward, some elements conservative and looking to the past for inspiration, others looking forward, discontent with their heritage from the past and feeling something new stirring within them. The historian should attempt to discern both impulses and to distinguish between them.

In the chapters that follow, the Middle Ages will be treated as a whole, as if the period were a separate civilization. Each chapter covers a single topic, or series of topics, from the fall of the Roman Empire to the last days of the Middle Ages. The writer is well aware that the centuries covered could have been treated separately, and within a chronological framework— for example, the early Middle Ages, to 1000 A.D.; the High Middle Ages, from 1000 to 1300; and the decline of the Middle Ages, from 1300 to 1500. From a strictly historical viewpoint such an arrangement might well have been preferable. But it would have entailed the separation of the older manorial system from the feudalism of the High Middle Ages, which rested upon manorialism as its economic base. A few paragraphs would have covered the towns of the early Middle Ages; a more extended treatment would have been reserved for the later periods, when the towns became really important and exercised much influence. The early kings would have become separated from the later kings; and so on.

Rather than make these separations, it has

been thought preferable to attempt to deal with the key institutions of the Middle Ages as a whole, and to depart from a strict chronological treatment. Chapter 9 begins with the early attempts to restore the universal empire and the failure of these attempts. It continues with a discussion of the fragmented Europe of feudalism and manorialism. The chapter concludes with an account of the revival of commerce and trade and the rise of towns—how they escaped from feudal control, and how trade and industry were organized within the towns. Chapter 10 is devoted to the Church, the key institution of the Middle Ages—its rise to supremacy in the thirteenth century, the means by which this dominance was attained, and the weaknesses to be observed in the ecclesiastical structure by the end of the century. Chapter 11 deals with the rise of the national state, the institution that put an end to the universalist aspirations of Church and State. This chapter is therefore concerned primarily with the medieval seeds of modern times and will provide a framework for the study of modern history, in which the national state has proved to be the key institution. Lastly, Chapter 12 is devoted to medieval culture as a whole, from the beginnings of this characteristic culture in the time of Charlemagne down to the close of the period.

There can be no doubt that this topical arrangement will present certain difficulties for the student, who will be expected to jump about somewhat in time. To assist him in his chronological orientation, a special chart appears on page 180. This chart shows the key events, century by century. It should therefore be consulted whenever it is desired to place any event in its proper historical perspective and to see what is taking place in some other sector of medieval life at the same time. The separate chapters also have their own charts, which deal in more detail with the events recounted in them. But for an over-all view of medieval history, it will be essential to turn back to this special chart. The time sequence of events and the relation between religious, political, economic, and other spheres are essential to an understanding of the period. By assigning the ordering of these events to a chart the writer has taken a calculated risk that the student will not neglect this task, which is necessary for his proper comprehension.

NINE

Political, Social, and Economic Structure
of the Middle Ages

❖ The political structure of the early Middle Ages

We have now considered the Roman Empire and the states that entered into its inheritance in the East, where a centralized government was still possible and the Roman governmental structure to some degree survived. In the West, however, such centralized rule was impossible. Throughout the period which followed the fall of the Roman Empire, which is conventionally known as the Middle Ages, all rule was local, based upon much smaller units than in Roman times. The only truly effective rule for many centuries was that exercised by the landowners over those who dwelt on their lands. Kings continued to exist; but though their title might be recognized and a formal allegiance paid to them, their authority was always challenged by some landowners in their kingdoms, and their writ seldom ran beyond the areas which they could control and threaten with their troops. No monarch until the late Middle Ages had any bureaucracy worthy of the name. He could call upon the services of the literate clergy to perform some of his administrative chores; but these men were not full-time paid servants. Tax collection was rudimentary, confined, as a rule, to a few indirect taxes and certain irregular obligations. Even the armies at the disposal of these monarchs were rarely paid. The troops were obligated to serve for a stated period and had to provide for their own subsistence during that period.

The papacy, on the other hand, retained at least a skeleton of the Roman organization. The papal court always had its quota of full-time bureaucrats, whose effectiveness increased in the later Middle Ages. Though far from strong in the early Middle Ages, as an organization it was always more effective than that of any contemporary medieval monarch. At the height of the Middle Ages it was by far the most efficient administrative system in the West, as its duties were more numerous and its interests more widespread than those of any monarch. The medieval Church was a unique institution, and its interests and tasks were both religious and secular. Its rise to power and its decline in face of the competition offered by the growing national states will therefore be studied in a special chapter. In the present chapter there will be occasional references to the position of the Church within the feudal system, and some of its relations with secular powers will be discussed. The fuller consideration of the Church itself will be reserved for Chapter 10.

THE FRANKISH KINGDOM AND EMPIRE

Mention has already been made of the kingdom established by Clovis at the end of the fifth century. This kingdom his successors were unable to hold together, and only for brief periods was it united under one ruler. The later Merovingian monarchs, although they retained their title of king, tended to lose any real authority they possessed to their chief ministers, who were called stewards of the household, or "mayors of the palace" (*major domus*). This position, in turn, tended to become hereditary. In the early eighth century one of these mayors, Charles Martel (the Hammer) was able to unite the whole Merovingian kingdom once more under his effective rule. For a few years he ruled without even troubling to fill the vacancy in the monarchy, and he increased his prestige immeasurably by defeating a Muslim expedition which penetrated into France (Battle of Poitiers or Tours, 732). However, Charles himself was of illegitimate birth and, perhaps for this reason, did not himself aspire to the title of king. His son, Pepin the Short, inherited the position of his father, but for some years was content to rule as mayor. He kept the old Merovingian monarchy in being by ensconcing a scion of the royal Merovingian house once more on the throne. The time came at last, however, when he considered himself strong enough to send his puppet to a monastery and legitimize his rule by having himself crowned king.

It should be recognized that Pepin, strong as he was, possessed a relatively limited authority in his domains. The Frankish nobles objected to any kind of control over them, and certainly preferred a merely titular ruler. Such power as Pepin was able to wield he owed to his control of royal lands, which were greater in extent than those of any other individual lord, and the military rights that went with his land and the royal position. He could command also the services of the higher clergy, who were appointed to their positions by him. These services were extremely useful to him, since literacy was virtually confined to the clergy at the time, and such administrative regulations as he was able to enforce had to be prepared in his chancery and promulgated in written form. It would therefore clearly be of the greatest value to him if he could secure the legitimization of his own position, and command not only the compelled support or acquiescence of his subjects, but their freely given loyalty.

As it happened, at this time a new king of the Lombards named Aistulf was engaged in consolidating his domains in Italy, and had built up a fairly effective fighting force. If he wished to rule a united kingdom even in northern Italy, two obstacles stood in his way. The exarchate of Ravenna, the old Roman imperial capital of the fifth century, had been in Byzantine hands since the conquests of Justinian; while Rome itself owed a nominal allegiance to the Byzantine emperor but was in all important respects independent. The popes might certainly in ordinary circumstances have hoped for help against Aistulf from their theoretical overlord in Constantinople, particularly since the emperor's own possessions in Italy were also threatened. But the imperial throne was occupied in 751 by a strict iconoclast, Constantine V, and his relations with the papacy were embittered by the controversy. Pope Zacharias, who occupied the papal throne, was of no mind to settle the controversy in the emperor's favor; but on the other hand his predecessors had not been able to persuade Charles Martel, Pepin's father, to give them any aid against the Lombard predecessor of Aistulf, since the latter was Charles' ally and had helped him against the Muslims. Thus the request of Pepin to the head of Christendom, asking his opinion "whether he who held the power should also hold the title," must have been recognized at once by the astute Greek from southern Italy who occupied the papal throne as a heaven-sent opportunity to gain the Frankish support he so sorely needed. He therefore replied in the affirmative, whereupon Pepin called together a group of Frankish lords, who duly proclaimed him king.

Stephen II, who succeeded Pope Zacharias the following year, followed his predecessor's policy with energy. Aistulf had already captured Ravenna, and it could be only a matter of time before he marched on Rome. Pepin's alliance must be secured by a more signal act of favor than mere acquiescence in his assumption of the throne. The aged missionary St. Boniface, the leading churchman in Frankish realms, who had spent much of the second half of his life in reforming the Frankish Church with the aid of Charles Martel and Pepin and with the full support of the papacy, was instructed to crown Pepin king of the Franks. This was accomplished early in 752. Soon afterward negotiations were begun between Pepin and the pope, while the Lombard monarch prepared to march on Rome and the papal lands in central Italy. In 753 Stephen addressed a last appeal to his overlord in Constantinople but took the precaution of sending emissaries to Pepin at the same time. When the overture to Constantinople met with no promise of support but merely instructions to demand the restoration of Ravenna by the Lombards, while the overture to Pepin met with a prompt invitation to visit him, Stephen decided to make the voyage to France. There he crowned Pepin once more with his own hands, threatening with papal wrath anyone who presumed in later times to dispute the crown against any of Pepin's descendants.

The negotiations having proved satisfactory, Stephen returned to Rome. The next year (755), Pepin came over the Alps with an army, and shut up Aistulf in his own capital of Pavia. He was permitted to emerge only when he promised to abandon his recent conquests. Having no intention of carrying out his promises, he returned to the attack as soon as Pepin's back was turned, to the extreme discomfiture of Stephen, who now addressed more piteous appeals than ever to the Frankish king. The latter came over the Alps again in 756, and again defeated Aistulf, imposing the same terms as before. But this time Pepin made an outright gift of the lands taken from the Lombard to the pope. This was the famous Donation of Pepin, a legitimate donation of lands won by conquest. Although it was some time before the popes were able to exercise full authority over this territory, the Donation remained the legal instrument by which the popes maintained their lands in Italy until the nineteenth century. It is probable that Pope Stephen had already asserted his rights to the lands thus given to him by presenting to Pepin a document known as the Donation of Constantine, which had evidently been recently forged by the papal curia. According to this document, the Roman emperor Constantine, having been cured of leprosy and converted to Christianity by Pope Sylvester I, granted to the pope and his successors all his western dominions. The pope was to be the

"highest and chief of all priests in the whole world." It is not known whether Pepin was impressed by this document, but much was to be made of it by the papacy before it was unmasked as a forgery by the fifteenth-century humanist Lorenzo Valla.

By the end of his reign Pepin was able to bequeath to his two sons a united kingdom which was now the recognized ally and supporter of the papacy. The emperor at Constantinople, having failed to respond to papal appeals and too weak to assert his own rights by force, had lost his exarchate forever. Neither king nor pope was ever to relinquish it again. The new monarchy had been twice sanctified, by the Church as well as by the nobles of the kingdom. The ground had thus been prepared for the reign of Charlemagne (Charles the Great) and the restoration of the empire in the West. His younger brother having died within three years of the joint accession of the brothers to the rule of the kingdom, Charles was able to enjoy undisputed rule thereafter.

The long reign of Charlemagne (768–814) is notable above all for the fact that for the first time since the fall of Rome, the West knew a ruler whose lands were greater than those of the emperor in Constantinople, but whose rule, as we shall see, was no stronger than the hands that wielded or the institutions that supported it. Charles was unquestioned master in his own realm. He kept his lords loyal to him by oaths and the threat of severe sanctions, which he had no hesitation in inflicting on the rebellious. He fought the Saxons for twenty-three years, compelled them to accept Christianity, and incorporated their territories into his empire. He defeated the Asiatic Avars to the east of Germany, and converted them to Christianity likewise. He was compelled to intervene in Italy again when a new Lombard monarch tried to retake his former possessions, deprived the monarch of his kingdom, and ruled it through his own nominees. He assured the undisturbed possession of the Donation of his father by the papacy, though reserving the right to see that it was well ruled. Only in Spain did he suffer a severe defeat when the Basques fell upon his rear guard at Roncesvalles. Even

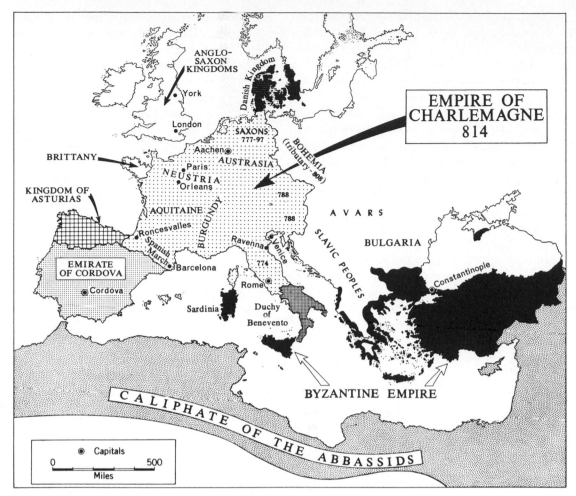

so, he was able to establish a Frankish zone on the Spanish side of the Pyrenees, in charge of one of his counts.

The administrative system of Charles was simple, but, as long as he himself lived, it was effective. Every freeman in his realms was bound to him by an oath of allegiance, and every lord had certain duties to perform for the monarch. The monarch saw to it that the lords did what was assigned to them, on pain of being charged not only with dereliction of duty but with perjury. He appointed counts to look after subdivisions of his realm, called counties. He issued ordinances (capitularies), giving all his officers detailed instructions on every matter that concerned him, from the management of his own personal estates to the duties of his emissaries when they were abroad on his business. At regular intervals he sent out personal emissaries (*missi dominici*), a count and a bishop or other leading clergyman from some other jurisdiction, to enquire into the administration of each county. For the frontier areas, where the counts needed to keep a military force in being against possible raids from beyond the empire, Charles appointed special "counts of the march," or margraves. These were responsible to him for the preservation of peace on the frontiers they guarded, and were entitled, when necessary, to the support of his own troops. As with the civil and military administrators, so with the Church. Charles appointed, or caused the local clergy to appoint, men of whom he approved to all the high positions in his realm. He had no hesitation in calling upon their services—as, for example, to serve as missi —often to the detriment, as some of them discreetly complained, of their dioceses. No one was spared from attending his annual assemblies of notables, save on grounds of illness or infirmity.

Charlemagne was one of the most autocratic of rulers the world has yet seen. He was one of the few who was able to exact absolute obedience from all his subjects. Yet, autocratic as he was, he recognized his responsibility to God. He felt himself to have been chosen by God to rule. His courtiers called him David, and frequently made allusion to his role as a second David, destined to lead the Christian people in a new age and to convert the heathen to the true religion. His favorite work was Augustine's *City of God*, which, being himself illiterate, he had read to him whenever he could, and always kept by him. He tried to rule with justice and administer his heritage according to the light that God had given him.

This did not mean that he regarded himself as in any way responsible to God's vice-regent on earth. On the contrary, he looked upon the pope as a useful collaborator, but in no sense his superior. He was willing to grant the pope every honor due to him as the representative of God and the head of the Church, but there is no evidence that any time he ever deferred to the pope's opinion on any subject. When an important heresy (adoptionism) was proclaimed by a Spanish archbishop and by a bishop within the empire, it was Charles who summoned a synod to declare the bishop heretical, and it was he who pronounced sentence upon him; it was Charlemagne who took a strong position on the procession of the Holy Spirit, thus forcing the pope into a more direct opposition to the Byzantine emperor than the more diplomatic pontiff desired. It was Charlemagne and his clergy who stated the moderate position on the iconoclastic controversy that was afterward adopted by the papacy. When Leo III became pope, Charles addressed a fatherly letter of advice to him as to how he should conduct himself. Later he restored this pope to the throne from which he

Portion of mosaic, dating originally from the ninth century, outside the Lateran in Rome. St. Peter is shown bestowing a pallium on Pope Leo III (left) and a banner on Charlemagne (right). According to the inscription St. Peter gives life to the pope and victory to the emperor. (PHOTO BY ALINARI)

had been violently driven by enemies who accused him of adultery, perjury, and other crimes. Yet the manner in which he handled this restoration made it clear that he was pleasing himself. Contrary to the advice of Alcuin, head of the palace school at Aachen, who reminded him that "the pope could not be judged by anyone," Charles required him to take an oath attesting his innocence, thus in effect sitting in judgment upon him. Throughout the affair he behaved as if the attack on the pope were an attack upon one who held his confidence and was entitled to be supported as a lord supports his vassal.

On Christmas Day, 800, Charlemagne was crowned emperor by Leo III in St. Peter's in Rome. His biographer Einhard claims that the new emperor was annoyed because he had not been consulted in advance. There has been much controversy among historians ever since as to why he should have been annoyed. It is held by some that Leo would never have acted without the sanction of Charles, and that the emperor had for years given every indication that some day he proposed to take the title. Others have pointed out, with justice, that Charles might well not have relished being crowned by a pope who only two days before had cleared himself of serious charges by an oath. There is no doubt that the coronation embroiled Charles further with the Byzantine Empire, whose ruler alone was entitled to be called emperor. It is also possible that Charles, without the gift of foreseeing the future, might have realized that coronation by a pope would come to be regarded as the legitimizing of the imperial position, and that subsequent popes could make their own terms for their participation in the ceremony. That this may very well have been in Charles' mind is suggested by the care with which he had his own son Louis crowned emperor before he died—a wasted precaution, since Louis in fact had himself crowned by the pope as soon after the death of his father as he could. It is a historical fact that all the subsequent emperors did not regard themselves as truly crowned unless the ceremony was performed by the pope, and many popes drove hard bargains before they would agree to it.

It does not seem that Charles ever gave much thought to what was to become of his empire after his death. It was the Germanic custom that an inheritance of land should be divided among the sons of the testator. Charles evidently regarded the empire as his own personal domain, of which he could dispose at will, as a landowner divided his land. In 806, while he had still three sons living, he decreed the division of his empire among them and forbade them to interfere with one another in their respective realms. Between 806 and 813 two of these sons died. Only then did he decide to crown his surviving son Louis emperor, and thus ensure the continuance of the empire which had been personally bestowed upon himself by God. Louis, on his own death in 840, did indeed divide it among his three sons, though the eldest was alone to have the title of emperor. Since these sons and their own sons fought constantly among themselves for the preservation and enlargement of their domains, and all had to fight against invasions of Northmen and Magyars, the Carolingian Empire, before the end of the ninth century, ceased to be an empire worthy of the name. Indeed, the Carolingian male line itself died out. None of the national monarchs who succeeded to the various subdivisions of the empire was descended directly from Charlemagne; all rose to power by their own efforts and by the choice of their nobles. Much of the territory given by Louis to his eldest son, Lothair, became a no man's land, disputed between France and Germany to this day (Alsace-Lorraine).

Yet Charles was in a very real sense right in his initial understanding that his empire was a personal possession. Although the Church was anxious to have a Western empire to replace the Eastern empire, which was powerless to protect it and adopted its own theological positions without reference to the papacy, it could not create such an empire when conditions for it did not exist. Obsessed as it was with the notion that there ought to be a universal State coterminous with Christendom, as there was a universal Church—a notion that derived largely from its early history in the Roman Empire— the Church did not see that the conditions in Europe were not ripe for the restoration of an empire. High clerics in the reign of Charle-

**DIVISION OF
CHARLEMAGNE'S KINGDOM
AT TREATY OF VERDUN—843**

0   100   200
Miles   ⊙ Capitals

magne and his successors did their best to make the empire of Charlemagne survive, but they could not succeed in their enterprise. For Charles had created no imperial institutions, no civil service that could rule once his strong arm was removed from the helm. The officials who performed services for Charles were not paid servants, but men who were given lands, the only form of wealth at the time, in exchange for their services. This land they could retain as their own private possession afterward, when the monarch had ceased to be able to compel their services. The landowners and nobles, who had wielded power in the Merovingian age, had not lost their power in the reign of Charles. They merely bided their time, while submitting with good grace to the obviously superior resources and greater military might of the emperor. Charles had conquered more lands outside of the Frankish kingdom, but had given them over to the rule of his subordinates. These

subordinates had little difficulty in throwing off the authority of his successors, and became rulers in their own right. The disputes among the successors of Charlemagne merely enabled them to obtain their independence sooner.

FOUNDATION OF THE HOLY ROMAN EMPIRE —OTTO I

Yet history was to show that the imperial idea had not been laid to rest. Though the title of emperor in the Carolingian succession was extinguished with the death of Ludwig the Child in 911, and the Germanic lords who had formally acknowledged him as king were by this time entirely independent, the latter nevertheless were accustomed to the idea of having a German monarch, even though they had no intention of giving him much power or authority. They thus returned to their ancient practice of electing a king as their acknowledged leader

Chronological Chart

Foundation of Venice	*ca.* 568
Reign of Pepin the Short	752–768
Pope Stephen II crowns Pepin king of Franks	754
Donation of Pepin to papacy	756
Reign of Charlemagne	768–814
Charlemagne defeats Lombards and assumes title of king	773–774
Battle of Roncesvalles—Defeat of Charlemagne's army under Roland in Spain	778
Charlemagne completes conquest of Saxons	785
First invasions of England by Northmen (Danes)	787
Charlemagne crowned emperor by Pope Leo III	800
Reign of Louis the Pious	814–840
Oaths of Strasbourg	842
Treaty of Verdun	843
Division of Empire at death of Lothair	855
Continuous invasions of England by Northmen	856–875
Foundation of Novgorod, traditionally by Rurik	862
Alfred the Great, king of England—Danes checked	871–900
Charles the Fat, emperor and king of East and West Franks (West Franks 884–887)	881–887
Foundation of Kiev by Northmen	882
Siege of Paris by Northmen	886
Deposition of Charles the Fat	887
Magyars cross Carpathians into Central Europe	*ca.* 895
Rollo becomes Duke of Normandy	911
Trading rights granted in Constantinople to Varangians	907

Robert, Count of Paris and brother of Odo, elected king of France	922
Battle of Augsburg—Magyars defeated by Otto I	955
Otto the Great crowned emperor by pope	962
Hugh Capet king of France	987
St. Stephen I king of Magyars (Hungary)—Completion of conversion of Hungarians to Roman Catholic Christianity	997–1038
Canute (Cnut) Danish king of England	1017–1035
Normans conquer southern Italy from Byzantines	1042–1068
Venetian war with Constantinople —extensive maritime trading rights granted to Venetians	1063
Invasion of England by Duke William of Normandy— Battle of Hastings	1066 (Oct.)
Normans conquer Sicily from Muslims	1072–1091
Norman sack of Rome (Robert Guiscard)	1084
Norman kingdom of Sicily	1091–1266
Diet of Roncaglia—Frederic I asserts imperial rights over Italian towns	1158
Alliance of Lübeck and Hamburg to protect Baltic trade routes	1244
Privileges granted to German towns in London	1282
Confederation of Cologne— League of Hansa towns against Denmark	1370
Richard II of England renews Hansa privileges	1377
Last assembly of Hanseatic League	1669

for occasions when they had need of one. The second such king, Henry the Fowler, formerly duke of Saxony (919–936), justified their choice by defeating the Magyars and was also able to win the land of Lorraine from France. Thus he bequeathed a strong position to his son Otto I, who was chosen king without opposition. Otto was by far the strongest lord in Germany, but his position would not be secure if his nobles decided to combine against him. He needed powerful allies, and there was one place where he might hope to find them. This was the Church.

The Church had certain manifest advantages as an ally. It possessed the best administrators in the realm; it had an efficient working organization; and it was controlled by the higher clergy under the nominal, but not in this age effective, control of the papacy. What was necessary if the Church organization were to be used for the benefit of the kingdom of Germany was that Otto as king should make all the appointments, without the approval of the papacy. The obvious way to accomplish this was to constitute himself, like Charlemagne, the protector of the papacy, and control the appointment even of the popes themselves. The higher clergy in Germany were drawn from the feudal families, but their position could not be inherited, in part owing to the canon law against the marriage of the clergy (which was not very strictly observed), and because in any case all appointments lapsed at the death of the incumbent. Otto here was in a strong position. He had the right to appoint all the higher clergy in his realm, and since they had no other regular source of income, they needed the land which he alone could give them.

Thus was inaugurated the policy of what was later called lay investiture, which, though it was not new with Otto, was carefully systematized by him. The bishops were tied to him by feudal tenure, required to provide both military and financial aid from their territories. Certainly the Ottonian bishops were not noted for their piety, but he was careful to appoint competent and loyal administrators—his first appointments, indeed, being made from his own very competent family. Many of these clerics actually went to war themselves on his behalf,

some of them becoming noted warriors, no doubt the envy of Otto's brother rulers in Europe. In short, the German Church, though partially independent, like other feudal magnates, usually lent its aid to the monarch, helping him to keep the lay feudal nobles in their place.

In 951 the first opportunity occurred to interfere in Italy. The Lombards had revived their kingship, but it was ineffectual; and the greater part of Italy had become the prey of rival lords. Taking advantage of a dispute over the Lombard crown, Otto made short work of the pretender, married the widow of the previous king, and became king of the Lombards himself, a title, it will be remembered, once held by Charlemagne. Recalled to Germany by renewed pressure from the Magyars, he was summoned for aid by a pope (John XII) in 961 against, as usual, the Lombards. This time, after his customary victory over the Lombard nobles, he forced the pope to crown him emperor. At the same time he extracted a formal promise, from a council called for the purpose, that his confirmation was to be required for all elections to the papacy.

The Roman nobles, who for many years had been accustomed to this privilege, usually electing one of the feeblest of their own number, objected; and as soon as Otto had left they proceeded to elect a pope of their own. Otto returned, ousted the Roman choice, and put in his own nominee. When this one, too, was driven out, the new emperor lost his patience, returned with yet another army, and inflicted a sanguinary punishment on the rebels. Thereafter Rome was quiet. The emperor had established the right to approve of the election of popes; he was likely to be untroubled by papal interference with his choice of the German clergy; and he was now the accepted overlord of Germany and Italy. And the Roman dream of Charlemagne had once more been revived, to the irreparable damage, as we shall see, of both countries.

The papacy still possessed its estates in Italy, now under the overlordship of the German emperor. But it had lost what authority it had over the German clergy, being no longer able to choose the appointees or invest them. A pope

ROMAN EMPIRE
OF THE GERMAN NATION
AT THE DEATH OF OTTO I
973

0　100　200
Miles

◉ Capital

could not even hold his own office without imperial approval. He was as much a servant of the secular power as ever the popes were under Charlemagne. Yet, from the papal point of view, there was one advantage, slight as it was, that Otto had over Charlemagne. He was no theologian, and his appointees were not chosen for their piety. The empire was thus vulnerable on religious grounds; a movement for the reform of the clergy would have the support of true Christians throughout Germany and the Christian world, and might even be fortunate enough to find some day a successor of Otto the Great who was himself a Christian before he was an emperor. Already, even in the darkest hour of the papacy, when the Holy See itself was a plaything of the Roman nobles, the reform movement had been set in motion which was ultimately to lead to the re-establishment of the authority of Church and papacy, and to the destruction of the empire itself.

RENEWED BARBARIAN INVASIONS— NORTHMEN AND MAGYARS

Before we come to the feudal system and the economic substructure that nourished it, a few words should be said on the invasions which helped to destroy the Carolingian Empire and made organized government on a larger scale than the county or duchy difficult for more than a century. Asiatic Magyars penetrated into Eastern Europe and were a constant menace, in particular to the Germans, before most of them settled down in the country now known as Hungary. Muslims working out of Tunis disrupted what Mediterranean trade survived, until their power was broken by the Normans and the rising Italian maritime cities. But the most important invaders were the Viking Northmen,

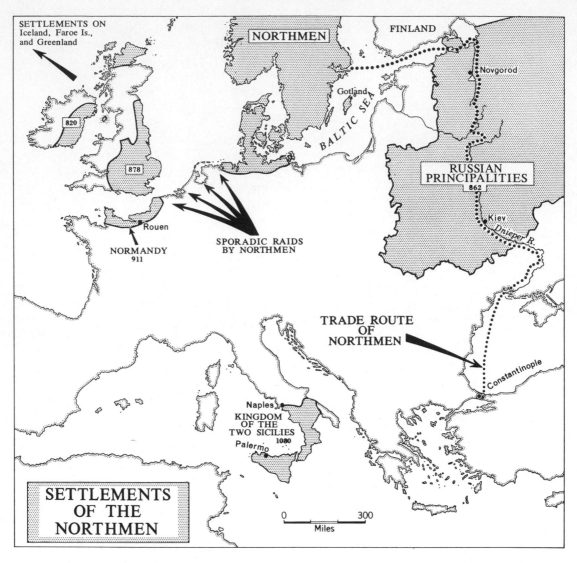

SETTLEMENTS ON
Iceland, Faroe Is.,
and Greenland

NORTHMEN

FINLAND

Novgorod

Gotland

BALTIC SEA

RUSSIAN
PRINCIPALITIES
862

820

878

Kiev

Dnieper R.

Rouen

NORMANDY
911

SPORADIC RAIDS
BY NORTHMEN

TRADE ROUTE
OF
NORTHMEN

Constantinople

Naples

KINGDOM
OF THE
TWO SICILIES
1080

Palermo

SETTLEMENTS
OF THE
NORTHMEN

0   300
Miles

who raided Western Europe constantly until they too finally settled down in various parts of Europe. It was they who founded the duchy of Normandy, which was received as a fief from the French crown. For a long time the Northmen terrorized much of England, Scotland, and Ireland, and exercised rule intermittently over considerable sections of those countries. Lastly, a group of Northmen in the late tenth century conquered Sicily and a part of southern Italy. Wherever they settled, they adopted the feudal system of neighboring countries, but adapted it to their own ends, making it far more systematic and efficient than in the countries of its origin. On the whole, the

Norman kingdoms were the best organized and managed of any realms in the early Middle Ages.

The renewed invasions of the Northmen and Magyars meant that the Europeans were compelled to band together under whatever local authority was in a position to offer resistance, since they could not rely on the weak central authority to come to their aid. Thus the Carolingian Empire, which for a time had postponed the full establishment of what came to be called feudalism, in the end succumbed to its advance. The empire of Otto the Great was itself a wholly feudal empire, in this respect differing in essential features from that of Charlemagne. Feudalism, in essence a substitute for central authority, came to full fruition in the centuries after Charlemagne, and persisted throughout the Middle Ages until it was gradually superseded by the national state and national monarchy of the later Middle Ages. The rest of this chapter will therefore be devoted to a discussion of feudalism as a form of government and social organization, followed by a brief account of the economic substructure which enabled it to function. In the following chapter we shall take up the history of the Church in the Middle Ages, and thereafter return to the national monarchies and the national states which were ultimately to replace the outdated concept of the universal empire.

❖ The feudal system

When the empire of Charlemagne disintegrated, and the successor monarchs were unable to establish effective rule over even their relatively small territories, power relapsed into the hands of the landowners who had been compelled to submit to the superior power of Charlemagne in the heyday of his empire. These landowners possessed private armies supported from their own resources and were thus able to maintain law and order to some degree within their own territories. This power, it should be understood, was not exercised in a completely arbitary manner; there was a network of customary and legal sanctions upon its exercise which, though not so strong as sanctions exercised by monarchs who had armies and bureaucracies at their disposal to enforce their will, were nonetheless adequate to keep powerful landowners from doing everything their fancy dictated. The relationship between lord (suzerain)[1] and vassal, between the bestower and receiver of the fief, is the heart of the medieval feudal system; and the duties imposed on each party to the transaction by feudal law

and custom are the chief sanctions on the arbitrary use of their power by either. A vassal had the power to go to war against his suzerain, and, indeed, only too frequently he did so; but, if he did, unless the suzerain had failed to perform his own duties, the vassal not only broke the feudal law and could be called to account for it in the feudal court of his lord, but also broke an oath of fealty which he had taken. And this itself, in an age when an oath was taken upon the Cross or upon holy relics, and was considered sacred, was enough to brand him as a false knight and hold him up to infamy.

So the sanctions in the feudal system were both material and moral, as under any effective law. The difficulty was that too often the law could not be enforced, and it never could be enforced without war; hence a man might brave the moral sanctions if his material interests were involved and if he thought he had a chance in the ensuing conflict. It was thus an ineffectual system rather than an arbitrary or immoral one; and since it was also an unequal one, in that the peasants and lower classes had few rights, and those unenforceable without military power to back them, it was not one that would obtain the assent of more than a small minority. It was likely to endure only as long as the effective power could be kept within the small class of nobles. Later medieval and modern history can be viewed largely as the attempt to destroy the privileges of the upper class and replace them with a more equitable system, giving more rights to ever increasing numbers of people. The national state, under a monarch backed by a middle class which hardly existed in earlier medieval times, provided such a system, however imperfectly; and the establishment of national states in several European countries, coincident with the destruction of the greater part of the feudal system, may be said to mark the real beginning of modern history.

THE ROMAN HERITAGE

The origin of the feudal system lies far back in the Roman and Germanic past. In the later days of the Roman Empire, as we have seen, there was a tendency for the large estates to

---

[1] The word *suzerain* is used in this chapter to denote the superior lord in a lord-vassal relationship, although the word has in certain countries a definite technical meaning not applicable to all such overlords.

This castle at Obidos (Portugal), only slightly restored, is now a government hotel.

grow larger, and for the independent small landowner to put himself under the protection of a larger one, who was better able to defend himself against the encroaching barbarians. This practice was called *patrocinium*, or patronage. As a rule, military services were not required so much as cultivation of land, whether such land was given to the farmer by the lord or already belonged to him. This relationship between patron and client is entirely a late Roman feature, and has little to do with the patron-client relationship in earlier days, when the client was usually of the same social class but inferior in worldly goods.

During the period of the Merovingian kings there was as much danger to a small independent man as in the late Roman Empire. So we find in the early Middle Ages an established practice of *commendation* by a poor and landless man, who asked for protection from a noble in a better situation. The more powerful nobles could gather large bands of followers in this way; the greater they were, the more men would commend themselves to them, for the safer would be the protection. Some of these followers were lesser nobles themselves and not farmers, but for some reason they had lost their land. In these cases the patron, after commendation, would take them into his service as military followers.

Another heritage from Roman times was similar to that of commendation. A free farmer who suffered from insecurity or had fallen into debt could yield up his land either to his creditor or to some noble, and ask for it back again as a tenant. This was called *precarium*, or requesting. Another form of precarium was simply the prayer by a landless farmer for some land to cultivate in exchange for goods and services. Since the noble had far too much land to cultivate himself, it was to his advantage to give it out to a good tenant. So the precarium helped him to take care of his needs, and was mutually advantageous. The Church, in particular, found the system valuable. It was forbidden to alienate Church lands altogether, but a precarious tenancy permitted it to have its lands cultivated without losing them; and in feudal times it had enough sanctions of its own peculiar kind at its disposal to permit it to protect its tenants as well as a secular lord.

The precarium, by the eighth century, had largely been replaced by the *beneficium*, or benefice, which was practically the same thing under a different name. Both were tantamount to leases of land for a limited period; but the later benefices rarely took land from freeholders and gave them back, for there was little such land available by this time. Benefices were given frequently by the great nobles to their officials and assistants in lieu of a money income. They were also given to lesser nobles who could provide great nobles with troops paid for out of the proceeds of the benefice. The Carolingian kings gave out such benefices freely, in many cases including an immunity from taxation and the performance of feudal services; then the land was held as a virtual freehold.

THE GERMANIC HERITAGE

The development from Roman times seems to be fairly clear. But in the system described above there seems to be an obvious parallel with the German custom of *comitatus*, already noted. Here, it will be remembered, the old warrior bands of Germans used to join the troop of an independent chieftain, to whom they were bound by ties of honor and fealty and for whom they were ready to fight and die. It would seem that in the early feudal period, before Charlemagne, Roman custom was predominant, and that the precarious system noted above arose in response to the definite needs of the time. But the necessity, under Germanic influence, became converted into a virtue; and all the ancient sanctions of the comitatus were gradually invoked to tie the lesser landholder and benefice holder to his lord. Moral sanctions now became established in addition to sanctions that were merely legal, and in addition to the ordinary ties of self-interest between landlord and tenant. The vassal, as he shortly came to be called, owed loyalty and allegiance to his lord, a virtue conspicuously missing from late Roman and Merovingian times. This development corresponded with the increasing militarization of the whole society and with the rise of a class of nobles whose interest ceased to be in land. Though of course he had to own land, the noble gave out most of it again to vassals in exchange primarily, not for goods and ordinary menial and farming services, but for military service under his command.

It is in this post-Carolingian period that feudalism based on the possession of fiefs comes to the fore. A fief was really only a hereditary benefice,[2] but almost invariably the obligation

upon the vassal or fief holder was to supply warriors. Knights who could ride on horseback and provide their own equipment were the most valued. Anyone who could not do this was unlikely to be given a fief. Hence fief holders finally became warriors belonging to the class of the nobility, or churchmen with such warriors under them, who could perform the same service.

RELATIONSHIP BETWEEN LORD AND VASSAL

The theoretical relationship—Practical complications—Subinfeudation The developed feudal system thus contained the lord or suzerain who held his land, originally or theoretically, by gift from the king, who was in theory the owner of all the land. This suzerain let out most of his land to vassals in exchange for military and certain other stipulated services to be described later; but he retained some land as a demesne from which he obtained the subsistence required for himself, his family, his personal landless military retainers, and his servants. The land received as fiefs by his vassals could also be subdivided, and let out again as fiefs to yet other vassals who would perform for them the same services as they themselves performed for their suzerains. This was a method of passing on some of the military obligations to others, and was called subinfeudation. At times the greater lords tried to check excessive subinfeudation, since by it they tended to lose control of their subtenants, who owed them no direct allegiance and could be reached only through their own personal vassals.

At this stage the process is not too complicated. Diagrammatically, it would look like this:

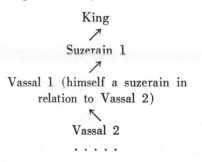

But unfortunately it was not in practice so simple. Any vassal could hold any number of

---

[2] A fief was not necessarily even land. Some honor or right could be held as a fief, entailing the usual obligations of a vassal.

fiefs from different suzerains; and sooner or later it would happen that, say, Vassal 2 in the diagram above would have let out part of his land as a fief to Suzerain 1, and would thus be in the relationship of a vassal to the vassal of this suzerain (Vassal 1), and yet be a suzerain in relation to the suzerain of his own suzerain! If this appears complicated, it is only a reflection of the actual state of feudal society, and may be illustrated in a more complex diagram (arrows indicate the direction of the services rendered). Part of Suzerain 2's land is held as fief from Suzerain 1, and another part, in a different locality, he has let out to the same suzerain:

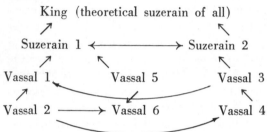

King (theoretical suzerain of all)

Suzerain 1 ⟷ Suzerain 2

Vassal 1   Vassal 5   Vassal 3

Vassal 2 ⟶ Vassal 6   Vassal 4

Puzzle: What happens when Suzerain 2 decides he will cease performing feudal services for Suzerain 1, and what will Vassal 3 do when called out by his respective suzerains?

The answer to the puzzle is that, if a vassal were anxious to do the right thing, he would give his personal service to one lord while allowing his own vassals to perform the remainder of his service. But clearly this would not hold good if he were called out by two lords at the same time who happened to be at war with one another.

It can be easily seen from these diagrams and examples that there was endless occasion for feudal wars. These could hardly have been avoided even if the feudal aristocracy had not in any case regarded war as a positive pleasure, their one great vocation in life, while they were content to hand over the management of their estates, from which they obtained their subsistence, to baseborn hirelings.

The legal structure—The feudal court In order to enforce his rights, the lord would periodically hold a court to which he summoned all his vassals. If any vassal did not appear, or if his equals in the court condemned him for

failure to perform his proper feudal services, his fief could be forfeited. If he were accused by another vassal in his lord's court, he could claim the right to single combat with his accuser. If he lost, he was presumed to be guilty.

The enforcement of the decree, however, was another matter. There were no means for driving him from a fief which he held in actual possession save war. It was thus of importance that all the vassals should sit on the court, since it was they also who would have to enforce the decree. If the guilty vassal had no greater lord to protect him, it was probable that the other vassals, fighting in unison under their suzerain, would succeed in compelling him to yield up the fief. It need hardly be emphasized how rough and ready such justice was; nor need it surprise us that many of the lesser nobility in later centuries supported the efforts of the kings to establish a king's justice, containing elements of Roman law, in preference to the feudal variety.

The duties of the lord toward his vassal The lord, of course, provided the vassal with his land in the first place. But it was also his duty to protect this land and the vassal from other lords or invaders. In this he was, in theory, only protecting his own land. It was also his duty to protect the vassal in other ways. If, for instance, a vassal were summoned to the king's court for an offense, as became possible when the kings began to hold courts for the administration of justice, it was the lord's duty to defend him. In theory, if the lord did not fulfill his obligation to protect the vassal, the contract was terminated, and the vassal no longer owed him allegiance. We find Pope Gregory VII later using this as an excuse for his deposition of the German emperor, and it is the basis for the much later idea of the supposed social contract, under which, as expounded by the English theorist John Locke, the people were released from their allegiance to the king if he did not maintain their "natural rights."

The duties of the vassal toward his lord The first duty of the vassal to his lord was allegiance, symbolized in the (Frankish) ceremony of homage. On being given, or on inheriting, a fief, the vassal would kneel, place his two hands within those of his lord, and declare himself his man. If the lord accepted the homage he kissed him as a sign of recognition of his vassalage. Since in theory a fief was not hereditary, an heir, on coming into his father's estate, had to do homage for his fief, which could, in theory also, be refused. In practice, the eldest son of a vassal inherited the fief of his father, and merely had to do homage for it, perform certain special services, and pay special dues, the equivalent of an inheritance tax. If a vassal died without male heirs, then the fief theoretically escheated (was restored) to the suzerain, even if there were a surviving daughter. But in practice this daughter inherited it, though the suzerain took her under his protection and saw that she was provided with a suitable husband, who then undertook the duties of the vassal. If there were no heirs, male or female, then the land did escheat. The fief was not subdivided between many sons, but passed down intact to the eldest (primogeniture), who could, of course, let it out by subinfeudation if he desired.

The chief duty for most fief holders was to provide a stipulated number of knights (mounted warriors), calculated in accordance with the size of the fief. The custom, however, varied in different parts, as indeed did all feudal arrangements. These warriors were bound to serve only for a definite, quite limited, period, a fact which made long campaigns difficult. The period, as a rule, was forty days in each year. However, the lord could promise booty or other rewards and then have his vassals follow him voluntarily—as, for instance, when William the Conqueror invaded England on the understanding that there would be new fiefs for all. In later medieval periods the military service could be commuted for a sum of money called scutage. The money was often more appreciated by the lord than military service, since it enabled him to hire mercenaries who would serve for a longer period of time. The Church also on occasion paid scutage instead of military service, since it had easier access to money than to warriors. Nevertheless, most ecclesiastical fiefs had some military service to perform, which was usually done by subinfeudation to lords who were willing to undertake the service.

The vassal had the duty of providing hospitality to his lord when the latter visited him. As this visit might be very expensive if the lord arrived with a large retinue, it was limited by custom and sometimes was commuted for a regular sum of money. The vassal also, as we have seen, had to attend the lord's court when requested.

When the lord was in financial difficulties—as, for instance, if he were trying to raise money to go on a Crusade—the vassal could be called upon for a gift, known as an aid. Aids were also given for the ransoming of the lord, for the knighting of his eldest son, and for the marriage of his eldest daughter. These again were limited by custom according to the size and value of the fief.

A further sum of money, known as a relief, was provided by the vassal on certain specified occasions. When an heir inherited his fief, it was customary to pay a relief, which might amount to as much as a whole year's revenue. When the lord himself died and was succeeded by his heir, a relief was also paid. Lastly, when a vassal wished to transfer his fief to someone else (the equivalent of a sale), then he had to give a relief to the lord in exchange for his permission to the transfer. All these reliefs were fixed by custom, and when the money economy began to take the place of the earlier commodity economy, the reliefs usually took the form of money payments. An heiress who wished to marry without the consent of the suzerain might persuade him to give it by offering him a sum of money. One of the best, if most irregular, sources of income for a lord was from the fief of a minor, or of an unmarried girl, whom he looked after till he or she came of age. The child for the time gave up what would have been his rights had he been of age to become a vassal, and the lord took the income from his estate. The lord did not have to reimburse the child for any losses he sustained during his infancy.

It should be emphasized that the lord did not live off the income provided him by his vassals, which was quite limited and given only at irregular intervals. He lived off the income from his demesne, which contained his personal manors run by his servants. These will be dealt with in a later section. Every vassal belonged to the feudal nobility himself, and he always possessed a demesne of his own unless he was a personal retainer living with his lord—a situation which became rare in the later feudal age. The primary purpose of the feudal system was to provide warriors for protection and prestige. It was the manorial system, the private demesnes of these feudal lords, which provided the economic base for the feudal system. The feudal nobility therefore was a military aristocracy which incidentally owned land, rather than a landed aristocracy which occasionally had to defend its property by military means. With the exception of the lord himself, the managers of the estates were of a different class from the nobility, were hired by them, and were treated as social inferiors. Most of the lords felt themselves too superior, and were too busy with their military affairs, to pay much attention to their estates. If this had not been so, they would not have given out so much of their land in financially unrewarding fiefs; they would, like the later Roman nobles, have lived in the lap of luxury from the intelligent exploitation of huge estates worked by laborers who could not rebel or leave the land.

THE SPECIAL POSITION OF THE FEUDAL KING

In view of the later importance of kings, a few words are necessary here on the anomalous position they occupied during the feudal age. Theoretically, as we have seen, the kings owned all the land, and every noble in a given country owed allegiance to his king. But, as a matter of historical fact, the greater nobles, perhaps the majority of them, had never received their land from a king, but had taken it for themselves during the period of disintegration following the breakup of the Carolingian Empire. The king, in fact, exercised very little power over them. The king's effective power was only what he derived from his own feudal estates, which were often, as in the case of France, by design of the nobles smaller in extent than those of many of the lords who owed nominal allegiance to him. The French lords, in choosing their king from the Capetian family, had probably agreed on the choice for the simple reason

that he was less powerful than they, and thus likely to present little threat to their power.

The king's position was naturally different in each country, according to the local conditions found there. The German king, who was usually also at the same time the Holy Roman emperor, was elected from among the German nobles; and, though there was a tendency to keep the office within certain families for long periods of time, it never did become formally a hereditary position. The king's power, as elsewhere, was derived from the estates of his house. His election as king conferred only prestige in addition to what he had had before, with two important exceptions. He had in his hands the appointment of the bulk of the higher clergy, a patronage that an astute monarch could manipulate to great advantage; and land left without heirs altogether escheated to him and not to any other noble. His prestige and title gave him the first refusal of the command in any all-German or all-European war, such as the Crusades. When the emperors tried to make good their claim to Italy, and sent a regular "Roman expedition" of German warriors over the Alps, their leadership was not challenged. For the rest, the only real feudal tie between the nobles and their elected monarch was the oath of allegiance which they took to him after election. The right to absolve from oaths, claimed by the papacy by virtue of its spiritual power, was indeed used as a political instrument for the deposition of an emperor. When Gregory VII wished to depose Henry IV of Germany, a prerogative naturally contested bitterly by this emperor, he solemnly absolved all the German nobles from their oaths of allegiance so that they could elect another emperor.

In England, after the conquest by Duke William of Normandy, the kings of his line actually did own all the land, since it had been acquired by conquest. They gave it out as fiefs, with certain restrictions on the raising of private armies which will be discussed in a later chapter on the rise of the English national state. It is only important here to note that in England the theory corresponded to the actual facts, with incalculable advantages for the monarchy.

The position of the French king, however,

is of greatest interest, since the Capetian kings used their theoretical powers and their prestige to such good effect that they were ultimately able to unify France under their rule. Hugh Capet and his successors actually owned only a small compact area around Paris. They owned this as counts, and their armies were only such as could be drawn from this comparatively small territory. Yet, as kings, they were socially of a higher rank than any of the more powerful lords in their realm. They were solemnly anointed as kings by the archbishop of Reims, and made to swear a coronation oath under which they promised to defend the humble, help the oppressed, preserve peace, maintain justice, and perform a number of other functions which were fantastically outside the scope of their real powers. But in theory they were expected to do this, and in their efforts they could usually count on the full support of the Church and the ecclesiastical officials, who had nothing, as a rule, to gain from the lawlessness created by the independent nobles. In addition, the king held in his hands much of the best patronage of the Church, especially in northern France.

The king, as theoretical owner of all the land in the territory vaguely called France, was owed allegiance by all the lords in his realm. His prestige was such that most nobles, at all events those of French origin, usually did perform the act of homage once in their lives; it cost them nothing, since the king was not in a position to take away their fiefs, and they did not have to give him anything substantial unless he was in a position to compel them. He was theoretically entitled to the usual military service from them, and could summon them to his court for the administration of justice. None of these rights was worth much as long as the kings were unable to enforce them. But in a society which laid so much store by custom and loyalty, they were not negligible. And the king had one immense advantage which was ultimately to prove crucial: If any lord did not obey the summons issued by him, then the lord was in the wrong. The king had the feudal law on his side if he went to war with the rebellious noble, and he had the right to call upon all the other lords in the kingdom to aid in punishing the rebel. Naturally the other nobles would consult their own interests in deciding whether or not they would obey the king; but it happened frequently enough that these interests would best be served by joining him and dispossessing the rebellious vassal. Philip Augustus used this power with extreme skill and effectiveness against his English vassal, John, king of England, as will be seen in more detail in Chapter 11. Philip in fact owned less land even in France than John himself. When John refused to obey his summons, Philip called upon the other French nobles to dispossess him; and since John commanded few French sympathies, Philip was able to take away the bulk of his lands and bestow them on his own followers as fiefs—with the great difference that Philip was now their real overlord, and not merely a theoretical one.

Finally, the king had all the social prestige belonging to his title. His wife would be queen, unlike the wife of any other noble—a position naturally sought after by heiresses. The king was often chosen as the most fitting protector of minors and of young women who had not yet found a suitable husband. And, like the German emperor, the French king was the natural leader for a crusade or other foreign war if he wished to go. It can be seen, therefore, that in shrewd and able hands the position of king, in spite of his relative poverty, had certain manifest advantages over the rest of the feudal nobility; and perhaps it will no longer seem so strange that from these small beginnings the French monarch was ultimately able to unify France and effectively control that feudal nobility which had elected him in the first place with far different expectations.

THE FEUDAL LORD AND LADY

The life of the feudal lord need not detain us long. Since their primary task was to provide protection for their family and retainers, all the greater lords tended to live in castles which were fortified to the best of their ability and surrounded by a moat. The castles themselves were often primitive enough. They were damp and unattractive inside, unless the lord was able to buy luxuries from the Orient, as many were

This medieval miniature shows the Israelite general Joab entertaining Abner, whom he is planning to murder. As in all these miniatures, the picture faithfully represents the illustrator's contemporary experience, and the feasting scene depicted here is no doubt authentically medieval. From a Picture Bible *(French), ca. 1250.* (COURTESY THE PIERPONT MORGAN LIBRARY. Ms. 638, folio 37)

able to do in the later Middle Ages. The lord himself, if he was a typical medieval aristocrat, enjoyed hunting and fighting; if there were no real wars to be fought, he engaged in jousting —mock battles which could be dangerous enough to the participants. He ate heartily, meat and venison predominating in his diet. His lady superintended the household, and busied herself in embroidery and needlework. Not infrequently she had to undertake the administrative duties of her husband as well as her own. If he went on a Crusade, she had to manage the fief; if he were killed on campaign, she had to undertake all his duties until she found herself a new husband or one was found for her by her relatives or by her late husband's suzerain. She might have to negotiate with her suzerain lord for permission to be allowed to remain a widow.

If a noble lady did not find a husband or did not care for the choices made by her male relatives, she could go to a convent. If she did not bear a child to her lord, preferably a male, then there was not usually much difficulty in finding some high cleric who would declare that the marriage was within the prohibited degrees and thus null and void from the beginning. This annulment was not too hard to reconcile with a clerical conscience, since so many members of the nobility were indeed closely related to one another.

In the later Middle Ages a code of chivalry, especially extolled by wandering troubadors and minstrels, sprang up, many features of which tended to glorify womanhood, making use of more romantic conceptions than were current in real life. The young knight was expected to form

Two knights do battle for a demoiselle, who is seen watching the combat. From a miniature, Tristan, ca. *1450.* (COURTESY THE PIERPONT MORGAN LIBRARY. Ms. 41, folio 49)

a romantic attachment to a lady of the court, who was to be his ideal and for whom he was expected to perform deeds of gallantry. He was always to observe perfect courtesy toward her, including the courtesy of loving and cherishing her above all other women. When he went out in the world, it was the custom for the knight to defend her honor and challenge to combat any who spoke words against her. The cult of chivalry glorified the feudal ideals, separating them from the practices of the day, which were far from noble in our sense of the word. And in turn this movement had its effect upon feudal practices, softening them and making them, in fact, more "noble" than they had been. Knighthood, with its many ceremonies, was stressed as the great and noble goal to which all youths of aristocratic rank should aspire, and knights were urged to keep faith, to speak the truth at all times, to protect the weak, and to practice numerous other virtues.

THE POSITION OF THE CHURCH IN THE FEUDAL SYSTEM

It has already been noted that the Carolingian monarchs appointed their own clergy and expected the clergy to perform duties on their behalf. In general it may be said that throughout Europe in the early Middle Ages the king and the nobility were the patrons of the Church and made all appointments, right down to the parish priests, who had the actual task of ministering to the spiritual needs of the people. The local higher clergy might have some say in the appointments, but since they too were drawn from the noble class, their choices were not likely to differ greatly from those made by the noble lords themselves. The quality of the clergy under these conditions was not likely to be high. Most appointments were given to relatives, to friends, or to those who could afford to buy them. The reason for this system of patronage was simply that the clergy, like everyone else, had to live. They could live only from the continuing income assured by the possession of land; and in order to possess land they had to fulfill the feudal obligations that went with it. In the early Middle Ages rulers and nobles certainly chose their appointees from those who were noted for competence rather than for piety.

So the Church itself became part of the feudal system, with the higher clergy drawn from the feudal class and performing feudal duties in addition to their tasks as clerics. On the other hand, the Church did have one manifest advantage in a rude age; it had at its disposal all the powers of compulsion wielded by the nobility. The clergy could discipline their flocks, even if they had to bow to their own feudal overlords; and they had their own courts in which to try offenders against ecclesiastical law and regulations. They could enforce their decisions either by exacting spiritual punishments (penances) or by handing over offenders to the secular authorities. On the whole, with certain notorious exceptions, it would seem that their influence was exercised in a more humane manner than that of the nobles; moreover, their influence on the nobility was not negligible, and probably greater than it would have been had they belonged to a different and more despised class.

❖ The manorial system—Economic basis of feudalism

Under the feudal system the entire noble class was supported ultimately by the labor of the peasantry, the sole producers in feudal society outside the few towns. As we have seen, most feudal lords gave away the greater part of their land to vassals in exchange for military service. But all lords, whether owning large or small estates, were compelled to keep some land which was cultivated for their own use. From this land they obtained the bulk of their income, since the feudal aids and reliefs were comparatively small in total and only reached them at irregular intervals. The income from their own estates or manors was, on the contrary, entirely regular, and under their own control, either directly or through officials appointed by and responsible to themselves. Only from the proceeds of their manors could they pay for the soldiers they were forced to furnish to their lords, and make the various feudal payments described above. It was therefore necessary for every lord to keep in his hands as many manors as was necessary for the purpose. A wealthy lord, with large obligations, might have a considerable number of manors, quite beyond his ability to supervise personally even if he had the competence. These manors were supervised by bailiffs and stewards, who in every respect drew their authority from him, and carried out his orders as his representatives.

MANORIAL SELF-SUFFICIENCY

The lord's demesne Every manorial estate had on it a manor house inhabited by the lord or his officials, a certain amount of arable and pasture land, and probably some forest land. There was probably also a parish church, whose priest lived in his own house and was appointed

Óbidos, in Portugal, stands at the top of a hill overlooking a valley. Within the walls, which completely surround the village, live a few hundred people; their houses are only slightly modernized from medieval times. This is one of the two European cities which still possess their medieval walls intact (the other being Carcassonne).

to his position by the lord. There was a village where the peasants lived, together with other workers required by the estate but not employed on the land—such men as blacksmiths, wheelwrights, shoemakers, and other specialized workers.

A portion of the land, fixed by custom, as everything else on a manor, was set aside as the lord's personal demesne. It was seldom more than a third of the whole property and might be as little as a sixth. This land was worked for him by the peasants, usually under the direct supervision of one of their number chosen by the other peasants, and according to the instructions of the lord or steward. When they were working on the lord's land the supervisor had authority to beat the peasants if they did not work hard enough. All the produce from the lord's demesne belonged to the lord and constituted the major source of his income.

The land of the peasants   The remainder of the manorial land was worked by the peasants for their own account, whether they were freemen or serfs, and was subject to taxation. Each peasant had a certain acreage allotted to him, varying from a half dozen to about thirty acres. But the acres were not all together, making up a self-contained farm. They were in strips, each strip containing about an acre, and each of the length that a team of oxen could plow before it needed to take a rest (from which comes the measure *furlong*—furrow long). A peasant's strips were separated from each other, sometimes by a quite considerable distance, perhaps in order to give each peasant his fair share of the best and the worst land. Among these strips were also the strips belonging to the lord, which had to be cultivated by the peasants without profit.

The peasant lived in the village in a small thatched hut. The hut had a small plot of land attached to it, which he could use as he wished. In this he grew vegetables and kept a few chickens or geese, which could pick up enough food to sustain life and yield a few eggs a year. He lived on black bread, fresh vegetables if he was thrifty enough to grow them, porridge, cheese, very occasionally meat or fish, and wine. The staple field crops to which he had access were rye and wheat, planted in the fall, and barley, oats, beans, peas, and sometimes spring rye, planted in the spring and harvested in the fall of the same year. Rye was the cereal used most for the peasant's bread, wheat for his lord's.

Subsidiary workers on the manor   Many of the menial tasks were done for the lord by free peasants and serfs. In the lord's mill millers were needed, and bakers for the lord's household. These men might receive full-time employment from the lord, or they might also have a few strips to cultivate. The blacksmith, carpenter, mason, and the rest had their houses in the village and might combine their specialized work with agricultural labor. The aim of the lord was naturally to be as self-sufficient on his manor as possible, for money was scarce and there were some items which must be imported, such as salt, spices, and all the luxuries for which he could pay. Moreover, it was only the surplus of the manor that provided him with such money as he had, and therefore it was not to his interest to keep more peasants working on the land than could be profitably employed. It was better to use any surplus labor on the manufacture of goods that could be exported and bring him some cash income. Indeed, one of the reasons for the later improvement of the status of the peasantry was the taste for luxury acquired by the lord, which forced him to improve his system of production; this often meant hiring free laborers, organizing them more efficiently, and allowing the manufacturing part of the village to become specialized into a town.

Status of the peasant   In practice, the peasant was not altogether without rights, though in theory his lord could do almost anything he wished with him. The lord could if necessary enforce his own rights in the manorial court, presided over by himself or his steward. Here also serfs could obtain justice against other serfs, and villeins against villeins.[3] But no class had any rights against a higher class.

---

[3] A *villein*, by derivation, means simply a "villager." Customarily it is used to designate a peasant who was theoretically not a serf, but was at the same time not wholly free, owing to his lord special manorial services not owed by the real freeman.

Dances in the street. From a Book of Hours *(French), ca. 1474.* (COURTESY THE PIERPONT MORGAN LIBRARY. Ms. 677, folio 137)

Amusements of the peasantry The peasant's life was hard, and, as we shall see, a very large percentage of the fruits of his labor was yielded up to the lord. But there were certain compensations of a simple kind. He did not have to work, and was indeed forbidden to work, on Sundays, and on the festivals of a considerable number of saints. On these festival days there was always dancing in the village—in the parish hall if there was one; if not, in the streets or even in the church itself. Two or three times a year most lords entertained their peasantry—especially at harvest time, or after the hay was in; after sowing; and at the great festivals, especially Christmas, when the peasants decorated the manor house and were allowed to enjoy themselves in it afterward. In wine country there was always a vintage festival. Some-

times jugglers and acrobats came through the village and performed for the villagers either in the manor house or in the parish hall. In the later Middle Ages fairs became common to which the peasants could take their produce and enjoy themselves in the towns for the day.

Though these occasional joys did not compensate for the hardness of the peasants' work and the scantiness of their reward, they did mitigate their lot. We should remember also the fact that every peasant had a secure place, however humble, in his society; that he belonged to the same religion as his neighbors and had to cooperate with them every minute of his life. He was dependent upon them, as they upon him. When one considers all that this means for psychological security, it can be more easily understood why, even in our own century, those who were compelled by circumstances to come to America have not always made their peace with it until the second generation.

THE INCOME OF THE LORD OF THE MANOR

From his demesne land The lord's land was cultivated by his peasants, and he took the produce from it. Though the lord in theory could make unlimited demands upon the labor of his peasants, custom usually regulated the limit placed on it in fact. The regular work was called *week work*, and limited as a rule to not more than three days a week. The time depended naturally upon the size of the lord's land and the number of peasants available. At certain times the peasant could be called upon for additional work, as at harvest time. This was called *boon work*, and included such extra duties as bringing in firewood and hay for the lord. Finally, the peasant was made to do forced labor on the estate, such as digging ditches and making roads, while his wife and children might be called upon for housework in the manor. This labor was called *corvée*. The amount of corvée required was again regulated by custom as well as by the need of the lord, and depended upon the status of the peasant—whether he was a serf or technically a freeman. The building and repairing of a castle were a very heavy burden on the peasant, but they were done by corvée.

From the peasants' land—Different forms of taxation The lord was not content with having his peasants work his own land for his benefit. In numerous ways he levied toll upon

Farm animals. From a miniature, Petrus Crescentius, ca. *1460.* (COURTESY THE PIERPONT MORGAN LIBRARY. Ms. 232, folio 212)

what the peasant produced for himself. The levies were not arbitrary, but fixed by custom; this, however, did not prevent them from being very heavy, and there was nothing except the probable resistance of the peasants, perhaps by armed revolt, to prevent the lord from increasing them.

There was usually a head tax paid annually by all serfs, and there was a direct tax upon the property of every peasant, known as tallage (French *taille*). There were many "gifts" to be made at specified seasons of the year, and there was a special tax to be paid when a serf inherited his land. The last two were similar to feudal aids. These taxes were seldom excessive, and could be regarded as the equivalent of rent, while the tilling of the lord's land could be regarded as a form of sharecropping—though a modern sharecropper does not have to pay rent too!

But far more annoying and probably more costly in actual cash or produce paid out were the payments that had to be made for the use of various facilities provided by the lord, whether the peasants wished to use them or not. The lord, for instance, provided a bake oven, and the peasant was not permitted to make one for himself. He had to use the lord's bake oven and pay a fee for the privilege. He was not permitted to grind his own wheat, but had to use the lord's mill and the services of his millers, who usually cheated him. He was made to buy wine whether he wanted it or not, use the lord's winepress, and use the lord's bull for breeding; moreover, the lord erected toll houses on his roads and bridges, which everyone had to use. These nuisance taxes were called *banalités* and were extremely difficult to get rid of. The French nobles never gave them up till the French Revolution, and they were largely responsible for the fact that the conservative peasants helped to foment it. And always, the lord could enforce the payment of fines for breaking his regulations, and impose fines for any other breach of the peace or misdemeanor brought to him for trial.

It is impossible to say what percentage of the actual produce of his manor went into the lord's pocket by one device or another. But it was certainly a large one, and kept the peasants from accumulating much that they could call their own. It sufficiently accounts for the ability of the feudal nobility to engage in their pleasant pursuits in spite of the low production of the manorial economy.

THE PEASANT'S INCOME

What he had left over after paying all taxes and fines belonged to the peasant. Though it was not much, there would be something if the land were fertile and he and his wife were good managers. He could convert his produce into cash at the fairs, and we do know that enough agricultural produce found its way into the towns to feed the townsmen, though some of it also came from the lord's demesne and what he had collected in kind from the peasantry. There might be enough in the peasant's sock or mattress to pay a small amount to the priest to educate his son, or to pay the apprentice's fee for his son to learn a trade in a town. But seldom do we hear of any luxury in the peasant's home. It would, in any case, only have invited unpleasant attention from his lord.

It should be noted that if a serf stayed away from his manor for a year and a day, he earned his freedom. This was probably the principal loophole through which he was able to put an end to his servitude. With the growth of towns (to be described in the next section), there was some other place for him to go. When Crusades were called, the lords were under great pressure from the Church and public opinion to allow the serfs to leave. Few returned alive, and those who did survive naturally did not return to the manors.

The lord's desire for luxuries beyond what an ordinary manor could provide under its generally inefficient management was also an aid to the peasants. More efficient management meant fewer serfs, and large numbers were freed, especially from the thirteenth century onward. In later times it was found that sheep raising earned larger dividends. This discovery gave rise to the enclosure movement, which turned many former manors into estates run by a few laborers, though at the cost of great hardship to peasants who found themselves deprived by legal means of their strips. When the kings began to establish their authority over the feudal nobility, they found themselves in constant need of mercenary soldiers. These again came from the ranks of the peasantry, and no lord could pursue and bring back a peasant who had joined the king's army. Other peasants were freed by the simple process of emigration to new lands in Northeastern Europe. These lands, settled from the thirteenth century onward, were in dire need of labor, which could be recruited only from the more thickly settled territories of Western Europe.

The manorial system itself survived for many centuries, but it was greatly transformed. The servile status of the peasants and the legal power of the lords disappeared first, and in most Western countries did not survive the thirteenth century. Tenant farmers and small proprietors took the place of serfs, the former still bound by the ancient customs and the ancient taxes, and still forced on occasion to do corvée and to pay the banalités. But when the taxes were raised, the peasants soon learned that they had the power to revolt. And though the revolts were usually mercilessly suppressed, reforms did come in time, for the lords as well as the peasants were the losers by them.

More than anything else, it was probably the inefficiency of the early manorial system that condemned it. With the growth of towns and the commercial revolution, a more efficient use had to be made of the land; and this could be provided neither by the warrior class of feudal nobility nor by the manorial system which nourished it.

❖ The urban sector—Rise of the towns

In the early Middle Ages there was very little industry; and because there was little industry, there was little trade. It was some centuries before the old trade and industry of the Roman Empire fell into complete decay. But by the time of Charlemagne almost all the manufactured goods in Western Europe were produced either in small villages or on the manors. In short, the economy of the early Middle Ages was overwhelmingly rural. The small agricultural surplus from the manors provided almost the only articles that entered into commerce, and the great bulk of what there was available was merely exchanged on a barter basis for the produce of other manors.

In the East, on the other hand, the Byzantine Empire was still a center of industry. But few of its manufactures could be taken by the West, which had so little to offer in exchange for them; the bulk of the meager supply of precious metals found its way to Constantinople and the East, and the gold, at least, could not be replaced from domestic sources. In the time of Charlemagne the only coins in general circulation were made of copper; the larger denominations of money were used simply as units for measurement. The one exception to the uniform lack of important cities in the West was Venice, a city built almost upon the sea itself, founded in the sixth century as a refuge for fugitives from the invasions. Unlike the Mediterranean seaports, Venice was immune from Muslim ravages; and it kept up a trade with Constantinople based on its own products as well as on those few items which were manufactured in the West. But Venice, though geographically in Italy, was a city whose civilization was far closer to that of Byzantine than of Western Europe. Indeed, for centuries it was nominally a part of the Byzantine Empire, although in fact self-governing.

By the eleventh century the Italian seaports of Genoa, Pisa, and Amalfi had begun a revival which culminated in the thirteenth and fourteenth centuries. The Crusades, to be described in the next chapter, were of great assistance to all the medieval maritime cities. Not only did they make profits from transporting those Crusaders to the East who could afford the cost, but they were able to bring back to the West the Oriental luxuries they found in the hitherto more prosperous and economically developed East. They also kept the Crusaders who stayed in the East supplied with those Western products which continued to interest them. In part as a consequence of the First Crusade, and in part as a consequence of the conquest of Sicily by the Normans in the eleventh century (a conquest aided by the Genoese), Genoa and Pisa increased their trade with the Muslim countries

The Palace of the Doge (Duke) of Venice. Note the Byzantine influence. (COURTESY ITALIAN STATE TOURIST OFFICE)

of North Africa and gradually ousted the Muslims from the carrying trade of the western Mediterranean. Venice, however, was the greatest gainer from the Crusades, and the notorious Fourth Crusade, which was diverted to Constantinople and will be described in the next chapter, was under Venetian direction.

In the rest of Europe there were still few towns of any size by the time of the First Crusade (1095). Milan, Florence, Lucca and other inland Italian towns had continued their separate existence from Roman times, but had shrunk in the early Middle Ages to a fraction of their former size. The manors were largely self-sufficient, and from most of them there was only a small surplus available for trade, far too little to support the needs of a whole group of specialized workers who would have formed the population of a town. Only a few nobles and higher clergy, with the produce of many manors to draw upon, could guarantee a regular supply of food and at the same time provide a market for the specialized wares of a town. In those days of poor transportation, it was essential that a surplus move regularly into a town, or that the townsmen themselves spend a large part of their time in agriculture. In the earliest medieval towns we find, as a rule, both of these conditions fulfilled. A noble or a bishop with his entourage would live in a town and provide it with its market from the produce of his lands. The workers themselves, who lived there under his protection, looked after some of their own food supply while at the same time producing various specialized wares for exchange. A very few continuously inhabited cities, centered in strategic places on trade routes, might be able to make their living from trade and industry alone, exchanging their products for agricultural goods drawn from fairly wide areas. But, on the whole, the vast majority of towns were of the first kind—the seats of lords or bishops who provided the food and protection needed by the townsmen.

During the period of the Viking invasions in the ninth and tenth centuries the towns suffered severely. It was the custom of the marauders to ascend the rivers in their boats, sacking and pillaging. At the end of the season they would return to their own countries. Al-

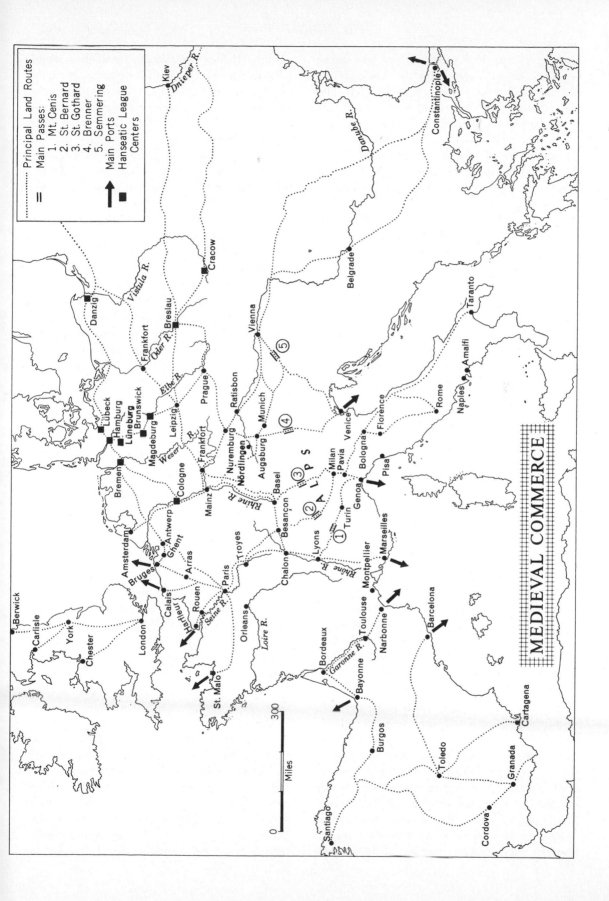

MEDIEVAL COMMERCE

Principal Land Routes
Main Passes:
  1. Mt. Cenis
  2. St. Bernard
  3. St. Gothard
  4. Brenner
  5. Semmering
Main Ports
Hanseatic League
Centers

most every city in Western Europe was sacked
at one time or another by the Vikings, and
defense against their raids was exceedingly difficult. Usually the Vikings did not wait to fight;
if any army approached it was easy to escape
by water, and it was impossible for an army
to pursue them. Only slowly did the feudal nobility and the townsmen learn to defend themselves against such aggression; and by the time
they had learned the Vikings themselves were
ready to settle down. The taming of the invaders, and the lessened interest of the feudal
lords in fratricidal warfare provided the opportunity for the towns to resume their growth.

THE ESCAPE FROM FEUDAL SERVITUDE

The majority of European towns, as has
been noted, owed their very foundation to feudal lords or to the higher clergy. As the towns
began to grow, merchants—men engaged exclusively in trade, who had been free for generations and had never been personally dependent
upon feudal overlords—began to settle there
permanently. It was natural that these men
should resent the disabilities placed upon them
because the town itself was subordinate to the
lords. They began to think themselves capable
of making their own defense without calling
upon their lord; and yet within the city the lord
had certain traditional rights of collecting tolls
and rents which seriously interfered with the
merchants' freedom and ability to make profits.
Lords, in other words, ceased to be worth their
keep, from the townsmen's point of view, and
at the same time, as their demands for money
and luxuries increased, especially after the Crusades, they tended to try to milk the burghers
or townsmen for more.

So we find from as early as the end of the
eleventh century onward efforts made by towns
throughout Europe to escape from the galling
restrictions of an earlier age. It was not difficult
for the burghers to recognize their strong position against the aristocracy. The lords possessed
military power, and they had the old feudal law
on their side. On the other hand, if they used
this military power, they would destroy the
source of their income. They needed regular
income, not one single great looting followed by

nothing. If they destroyed a town, they would
have to rebuild it afterward or forego their income. If traders refused to trade because conditions were made too onerous, then likewise no
tolls could be collected. Most independent lords
in these circumstances found it better to compromise with their towns, drawing up a charter
stating exactly what the towns had to do for
them, what rents and tolls had to be paid, what
scutage or commutation of military service had
to be paid, if any, what hospitality and similar
feudal services were owed. They thus saved
themselves from possible total loss through successful revolt.

Very great lords, and kings, not being
dependent in the same way upon their income
from any particular town, could hold out against
the demands of the towns and could even afford
to inflict punishment upon them. On the other
hand, these great lords could provide the towns
with more efficient protection and were thus
worth more of what they cost the burghers than
was the smaller lord. So we find that in countries where there was an efficient central government under a king, the towns maintained only
a limited independence and usually did not have
their rights confirmed by charters. This was the
case in England, and in France after the thirteenth century—where, indeed, many towns lost
their charters after the king had established his
supremacy over the whole country. On the other
hand, the Italian and German burghers, living
in countries where the official ruler exercised
only sporadic and never very efficient control,
were able to secure and maintain their independence far more effectively. The northern
Italian towns united in the Lombard League
were able to defeat and force concessions from
even such a powerful ruler as Frederic Barbarossa, and in a later age were able to hold
their own against the even more powerful
Frederic ii.

Some cities, however, had to fight long and
hard for their freedom. Many of the higher
clergy and the nobility refused to accept the
inevitable peacefully, and resisted the rising
power of the bourgeoisie with all the force at
their disposal. Bishops, especially bishops who
had purchased their office and expected to make
the town pay their debts, were often the last to

accept the new order. Many towns had to fight hard against the bishop and his hired mercenaries, and cases of a victorious bishop's looting his own town are not unknown.

THE GOVERNMENT OF A COMMUNE

Self-governing towns, with or without a charter, are usually called communes. The essential element of a commune was its right to be treated as a whole, a corporation, as distinct from its constituent members. The town as a whole undertook obligations toward the lords and received privileges in return, thus making a distinct break with feudal traditions, whose obligations were always binding upon individual persons and not on groups. To fulfill these obligations the town had to be self-governing, assessing taxes and duties upon its citizens and paying them in a lump sum to the lord. Though its independence might be limited by the terms of its charter, and it might not have full control of its foreign relations, within the city itself the government was substantially autonomous. And when the charter could not be easily enforced, as in the cities of northern Italy, they became for all practical purposes city-states not unlike those of the ancient world.

The government of the towns varied in different parts of Europe; almost the only generalization that can be safely made is that the richer merchants usually had effective control, unless the town was still ruled by its hereditary feudal aristocracy. As early as the twelfth century efforts were made by the lower classes to take away the monopoly of power from the richer merchants, who were able to use it tyrannically in the interests of their class. At one time the commune of Milan was ruled briefly by a kind of trade union of workers. But none of these efforts was permanently successful, and the oligarchy was eventually replaced, not by a

The Cloth Hall of Ypres (Belgium), one of the most perfect examples of a medieval commercial building. The hall was destroyed during World War I. (COURTESY BELGIUM GOVERNMENT INFORMATION CENTER)

more democratically based government, but by
the one-man rule of the despot, merchant, feudal prince, or some adventurer.

THE MERCHANT GUILDS

In a static society, in which it was generally
believed that only a limited quantity of trade
and industry was possible, all efforts were directed toward ensuring that foreigners should
have as little share of it as could be managed,
and that the workers in the city should all be
assured of a reasonable living and secure employment. Competition was frowned upon, especially unfair competition by such means as price
cutting. Rather, cooperation was the ideal, enforced by strict regulation on the part of the
authorities.

The earliest form of organization within the
towns was the merchant guild, or guild merchant. This was originally a union of merchants
and traders, including also the upper class of
artisans; and its purpose was to prevent foreign
competition and to divide up the home trade
equitably among the members. In some cases
the merchant guild came into existence even
before a town had a charter, and indeed it was
often the guild which succeeded in extracting
the charter from the overlord of the town. In
many towns the guild afterward became the
actual municipal government. The merchant
guild, like the later craft guild, was a closed
shop; traders who did not belong to the guild
found themselves excluded from trade within
the city.

The monopolies held in trade matters varied
from town to town. Reciprocal privileges could
be granted to foreign traders when they seemed
to be in the interest of the guild, but severe
penalties were always enforced against price
cutters. It was possible to enforce penalties because exclusion from a guild meant that the
offending trader lost his business. Cases are also
known of the assaulting and beating of offenders.

THE CRAFT GUILDS

Purpose and function   The craft guild was
an organization formed to protect the working

conditions in a particular industry and also to
protect the public. Not all industries were
formed into guilds, and the guild organization
was not uniform throughout Europe, being
strongest in the German and northern towns and
weakest in Italy. The regulations of the craft
guild were very rigid and very strictly enforced,
but always logically worked out to attain certain
objectives.

The product had to be sold at a just price,
which included the cost of labor and raw materials. It is clear that if any artisan skimped on
his material, used inferior workmanship, or cut
wages, then the resulting product would be
priced too high in relation to its actual value if
the price were the same as for goods of standard
quality; and of course price cutting was strictly
forbidden. Regulations governing the standard
of quality were set up by the guild masters in
each guild, since only these experts could determine what was the correct quality in their
particular craft.

Hours of labor were prescribed and enforced. Nightwork was, as a rule, entirely forbidden, both because it tended to spoil the
quality of the work and because the worker who
labored for additional hours would in this way
be able to get ahead of his neighbors. If one
group of workers did overtime, it was clear to
the medievals that others would have to do the
same, in the same way that one price cutter
would force all others to cut their prices too.
Improved methods of manufacture were not
regarded kindly if introduced by individual
craftsmen; it was therefore usual to insist that
any such improvements should be agreed to by
the guild, which would have the opportunity
of spreading the information among all its
members.

Advertising of all kinds was forbidden. No
salesman could draw attention to his wares in
any manner whatever; even a diplomatic sneeze
when a customer passed was considered im-
proper and, in one place, was forbidden. Craftsmen had to do their work in shops which were
visible from the street so that their practices
were at all times open to inspection. Shops were
limited in size so that no master could become
a regular employer of labor, and thus drive

down his costs and perhaps cut prices; and it was forbidden also to attempt to entice away workers from a rival shop.

In brief, the central ideas of the craft guilds were that there was enough work for all if everyone worked for reasonable hours and produced goods of first-rate quality; that every article had a fair price which customers should be able to pay; that the customer who paid this fixed price should be protected from his probable ignorance of the quality of his purchase; and that there was no need to cut this price, since everyone would suffer, and in a limited market no increased business for all would result.

Internal organization of the craft guild
The young artisan first entered the guild by becoming apprentice to a master, on payment of a fee. The apprenticeship might last for as long as twelve years, depending on the nature of the particular craft; the usual period for most crafts was seven years. The boy, however, became an apprentice when his family signed an indenture. It was the master's task to supervise the boy's morals and behavior as well as his work. The apprentice boarded at the master's home, and had to obey his orders in everything. When the apprenticeship was over and the boy was thoroughly trained in his craft, he became a journeyman (dayworker) and was free to leave his master and take work at regular wages wherever he could find it. He could stay on with his master, and perhaps it was the usual custom in early times for him to do so. But in certain trades, especially the building trade, it was of great advantage for the journeyman to work in foreign cities, improving his knowledge of his trade by examining or taking part in the building of churches, cathedrals, and public offices.

In the early Middle Ages there was no difficulty in the way of a journeyman who wanted to set himself up as a master. While business was gradually increasing, there was enough work for all; and the guild had no objections, provided the journeyman had sufficient savings to enable him to purchase the shop and the raw materials and had a wife who could take care of his apprentices. He had to pass an examination before the guild master (or warden), demonstrating his efficiency and his good character and financial standing. Foreign journeymen were sometimes admitted as masters in early times, though in later times, when the market had become saturated, this practice was abandoned.

All artisans were theoretically members of the guild, though apprentices could not take part in elections or in the management of the guild until they became journeymen. In later times journeymen were also excluded, leaving the guild a monopoly of the masters. As trade increased and serfdom declined it became increasingly difficult to maintain the monopoly; but for a long time the masters attempted to maintain it by every means at their disposal. Before the middle of the fourteenth century apprentices and journeymen probably did not feel the guild as a restriction upon their freedom. There really was enough work for all at a fair price, and an apprentice could look forward to a secure future and ultimately a mastership in his chosen craft. However, by the end of the Middle Ages, this was no longer true, as the student of modern history will discover.

MARKETS AND FAIRS

So far in this section we have considered primarily the larger towns and the manner in which industry came to be organized in them. But it should always be remembered that until the later Middle Ages the towns were scarce. Much more common were very small towns, or large villages, which acted almost exclusively as centers for the exchange of the surplus produce of the manors. But even people in the larger towns had to eat; and though some food was always produced within the borders of the towns, for the most part the townsmen bought their supplies in the markets, which existed in every town of any size.

The lord of the manor, as we have seen, had his own land worked by the peasants. But he also required payment in money from his peasants for many of their manorial dues, and the peasants on most manors had only one place to go for money—the town. Likewise, if the lord had many manors and wanted to convert his surplus produce into cash for luxuries, he too had to patronize the town. The townsmen also displayed their wares for the countryfolk, and supplied them with the few things they could afford.

In the early Middle Ages the towns and their markets were usually under the protection of some lord, or even the king. The lord gave his permission for a regular market to be held, usually once a week, in exchange for market dues to be paid to him. If the market was the center of a flourishing area with many manors, there was probably enough surplus food, as well as agricultural raw materials such as flax, for the merchant to buy in quantity for export. The markets therefore to some extent served as feeders for the export trade as well as centers for the exchange of agricultural and urban goods.

A market on a much larger scale was the international fair, held in some area with easy access by boat or road. Preparations for these fairs might take weeks, while the goods were being assembled from all parts of the country, or indeed from many parts of Europe. Transactions were carried out on a considerable scale and needed many special arrangements. Certain lords took a keen interest in these fairs, since they could be made into an excellent source of income if handled honestly and with benefit to all concerned. The greatest European fairs during the twelfth and thirteenth centuries were those held in the plain of Champagne, under the patronage of the counts of Champagne, who were responsible for their management. Safe passage to the fair through the count's territories was guaranteed, and extended as far as possible beyond them. The Church also lent what protection it could. The fairs were under the management of a warden, with a considerable staff under him made up of weighers, measurers, porters, and such; and they were well policed. A special seal of the fair was used to authenticate all purchases made by contract; and, of course, money-changers had to be present to facilitate trade between the participants from countries with different monies. Moneylenders were also to be found for those

who needed quick cash. Storage facilities were provided, as well as entertainment of all kinds —minstrels, jongleurs, dancers, clowns, and all other amusements which appealed to medieval people. Peasants were usually permitted to make at least one trip to the fairs by their manorial lords. Even though they might lack money to make purchases, they could always enjoy themselves at small expense.

ATTITUDE OF THE CHURCH TO URBAN ACTIVITY

A few words should be said in conclusion regarding the attitude of the Church toward business activity. In general, it may be said that the Church was in full sympathy with the monopolistic tendencies of the guilds. It was the belief of the Church, as of most people in the Middle Ages, that every man was born to a certain position in society, in which he was expected to remain. His economic needs were determined by his status. A noble was naturally entitled to consume more than a peasant, and it was permissible for him to indulge in display and to consume luxuries which would have been out of place in the life of an artisan or a peasant. If the latter had aspirations beyond their station, then it was likely that these were dictated by envy or pride, deadly sins condemned by the Church and society. If the common man had a desire for luxury or display, he must be actuated by some form of sensuality, another sin. If he simply wished to accumulate wealth, then he was motivated by avarice; or if he wished to consume too many of the good things of life, then he was a glutton. Finally, if he wished to save enough money for a comfortable old age, then he was slothful and lazy; he wished to avoid work, and this desire, too, was a deadly sin. In view of such restrictions, it is clear that public and ecclesiastical opinion would condemn any enterprise undertaken by the poor and lowborn man for the sake of profit. Life on earth, according to the teachings of the Church, should not be too pleasurable; the proper task of man was to prepare for the hereafter and endure whatever came to him in this life without expecting too much of it.

The Church likewise objected to the making of profits by merchants, unless the profits were a payment for work honestly performed. Like Karl Marx, the Church held a labor theory of value. The cost of an article, plus a reasonable wage, was all that the merchant was entitled to. Thus it was possible to calculate a fair and just price for every piece of merchandise. Any price fixed above this was profiteering. It was particularly reprehensible to engross, or try to corner the market, since the increased price represented no honest labor; the practice was morally evil in that it meant taking advantage of the necessities of poor men and charging them highly because the goods which they needed had been made artificially scarce. Forestalling was a similar crime; this was the practice of buying up goods from the peasant before they reached the market, and for the same purpose of pushing up prices. Even coming between the producer and the consumer unnecessarily and buying and selling at a profit was considered wrong, unless there was an obvious need for a middleman's service. The practice was called regrating.

Lending money at interest had always been considered wicked by Christians because money was supposed to be sterile, having no value in itself; and, further, to take money for helping others when such a service should be provided free was contrary to Scripture. It was taking advantage of the poor; and indeed, since loans for consumption purposes—the type of borrowing a poor man usually does—were poorly secured, the interest rates for consumer credit were high then, as now. In the early Middle Ages, since it was impossible to do without some form of consumer credit, this business was in the hands of Jews, who were, of course, not bound by ecclesiastical regulations, and who were prevented by various restrictions from making a living in other fields. All lending of money was called usury, whether for high or low rates of interest, and was considered sinful. Secular and clerical authorities constantly condemned and attempted to regulate it. But in an age of growing capitalism, it was found impossible to maintain all the artificial restrictions which were suited to a static society. For several centuries, however, the guilds followed faithfully the rules laid down by the Church, with which, indeed, they were not unsympathetic, since they too believed in a static society.

In the next chapter we shall consider the nature of the medieval Church, and how it came to have such influence that it was able to compel respect for its views not only from the towns but from the secular rulers. In Chapter 11 we shall deal with the national states, and thus resume our account of the political institutions of later medieval times. In the later Middle Ages there were numerous economic changes which, though unspectacular if considered by themselves, in their totality achieved nothing less than a new orientation for the economic striving of the West. But these lie outside the scope of this book.

Suggestions for further reading

PAPER-BOUND BOOKS

Adelson, Howard. *Medieval Commerce*. Anvil. Narrative and source material by an American historian, an expert on coinage.

Bark, W. C. *Origins of the Medieval World*. Anchor. Interesting study emphasizing the new life brought into a declining civilization by the invaders who were later to bring forth the new western civilization.

Coulton, G. G. *Ten Medieval Studies* (Beacon), *Medieval Panorama* (Meridian), *Medieval Scene* (Cambridge University Press), *Medieval Village, Manor and Monastery* (Torchbooks). To some degree these books duplicate one another. All are based on solid research by this leading English medievalist, who was always at his best in English social history.

Easton, S. C. and Wieruszowski, H. *The Era of Charlemagne: State and Society*. Anvil. Narrative and documents, including Donation of Pepin and several capitularies.

Einhard. *Life of Charlemagne*. Ann Arbor. Brief contemporary life by a member of the emperor's entourage. Anecdotal but well informed.

Fichtenau, H. *The Carolingian Empire*. Torchbooks. Scholarly study of all aspects of the reign of Charlemagne.

Ganshof, F. L. *Feudalism*. Torchbooks. Excellent introduction by a noted modern scholar.

Holmes, U. T., Jr. *Daily Living in the Twelfth Century*. University of Wisconsin Press. An interesting picture based on the observations of Alexander Neckam, a medieval traveler and indefatigable student.

Lopez, Robert S. *The Tenth Century: How Dark the Dark Ages?* Holt, Rinehart and Winston. Extracts from contemporary sources with interesting commentary.

Painter, Sidney. *French Chivalry: Chivalric Ideas and Practices in Medieval France; Medieval Society;* and *The Rise of the Feudal Monarchies*. Cornell University Press. Three very valuable studies by one of the leading American medievalists.

Pirenne, Henri. *Economic and Social History of Medieval Europe* (Harvest) and *Medieval Cities*. (Anchor). Two pioneer works by a noted Belgian historian. Although his famous "Pirenne Thesis," which held that Mediterranean commerce persisted substantially undiminished until the Muslim conquest, is no longer widely held, Pirenne's book on the cities remains almost the best on the subject within a small compass.

Power, Eileen. *Medieval People*. Anchor. Presentation of the lives of six medieval people, drawn from original sources but embellished by the author. One of the best books for getting the feel of medieval society.

Stephenson, Carl. *Medieval Feudalism*. Cornell University Press. Clear account, one of the best short surveys.

Usher, Abbot P. *A History of Mechanical Inventions*. Beacon. Several chapters in this admirable book cover medieval inventions, especially those on water wheels, mechanical clocks, and printing.

Wallace-Hadrill, J. M. *The Barbarian West: The Early Middle Ages* A.D. *400–1000*. Torchbooks. Useful brief survey of the period, emphasizing the manner in which the barbarians helped to preserve the Roman heritage.

White, Lynn, Jr. *Medieval Technology and Social Change*. Oxford University Press. This spirited and well-written series of essays on such medieval inventions as the stirrup and their effect on medieval life and history is no doubt a purposeful overstatement of the case for medieval inventiveness but very well worth reading as an antidote for those who continue to regard the Middle Ages as a period of economic and technological stagnation.

HARD-COVER BOOKS

Baldwin, John W. *Medieval Theories of the Just Price*. Philadelphia: American Philosophical Society, 1958. An important brief study.

Clough, S. B., and Cole, C. W. *Economic History of Europe*, 3d ed. Boston: D. C. Heath and Company, 1952. This good economic text contains much out-of-the-way and useful information. It should be consulted whenever supplementary economic information is needed. Clough's more recent book, *The Economic Development of Western Civilization* (New York: McGraw Hill Book Company, Inc., 1959) is more up to date, but the medieval period is largely an abbreviated version of the material in the Clough and Cole text.

Davis, H. W. C. *Medieval Europe*, 2d ed. New York: Oxford University Press, 1960. A Home University survey (1911). Still one of the best introductions to the subject.

Davis, W. S. *Life in a Medieval Barony*. New York: Harper & Row, Publishers, 1928. Imaginative picture of a French seigniory drawn from authentic feudal sources.

Haskins, Charles Homer. *The Normans in European History*. Boston: Houghton Mifflin Company, 1915. Still the only accessible book covering the various settlements made by the Normans in the different parts of Europe. By a fine medieval scholar of the last generation.

Heaton, Herbert. *Economic History of Europe*, rev. ed. New York: Harper & Row, Publishers, 1948. Excellent text, topically organized.

Lopez, R. S., and Raymond, I. W., eds. *Medieval Trade in the Mediterranean World*. New York: Columbia University Press, 1955. Collection of useful source material.

Roover, Raymond de. *Money, Banking and Credit in Medieval Bruges*. Cambridge, Mass.: Medieval Academy of America, 1948. This book and other works by the same author scattered through many articles have been instrumental in changing our picture of medieval banking and credit institutions. Through the analysis of numerous account books, the author has succeeded in demonstrating not only the different kinds of credit available and their relation to the usury laws but how the various institutions must have operated. While this book, which is concerned primarily with the operations of Italian bankers in Flanders, is not easy reading, it should be attempted by all those who wish to have an accurate knowledge of the subject.

TEN

The Church to the End of the Thirteenth Century

❖ The Church in the tenth century

ECCLESIASTICAL ORGANIZATION IN EUROPE— LAY INVESTITURE

It will be clear from the last chapter how completely the Church had become integrated into the feudal system. Throughout Europe the emperor, kings, and chief nobles appointed the bishops and the archbishops; the clerical assistants in the episcopal sees (cathedral chapters), who were responsible for the administration of the diocese, were appointed by the bishops; while the parish priests, chosen by local lords, usually from their own free peasantry, were ordained priests by the bishops whenever the latter found time for it, without inquiring too closely into the qualifications of the priests. There was no way in which the papacy could interfere in the process, though in theory all the high clergy were at least subject to confirmation by the Holy See. If the rulers desired to sell the offices of the Church or give them to their friends and relatives, no papal wrath could stop them; if the bishops accepted fees illegally for the performance of their ordinary duties, if they inflicted fines as penance and put the proceeds into their own pockets, perhaps to pay the sum exacted from them by the kings in exchange for their appointment, no one could

insist on their obedience to the laws of the Church, which forbade such practices. If the parish priest had no qualifications for his office, knew no Latin, permitted gaming and dicing in his church, was unable to celebrate mass with due order and dignity, and betrayed the secrets of the confessional for private gain— if his manorial lord did not discipline him, no one else would. All these practices were common, and there was not much that anyone in high authority in the Church could do about it.

THE PAPACY IN THE FEUDAL SYSTEM

The papacy itself was in no position to institute reforms. When the pope was not chosen by the local Italian nobles and people, he was chosen by the emperor. If he offended the emperor, he could be deposed; if he offended the local nobles, they also could depose him by force unless the emperor objected. The revenues of the Papal States in Italy were collected through the papal bureaucracy; but this also was composed of local nobles, who could direct them into more suitable pockets than the pope's.

In such circumstances few would have ventured to predict that in little more than a century a pope would have brought an emperor to beg his forgiveness in the snow, still less that in two and a half centuries Pope

Innocent III would be successfully disciplining every monarch in Europe. Such an achievement therefore deserves a careful analysis in itself as a political event of the first magnitude. Moreover, the swift collapse of papal power that followed Innocent's triumphs may also reveal the necessary limitations on the exercise of political authority by a power whose claims were spiritual, and whose sanctions depended on moral rather than on military and political force.

THE THEORY OF SALVATION

The means of salvation   In our modern age, when Christianity has been split into numerous sects, when a large number of people are religious skeptics, and when power rests firmly in the hands of secular authorities, it is clear that the moral reform of the individual can only be enforced, if at all, by secular authority through legislation. A Church can only hope to induce moral reform by persuasion, and by the threat of cutting off such ecclesiastical comforts as it can supply. In the Middle Ages, however, Catholic Christianity was a religious monopoly, and there is no evidence that anyone in the whole of Christendom in the tenth century doubted its main teachings, so far as they were understood. The central teaching understood by all was that there was a God in Heaven, a Devil in Hell, and that after death human beings went to either Heaven or Hell according to a verdict given by God in his capacity as judge. The supreme aim of man's life on earth was to win a favorable decision at this last judgment. And it was universally believed that the purpose of the Church was to help man win the decision and thus attain Heaven.

Largely on the authority of Pope Gregory I a further important doctrine had been propounded for the belief of the faithful, though it was not widely understood: the doctrine that there was an intermediate place between earth and Heaven through which those who were destined for Heaven would pass. This was called Purgatory, the place where sins were purged through punishment, leaving a purified soul to pass on to Heaven. It was only a temporary abode, but the period passed in it varied according to the sins committed on earth. The Church could also help mitigate the punishment in Purgatory.

The role of the Church in the attainment of salvation   According to the theory of salvation put forward by Augustine in the fifth century, modified by Gregory I, and generally accepted as the true teaching of the Church, man was saved only through grace, bestowed as a heavenly gift by God, a gift made possible by the sacrifice of Christ. Grace, however, was given to man only through the medium of the sacraments of the Church, which had been founded by Christ for this purpose.

There were seven sacraments: baptism, by which the newborn child was redeemed from original sin, with godparents accepting Christianity on his behalf; confirmation, when a child of about twelve accepted Christianity for himself; the Eucharist, the most sacred and important of the sacraments, offered daily, in which through the miracle of transubstantiation bread and wine were made into the body and blood of Christ; matrimony; penance; and extreme unction, which prepares the Christian for death and wipes away what is left of his sins. The seventh sacrament (holy orders) was the ceremony by which a layman was made into a priest, setting him apart from ordinary men, and enabling him to celebrate the Eucharist and grant absolution from sin.

The sacrament of penance needs a few words of explanation because of its role in the disciplining of the Christian by the Church, and the consequent power conferred by it on the clergy. In theory the Church could not guarantee salvation; all that was sure was that salvation could not be won without the aid of the Church—a distinction not always clear to the unschooled Christian. But the Church could save the Christian sinner from having to suffer the consequences of his sin in Purgatory—provided always that God had chosen to grant him salvation and an entry into Heaven. Christ and his saints, according to Church doctrine, had made full satisfaction to God for the sins of every man on earth, and thus a treasury of merits had been accumulated which was at the disposal of the Church for helping repentant sinners through Purgatory.

If a sinner repented truly and confessed his sins to a priest, then it was the duty of the priest to absolve him. This was the sacrament of penance. But the consequences of the sin still remained, and in the absence of any intervention by the Church, full punishment for it would be exacted in Purgatory. But the Church could remit the punishment by assigning some temporal punishment on earth, in the form of the repetition of a certain number of prayers, the undertaking of special fasts, the performance of a useful social work, such as building a bridge, or even a pilgrimage to some sacred place such as Rome or Jerusalem. Such an act would relieve the sinner of some period of punishment in Purgatory. The statement of this remission of punishment was called an indulgence. A plenary indulgence, which was the chief inducement offered to Crusaders, remitted the whole time of punishment in Purgatory. If, therefore, God has chosen to save a sinner who had been given a plenary indulgence, then he would enter Heaven at once without having to spend any time in Purgatory.

It is clear that this complex theory would not be understood by the ordinary ignorant layman. It is not, therefore, to be wondered at that only too often the sinner who possessed an indulgence regarded it as a safe passport to Heaven; and it is also not too surprising that the temptation to abuse the sacrament of penance and sell the indulgences for money was sometimes too much for a Church that had many uses for money. It was the flagrant abuse of the indulgence in the sixteenth century that was the principal factor in the rebellion of Martin Luther against the Church which began the Protestant Reformation.

Since the receiving of the sacraments was necessary for salvation, the most severe penalty that could be meted out to a Christian was to withhold them, a penalty known as excommunication. Complete excommunication, which could be pronounced by the higher clergy or by the pope, meant that the offender was severed from all services performed by the Church. No Christian might have any dealings with him on pain of excommunication himself; he could not attend services of the Church or receive any sacraments; and he could not be buried in holy ground. If the State accepted the excommunication it would sometimes withdraw the benefits of secular law from him also, making him an outlaw. He could then be killed with impunity, and by the Church action he was necessarily condemned to Hell. If excommunication was to be lifted by the Church, the offender would be expected to make a complete submission, and undergo severe penance.

As a supplement to excommunication when directed at a monarch or an independent feudal lord, the Church could also declare an interdict upon his whole territory. This was a kind of excommunication en masse of a whole population, and its purpose was to bring the pressure of public opinion to bear on the offending ruler. In a land laid under an interdict the Church performed none of its duties at all—though exception might be made by special dispensation for some of the essential sacraments, such as baptism and extreme unction. When it is remembered how many duties the Church performed in the Middle Ages that we now regard as functions of the State, it can readily be seen how effective this weapon might be in the hands of a Church obedient to its leaders.

Clearly neither of these disciplinary powers, however, would have any effect at all if the local clergy did not cooperate. When, as in the tenth century, the clergy were nominated by local lords, they could not be used; and probably no cleric could even be found who would read a bull excommunicating a high noble or a monarch.

In addition to these weapons, the pope, who alone could pronounce an interdict, claimed the right to depose a king. No king, theoretically, could hold office from the moment of his excommunication; and the oath of allegiance made to him by his subjects became automatically void. Naturally this right was never admitted by the rulers, who themselves claimed to hold their power from God and not from the Church. The pope's ability to make his decree effective depended entirely upon the conditions in the country concerned—as, for instance, whether there was any rival for the throne, or whether any foreign king could be induced with papal support to overthrow the offending and deposed monarch.

THE CHURCH AS REGULATOR OF CHRISTIAN MORALITY—CANON LAW

The Church had always claimed jurisdiction throughout Christendom in all matters which concerned faith and morals. In the early centuries of Christianity authoritative creeds—statements of what Christians must believe—had been drawn up by councils. But gradually it was recognized that a single authority must be accepted in such matters, and this, after many centuries of doubt as to where the authority lay, was granted by consent in the Western world to the pope. From time to time popes also promulgated new dogmas which must be believed by the faithful. Those who refused to subscribe to these beliefs could be charged with heresy, and handed over to the state for punishment. If they did not recant, they could be put to death by burning (without the shedding of blood, forbidden to churchmen). Before the establishment of the Inquisition in the thirteenth century, heresy trials were in the hands of the bishops. By such means the Church attempted to guard the purity of the faith.

In the realm of morals, which covered a very wide field and which the Church in the days of its power sought to make ever wider, the authority was the canon law, the rules laid down by the early councils, combined with decrees made by various popes. These were codified by Gratian in the twelfth century.

Canon law stated that all clerics, both regular and secular, and even those in minor orders—assistants of the higher clergy and even, later, students at universities—were subject only to the jurisdiction of the Church and were not to be tried for any offense whatever by the temporal powers. It claimed that all crimes against religion, whoever committed them, were to be tried by the Church. These crimes included not only heresy, simony, and blasphemy; but also sorcery, adultery, and sexual crimes, usury, and even the illegal fighting of duels. If these were not punished by the state of its own accord—and in the early Middle Ages many of the chief offenders were rulers and nobles in high position who did not even recognize these acts as crimes—then the Church claimed the right to try the offenders instead.

Finally, canon law regulated all civil cases connected in any way with one of the sacraments—as, for instance, marriage settlements and divorces, wills, and civil contracts which concerned inheritance. The canon law, observing Roman principles and taking into account such things as motives (not recognized as important under feudal law), served to mitigate some of the evils of feudal law, besides adding to the power of the Church.

Again, however, it must be emphasized that the Church was able to regulate such matters only if the State permitted it to do so. In general, the Church was allowed to have its way in matters that were not of great moment to the rulers. The higher courts were always crowded with legal business at a time when feudal law was only rudimentary, and incompetent to deal with much that occupied the Church. The Church, however, was rarely allowed much say in the matter of feudal inheritance; but when a quarrel was precipitated with Henry II, a strong king of England, over his efforts to establish a uniform law for clerics and laymen alike, it was the Church, not the king, who won the victory.

REQUIREMENTS FOR THE ESTABLISHMENT OF PAPAL AUTHORITY IN EUROPE

From the above it can be seen what relation the claims of the Church had to the reality of its power in the tenth century. It remains to be considered what essential changes had to be made if the pretended power were to become real. First, and underlying all the rest, the Church had to re-establish its moral supremacy in Europe, so that Christians throughout the whole area could see that it was not just an oppressive secular institution, demanding tithes and feudal dues and contributions, but a body with a true spiritual mission, able to help in the saving of souls. It must renew the faith of the people both in Christianity itself and in the mission of the Church.

Second, and as a consequence of this, it must attract to itself as a body sufficient voluntary financial support to enable it to carry out its duties and maintain some independence from the feudal lords. Voluntary support would be forthcoming only if the people believed in its efficacy for salvation. And the Papal States, the best immediate source of income, must be thoroughly subjected to the pope and firmly administered.

Third, the papacy must free itself from the domination of the German emperor and the Roman nobles and people. This would enable it to carry out a consistent policy, dependent not on imperial or local desires, but upon what it considered best for the Church. The most obvious way was for a pope to name, or have a large share in naming, his successor.

Fourth, the control of appointments to the higher clergy must be taken out of the hands of the feudal lords and kings and put under the control of the papacy. If the higher clergy were papal appointees, then the lower clergy would likwise become responsive to papal policy through these nominees. This policy meant, of course, the suppression of such practices as the sale of Church offices (simony), the bestowal of them on relatives (nepotism), and incelibacy, since a Church office might become hereditary if a clergyman had sons to succeed him.

This tremendous program was substantially carried out in the next few centuries. Its instrument, as so often in the Church reforms of the Middle Ages, was found in the monastic system. The monastic system had for a long time ceased to play any important part in the public life of the Christian world, but it was now to show itself capable of a self-renewal that was as unexpected to the papacy as it was welcome. In the end, as it happened, it was the monastic reform that took over the papacy, instead of the papacy's taking over and exploiting the reform.

❖ The Cluniac reform and its consequences

For a long time the monasteries had been trying to reform themselves, but they were so deeply influenced by the social conditions of the time that they had experienced little success. Then, in 910, a feudal lord, Duke William of Aquitaine, died, leaving a considerable piece of land at Cluny, in eastern France (Burgundy), to the abbot of a monastery of the Benedictine Order in exchange for prayers to be said for his soul. The land was to be entirely free from either royal or feudal jurisdiction, and subject only to the papacy. From this modest beginning the Cluniac movement spread with great rapidity. The abbot of Cluny insisted on maintenance of the strict Benedictine Rule, although manual labor was not stressed as much as in the original Rule. Soon the abbot began to found daughter houses, called priories, which attracted churchmen who were ready to make their lives a moral example to the Christian world. No land was acceptable to the Cluniac Order unless it was given free from feudal obligations. But the terms were met, since the donors believed, as William had, that the prayers of the Cluny monks would be more efficacious for salvation than those of the ordinary churchman, busied as he was with secular affairs.

The Cluny movement from the beginning was interested in ecclesiastical reform, and it had a free hand to do what it could. The sanctity of the monks was, as a rule, sufficient safeguard against actual violence offered by the nobility; and violence was the only way available for hindering their work. They were able, by their preaching and wide influence, to effect an improvement in the whole religious life of Europe; but, even more important, they trained a body of sincere clergymen to fill the high offices in the Church when they became vacant. It was not at first of much significance that the papacy itself was sometimes in the hands of unworthy appointees of the emperor, since the movement, although theoretically subject to the papacy, was not in practice under papal control. The second stage of the Cluniac Reform involves the reform of the papacy itself. Since

Chronological Chart

Foundation of monastery of Cluny	910
Growth of Cluniac influence	910–1050
Henry III appoints four successive reform popes	1046–1054
Schism between Eastern and Western Churches	1054
Treaty of Melfi—Robert Guiscard invested with southern Italy by Pope Nicholas II	1059
Norman conquest of Sicily	1072–1091
Saxon rebellion against Henry IV	1073–1075
Gregory VII becomes pope	1073
Synod of Rome—decrees against simony, clerical marriage, and lay investiture	1075
Henry IV quells rebellion of Saxon nobles	1075
Dictatus papae by Gregory VII	1076
Synod of Worms, called by Henry IV, deposes Gregory	1076
Penance of Henry IV at Canossa	1077
Second deposition of Henry IV by Gregory VII	1080
Sack of Rome by Normans	1084
Proclamation of First Crusade by Urban II	1095
Capture of Jerusalem by Crusaders—Kingdom of Jerusalem	1099
Compromises over lay investiture in England and France	1107
Concordat of Worms	1122
Conrad III first Hohenstaufen emperor	1138–1152
Muslim reconquest of County of Edessa	1144
Second Crusade	1147–1149
Frederick I (Barbarossa) emperor	1152–1190
Frederick states claims on Italian cities at Diet of Roncaglia	1158
Peter Waldo organizes "Poor Men of Lyons"	*ca.* 1176
Battle of Legnano—Defeat of Frederic by Lombard League	1176
Peace of Constance	1183
Pope Lucius III condemns Waldensians	1184
Saladin recaptures Jerusalem	1187
Third Crusade	1189–1192
Henry VI emperor	1190–1197
Capture of Richard I of England by Henry and payment of heavy ransom	1192–1194
Pontificate of Innocent III	1198–1216
John King of England	1199–1216
Fourth Crusade	1202–1204
Capture and sack of Constantinople	1204
Innocent lays interdict on England	1208
Albigensian Crusade	1208–1213
Frederick Hohenstaufen becomes king of the Romans	1212
Innocent deposes John and invites Philip Augustus to execute the sentence	1213
John submits, doing homage to Innocent for throne	1213
Battle of Vouvines—victory of Philip over allies of John	1214
Magna Carta	1215
Deaths of John and Innocent	1216
Louis, son of Philip Augustus, abandons efforts to gain English crown	1217
Fifth Crusade	1218–1221
Frederick II crowned emperor by Honorius III	1220
Dominican Rule confirmed by Pope Honorius III	1220
Franciscan Rule confirmed by Pope Honorius III	1223
Sixth (Frederick's) Crusade	1227–1229
Excommunication of Frederick by Gregory IX	1227
Frederic negotiates ten-year truce with Muslims	1229
Foundation of medieval Inquisition by Pope Gregory IX	1233

Defeat of Lombard League by Frederic at Cortenuova	1237	Conradin, last Hohenstaufen prince, executed	1268
Death of Gregory IX	1241	Rudolf of Hapsburg elected emperor	1273
Two-year interregnum in papacy	1241–1243	Sicilian Vespers	1282
Synod of Lyons—deposition of Frederic by Innocent IV	1245	Peter III of Aragon conquers Sicily and becomes king	1282
Ferdinand captures Seville	1248	Pontificate of Boniface VIII	1294–1303
Lombard cities defeat Frederick at Parma	1248	Boniface issues bull *Clericis laicos*	1296
Death of Frederick II	1250	Philip forbids export of precious metals from France	1297
Conrad IV emperor	1250–1254	Papal jubilee	1300
Manfred regent, later king, of Sicily	1250–1266	Philip summons States-General	1302
		Boniface issues bull *Unam sanctam*	1302
Interregnum in Empire	1254–1273	Death of Boniface VIII (Anagni)	1303
Battle of Benevento—defeat and death of Manfred	1266	Clement V elected Pope	1305
		"Babylonian Captivity" of papacy	1305–1376

this is associated with the name of Pope Gregory VII (1073–1085), it is sometimes called the Gregorian Reform, though it was a natural consequence of the Cluniac Reform and involved no change in policy.

As mentioned earlier, the main line of the attack on secular control of the clergy was directed verbally against the abuses in appointment—against simony, nepotism, and incelibacy. This criticism had for a long time little effect. The secular clergy had been accustomed to living openly with their wives or concubines, and considered the monkish demand for celibacy inhuman. Most rulers also were not willing to give up their patronage so easily, though there were some notable exceptions who greatly advanced the cause of the reform.

But, slowly and carefully, the ground was prepared; and at last it was possible for the popes, several of them from Cluny, to decree that only the pope was entitled to appoint the higher clergy. There must be no more appointments to Church positions by the laity. Thus was precipitated the quarrel between rulers and the papacy over lay investiture.

It was a demand for more than the popes could hope to gain. The clergy required an income, and income could at this time be obtained only from land. The Church had no land to give to its clergy. Hence the feudal lord must give the land, and the Church was willing to allow him to invest with the symbols of sovereignty. But the reformers nevertheless went boldly ahead, demanding the abolition of lay investiture altogether.

RELEASE OF PAPACY FROM SECULAR CONTROL—ELECTION BY CARDINALS

It was not possible for the papacy itself to be independent until it could free itself from control by the emperor. The reformers therefore waited patiently for a suitable opportunity to throw off the shackles. This presented itself when a child (Henry IV) was elected emperor. The papacy then announced (1059) that the pope henceforth would be elected by the cardinal-bishops (later by the whole College of Cardinals). The cardinal-bishops at this time were the heads of certain Roman churches, and the other cardinals held important positions in the papal court. In time the cardinals came to be chosen from all the clergy of Christendom, and the title became an honorary one, carrying great prestige and power because of the cardinal's role in the election of a pope, but held in conjunction with any other office in the Church he might possess. The importance of the announcement at this time was that cardinals could be appointed only by the pope, and they held office for life. Thus continuity of policy could be maintained. The papal appointees of the previous few reigns chose the next incumbent; the emperor had nothing to do with the choice.

ROLE OF THE PAPAL LEGATES—BY-PASSING OF THE SECULAR CLERGY

A third feature fundamental to the program was the growth of a new position in the Church, that of papal legate. The legate was a personal representative of the pope and had precedence over any clergyman in the country to which he was sent. The local clergy and nobles might not like these ambassadors, but they could neglect them only if they also intended to defy the pope. Legates could proclaim the announcements of the pope in the churches of their diocese; they could read the bulls which the local clergy might have wished to suppress; and they could excommunicate or lay an interdict upon the country by the direct authority of the pope himself. By means of the legates the pope could make a direct appeal to public opinion over the heads of the clergy.

The reform movement could not now fail for want of publicity given to the decrees of the pope in the countries for which they were intended.

THE EMERGENCE OF A STRONG PAPACY UNDER CLUNIAC INSPIRATION— HILDEBRAND (GREGORY VII)

From the middle of the eleventh century all the popes were serious reformers. One of the powers behind the papal throne for much of the second half of the eleventh century was a monk named Hildebrand, who did not, however, himself take the chair as Gregory VII till 1073. But as assistant to several popes, he had a share in the determination of papal policies.

When Henry III died, his son was only a child, and during the regency of the child's mother the popes were able to prevent the Germans from playing any active part in papal affairs. When Henry IV grew up, he found himself in trouble with his own nobles, who constantly rebelled against him. He wished for a united Germany under his leadership, and full control of his own clergy and the nobility. He saw at once that he needed his clergy to help control the nobles, in the manner of Otto the Great. He also needed money, most easily obtained by simony, for the purpose of keeping always at hand a body of faithful servants who would help him when necessary to crush the feudal nobility, especially the Saxon lords, who resented the fact that they no longer provided the emperors.

It was thus very difficult to retain control of Italy as well, nor could Henry usually find the time to curb the reformers. Indeed, it was necessary for him even to recognize the reforming popes, in spite of the fact that, in his view, they had been illegally elected since 1059, when election was handed over to the cardinals without his permission. But in Germany he continued to ignore the fulminations of the reformers. He did nothing about clerical marriage; he continued to sell Church offices for money for his campaigns; and of course he made all clerical appointments without reference to the popes. He thought he could afford to wait to deal with the papacy; when it suited him, he could always repudiate his recognition of the popes since 1059, and claim they had all been illegally elected, including any pope who tried to discipline him.

Gregory VII, who was now pope, was ready for the encounter. He was certainly well aware of Henry's difficulties with his own nobles, and he knew that the German clergy, though not in any sense loyal to the pope, were not likely to support Henry against the nobles if the latter were supported by the pope. At the right moment, after formally forbidding lay investiture altogether and making a full statement, circulated by his legates, of what he held to be the true position of the papacy in relation to secular rulers and its right to discipline them, he excommunicated Henry and deprived him of his kingdom. At the same time he released the German nobles from their vows of allegiance, which they had taken when Henry was elected king. Since the German clergy wavered and showed signs of deserting the monarch who had appointed them, and the nobles, led by Rudolph of Swabia, took active

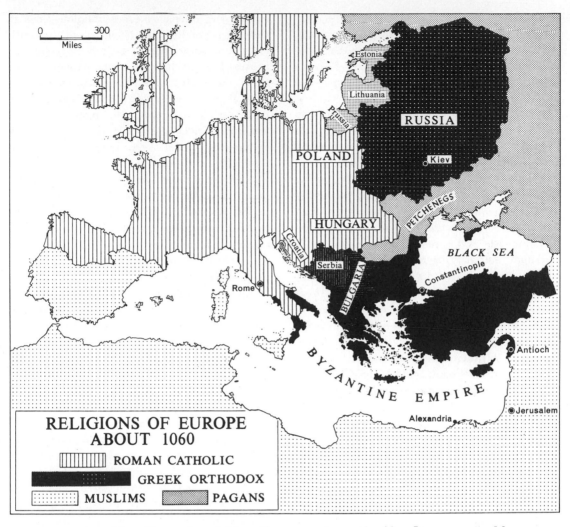

RELIGIONS OF EUROPE
ABOUT 1060

ROMAN CATHOLIC
GREEK ORTHODOX
MUSLIMS   PAGANS

measures against him, Henry found himself isolated and without means of resistance. The nobles took him into custody and called upon the pope to come to Germany and preside over the election of a new king.

Gregory was therefore on the point of triumphing and establishing once and for all his right to discipline rulers. Unfortunately for him, Henry escaped and made his way to Canossa, in northern Italy, where Gregory was spending a few days on his way to Germany for the election (1077). This presented the pope with a cruel dilemma. Since Henry expressed his penitence, it was his duty as a priest to absolve him, even though it might mean the collapse of his German policy and result in a civil war within Germany. Nevertheless, absolve him he did, and Henry re-

turned over the Alps. It was assumed by everyone that the pope had restored him to his kingdom. Some of the nobles and the bulk of the German clergy hastened to join him, giving him enough strength to defeat and kill Rudolph. Although Gregory excommunicated Henry again in 1080, the moment of decision had passed, and this time the action was ineffectual. As a final irony, Henry himself crossed the Alps with an army in 1083 and drove Gregory into exile.

But Gregory's work did not die with him in 1085. Henry was still excommunicated, and, in the eyes of the papacy, still dethroned. Rebellions continued against him for the rest of his life. Finally, his son was elected king by the nobles with papal support, and Henry died a year later, without a throne. The new king, later Emperor Henry v, had to take forceful action in Italy on several occasions. But the cardinals continued to elect the popes without hindrance, establishing enough precedent for the practice to make it impossible for any emperor later to question its legality.

Meanwhile, a series of popes continued to negotiate on the matter of lay investiture with Henry v. After a number of agreements had been made, which were later repudiated, a lasting compromise was arranged, embodied in the Concordat of Worms of 1122. Under this settlement the emperor invested the clergy with land and secular authority, symbolized by the scepter; while the pope invested them with spiritual authority, symbolized by ring and staff. Thus each had a veto on the other's appointments—a clear gain for the papacy, for it now gained something it had never previously held—while the emperor lost his right to make nominations without reference to the papacy. As long as the popes remained reformers, simony and incelibacy could be held in check, since they could refuse to invest any priest who did not fulfill their moral and religious requirements. A similar compromise was arranged with the kings of England and France, who had, like the emperor, been accustomed to making clerical appointments in their realms.

❖ **The expansion of Europe—
The Crusades**

Meanwhile, in 1095, only ten years after the death of Gregory VII, the papacy was provided with an opportunity to give leadership to a movement for the expansion of Christendom to the East. The Crusades could be described from any of several points of view. They have been regarded as an early example of typical European imperialism—as efforts by feudal lords to obtain new lands and new sources of income at a time when the fertility of their manors was decreasing, as efforts by merchants to find new trade routes and new items of trade. The Crusades, incidentally, were all of these things. But they were unique in being summoned by a religious leader with ostensibly solely religious ends in view. It is true that the later Crusades escaped altogether from papal control, and in the process brought discredit to the papacy as well as to the participants. Their ultimate effects upon Western Christianity and the Church were relatively unimportant. Far more important was their incidental effect in opening up a part of the East to the West, stimulating Western commerce, and assisting the spread of towns.

The reformed Cluniac papacy was still in power and the investiture struggle not yet settled when Pope Urban II called the First Crusade in response, in part, to an appeal from a pilgrim named Peter the Hermit. Peter had reported that Christians were finding it hard to deal with the Seljuk Turks, who had captured Jerusalem from the Abbasid caliphs of Bagdad. The latter had interfered little with Christian pilgrimages to the Holy Sepulcher— a fairly common penance undertaken by Christians. But the Turks who now controlled the Asiatic dominions of the Abbasids were more fanatically Muslim than the later Abbasids, and did not look with favor on the Christian interest in Palestine. Urban had also received an appeal from Alexius Comnenus, the Byzantine emperor, many of whose lands had been overrun by the Turks. Although by 1095 the Eastern and Western Churches had been separated for over forty years, the pope no doubt cherished the idea of a possible reunion and increased influence at Constantinople if the Crusade were successful.

In an impassioned speech, therefore, Urban urged all Christians to unite in driving the infidels from the Holy Land, and promised a plenary indulgence to all those who went on the Crusade. The appeal met with a wide response from most classes in society. The traders and merchants could envisage new markets and new products, as well as profit in transporting some of the Crusaders by sea and keeping them supplied. The proper business of feudal lords was fighting, and land was becoming short in Europe. Perhaps they could win new fiefs for themselves. The peasants had little to lose, and if they won nothing else they might win freedom from serfdom if they survived. Only the kings and

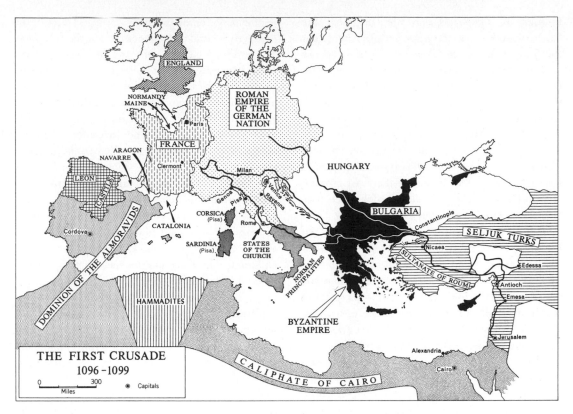

THE FIRST CRUSADE
1096–1099

0   300
Miles   ⊚ Capitals

greater lords hesitated, for they might lose much by absenting themselves from their realms. If they stayed, they might hope to gain the lands of Crusaders who never returned. But beyond and above all these private considerations the religious zeal was unmistakable. Many in the full flood of enthusiasm went against their material interests. With scarcely the vaguest idea of where Jerusalem was, still less of what they would find there (never having seen an infidel), they received absolution from the Church, donned the sacred emblems which showed they were Crusaders, and set out by land, determined to recover the Holy Sepulcher. Afterward it became necessary for the popes to use coercion, and leadership fell into the hands of kings who went because it was expected of them. But no one was coerced for the First Crusade; and it was the only Crusade that was successful.

The First Crusade was not very well organized, and the Byzantine emperor gave only limited help. But the Crusaders reconquered most of Asia Minor, which they had to return to the emperor, and the following year moved

into Palestine. Since the Seljuk Turks made only a token resistance, leaving the unfortunate Egyptians and others who lived in Jerusalem to bear the brunt of the Crusaders' fury, Jerusalem was captured without much difficulty. A kingdom of Jerusalem was then established as a fief of the papacy, with the leading Crusader, Godfrey of Bouillon, duke of Lorraine, as king (1099). Other nobles won fiefs for themselves, and several religious-military orders were founded to assist in the defense of the Holy Land. The Venetians, Genoese, and Pisans brought out regular reinforcements from Europe each year, and began to take back Oriental products for the European markets. Lacking religious zeal, the merchants encouraged fraternization and peaceful relations with the infidels. In due course the Crusaders themselves began to relax their severity, adopt Muslim customs and dress, and lord it over their realms like Oriental princelings, leaving defense to the new military orders and to mercenary armies locally recruited from the Oriental population.

As it happened, the success of the First

Crusade had been due to the fact that the Turks were so heavily involved elsewhere that they could not undertake the effective defense of Palestine. But Muslim power was far from broken. As soon as the Muslims had secured their own position, they began to encroach upon the lands recently conquered by the Crusaders. Edessa, an outlying fief to the northeast of the kingdom of Jerusalem, fell to Muslim arms in 1144. Thereupon a second Crusade was called, in which the Holy Roman emperor and the French king took part. The Crusade was completely unsuccessful, and Edessa remained in Muslim hands. Toward the end of the twelfth century a great Muslim prince named Saladin united the two countries of Syria and Egypt under his rule and marched on Jerusalem, which fell to his arms without much difficulty (1187). Immediately, another Crusade was called, to which Frederic Barbarossa, the French king Philip Augustus, and the English king Richard I (the Lion-Hearted) responded. The old emperor was killed while crossing a river in Asia Minor. The two kings, who had gone separately, had different motives for joining the Crusade. Philip had no interest in the Crusade as such. He was primarily interested in seeing that Richard became thoroughly involved in it so that he could return to France and try to conquer Richard's lands in France. Richard, on the other hand, was interested in performing knightly deeds. He was successful in taking Acre from the Muslims but had no success in his efforts to recapture Jerusalem. Finally, without accomplishing his objective, he began the journey home, and on the way he was captured and held for ransom by the new Holy Roman emperor, Henry VI.

By this time it was clear to many in Europe that the crusading spirit was almost dead. Kings had to be threatened with spiritual sanctions if they did not obey papal commands. The nobles recognized that there was little opportunity left for new lands. Jerusalem was too difficult to conquer, and if they went on the Crusade there was a good chance that some rival lord would filch their European fiefs from them. Only the traders were still interested. But the eyes even of some of these, notably the Venetians, were evidently already straying

in the direction of Constantinople, an important competitor and perchance a source of loot. These facts of life did not, however, deter Pope Innocent III from calling another Crusade, and popes were to continue calling them until all hope had been lost of capturing the Holy City. The Fourth Crusade, however, was a disgrace in all respects. The Crusaders who accepted the call assembled at Venice, hoping for transport, and heavily in debt for their initial expenses. The Venetians agreed to transport them to what they believed would be the Holy Land. In fact, the Venetians had no intention of going there. They did not, however, reveal their intentions until the Crusaders were safely embarked. In the end, for reasons that do not need to be detailed here, the Crusaders went to Constantinople and, through intervening in a disputed succession at the request of the ousted monarch, were able to enter the city without fighting. A few days later, dissatisfied with their spoils, they fell upon the defenseless city and sacked it. The Byzantine emperor fled, and the Crusaders established the Latin Kingdom of Constantinople, which lasted from 1204 to 1261. Innocent III was unable to prevent the Venetians and the Crusaders from completing their nefarious enterprise in spite of threats of excommunication. Ultimately he accepted the new kingdom as a blessing, since it reunited the Eastern and Western Churches for the first time in a century and a half.

Nothing daunted, Innocent again proclaimed a Crusade at the Lateran Council of 1215. The king of Hungary agreed to go by way of Egypt, but so bungled the enterprise that after capturing the key city of Damietta, his armies were defeated and Damietta was lost. Later in the century the Holy Roman emperor Frederic II—threatened with excommunication if he did not go on a Crusade, as he had promised Innocent in his youth—returned after starting his voyage, whereupon he was in fact excommunicated by Pope Gregory IX. Frederic proceeded to Jerusalem shortly afterward and recovered it by negotiation—a feat which was regarded unfavorably by the pope, who preferred more spectacular ways of treating infidels. The Holy City remained in Christian hands for only fifteen years. Thereafter it was never again recovered, despite the efforts of other Crusaders, including the saintly French monarch Louis IX. The last Christian possession in Palestine, the city of Acre, fell in 1291.

CONSEQUENCES OF THE CRUSADES FOR THE PAPACY

The economic results of the Crusades will be dealt with elsewhere. Here we are concerned with their effect on the power of the Church and the papacy.

There is no doubt that the success of the First Crusade redounded to the prestige of the papacy, which had called it, as the failure of the others to some extent discredited it. The overlordship exercised by the popes over the Latin Kingdom of Jerusalem was never more than nominal. The papacy was unable to prevent the Crusaders from tolerating and fraternizing with Muslims, once the early fanaticism was over. Very little attempt was made to convert the Muslims themselves to Christianity. Many Crusaders married Muslims and took over some of their customs. They were far more influenced by the superior Muslim civilization, even in its decay, than they themselves influenced the Muslims. It has also been suggested that contact with the Greek Orthodox Church and with the various heretical groups that had been living peaceably in Palestine for centuries under Muslim rule made them realize that Western Catholicism was not as universally accepted as they had been led to believe, but actual evidence is necessarily missing for this assumption. There can be no doubt that the inability of Innocent to control the Crusaders who sacked Constantinople was a blow to his prestige for which even the temporary forced union between Greek and Roman Churches was but a slight compensation. This failure did not, however, prevent his subsequent success in dictating to the kings of Europe.

The times had changed. The true crusading spirit had disappeared from all but a few remaining knights-errant, such as St. Louis IX of France. The commercial spirit symbolized by the Fourth Crusade showed that men now had other interests than salvation. Indulgences had been cheapened by their indiscriminate bestowal on the Crusaders, the purity of whose deeds and motives was questionable. The political activities and worldliness of the Church did not escape the notice of the more earnest Christians. And, as we shall see later, the faith of the people, which was ultimately the only basis upon which all papal claims must rest (a truth which had been recognized by Gregory VII but forgotten by Innocent), had been put to a severe test by the actions of the papacy. Within the Church and outside it a movement had been growing since the eleventh century which called for a return to an earlier and more ideal Christianity. But discussion of this movement will be left to a later section of this chapter, after we have considered the position of the papacy at the height of its power under Innocent III.

❖ Growth of the papacy to supreme power in Europe

CONFLICT WITH HOHENSTAUFEN EMPERORS

Having considered the role of the papacy in the Crusades, it is now time to return to the Church as it was at the time of the First Crusade. We have dealt with the Concordat of Worms in 1122, under which the investiture struggle between the emperor and the papacy was settled. The pope was therefore in a stronger position than before the reign of Gregory VII. But, as it happened, the papacy now had to meet a challenge of a different kind, for which it was ill-prepared. The empire, having been for a time in the hands of relatively weak rulers, who had difficulty in holding their own within Germany itself and could hardly aspire to rule beyond German boundaries, in the twelfth century fell under the rule of the family of Hohenstaufen, one of whose members, Frederic Barbarossa, reigned for thirty-eight years (1152–1190). This emperor desired nothing less than the restoration of a truly Roman Empire, called in his day the Holy Roman Empire. This meant that he must subject Italy, which was dotted with prosperous towns, mostly independent, to his sway. The

HOLY ROMAN EMPIRE
AT DEATH OF
FREDERIC BARBAROSSA
1190
★ LOMBARD LEAGUE TOWNS

ADDED TO EMPIRE
UNDER HENRY VI
1190-97

pope, possessor of lands in Italy (including Rome, presumably the capital of an empire called Roman) which he had no intention of yielding to the emperor, was compelled to aid the Italian towns in their resistance to Frederic, while the latter attempted to control the papacy once more through his own nominees.

In 1178 Frederic was severely defeated by the Lombard League, and thereafter abandoned his ambitions. But before he died he had arranged for the marriage of his son Henry to the heiress of Sicily, a well-managed Norman kingdom which included parts of southern Italy. This combination was too much for the Italians and the papacy to resist; and for a brief period, 1190–1197, the new emperor Henry VI kept Italy in submission. The popes of the period had no alternative but to accept the situation. The feeble weapons available to them would not have been effective to change

it, but the expansionist policy of the emperors had brought the papacy into the thick of Italian and imperial politics. The papacy, in short, was rapidly becoming a secular power, wielding what spiritual weapons it had, but in the interests of secular and not religious policy. Then Henry VI, who was only thirty-two years of age, suddenly died, leaving a son of three in Sicily and no one of his family strong enough to hold the empire together. One year later, in 1198, Innocent III ascended the papal throne.

Innocent's policy was thus all prepared for him. His task was clearly to prevent Sicily and the empire from ever falling into the same hands again, and to keep the two chief German families at each other's throats. He accomplished the second not very difficult task by throwing his support first to one family and then to the other, while Germany fell into the throes of a civil war. He kindly took the infant

Frederic Hohenstaufen of Sicily, son of Henry VI, under his personal patronage, made him his ward, and promised to keep the kingdom of Sicily for him until he was grown up—with the determination that at all costs he must be kept from the empire.

In the century since Gregory, the papacy had gained no new weapon; it could exercise its influence to disrupt, and hope to make incidental gains from the discord. Nevertheless, the breathing space after the extreme danger of the reign of Henry VI was enough for Innocent to display the papacy at the height of its temporal power; even though to hindsight its foundations were no stronger than the temporary division among the natural opponents of papal prerogatives in the secular realm.

THE PAPACY AT THE HEIGHT OF ITS POWER

In 1198 Innocent, who regarded himself as the spiritual lord of Christendom, commanded the French king Philip Augustus to take back his Danish wife, whom he had repudiated without papal consent. When Philip refused, Innocent laid an interdict upon his territories. Philip then submitted. Soon afterward, John, king of England, insisted on choosing his own archbishop of Canterbury, contrary to the wishes of Innocent. When the pope laid an interdict on England, John resisted; whereupon Innocent "gave" his kingdom to Philip, with whom John had been constantly at war in an effort to retain lands in France that had been acquired by the English crown as part of the dowry of John's mother. In danger of invasion and deserted, for reasons that will be discussed in the next chapter, by most of his barons, John finally submitted, yielding his kingdom to the papacy as a fief. Innocent then tried to protect his new vassal against Philip's son, who was preparing to invade England, and against John's rebellious barons. He also declared Magna Carta, a document which John had just been compelled by his barons to sign, null and void. Innocent was unable to achieve any of his aims in England, and even his own appointee to the archbishopric of Canterbury sided with the rebellious barons. Innocent himself died in the year following Magna Carta.

It is clear that it was Philip who was the gainer from Innocent's intervention, not the pope himself. Although the interdict damaged England severely it would not have forced John to submit, in spite of the difficulties he was having with his barons. Philip took back his wife because he looked forward to papal support in his struggle with England, not because he recognized the papal right to interfere in his marital affairs. Moreover, it is doubtful whether these ventures into national politics increased either the power or the prestige of the papacy. Papal taxation in England, which resulted from her position as a papal fief, was certainly extremely unpopular in that country. It gave rise to numerous complaints against papal avarice in the thirteenth and later centuries. It contributed to baronial resentment against John's successor, the pious monarch Henry III, who strove to fulfill his papal obligations. Innocent's policy, therefore, was distantly responsible for the baronial revolt which led to the first English Parliament.

Finally, it should be noted that Frederic, son of the emperor Henry VI, was able to have himself elected Holy Roman emperor, in spite of Innocent's efforts to divide and rule in Germany. Ironically enough, Innocent himself was left no option but to support his candidacy.

❖ Reactions to the worldliness of the Church

THE FAILURE OF THE MONASTIC ORDERS

It was not possible for the Church to become so heavily embroiled in secular affairs without losing some prestige as a spiritual organization. The papacy was compelled to enter into alliances, especially with the Italian towns or with some faction in the towns; it was in constant need of money; and its religious sanctions, such as the interdict used so freely by Innocent III, necessarily brought it into constant conflict with secular powers. As an organization, the Church was becoming wealthier and more powerful, thus moving, in the opinion of many sincere Christians, ever further away from the Christian ideal of poverty that had been stressed by its founder. Even the monasteries, which in earlier years had appealed to those religious men who had wished to follow a purely religious life, were growing wealthy. The monks too often were worldly. Almost every religious order at one time or another had had to be reformed, and forced back into a stricter observance of their Rule.

In the twelfth century an ascetic and mystic, St. Bernard of Clairvaux, for a time acted as the conscience of the Church. Despising earthly power, possessions, and wisdom, he did not hesitate to attack the secular clergy for its excessive interest in worldly matters and for neglect of its religious duties. He was instrumental in aiding a new religious order, the Cistercians, to set itself upon a more spiritual path. For a time the Cistercian Order maintained its austerity, but, as with all the other successful orders which did not keep themselves separated from the world, the wealth that flowed into it from the faithful undermined its discipline. Long before St. Bernard's death the Cluny Order that had started so auspiciously had likewise fallen into decay and become involved too exclusively with ecclesiastical politics and other worldly affairs. So, in the twelfth century, it was to a considerable degree the heretics rather than the Church that set the example of unworldly living.

THE GROWTH OF HERESY

As early as the eleventh century attacks on the worldliness of the Church and the failure of the Church to heed them had driven occasional reformers into an uncompromising position which could only mean actual separation from organized religion. There were no other Churches to join; only one great Church, authoritarian and dogmatic, which had to be accepted or rejected. And the penalty for rejection, or heresy, was death if the heretic refused to change his views. Many heretics no doubt found their way into the reformed monasteries, where they could spend their lives in personal worship and outward conformity. If no such monastery appealed to them, then there was no other recourse than heresy.

Earlier heresies, in the main, concerned questions of theology; at a time when Christian theology had not yet crystallized into dogma, or beliefs necessary for salvation promulgated by authority, such heresy was to be expected until the authority was universally accepted. Twelfth-century heresy is of a different kind. With a few minor exceptions it was anticlerical in origin. It was above everything against the established Church; and though in some cases a different doctrine was preached, the doctrine was subsidiary to the anticlericalism, and usually grew out of it. The common element in all twelfth-century heresy was the belief that true Christianity consisted in leading a life more consistent with the life of Christ as it had been portrayed in the Gospels. It was, then, a reaction against the apparently non-Christian life of the Church and its clergy.

The Waldensians Of the two important heretical groups of the twelfth century, the Waldensians moved a shorter distance from the doctrines of the Church. The founder, one Peter Waldo, had discovered in the Gospels that Christ had owned no property but given all his goods to the poor. Waldo, who had been a merchant, followed his example; then, gathering around him a number of disciples, began to preach poverty. He applied to Pope Alexander III for permission for himself and his followers, who were known as the "poor men of Lyons," to take vows of poverty and to preach. The pope gave his permission but insisted that the Waldensians first obtain permission from the local clergy. This they neglected to do. Their opinion of the local clergy was a low one and they did not attempt to conceal it, thus exciting the wrath of all those who did not care to follow the Waldensian example. Faced by such opposition, the Waldensians in time began to insist that there need be no clergy at all; and they gained adherents among all the anticlerical groups in society, especially in the towns and among the poor. It was no great step to organizing their own churches, based on the ideal of the early Christian Church as far as they understood it. Waldensianism was condemned by a Church council, and in later years pursued by the Inquisition. But the movement was never altogether suppressed. In later years it became part of Protestantism, and even today a small Waldensian Protestant sect is still in existence.

The Cathari The heresy of Catharism was for a long time far more dangerous to the Church. The teachings of the Cathari (the "pure ones") stemmed from Manichaeism, a Persian cult with a central teaching that there were two great powers in the world, good and evil, light and darkness, and that it was the task of mankind to cast out everything that pertained to the realm of darkness. For the Cathari this included such things as certain kinds of food, sexual intercourse, and private property. From the first the movement was anticlerical, regarding the Church as an instrument of the powers of darkness. Naturally not all Cathari adhered strictly to the list of permitted and forbidden practices. There were degrees amongst them, consisting of "believers," who did not have to live a fully Catharist life, and of "perfected ones," who had undertaken the full ideal of austerity.

Catharism may be considered as a heresy if it is taken into account that Christ appears in it as the emissary of the forces of light, or as a separate religion if one considers mainly its Manichaean origin. It obtained a surprising success in parts of Europe, notably southern France, where it set up its own Church and clerical hierarchy. It was protected by secular powers, especially by the counts of Toulouse, within whose feudal jurisdiction the majority of Cathari lived. For this reason the Cathari are also called Albigensians, since the city of Albi was one of their centers.

For a long time the heretical activity in southern France had troubled the papacy, and several attempts had been made to turn the Albigensians from their heresy. But public debates between representatives of the Catholic and Catharist Churches invariably ended in victory for the latter, and the Catholics were often roughly handled. Innocent III was not the man to permit such a heresy to exist side by side with the Church without taking action against it. He attempted first to work through

a special evangelical mission. But since this was in the hands of Cistercians, who were not trained for such work, it failed like all the others. Finally, Innocent proclaimed a "Crusade" against the Albigensians. Since the lands they occupied were some of the fairest in France, and the lords who obeyed the papal call might expect to win fiefs for themselves from the rebellious count of Toulouse, who continued to try to protect his subjects, there was no lack of volunteers. There was little danger, for most of the Cathari were pacifists and would refuse to fight, whereas the nobles and their retainers were relatively few. After a number of terrible massacres by the "Crusaders," and some fighting with the nobility, the Albigensian movement was eradicated from that part of France. The entire territory was not pacified until 1229, however, long after the death of Innocent. By that time the son of that count of Toulouse who had protected the heretics had inherited his father's lands, and, by aiding in the last suppression of the Albigensians, was able to oust the crusading nobility who had temporarily occupied the lands.

THE MENDICANT ORDERS

The Dominicans When the first phase of the crusade was over Innocent did his best to help in the work of reconverting those Albigensians who had survived. He permitted St. Dominic (1170–1221), a young Spaniard who had formed part of the earlier Cistercian mission, to form a new order for the purpose of preaching to the heretics, although the Dominican Order (Order of Preachers) was not given official sanction until the reign of Innocent's successor (1216). The Dominicans took vows of poverty, thus setting an example to the worldly clergy; and though they, in turn, became unpopular with the secular clergy, throughout the thirteenth century they were strongly supported by the papacy, and undertook many missions for the popes. Together with the Franciscans, who also took vows of poverty, they were the most influential churchmen of the thirteenth century.

The religious life of the towns had been seriously neglected for centuries. The parish priest had far more difficulty in the towns than on a compact manor in keeping in touch with his flock, and the higher clergy had too many other duties to give the townspeople much attention. The monasteries were, as a rule, founded in country districts, and had no influence in the cities. But these new orders of friars (brothers), as they were called, went out preaching to the people directly in the market place or in the local church. The Dominicans early became noted for their learning, and were able to give instruction in a manner hitherto unknown. As missionaries, first within Christianity and then to heathen countries, their influence and activity were enormous. Convents were founded throughout Europe where the friars could live, and which they could use as their headquarters for missionary activity. But unlike the monasteries, the convents were modest institutions. Very little land was required, nor was regular income needed from feudal dues, since the brothers lived at the beginning entirely from begging (hence they were called mendicant orders). From the first they were directly subject to the papacy through their chief officer, called a minister general, who ruled authoritatively through provincial ministers in each country.

The Franciscans The Franciscan Order was founded by St. Francis of Assisi (1182–1226), the son of a merchant in good circumstances who was able to provide Francis with a life of modest luxury. But Francis was suddenly converted from this life of ease by reading the Gospels. At once he gave away all his possessions save the coarsest and simplest of clothing, took, in his own words, Lady Poverty for his bride, and began to preach.

If there has ever been a true Christian saint since the founding of Christianity, then St. Francis was he. By his example and utter sincerity, and by the simplicity of his life, he won the hearts of all those who listened to him, and a band of disciples quickly grew up around him. It was not only that he was kind to everyone, even the outcasts of society—the sick and the maimed and the lepers, whom no one would touch. The quality of love seemed to shine out from him in a way that no one could resist or wished to resist. But behind this genuine simplicity there was also a rare intuitive understanding of the life around him. He knew that it was impossible for the Church ever fully to accept him, he knew what dangers and temptations his order would have to meet; he knew to how few it is given really to lead

An almost contemporary (ca. 1265) *miniature of St. Francis of Assisi preaching to the birds. From a* Psalter *(Franco-Flemish).* (COURTESY THE PIERPONT MORGAN LIBRARY. Ms. 72, folio 139)

such a life of absolute poverty as his. He did not want to organize his order formally; he did not want it to have rules and regulations which would inhibit the spontaneous outpouring of love in which lay his own special genius. He did, however, have an interview with Innocent; but it was only natural that the pope should be hesitant, his shrewd diplomatic mind grasping the dangers that such a movement held for his Church. Dominic was dangerous enough, but a leader like Francis was a hundred times more so. It is said that Innocent had a dream in which he saw the Church supported by only these two orders, a dream later enshrined in a famous fresco of Giotto. Whether be heeded the dream or not, he temporized, and it was his successor who drew up the Franciscan Rule and confirmed the order (1223). Francis himself refused to be minister general, and insisted on appointing the most worldly of his band to the position, because, as he said, it was right for himself also to be subject to discipline as a Christian duty.

Francis disapproved of learning as unnecessary in a pure gospel of love, and the preaching of his order in his lifetime corresponded to his own. The task of Franciscans was rather to help and heal, to teach by example and not by precept, to go about among the poor bearing the Gospel and praising God for his blessings, and encouraging them to do likewise.

It was inevitable that after the death of Francis there should be a schism within his order. No organized body, but only rare individuals, could live up to such an ideal. Money poured in upon the order, which was not permitted by its Rule to keep it. The appointment of a papal procurator to handle the funds of the order did not solve the problem, and in the eyes of the uncompromising followers of St. Francis, this subterfuge was a betrayal. With the resounding success of both the Dominican and Franciscan Orders and the support given them by the papacy, privileges showered in upon them, and ever more recruits flocked to the Franciscan Order. The life of primitive simplicity had to be abandoned; and the begging of the friars before long became a scandal to those who knew of the order's wealth. Friars of both orders began to seek learning, and the

influence of the papacy was able to gain them chairs in theology even at Paris. The secular professors, resenting this unfair competition, unleashed a torrent of scurrilous pamphlets on their way of life and their hypocrisy, which was replied to in kind by the leading friars. In the convents of both orders learning was approved, and preaching to the people ceased to be universal; friars were permitted to hear confessions, and before the end of the century a friar was pope.

The Dominicans, to whom in any case poverty had never been such an essential part of their movement, accepted the inevitable; the Franciscans split in two. For a while most of the ministers general were men who had known St. Francis and knew what poverty had meant to him; and those dissident Franciscans who objected to the ownership of property, whether by brothers or by the order itself, were protected by them. But by the end of the thirteenth century it was clear that the order was doomed if it could not heal the schism. The path that was probably inevitable from the first was chosen. The Conventuals, who accepted the compromise on absolute poverty and who were in a majority within the order, expelled the Spirituals, who wished to retain strict poverty and were ultimately treated as heretics by the Conventuals. By the early fourteenth century the Spirituals had been formally declared heretical.[1] Some were handed over to the Inquisition, while many more languished in Franciscan prisons. Their movement persisted for a long time, being used by secular powers against the Avignon papacy when they wished to castigate its pride and luxury. Ultimately, the remnants found refuge in Protestantism.

THE INQUISITION

Great though the influence of the mendicant orders was, heresy did not disappear as a result of their efforts. In the early thirteenth century Pope Gregory IX established a regular

---

[1] By this time, indeed, they had accepted certain prophetic teachings which could be considered formally heretical, although the Spirituals themselves denied that they were.

Inquisition into the beliefs of supposed heretics, which was entrusted first to the Dominicans, and later to both orders. The purpose of the Inquisition was to fix a procedure for the detection and punishment of heretics. The Inquisitor, a papal appointee, paid periodical visits to the various cities within his jurisdiction, calling upon heretics to declare themselves and upon the faithful to denounce those suspected of heresy. If a heretic confessed and recanted, he was usually let off with a comparatively light penance imposed by the Church. If he refused to recant, then torture was permitted to compel the confession. Testimony was taken, but the defendant was not allowed a lawyer nor was he permitted to know the names of his accusers or the nature of the evidence. If two witnesses of good character agreed, then he could be condemned.

The purpose, however, was always to obtain a confession and to persuade the heretic to recant, in which case, if he had been a long time making up his mind to confess, he might receive a severe, but not a capital, punishment. Except when in later years the Inquisition became a tool of the secular powers, who used it to confiscate the property of heretics, this provision was usually carried out, and there were far fewer death sentences imposed than penances. If the heretic refused to recant, he was handed over to the secular authorities to be put to death, customarily by burning. If a heretic recanted and then relapsed into heresy he was regarded as incorrigible, and likewise handed over to the secular authorities.

The Church, however, was not all-powerful in the medieval period; it could not impose the death penalty itself. Only when the secular authorities agreed could the death penalty be exacted. They must therefore share the opprobrium for the Inquisition with the Church. That they backed it up as much as they did is because they too regarded heresy as treason, and heretics as rebels against the established order.

❖ The papacy and secular powers in the thirteenth century

THE IMPOSING EDIFICE OF INNOCENT III

In the last section we have, for the sake of convenience, included events after the death of Innocent III, and it is now time to consider and summarize the position of the papacy as it was left by Innocent. In 1215 the pope summoned

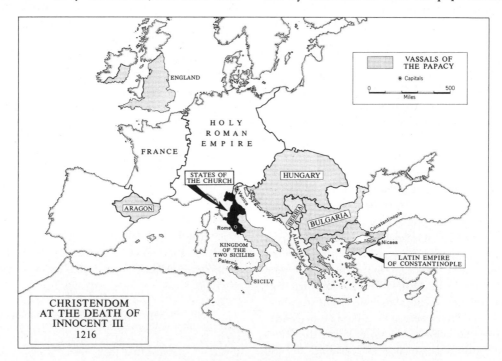

CHRISTENDOM
AT THE DEATH OF
INNOCENT III
1216

a council to be held at the Lateran in 1215. All the potentates of Christendom came or were represented. The pope proclaimed a new Christian dogma and gave fatherly advice to all the rulers present. It might have been thought by any contemporary that Christendom was close to becoming a true theocracy, ruled by the representative of God upon earth. At the time the pope was the feudal suzerain of England, Aragon, the Two Sicilies, Hungary, Serbia, Bulgaria, and the Latin Kingdom of Constantinople. The English and French monarchs had to all appearance been successfully disciplined by him. He had so weakened the Holy Roman Empire by his political interference that it seemed likely that no emperor could again win the power that had rested in the hands of Henry VI. When he summoned a new Crusade at the Lateran Council there was some show of enthusiasm, and the king of Hungary promised to go. Southern France had been restored to the Catholic fold after several generations of heresy, even though at the cost of many lives. Finally, the Eastern and Western Churches had been reunited as a consequence of the Fourth Crusade.

It was an imposing edifice that Innocent had built. Yet history was to show that not one of the triumphs was really significant or proved to be lasting. The Latin Kingdom of Constantinople came to an end in 1261, when the Greek emperor was restored, and the empire itself had been so seriously weakened by the Crusade that it was never able fully to recover. The two kings of England and France were not in fact properly controlled. They had given way when it suited them, and another time they could resist the same weapons. The quarrel between England and France had been the pope's opportunity, as the premature death of Emperor Henry VI had been his opportunity in Central Europe. He had crushed the Albigensians because he offered land to the nobles, not because they were the obedient Christian executors of his wishes. He had been unable to prevent the Venetians and Crusaders from sacking Constantinople, though he had been willing enough to take advantage of their victory. In short, whatever the appearances, the secular powers held all the sources of power in their hands,

and they only needed a more favorable moment to throw off the illusory yoke of the pretended theocracy.

Innocent III betrayed no real understanding of this state of affairs. Even if he had, there was still little that he could have done about it save the last thought that would have occurred to him—to become a spiritual power alone, the moral arbiter of Europe and not its dictator. When a hint of this other way was revealed to him by St. Francis, he looked hastily in the other direction.

He had no understanding of the growth of commercialism in the century before his day; his eyes were on the past glories of the Crusades, and not upon the present reality that the crusading spirit had disappeared from Europe. His political interferences without exception led in the longer run to exactly those results most dangerous to his office and authority, as when he made the English king his vassal; he failed to understand the basis of heresy in a justified anticlericalism, and preferred to wipe out heretics with the sword.

The heritage he left to his successors was a long struggle with the secular powers which could never be won, a universal Church with ambitions beyond its power to achieve, and a tradition of authoritarian dictation which made an ultimate schism inevitable.

By not understanding the nature of the City of God, he helped to make it forever impossible.

RESUMED STRUGGLE OF PAPACY WITH THE EMPIRE

Trouble between the papacy and the empire was not long in coming. Before the end of the reign of Innocent, Frederic Hohenstaufen, his young ward, was chosen king by the Germans, with Innocent's approval. Honorius III, who succeeded Innocent in 1216, could not prevent the young king from being crowned emperor also, thus uniting the Norman kingdom of Sicily with the empire, as in the time of Henry VI.

Frederic II was one of the most remarkable of medieval rulers. Scientist and freethinker. educated almost as much by Muslims as by

Christians, with an excellent understanding of both his Sicilian and his Germanic heritage, in his day he was known as the "wonder of the world" (*stupor mundi*). He was unfortunate in the opposition of two popes who were anxious to curb his power. Gregory IX appears to have been as horrified by his freethinking as he was opposed to his policies. He it was who excommunicated Frederic for not going on a Crusade as he had promised Innocent, and kept the ban on him even when he later fulfilled his promise. While Frederic was away on the Crusade, Gregory attempted to deprive him of his Sicilian lands. When he returned, he engaged in war with the Lombard towns and attempted to add them to the empire. In this enterprise, too, he was naturally opposed by the pope, who raised money and troops for the defense of the revived Lombard League. Finally, the pope attempted to depose the emperor, whereupon the latter seized and imprisoned a boatload of cardinals. At this point Gregory died and Frederic insisted that the cardinals elect a man acceptable to himself. But when such a man had been elected under the name of Innocent IV, the new pope escaped to France, from which safe haven he proceeded to depose the emperor again, and tried to raise a rebellion against him in Germany.

Meanwhile, Frederic had run into trouble in Italy. In the early part of his reign he had subdued almost the whole of the peninsula. But in his last years he lost an important battle, and had not recovered his position when he died at the age of fifty-six (1250). The pope was able to prevent the Sicilian crown from going to the same man as the empire. But Frederic's illegitimate son Manfred, who ruled Italy, could not be dislodged until a later pope, Clement IV, called in a French noble, Charles of Anjou, to dispossess him. Thus Hohenstaufen influence in Italy was exchanged for French. Charles killed Manfred in battle (1266) and captured the last Hohenstaufen of the direct male line. With the approval of the pope, he had him beheaded in Naples. Meanwhile, the Hohenstaufen who was on the imperial throne died, and the electors could agree on no other ruler. Thus from 1254

to 1273 there was no Holy Roman emperor, while a French noble ruled over Sicily and much of Italy. To such a pass had papal imperial policy led. The empire was virtually destroyed, and its influence in Italy seemed to be over.

In 1273 the first prince of the House of Hapsburg was chosen emperor—a minor lord who was the choice of the nobles primarily because he held little initial power or land of his own. French influence in Sicily was not to be broken until 1282, when the Sicilians staged a massacre of all Frenchmen who could be found (Sicilian Vespers). By a remarkable irony, the daughter of Manfred married the heir to the throne of Aragon, who inherited the lands of the Hohenstaufens in Sicily and maintained his rule even when the pope of the day called a Crusade against him.

CONFLICT WITH FRANCE AND ENGLAND

If the popes had but known it, not the empire but the national states presented the real danger to papal interests. It is true that the popes in the thirteenth century were secular rulers, and therefore the interests of the Papal States were the equivalent of national interests, to be maintained with all the power available to their rulers. But papal interests in fact were far wider than those of any national state or ruler. Only by virtue of its position as spiritual leader of Europe did the papacy have at its disposal the services of the ecclesiastical bureaucracy, the clergy, and the religious orders. These latter groups were dragged along behind the papal chariot to their own irreparable damage. The empire had been destroyed, for what the victory was worth; but it had not been destroyed by the united forces of an outraged Christendom, nor even by the authority of the pope, entitled as God's vicegerent on earth to see that the monarchies of the world were in worthy hands. It had been broken by the naked swords of Charles of Anjou and his feudal vassals, and by papal mercenaries whose wages were paid out of the gifts and tithes of faithful Christians.

Naturally the political warfare waged by

the papacy was well understood in royal chancelleries. The pope was treated with respect for the power that he commanded. But he could expect little more consideration than secular rulers if his power should wane. Even though he still commanded the same spiritual sanctions as in former days, the monarchs and their advisers naturally tended to regard these as political weapons, and estimated them accordingly. The popes would have only themselves to blame when political weapons available to the monarchs were used against them.

At the close of the thirteenth century Boniface VIII, an Italian jurist on the papal throne, engaged in a trial of strength with the French monarch. The contest cost him his life, and cost the papacy a long period of exile from Rome in Avignon, under French protection. Both French and English monarchs resented bitterly the efforts of the papacy to lay taxation upon their peoples. Both Philip IV (the Fair, 1285–1314) and Edward I of England (1272–1307) were engaged in an important work of national consolidation, which will be considered in more detail in the next chapter. Neither wished to allow any revenues to leave their country to be swallowed up in the papal treasury, probably to be spent in unprofitable wars in Italy. Both Philip and Edward made the decision to tax the clergy, which was forbidden under canon law. Boniface promptly issued a bull (*Clericis laicos*, 1296) reasserting the principle that secular rulers had no right to tax the clergy, adding that kings who did so would be automatically excommunicated. Edward responded by withdrawing the protection of English law from the clergy, which soon afterward submitted. The only exception, the archbishop of Canterbury, could be safely ignored, since Edward was ready to antagonize the pope, the Archbishop's only protector.

Philip, however, went further, laying an embargo on all silver, gold, and bills of exchange leaving France, thus effectively shutting off French money from the papacy—a procedure which would not have been possible in

The Palace of the Popes at Avignon, used during the "Babylonian Captivity" and the Great Schism.

earlier reigns, before the country was as well organized as it was at the end of the thirteenth century. The pope submitted temporarily, withdrawing his edicts and permitting taxation of the clergy in certain circumstances. A few years later, after Philip had suffered a serious military reverse and the papacy had improved its financial position, the quarrel was renewed. Boniface announced that he would call a council to pronounce upon Philip's crime in prosecuting a bishop for treason, and Philip summoned a special assembly of the three estates of his realm, including the bourgeoisie and the clergy, for the purpose, among other things, of sending a protest to the pope. Boniface then issued the bull *Unam sanctam* (1302), in which he reiterated his claim that both spiritual and temporal powers were in the hands of the pope, and followed this up with the startling declaration that "we state, define and pronounce that it is altogether necessary for salvation for every human being to be subject to the Roman pontiff." He then demanded complete submission from Philip under the threat of excommunication.

Philip's patience was exhausted. Even while the pope was preparing a final bull of excommunication, which would release Philip's subjects from their allegiance to him, Philip sent his chancellor Nogaret to take possession of the person of the aged pope and bring him to France. With the aid of some Italian opponents of the pope, Nogaret forced his way into the papal presence at Anagni. After a scuffle during which the pope was manhandled, the royal emissaries were driven from the city by the townsmen. But the pope himself survived only a month.

Clearly Italy was a dangerous place for the popes. Papal opponents from the Italian nobility were not above laying sacrilegious hands on the person of the vicegerent of God; while the powerful French monarch had evidently had his fill of papal interference. After much hesitation the cardinals elected a French pope, who tried for a short time to resist Philip's demands while settling the monarch's quarrel with his predecessor. Finally, he decided to leave Rome and go to France, where

the city of Avignon was placed at his disposal. Thus began the exile of the popes in France which was not brought to an end until the Council of Constance (1414–1418).

THE PAPACY AT THE END OF THE THIRTEENTH CENTURY

In less than a century, the position to which Innocent III and his predecessors had lifted the medieval Church had thus been eroded to the point where the pope was no longer master even in his own realm. Instead, he had to seek the support of a secular ruler who was himself fully in command of his own kingdom and regarded the support of the pope as unessential, even though he continued to make use of the local Church for his own purposes. As we shall see, the monarchs made deals with the popes for a share of papal revenues, and the papacy, even at Avignon, retained much of its formidable financial and organizational strength. But it was no longer deferred to by secular rulers, who consulted their own national interests first.

Although new heresies were to arise in the fourteenth century, the Christian religion was to remain a Catholic monopoly for another two centuries. But interests had shifted from religious to secular affairs, and the Church could no longer command the consciences of Christians and their unquestioned obedience even in religious matters. For this the worldliness of the Church and the political activities of the papacy must bear some of the blame; and though the interests of the people of Europe had changed and the medieval Church could never have prevented the change, it might perhaps have been possible for the Church to have reformed itself into a purely religious institution and thus have avoided the degradation of the papacy in the Babylonian Captivity and the Great Schism. When it reformed itself later it was under the spur of Protestantism, and at a time when Protestantism had become too strong to be dislodged even by the reformed Catholic Church. The historian may speculate on whether the Church could have remained the only Christian Church, and thus retained the full right to the word Catholic (universal), if it had listened to the heretics and the anti-clericals and read the signs of the times aright. But the question, like so many others, must remain an idle speculation. The Church did not reform until reform was thrust upon it, and the medieval Church, one and universal, comprising the whole body of Christian believers, has passed into history.

Suggestions for further reading

PAPER-BOUND BOOKS

Bainton, Roland H. *The Medieval Church*. Anvil. Brief narrative and valuable documents.

Baldwin, Marshall W. *The Medieval Church*. Cornell University Press. Treats the history handled in this chapter in greater detail. By a noted American medieval scholar.

Bryce, James. *The Holy Roman Empire*. Schocken. Although some of Bryce's comments are not accepted today, this nineteenth-century classic remains valuable for its insights into the nature of the Empire and the anachronism involved in the attempt to revive the Roman Empire in an age no longer suited to it.

Chesterton, G. K. *St. Francis of Assisi*. Image. A brief and eloquent appraisal by the famous English Catholic man of letters.

Cheyney, E. P. *The Dawn of a New Era, 1250–1453*. Torchbooks. The first and one of the best of the series, The Rise of Modern Europe, edited by William Langer. Several chapters deal effectively with the decline of the medieval Church and the rise of the heresies.

Lamb, Harold. *The Crusades*. Bantam. Two volumes in one, the first (from *Men and Saints*) concerned with the First Crusade, the second (*The Flame of Islam*) with the struggle between Christians and Muslims for possession of the Holy Land. Popular and stirring account.

Lea, H. C. *A History of the Inquisition of the Middle Ages*. Citadel. Somewhat anticlerical and in a few respects outmoded but still the fullest and most accurate account. By a businessman turned historian.

McLaughlin, Mary, and Ross, J. B., eds., *The Portable Medieval Reader*. Viking. There is a useful extract (pp. 202–216) in this book from the manual of Bernard Gui, an inquisitor, concerning his procedure.

Runciman, Steven. *A History of the Crusades*. Vol. I. (Torchbooks) covers the First Crusade. Vols. II and III are available in hard-cover edition (Cambridge University Press). Very readable, and the most up to date and the fullest of the complete histories.

Runciman, Steven. *Sicilian Vespers*. Penguin. Scholarly account of the massacre which brought an end to French rule in Sicily, including useful background material.

St. Francis of Assisi. *The Little Flowers of St. Francis*. Image and Penguin. Two translations of the fourteenth-century tales of St. Francis, compiled a century after his death from the accounts of those who had known him.

Villehardouin, Geoffrey de, and Joinville, Jean de. *Memoirs of the Crusades*. Everyman and Penguin. This book contains Villehardouin's *Conquest of Constantinople*, an eyewitness account of the Fourth Crusade, and Joinville's story of the crusade of St. Louis ix from the writer's *Life of St. Louis*, which he wrote when he was in his eighties.

HARD-COVER BOOKS

Cantor, N. F. *Church, Kingship and Lay Investiture in England, 1089–1135*. Princeton, N.J.: Princeton University Press, 1958. Detailed scholarly book on the controversy as it affected England.

Crump, C. G., and Jacob, E. P., eds. *The Legacy of the Middle Ages*. Oxford, England: The Clarendon Press, 1926. The first essay, by Sir Maurice Powicke, is especially valuable for its lucid presentation of the necessary conflict between Christian ideals and the organized Christian Church.

Kantorowicz, Ernst. *Frederick the Second*. New York: Frederick Ungar Publishing Co., 1957. A fine scholarly biography of the emperor, which provides a great deal of information on the relation between Church and State in the thirteenth century.

Mandonnet, P. F. *St. Dominic and His Work*. St. Louis, Mo.: B. Herder Book Company, 1944. By a noted Dominican scholar. Fair and accurate.

Oldenbourg, Zoë. *Cities of the Flesh*, trans. by Anne Carter. New York: Pantheon Books, Inc., 1963. Both this novel and the author's earlier *Destiny of Fire* (1961) from the same publisher are harrowing and realistic accounts of the Albigensian Crusade. Scholarly and readable, with Pope Innocent III as the villain of the piece.

Oldenbourg, Zoë. *The Cornerstone*, trans. by Edward Hyams. New York: Pantheon Books, Inc., 1955. One of the very best novels of the Crusades and the contemporary medieval world. The story of an old man who went on a Crusade and the family he left behind him. Scholarly and evocative.

Packard, S. R. *Europe and the Church under Innocent III*. Holt, Rinehart and Winston, Inc., 1957. An excellent brief survey.

Sabatier, P. *The Life of St. Francis of Assisi*. New York: Charles Scribner's Sons, 1901. This book, by a Franciscan, remains the most scholarly and complete of numerous biographies.

Smith, Lucy M. *The Early History of the Monastery of Cluny*. Oxford, England: The Clarendon Press, 1920. This is a useful account that is not too specialized for the beginning student.

Tellenbach, G. *Church, State and Christian Society at the Time of the Investiture Controversy*. New York: Humanities Press, Inc., 1940. Most important single study of the aims of the papacy in the struggle and the effort to Christianize Europe.

Ullmann, Walter. *Growth of Papal Power in the Middle Ages*. New York: Barnes & Noble, Inc., 1955. A noted German scholar's evaluation of the success of the investiture struggle from the point of view of the papacy.

ELEVEN

The Evolution of National States in the Middle Ages

❖ **The national state as the key political institution of Western civilization**

CONTRAST WITH CITY-STATE AND EMPIRES

Prior to our own Western civilization the governmental institution which developed the most advanced political forms was the city-state, whose weaknesses were discussed at length in the chapter on Greece. City-states, unable to solve their problems, and especially unable to refrain from fratricidal warfare, were usually replaced by great empires, of which we have seen many examples in this book. But it is difficult to point to many instances in the ancient world of the true national state, whose inhabitants were bound by ties of loyalty to their fellow nationals, who felt that they had some kind of common kinship merely because they inhabited a certain area of land, larger than a city.

Perhaps the nearest to the modern national state was ancient Egypt, which was considerably more than a mere geographic entity. The Pharaoh of Egypt was a king-god who was responsible for the welfare of Egypt and not that of other countries; he commanded loyalty from his people as their protector. The Egyptians, in the manner of some modern states, despised the people of Babylonia, who were

unfortunate enough to have a "Nile in the sky," and called them "wretched Asiatics." The ancient Hebrews also had a patriotic feeling beyond that of the city-states, and again they had a national God to lead them. But their loyalty was religious and cultural rather than based on the possession of a particular territory, and Northerners soon separated from Southerners when political and economic conditions suggested a division.

The national state, therefore, is a relatively modern phenomenon, and is not even necessarily the final political form to be evolved by the human race. But its achievements up to this time have been impressive enough, even though it too has failed to solve the problem of fratricidal interstate warfare. The national state, possessing within its borders economic resources far greater than those commanded by city-states, has proved superior to the city-state in being able to support comparatively efficient governments manned by professional officials, free from excessive dependence upon foreigners and possible enemies for essential supplies; and it has been able to maintain public security better than the empires. But, above all, the national state has not proved too large to permit individual citizens to feel they have some share in the government. As a consequence of this added sense of responsibility on the part of the public, the modern national government has been able to enforce certain basic human rights in a way that even Roman law could not, since Roman law was not written in Heaven, as the philosophers claimed, but drawn up and administered by servants of the ultimately irresponsible empire.

Although a national state must always have a national government in effective control of the whole territory, a government which is recognized as such by the people of the state, there are otherwise no acceptable criteria for what constitutes a national state. A common language may be an important aid to the establishment of such a state, but multilingual national states, such as Switzerland, exist; and, conversely, many different states speak the same language. If culture is taken in the widest sense, a common national culture and common ideals are an even greater aid; and it is perhaps arguable that no state has ever been permanently united without them, though, for instance, present-day Yugoslavia has a partly Catholic and a partly Orthodox religious culture.

If the national state is the dominant institution in the world at any given time, as it is at present, then it is likely that all countries which feel that they have enough in common will desire to organize themselves into separate sovereign states. This creates difficulties when empires break up and each minority people desires to have a national state of its own, however small; likewise difficulties occur when peoples whose natural loyalties are to their tribe wish to form national states large enough to command world attention. But, one and all, the inhabitants of those countries, especially in Africa, which are not yet independent national states feel that they should belong to a nation, and that the nation is entitled to all the prerogatives of nationhood, including separate diplomacy and a seat in the United Nations.

It is therefore of importance for us to consider how the national states evolved in the Middle Ages, what institutions they developed, and how their inhabitants came to feel that the national state is the natural form of government to which all peoples should aspire.

THE FAILURE OF GERMANY AND ITALY TO ATTAIN NATIONAL STATEHOOD

Three major national states, whose history as national entities has been continuous to this day, came into existence in the Middle Ages—England, France, and Spain. The more populous and in some ways more advanced countries, Italy and Germany, did not become national states until the second half of the nineteenth century. Germany was bedeviled by the ghost of the Roman Empire. At a time when both France and England were relatively unimportant, the Germans under the Holy Roman emperors were trying to establish their dominion over territories whose geography made permanent union unlikely. After the imperial dream was over, the German feudal nobles had grasped so much substantial power that for centuries it was impossible to dislodge them; and German towns constituted a league of states beyond the control of German monarchs for two crucial centuries. No one lord was powerful enough to rule the whole. The emperor was elected by the very nobles to whom he presented a threat, and they were therefore careful to elect only those of their peers who seemed to be least dangerous; if a family made gains while it held the imperial throne, an effort would be made to see that none of its members were elected next time. It was not until the middle of the seventeenth century, as one of the results of the Thirty Years' War, that the feudal lords of Germany became finally free of the emperor. But it took more than half a century of patient work by the largest German state, masterly diplomacy, a modern army, and three wars before Germany could be united as a nation in the nineteenth century.

Italy, at first forced to defend herself against the regular invasions of the emperor, for a while experienced freedom under city-state government, and for two centuries led Europe in commercial development. But the country was divided. Venice always dominated the northeast, the Papal States stretched across the backbone of the country from the Mediterranean to the Adriatic, extremely resistant to any moves looking toward the unity of the country as a whole. The south was under the domination of foreigners, either Spanish or Angevin princes who could usually count on foreign aid to bolster their kingdoms. Several times the possibility of union seemed to open, and Italian writers and publicists from Dante to Machiavelli were well aware that Italy desperately needed unity. But not until Napoleon was the dream almost realized; and after his collapse more than half a century of propaganda, war, and diplomacy was needed to achieve it.

In this chapter, therefore, we shall discuss those states whose development was continuous. In England national unity under a strong monarchy was achieved early, and interest is centered both upon the means by which this early achievement was possible and upon the efforts made by the nobles to curb the power of the monarchy. In France the central monarchy had difficulty in establishing itself, but once it had done so, the king's power remained intact until the French Revolution in the eighteenth century. Unity in Spain was attained largely through the shared experience of driving out the Muslims; and though partially representative institutions were developed, the kings retained almost absolute power until recent times. The contrast, especially between England and France, will serve to explain much of the modern political history of these countries: the strength of representative government in England, based upon so many centuries of tradition, and the weakness of French representative government in a country whose traditions until recent times were all absolutist and monarchical.

❖ The Anglo-Saxon monarchy

The English national state is the oldest in Europe. It arose at the end of the ninth century as a result of the invasions of the Vikings and the resistance offered to them by the Anglo-Saxon kings of Wessex. For a period, the whole of the eastern part of England was subject to the Danes, as the English

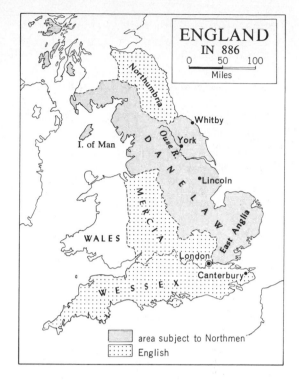

called them. The ancient northern and central kingdoms of Northumbria and Mercia were unable to withstand the Danes, but the kings of Wessex retained their independence and staged a counterattack. King Alfred the Great (871–899) ruled over a united kingdom which included Danes who had been permitted to remain. Thereafter the throne of England was occupied by descendants of Alfred until the conquest of the country by Sweyn and Canute in a renewed invasion by Scandinavians. After the death of Canute, who ruled as king of England from 1042, Edward the Confessor, a descendant of Alfred, reigned until his death in 1066. Soon afterward William of Normandy conquered England and established a new dynasty that lasted almost a century.

The Anglo-Saxon kingdom of England had developed certain institutions not unlike those of the feudal Continent, although differing in some important respects. The king was advised by a council of great lords, or thanes, called the Witan. This council constituted an important check on royal authority, which, in England as elsewhere, was not as great in practice as in theory. The king could summon a na-

Chronological Chart

The English National State		The French National State	
Reign of Edward the Confessor	1042–1066	Reign of Hugh Capet	987–996
Norman Conquest of England	1066	Dissolution of marriage between Louis VII and Eleanor of Aquitaine	1152
Domesday Book completed	1086		
Oath of Salisbury	1086		
Reign of Henry I	1100–1135	Reign of Philip Augustus	1180–1223
Interregnum in English monarchy (reign of Stephen)	1135–1154	Reign of Louis IX	1226–1270
		Reign of Philip IV, the Fair	1285–1314
Marriage of Henry Plantagenet to Eleanor of Aquitaine	1152	Summoning of States-General	1302
Henry II king of England	1154–1189	End of Capetian monarchy	1328
Assize of Clarendon (grand jury)	1166	Hundred Years' War with England	1337–1453
Murder of St. Thomas Becket	1170	Battle of Poitiers—capture of King John II	1356
Richard I held to ransom by Emperor Henry VI	1194	The Jacquerie—murder of Etienne Marcel	1358
Reign of John	1199–1216	Treaty of Brétigny	1360
Loss of French lands to Philip	1202–1204	Duchy of Burgundy granted by John II to his son Philip	1363
Struggle with Pope Innocent III	1205–1213		
Magna Carta	1215	Reconquest of most of territory lost to England	1369–1380
Provisions of Oxford	1258		
Simon de Montfort's Parliament	1265	John the Fearless becomes Duke of Burgundy	1404
Reign of Edward I	1272–1307	Intermittent civil war in France between Burgundy and House of Valois (Armagnacs)	1407–1435
The Model Parliament	1295		
Outbreak of the Hundred Years' War	1337	Henry V of England invades France	1415
Treaty of Brétigny	1360	Reign of Charles VII	1422–1461
Reign of Richard II	1377–1399	Joan of Arc at siege of Orléans	1429
Renewal of war with France	1383	Coronation of Charles VII at Rheims	1429
Henry V claims throne of France	1415	Death of Joan of Arc	1431
Treaty of Troyes—Henry V regent of France	1420	Peace of Arras between Charles and Burgundians	1435
Deaths of Henry V and Charles VI of France	1422	Reform of French army	1445–1446
Joan of Arc burned at Rouen	1431	Expulsion of the English	1449–1461
Loss of all France except Calais	1453	Reign of Louis XI	1461–1483
Wars of the Roses	1455–1485	Charles the Bold, Duke of Burgundy	1467–1477
Henry Tudor, Henry VII of England	1485	Edward IV of England bought off by Louis	1475
		Battle of Nancy—defeat and death of Charles the Bold	1477
		Unification of France as a national state	1480

Spanish and Portuguese National States

Muslim conquest of Spain	711–719
Christian kingdom of the Asturias reconquered	718–737
Partial conquest of northeastern Spain by Charlemagne	778
Expansion of Christian kingdom of León	910–914
Reign of Abdu-r-Rahman III (height of Muslim power)	912–961
Rise of Castile to independence	930–966
Conquest of León by Castile	1037
Capture of Toledo by Alphonso VI of Castile	1085
Christian advance into Muslim Spain	1072 onward
Union of Catalonia and Aragon	1137
Earliest Cortes in Castile	ca. 1188
Battle of Las Navas de Tolosa— decisive defeat of Muslims by Alphonso VIII	1212
Capture of Cordova by Ferdinand III of Castile	1236
Capture of Seville by Ferdinand	1248
Conquest of Sicily by Peter III of Aragon	1282
Portuguese independence secured by decisive victory over Castile	1385
Marriage of Isabella, heiress of Castile, to Ferdinand, heir of Aragon	1469
Isabella succeeds to Castilian throne	1474
Establishment of Spanish Inquisition under royal control	1478
Ferdinand succeeds to throne of Aragon	1479
Fall of Granada, last Muslim stronghold in Spain	1492
Expulsion of Jews from Spain	1492
Expulsion of Moriscos from Spain	1609

tional militia for the defense of the realm. But the service the militia owed him was limited; after the service had been completed, the lords and their servants were entitled to return home. Often the king had to rely upon special troops known as housecarls, who formed his personal retinue and were dependent upon him. The latter were not, however, the king's personal feudal vassals, as they were in France.

The king was also the theoretical head of the justiciary, and certain kinds of lawsuits were always referred to him for decision, in spite of the fact that other law courts existed with their own systems of law. In general, however, almost all law was local, and enforced locally, until the Norman and Plantagenet kings were able to make inroads into local and feudal courts and establish the king's justice as the supreme law of the land.

The central government was rarely strong enough to control the whole country, and though the king had many rights owed him by villagers in the country, he usually granted these rights to his lords, or thanes. It was the thanes who maintained order and executed justice in their territories. According to an Anglo-Saxon law, every man must either have land which he possessed freehold, or have a lord. This lord must give him the protection that the king, too distant and with too little authority, was unable to provide.

One of the greatest achievements of the Anglo-Saxons in England was their system of local government, much of which was maintained by the Normans. The country had already been divided into shires, later called counties, which differ little from those of the present day. The shires were administered by the bishop, the earl, or the chief lord, and an appointee of the king known as the *shire-reeve* or sheriff. The latter had the important function of looking after the king's business in the shire, especially the mustering of the national militia and the collection of such taxes as the Danegeld, originally paid to keep the Northmen away but continued, like so many taxes in modern times, long after the immediate necessity had passed away. There was also a shire court that tried civil and criminal cases which came under its jurisdiction, presided

over by the sheriff with the aid of the bishop
and occasionally, when necessary, the earl.
Minor cases were handled in a subdivision of
the shire, called a hundred. It was in the hundred that the apportionment of taxes to each
person was made by men of local knowledge
under the guidance of the sheriff. These administrative divisions had since early times
given the kings a means of enforcing their
will; and because the sheriff in most cases, and
the assessors in all cases, were local men, the
germ existed for the combination of decentral-
ized government and responsibility to the central government which made representative
government possible later, and provided a
vehicle by which consent for taxation could
be asked and given.

THE NORMAN CONQUEST
AND ITS CONSEQUENCES

Imposition of feudalism By the time of
the Norman Conquest there was no fully developed feudal system in England. The relationship between lord and vassal existed, but
in primitive form; courts presided over by the
lords operated in cases involving themselves
and their dependents, while other courts
operated for different offenses not concerned
with land tenure. The king had certain rights
over the common land of England, and these
rights had real meaning; but he was not even
the theoretical owner of the remainder of the
land, as in France. The English thanes owed
him military service as a national obligation
rather than because they held land from him;
they owed it to him as chief warrior, who was
constantly having to call upon them through
the persistence of national danger from the
Danes.

The great change made by the Norman
Conquest was therefore not the establishment
of an entirely different system, but the imposition of order upon a mass of customs which
had been gradually growing up, and the speed-
ing up of the feudalization process by a series
of able kings, in whose French possessions
there was already a well-developed feudal system.

When Edward the Confessor died, leaving

POSSESSIONS OF
WILLIAM I OF ENGLAND
1066–1087
★ Battles

no direct heir, the Witan elected as king the
most noted warrior in the country, son of its
greatest earl. Harold, the new king, however,
was faced by two threats, one from Scandinavia and one from Normandy, whose rulers
both claimed the English crown. Harold was
able to defeat and kill the Scandinavian claim-
ant, but his army was too exhausted to stand
against William of Normandy, whose feudal
army, swelled by adventurers from all parts
of France, defeated and killed Harold at the
battle of Hastings (1066). After subduing the
rest of the country, a task that occupied five
years, William (called the "Conqueror") declared that all lands were forfeited to himself.
Any English lords who wished to retain their
land were compelled to swear allegiance to
him and do homage as his vassals. The remainder of the lands were given to William's
Norman followers in return for the same recognition of himself as their suzerain. Thus

the Conquest made what was elsewhere only a theoretical position real in England. William was the actual lord or suzerain of the entire land of England. Under the Norman kings there was no land whatsoever that was free (or alodial); every land had at least one lord, the king.

The king, however, could not administer such a vast estate himself through his nominees or servants. He retained the greater nobles as his direct vassals, or tenants-in-chief. But these were permitted, indeed encouraged, to let out the land again to subvassals (subinfeudation), who owed service to the king's tenants-in-chief as vassals. The service was composed of the usual feudal aids, and these subvassals were said to hold their land, as customary in the feudal system, by knight or military service. But, in William's eyes, this did not justify the subvassals' fighting on behalf of their lord in his private quarrels. Though private warfare was not altogether quelled, especially under later kings, it was never legal for a vassal to fight for his lord unless the king himself had authorized the calling out of troops. And this he did only in national wars. A subvassal under this system therefore owed military service only to the king; but he was called upon for military service by his own overlord on behalf of the king. Thus the king had the advantage of indirect control over his subvassals, saving him the labor of administration involved, while at the same time he had all the benefits which accrued to a mighty feudal landowner, able to command the military service not only of his own tenants-in-chief but of every landowner in the country.

Through the sheriffs the king likewise exercised the old Anglo-Saxon privilege of direct taxation of the people without the intervention of the vassals and subvassals, and he retained and extended the power of the king's courts, though feudal lords could hold their courts to deal with matters within their own jurisdiction. No lord could erect a castle except with the king's license, and theoretically every castle in the country belonged to him. It will be seen, therefore, that, with customary Norman intelligence, William made full use of everything that could help him in the existing Anglo-Saxon system, while adding to it elements of Norman-French feudalism which could be used with profit to himself. He took full advantage of the Anglo-Saxon system of sheriffs. Bishops and earls were far harder to control than his own appointees. He therefore excluded the former from the government of the shires and hundreds, and made the sheriffs supreme, subject to dismissal only by himself. Hoping to make it entirely clear that the members of the new English nobility were no longer to have the privilege of making private war, and that all military service was owed only to himself, in 1086 William summoned to Salisbury all the landowners in the country, whether tenants-in-chief or only subvassals, and made them swear fealty to himself. They swore that they would be loyal to him even against their direct suzerains. Thereafter every tenant doing homage to his own lord for his fief had to add, "Saving the faith that I owe to my lord the king," which, of course, expressly covered military service, taxation, and legal appeals, which were the prerogatives of the Crown.

In order to have an exact knowledge of the dues of all kinds owed by every man in the kingdom, whether to himself or to any of his vassals, William sent out clerks into his shire courts. Every landholder, whether free or serf, had to appear and, under oath, answer certain questions about his land—how many people worked on it, how much meadow and forest it contained, how many streams, and who had the various rights involved. All this information was written down in the Domesday Book, a magnificent example of Norman administrative genius altogether unique for that period, and only possible in a country which had developed the necessary local institutions through which the information could be collected. The king now had his hands upon the pulse of the whole realm, but few English kings ever had such power again. The lords, who had been robbed of so much that belonged to their class elsewhere, did not hesitate to take advantage of any later weakening in the central government, and in so doing ultimately paved the way for the limited monarchy and representative institutions which have been the special glory of the English political genius.

Machinery of government The king had so many tenants-in-chief that the customary feudal council, made up of the king's vassals, would, in England, have been a most cumbersome body. William did call it on occasion, but preferred to work with a committee of these tenants-in-chief, which took the place of the Witan. The whole body was entitled to be consulted, but few lords desired the privilege, and it became the custom for this smaller council to give advice to the king when he summoned it for the purpose. The whole assembly at this time is known as the *Curia Regis*, or Court of the King, but in practice the Curia was made up of those tenants-in-chief whose presence William especially desired, and the majority did not attend. William's younger son, Henry I, made this committee a formal institution.

William used a small number of regular officials in a full-time capacity. Chief of these was the justiciar, who ruled England in the king's name when, as fairly often happened, he was forced to look after his ducal interests in Normandy. The justiciar also became head of the departments of finance and justice in William's time, though these were separated by his younger son. The chancellor and chamberlain, two important officials in later centuries, at this time had duties in the king's household. Whenever the king needed any further help he called upon his higher clergy and members of his Curia, whom he authorized to perform special limited tasks in the country, usually in conjunction with the sheriffs. With the feudal system working so efficiently in his behalf, William did not need a great corps of officials in his employ. All that was really needed was competent supervision of the work carried out for him by his tenants-in-chief in return for the land they had received from him, and this was provided by the few officials that he had.

The institutions of William the Conqueror have been discussed at considerable length because they gave the English monarchy a strength which was to endure for many centuries, in spite of rebellious nobles. They established certain principles which outlasted even the conversion of the monarchy into a constitutional kingship in the eighteenth century. For many centuries it was held that the king ought to live from his own resources and was entitled only to specified dues from his people unless they agreed to grant him temporary assistance, that only the king could raise an army, and that all acts were done in the king's name. Even today the king, not the government or people, is the owner of the colonies beyond the seas; and constitutional changes in the colonies are effected by orders-in-council—that is, by orders issued by the king in the presence of, and by the advice of, his chosen councilors. The king chooses his own prime minister, although his choice is necessarily based on the result of the most recent parliamentary elections. He invests the ministers chosen by the prime minister with their offices, and the cabinet remains in theory the king's council. The advice it offers to the king he is, however, now bound to accept. No legislation is valid unless it has received the king's assent, and it is in theory the king who legislates by the advice of and with the consent of his ministers.

CONSTITUTIONAL AND LEGAL DEVELOPMENT UNDER SUCCEEDING MONARCHS

Reign of Henry I The work of the monarchs of the next few centuries was a continuation of what had been begun so auspiciously by William. It may therefore be discussed more briefly, with indications of the major developments effected in each reign.

In the long reign of Henry I (1100–1135), the younger son of William the Conqueror, there was a considerable improvement in administration. By appointing to his personal staff a number of gentlemen who were not of the highest nobility and granting them lands as his direct vassals, and by paying careful attention to his ecclesiastical appointments so that they were occupied by the best administrators in his realm, Henry succeeded in creating a council of advisers whose positions were not hereditary and who were thus closely tied to himself. This small council was the governing body of the realm under the king, who rarely called together the great council composed of all his tenants-in-chief. The small council ultimately became the Privy Council and in modern times the cabinet. Henry also reorganized the treasury, so that at all times he was aware of how much money was due to him and how much had been collected on his behalf. Twice every year his treasury officials met to scrutinize his accounts, using a table covered by a cloth divided into squares, representing the pounds, shillings, and pence he had received. The cloth gave rise to the word *exchequer*, which has ever since been used for the English treasury.

It has already been noted that many different kinds of law were in use in England. Henry made a serious effort toward unifying the law. He granted writs to complainants to enable them to use the king's courts in cases where they believed they had not received justice. He was the first to send out justices

to try cases in the country, and to observe the conduct of the local sheriffs—a practice similar to that employed by Charlemagne, who, as recounted in Chapter 9, sent out *missi dominici* to observe the behavior cf his counts. The sheriffs on occasion were also instructed to hold sworn inquests, in the course of which neighbors were summoned to give testimony under oath that a crime had been committed. Thus, in the reign of Henry I, we find already the germ of the grand jury and the beginnings of what later came to be called the common law—that is, the law common to the whole realm.

The interregnum of Stephen and restoration of royal power by Henry II Henry's work, however, was almost undone in the anarchy that followed his death. It had not yet been established in England that a woman

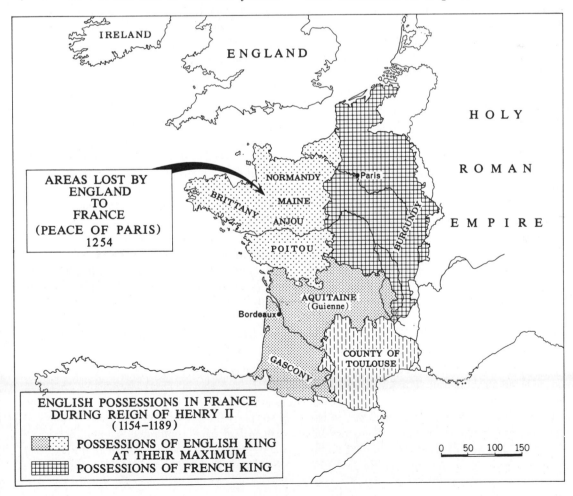

AREAS LOST BY
ENGLAND
TO
FRANCE
(PEACE OF PARIS)
1254

ENGLISH POSSESSIONS IN FRANCE
DURING REIGN OF HENRY II
(1154–1189)
POSSESSIONS OF ENGLISH KING
AT THEIR MAXIMUM
POSSESSIONS OF FRENCH KING

0   50   100   150

could succeed to the throne, and Henry left a daughter, but no son, on his death. Henry's nephew, Stephen, supported by a considerable number of the nobles, claimed the crown, as did also Matilda, his daughter, supported by other nobles. In the ensuing civil war, which persisted for the greater part of the reign that appears in English records as that of Stephen (1135–1154), the nobles recovered all the power that they had lost since the time of William the Conqueror, and were a virtual law to themselves. They erected castles, contrary to royal decrees of the past, and Stephen was never able to exercise an effective administration. Each noble was lord in his own area, and submitted to no authority from others. The English monarchy might never have recovered from this setback had it not been for a number of fortuitous events which resulted in the establishment on the throne of Matilda's energetic son, Henry II (1154–1189), with the aid of French nobles who were the vassals of his wife, Eleanor of Aquitaine.

Eleanor was the sole heir to much of France when she was married at an early age to Louis VII of France. After the failure of the Second Crusade Louis, dissatisfied with the behavior of his wife during the crusade, divorced her. She thereupon married Henry, who was several years her junior, taking her possessions, including Aquitaine, with her. Henry himself inherited further French lands from his father, Geoffrey of Anjou, a French noble. Armed with such might from his French possessions, Henry was able to force Stephen to recognize him as his heir to the English throne and, on the death of Stephen, he was able to compel the English lords to recognize him as king—the first of the Plantagenet line. Henry promptly restored the lords to their obedience and ruled the English with an even stronger hand than had his grandfather, Henry I, and great-grandfather, William the Conqueror. He restored the administration to efficiency, incidentally dismissing almost every sheriff in the realm. But his greatest claim to fame is his reform of the judicial system on the lines indicated by his grandfather, and the institution of many new arrangements which laid the

foundation for the entire modern legal system of all English-speaking countries.

Reformation of the legal system Influenced by Roman law, which was beginning to be studied in England, Henry nevertheless retained the bulk of the English law, thus making the English system in some ways superior to the ancient law of Rome, and capable of very great modification and development. From the beginning Henry seems to have realized that the enforcement of the common law above all earlier systems of law was essential to his power, and this unification was fundamental to all his reforms.

Though the sheriff's courts remained, any complainant could apply to the chancery of the king to set a legal case in action within these courts. A writ could be purchased from the chancery for any of a great number of cases, and these at once became cases in which the king was interested, to be settled by the king's law. Writs could even be obtained in which the king directed the sheriff to enforce judgments which were the results of lawsuits, thus giving the king a hand in legal matters previously under the jurisdiction of local courts and accustoming the people to the idea that the king was the source of all justice.

The grand and the petit, or trial, jury both have their origin in Henry II's reign, although the grand jury of Henry is much closer to the modern grand jury than was his small jury to the modern counterpart.

The grand jury's primary function was to ascertain what duties were owed to the king and whether they were being fulfilled. This was the sworn inquest of the earlier Norman monarchs in a different form. The sheriff was instructed by the king's writ to call a body of jurors together who were to swear such matters before the royal justices. But under the Assizes of Clarendon and Northampton (1166 and 1176), the sheriffs were instructed to bring before the king's justices a group of men who were to swear whether any of various specified crimes had been committed in their neighborhood, and to say who, in their opinion, had committed them. The accused would then be subjected to the ordeal or trial by combat. But as time went on, perhaps not at all in the reign of Henry, certain pleas could be made by the accused in front of a sworn jury —such as that he had been elsewhere at the time (alibi), or that his accuser had been actuated by malice. He was finally allowed to appeal to a jury of his neighbors on the whole question of guilt or innocence; but it should be emphasized that for a long time the accused did not need to submit to the new procedure but could demand the old trial by ordeal or combat. Nevertheless, even if the accused were successful in the ordeal, the king could order him banished from the realm.

Under Henry I, as has been seen, the king's justices paid visits to the shires to see that justice was done. These visits, however, in Henry I's time seem to have been spasmodic and not regular. Henry II sent out justices regularly into each shire to hear criminal cases brought before them by the grand jury, and he sent out members of his own Curia irregularly to check upon officials, again using the device of the grand jury or sworn inquest. These judges even listened to complaints about the quality of beer sold in a shire, and a check was supposed to be kept on every matter of public importance; but, needless to say, this court was popular with few, and in later years its visits became rare, though it remained a salutary reminder to the people that the king's justice was capable of reaching them in any case of offense against the public interest.

It was as a result of his attempts to make a uniform law code for England that Henry quarreled with the Church in the person of his Archbishop of Canterbury, St. Thomas Becket. Becket had been Henry's chancellor, and the king felt sure that he could rely upon him as archbishop to support the royal reforms. But Becket at once upon investiture

The murder of Thomas Becket by the knights of King Henry II of England. From the Ramsey Abbey Psalter *(English), 1285–1300.* (COURTESY THE PIERPONT MORGAN LIBRARY. Ms. 302, folio 4)

became a stubborn supporter of all papal claims, and in particular of the right of the Church to try all offenders, whatever their crimes, as long as they were ecclesiastics. Becket refused to accept the Constitutions of Clarendon (1164), the main provisions of which deprived the ecclesiastical courts of the right to try "criminous clerks," or clerics who had committed a crime against the king's law. The archbishop's recalcitrance ultimately resulted in his murder, after the king had in a rage incited some of his knights to the deed. The murder shocked the country. Henry had to do severe penance, and he withdrew part of the Constitutions. The remainder continued in force, allowing the king to make ecclesiastical appointments and preventing the papacy from directly taxing the English Church without the king's consent. In addition, certain important regulations regarding the possession of property by the Church were allowed to stand. The ecclesiastical courts experienced a continuous growth for some time in England after the murder, and Henry was effectively prevented from establishing his jurisdiction in the matters which had customarily been allowed to the Church.

DIMINUTION OF ROYAL POWER UNDER LATER PLANTAGENETS—MAGNA CARTA AND THE BEGINNINGS OF PARLIAMENT

The system set up by Henry II was strong enough to survive an absentee monarch (Richard I, 1189–1199) and a monarch who was uniformly unsuccessful in everything he undertook (John, 1199–1216). But the English nobles in the latter reign were able to force some recognition of their traditional rights from the monarch. Richard (called the Lion-Hearted) had been captured on his way home from the Third Crusade and delivered to the Holy Roman emperor Henry VI, who had exacted a huge ransom before permitting him to return to England. Richard's officials were able to raise the money, but only with great difficulty, and with the aid of new taxes, which were doubtfully legal and greatly resented.

When John came to the throne, the treasury was empty, and it was virtually impossible to find new sources of income to enable him to retain his French territories against the attacks of Philip Augustus, king of France. This struggle was of little or no interest to the English nobility, since no loot could be taken and John, in any case, was an inefficient leader. They insisted on sticking to the letter of their ancient rights, namely that they had to serve for only forty days a year, and could not be compelled to pay scutages beyond what was customary.

Finally John embroiled himself, as we have seen, with Pope Innocent III, and the land was laid under an interdict. This again decreased the means of the people to pay for John's wars and other expenses. When Innocent bestowed the kingdom on Philip Augustus and Philip's son Louis made preparations for attacking England, John submitted and gave the kingdom to the papacy as a fief. This in no way lessened John's expenses, but rather increased them.

By 1215 his powerful enemies among the barons were strong enough to force him to meet with them on a small island in the River Thames called Runnymede, where he signed the Magna Carta ("great charter"). In essence, Magna Carta was a document signed by the king stating that he would not do certain things which he had grown accustomed to doing but which were forbidden under feudal law and custom. The nobles compelled John's successor, Henry III, to bind himself by an oath not to do the things forbidden by the Charter, an oath which he repeated several times. In later years the Charter came to be regarded as the cornerstone of English liberties, but of course it was nothing but a declaration made by the king concerning what he would not do. It could not be enforced save by a rebellion, which, indeed, the king himself was required by the Charter to sanction, if he did not abide by his promises. Such a rebellion as was staged by the nobles against Henry III could be defended as in accord with this provision of the Charter, since the monarch had refused to observe his promises, in spite of their repeated remonstrances. The king himself of course never did sanction it, but resisted it to the best of his ability.

Toward the end of his reign John ceased to choose good men as officials, and his administration became weaker than in the days of his brother and father. This tendency became even more marked in the reign of John's rather feeble son, Henry III (1216–1272), who was much influenced by foreign friends of his wife and appointed many of his personal favorites to high positions which they were not qualified to fill. Henry tried also to live up to his obligations as vassal to the papacy and to provide his suzerain with money for his Italian wars. At one time he was even willing to accept the Sicilian kingdom on behalf of his son, who would have had to fight hard for the position—as usual at the expense of the English people. The nobility therefore were always restive during Henry's reign, and when they found a leader in the person of Simon de Montfort, formerly one of Henry's French favorites, they decided on direct action to compel the monarch to observe Magna Carta and to take greater account of the wishes of his nobles and people. In 1258 a number of feudal lords summoned other barons to a gathering, known as the Mad Parliament, to concert measures for keeping the king under control and restraining his taxation. They proceeded to issue the Provisions of Oxford, a series of reforms which the king was forced to accept. Some of their grievances he was compelled to redress, and for a while he was virtually controlled by this self-constituted committee of greater barons.

Two years later the barons evidently felt that they, too, needed a wider basis of support and authority. They therefore summoned to a special assembly three knights from each shire, who would represent the interests of the lesser lords of the realm who were not tenants-in-chief of the king. The king issued counterinstructions to the knights to come to meet him instead, thus adding to the confusion. It was impossible for the king to accept indefinitely this kind of dictation from his vassals, and it was clear that civil war could not be long delayed.

When it came, in 1264, Simon de Montfort and the barons were at first successful, defeating the king in the battle of Lewes and imprisoning him. But there was no intention of harming the monarch; the sole interest of Simon and the barons was in forcing Henry to yield some of his powers to the feudal aristocracy. The king's own son, later to become Edward I, supported the lords against his father for a time. Simon summoned four knights to be elected to meet the king during 1264, but nothing came of the effort. Then he summoned a full parliament, of lords and higher clergy, though he was careful to choose only those who favored his party. To these he added representatives from the shires (two knights from each, to be elected in the presence of the sheriff) and, for the first time, two representatives from each city and borough. This Parliament of Simon de Montfort was the most representative assembly that had been called since the Conquest, but it came to nothing. Edward deserted him, returning to his father, and Simon was defeated and killed in the battle of Evesham in 1265. But Edward seems to have remembered the salutary lesson, and it was in his reign that Parliament first became an established institution, giving advice to the king, who was expected to legislate only after having taken careful consideration of its advice.

THE MODEL PARLIAMENT OF EDWARD I

In 1295 this same Edward, now Edward I (1272–1307), summoned the most inclusive assembly yet called in England, known as the Model Parliament. This did not mean that he considered Parliament as the legislature of the realm. He himself had already promulgated the majority of those fundamental laws which have earned for Edward I the name of the English Justinian. These laws he declared he had made only after consultation with various great men of his realm, without reference to any parliament. For more than a century the king continued to draw up the statutes himself with the aid of his council, but the statutes were supposed, after the time of the Model Parliament, to be in conformity with what Parliament had advised him. When members of Parliament complained that the statutes did not conform, it was with a sense of grievance, as if the king and council had cheated them; ultimately they forced the king to allow them to make the statutes, to which he had only to give his assent.

In the Model Parliament the sheriffs were instructed to cause two knights of each shire, two citizens of each city, and two burgesses of each borough to be elected. In addition, the monarch summoned the nobility and the clergy as in earlier times; but by no means all of the king's tenants-in-chief were summoned. Indeed, the nobility was considerably outnumbered by the clergy. It is not known whether the members who were summoned by virtue of their rank or position sat separately from the elected members from the beginning, but before long this was the custom.

The knights of the shire were, of course, landholders, and might be presumed to have many interests in common with the larger barons. But they also had divergent interests as subvassals rather than tenants-in-chief; though they might also be minor tenants-in-chief of the king, they usually were not. At all events, these knights decided—and it was a decision of supreme importance for the development of constitutional government—that they would throw in their lot with the townsmen, by whom they were outnumbered, but to whom for centuries they supplied leadership in Parliament. These two groups grew into the modern House of Commons, and both were classified as part of the third estate. while the higher clergy (the first estate) and the higher nobility (the second estate) became the House of Lords.

As a member of either House would have considered it in his time, the primary purpose of having a Parliament was to regulate and minimize the power of the king, especially in matters of taxation. The Parliament presented petitions to the king and could ask for justice even in minor complaints, which the king would refer to the suitable court or department of state. In time these petitions became a means of initiating legislation; the petitions would be discussed and recommendations given, and the king was then expected to act upon them. But the king usually called Parliament only when he needed money, and thus gave Parliament the opportunity to go into the whole question of his expenditures. It gradually became accepted that the power of taxation was in the hands of Parliament, except for those taxes which belonged to the king from ancient times and were his under feudal law. It was this principle, and its acceptance, that led directly to the limited monarchy at the end of the seventeenth century; and it was also ultimately to make the House of Commons superior to the House of Lords, since revenue from the former was far more elastic than anything a few lords and bishops could hope to raise. Only two years after the Model Parliament, at a time when the Crown was in great need of money and was engaged in controversy with Pope Boniface VIII over the taxing of the clergy, Edward tried to collect money without the consent of his Parliament and to force his barons to serve in a foreign war. The barons took to arms, supported by the merchants whose commodities the king had claimed to be able to tax. The king was forced to give way, swearing an oath that he would not make such new taxes in the future without the common consent of the realm. His grandson later had to confirm the promise, and it became generally accepted as the law and custom of the land.

WEAKNESS OF LATE MEDIEVAL MONARCHY— FORCED ABDICATIONS, DISPUTED SUCCESSIONS, AND CIVIL WARS

It is unnecessary to go in detail into the growth of Parliament once it had been established as a going institution, entitled to be called regularly for the purpose of petitioning the king, even if he himself had no demands to make on it. The son and successor of Edward I, Edward II (1307–1327), was deposed by the barons led by the queen and one of her favorites. The only point of constitutional interest in his reign is the insistence of the heir to the throne that his father must abdicate before he could take the position. This heir, who reigned from 1327 to 1377 as Edward III, was in constant need of money for the Hundred Years' War with France—a war begun by Edward, as discussed later in this chapter. The war was, for the most part, popular with the soldiers and nobility; it was usually successful, and loot was available. But the townsmen were not always so contented with the war, and Edward had to find many new sources of revenue. It is at this time that the customs and excise (tunnage and poundage) became a regular imposition, though granted by Parliament for only limited periods and not intended to be a permanent source of revenue for the king. There were a number of other experimental taxes, including income, personal property, and poll taxes. But, as always in the Middle Ages, the new taxes were only temporary grants for definite needs. A permanent source of revenue beyond the king's regular income from Crown resources and the proceeds of his courts of justice, was never acceptable until comparatively modern times. Edward even resorted to loans from Italian bankers, then found himself unable to repay, in spite of their acceptance of the English crown as security.

The reign of Richard II (1377–1399), short as it was, was of considerable constitutional importance. Coming to the throne as a boy of eleven, Richard was at first dominated by his council, which was constantly opposed by the great lords in Parliament who were not in the council. When he finally came of age, he attempted to rule personally, calling Parliament irregularly or not at all, and trying to use his executive power to collect sufficient money for his needs. But a baronial revolution overthrew him, and the indictment drawn up against him in Parliament declared that he had offended against the laws and customs of the realm by trying to rule and tax without the consent of Parliament. Again, as in the case of Edward II, Parliament deposed him and compelled him to abdicate, choosing as king, under the title of Henry IV (1399–1413), a noble of the House of Lancaster who was clearly not the best heir to the throne. No doubt Parliament was influenced in its choice by the fact that Henry had led the revolt against Richard, who was murdered shortly afterward.

Owing his position to parliamentary support, Henry allowed Parliament to perform all the functions it claimed for itself, and rarely succeeded in imposing his will upon it. He was the only fully constitutional king of the Middle Ages. The House of Commons began to audit the king's accounts, and directed the expenditure of the money it voted to him. The wording of legislation was now determined by Parliament before a bill reached the king for signature.

Though Henry V (1413–1422) safely succeeded to his father's position, it was not without opposition from another noble house, which had, in its own opinion, a better right to the throne—the House of York. At least in part in order to head off such dynastic opposition, Henry V picked a quarrel with France and plunged his country into a foreign war, in which he was brilliantly successful, winning by the Treaty of Troyes (1420) the consent of the deranged French king to his own succession to the throne of France. Henry, however, died prematurely, and, as we shall see, his son was unable to make good his father's claim to the French crown. As this son, Henry VI (1422–1461) was intermittently insane and never exercised an effective control over it, Parliament in his time was usually supreme.

When Henry VI became permanently insane, the House of York decided to take matters into its own hands. The whole of France except Calais had been lost; mercenaries defeated in France returned to England, where they preyed upon the countryside almost with impunity; the officials of the government were unable to exercise their functions and were frequently unpaid and corrupt. In these circumstances Richard, Duke of York, claimed that the country required a competent king and that this should be himself, by a hereditary right superior to that of the actual reigning monarch, Henry VI. The supporters of the Lancastrian house did not accept his claim and war broke out.[1] Richard was killed. His son and heir Edward (IV) proclaimed himself king in 1461. But his title was not uncontested, and he continued to wage the War

---

[1] This war is called the War of the Roses because the Lancastrian emblem was a red rose, while that of the House of York was a white rose.

of the Roses until his chief opponent, the Earl of Warwick (the Kingmaker), was killed at the battle of Barnet (1471). Henry's wife and young son were defeated in the same year at the battle of Tewkesbury. Edward's title to the throne was then formally acknowledged by a subservient Parliament.

Edward may be considered as the real founder of the absolute monarchy. Henry VII, the first Tudor king, merely followed Edward's policy, with various improvements. Edward called Parliament rarely, and used various indirect means for gaining money for his rule, especially from the townsmen. The latter did not mind taxation, even severe taxation including forced loans (called benevolences!), provided the War of the Roses did not break out again and ruin everyone.

Edward's monarchy was strong, and it was far from constitutional. He had come to power by violence and he did not mind using some violent means to maintain his throne. He no longer had any wars with France on his hands, and his increased revenue obtained from the towns, plus a merciless use of his judicial powers to extract further income, enabled him to be free of Parliament, as Henry VII was also able to be when he wished. When Edward died his sons were children, and they were imprisoned and are generally believed to have been murdered by their uncle, Richard III, who usurped the throne but reigned for too short a time (1483–1485) and with too little security for any constitutional changes to take place in that period. He called only one Parliament. In 1485 he was killed at the battle of Bosworth, and an outright usurper, with hardly more than a shadow of a claim to the throne through his mother, was accepted as king by Parliament, on the condition, or at least after a promise, that he would marry the heiress of the House of York. Thus began the great Tudor monarchy, and the establishment of an absolutism, under which Parliament was clearly an unequal partner in the rule of the country. This in turn gave place to the Stuart dynasty, by the end of which Parliament had clearly become the superior partner, leaving the monarchy with few powers, and even those it was unable to use effectively.

ENGLAND AND FRANCE

We have now studied the English national state up to the end of the Middle Ages, concentrating on the development of the characteristic English political institutions. A few words should also be said on the relations of the English monarchy with France, although these will be dealt with in rather more detail in the French section of this chapter. In the reign of Henry II, as we have seen, more than half of France was made up of fiefs of the English crown, for which the English monarchs had to do homage to the French king. The latter had certain rights over the English king as a vassal, but these were not of much use to him unless he had the power to enforce them. The English kings usually performed the act of homage in the prescribed manner, since there was nothing derogatory to their dignity in this in a Europe still in the feudal age. On the other hand John, king of England, married a noble lady who had already been promised to a French baron. This brought Philip Augustus into the picture since he had to protect the rights of the baron, who was also one of his vassals. He summoned John to his feudal court to answer for his crime. When John refused to appear, Philip was given a legitimate cause of war against him as a faithless vassal. Furthermore, when John murdered or caused to be murdered the young count of Brittany, his own nephew, who had possibly a better right to the English throne than himself, Philip was able to have John condemned by his feudal court since the count was likewise a vassal of the French king. Thus the English king's position as a French noble might bring him into difficulties in circumstances where the French king would have the support of his other vassals. On the other hand, the French nobles and people did not regard the English king as a foreigner against whom could be stirred up xenophobic feelings —not at least until the later Middle Ages, when, as we shall see, nationalism was rising in France.

Once Philip had deprived John of most of his French possessions by war, it was difficult for the English king to recover them. Henry III agreed by treaty to relinquish his right to most of the lands taken from his father, on condition that he be allowed to keep Aquitaine. Gascony and Guienne, in southwest France, had not yet been taken over by the French monarch.

In the fourteenth century various quarrels between the French and the English, including one over the French king's rights in Flanders, where much of the English wool crop was manufactured into cloth, culminated in the claim by Edward III of England that he was, through his mother, the rightful king of France. This set off the so-called Hundred Years' War, the first phase of which went strongly in favor of the English. But in the later phases, after England with the aid of French (Burgundian) allies had occupied much of France and had the English king's right to the French throne accepted by treaty (Treaty of Troyes, 1420), there was a sudden national revival in France under the inspiration of Joan of Arc, which resulted in the expulsion of the English from all France except Calais.

There can be no doubt that this expulsion was to the eventual benefit of the English, who were thus enabled to build up a national state apart from the Continent. Under the Tudor dynasty of England (1485–1603) the English were able to develop an exclusive patriotism and nationalism of their own which was to stand them in good stead in later centuries. However, these developments lie outside the scope of this volume.

❖ The French national state

THE EARLY CAPETIANS

It has already been noted that the French royal line is not descended from Charlemagne, although the grandson of the great Charles was the first king to reign over a kingdom not far different from what was later to be France. The crown left the family of Charlemagne when Charles the Fat was deposed by his nobles in 887 for cowardice and inertia. It was later given to the descendants of Odo, who had defended Paris against the Vikings. One

of Odo's descendants, Hugh Capet, founded the Capetian dynasty in 987. The direct descendants of Hugh Capet ruled France, eldest son succeeding eldest son, until 1328, when the crown went to the collateral house of Valois. In 1589 the house of Bourbon inherited the crown, retaining it in that branch of the old Capetian family until the Revolution.

The early history of the French monarchy need not detain us long. The Capetians were not among the great landowners of France when the crown passed to them. Before very long they had lost some of their possessions to other great lords, and were confined to little more than the Ile de France, the area around Paris, and the title of king. This latter meant that the monarch was the titular overlord of every noble who had any possessions in an area generally conceded to be that of "France," and that the other lords had to do homage to him at some time in their lives for their lands. In early years the Capetians could not compel their nobles to make even this gesture of respect to them. But they did at least have, in addition to the perquisites of a feudal king described in Chapter 9, a fair amount of ecclesiastical patronage in their hands, and the French clergy on the whole favored a monarchy over feudal decentralization. The clergy were continually urging the kings to establish and maintain justice beyond their mere feudal domains, and were, for the most part, willing to lend what aid they could.

The early Capetians, very sensibly in view of their position as relatively small landholders, rigidly refused to take part in foreign adventures in which their vassals were gaining glory and even kingdoms for themselves. The kings stayed at home looking after their affairs, and the fact, already mentioned, that there was never any doubt as to the succession and that most of the kings lived to an advanced age, thus obviating the need for a regency, aided them in their policy of gradually improving their position. In the early Middle Ages the French kings used the old Germanic custom of appointing household officials and giving them charge of various departments connected with the management of their feudal estates. But for a long time they did not even have control over these appointments, which tended to pass from father to son, like the old "mayors of the palace." However, the king also gave appointments to clergymen, who were barred by celibacy from handing down such appointments. As the kings from the twelfth century onward managed to establish some order in their own territories, a task in which some of the earlier kings had indifferent success, so they were able to obtain control over their official appointments and began to appoint commoners who were more susceptible to royal control.

Louis the Fat (1108–1137) was the first French king who fully controlled his own territories, and he began to extend his jurisdiction beyond them, summoning to his court occasionally vassals who only owed him allegiance as king, and sometimes succeeding in enforcing his will. His son Louis VII married Eleanor of Aquitaine, adding to his kingdom for a time territories far greater than his own. This marriage was the direct result of his position as king, since the lady's father had asked Louis to look after her when he died. But Louis divorced her after the Second Crusade, as we have seen, and she married Henry II of England, taking her lands with her.

Louis had little success in dealing with Henry. But his successor Philip Augustus (1180–1223), by shrewd diplomacy and occasional military campaigns, was able to take back from Henry's sons almost all the land that had gone to the English crown through the action of Louis VII. More English possessions were also added by Philip's successor, Louis VIII. As we have noted in the last chapter, Philip was also the beneficiary of the Albigensian Crusade, when he became the overlord of the southern French lands formerly belonging to the count of Toulouse. The important county of Flanders fell into his hands as a result of a military victory in 1214. Philip was thus the actual rather than the merely theoretical suzerain of the greater part of France. He developed an administration that was efficient and in keeping with his needs, thus bequeathing to his successors a nearly united kingdom and a strong monarchy of a feudal type. In view of his effective work for the monarchy during his long reign, it is not without justification that he was called Augustus, after the founder of the Roman principate and organizer of the Roman Empire. It should be understood that Philip Augustus and his Capetian successors were, however, feudal monarchs, and far from absolute. It was left to the Valois kings, Charles VII and Louis XI, to lay the foundations of that absolutism which is characteristic of the *ancien régime* of France, and which endured substantially to the French Revolution. In this chapter more attention will therefore be paid to the latter phase, which just falls within the traditional period of the Middle Ages, although the basis laid by the Capetian monarchs will also be dealt with as far as is necessary to explain what came later in the fifteenth century.

CONTINUED GROWTH OF POWER OF CAPETIAN KINGS

Full exploitation of feudal powers The French king, unlike the English, had no ancient customary rights to enforce, nor had he hedged his barons with restrictions on their independence like William the Conqueror of England, for his vassals owed a more direct obedience, more easily enforceable, to their own suzerains. So the kings had to concentrate their attention on trying to make their own domains at least subservient to themselves. Within this domain they did provide an administration far superior to those of other ordinary feudal lords, one which was capable of being extended as soon as the domain itself was enlarged. The earliest official was the *prévôt*, who looked after the king's interests in matters of justice and finance. As prévôts were paid by the grant of fiefs, their offices became hereditary, and it was not possible to do much to improve their administration until the king was in a position to pay them in money, and appoint and dismiss them at will. This reform was largely the work of Philip Augustus, who, by the help of his new feudal possessions, was able to find for the first time enough money for royal needs. He appointed *baillis* to watch the prévôts. These new officials at once became the chief instruments of royal policy. Their instructions were to support not only the king's feudal prerogatives but also as many of his kingly ones as they could, including within their jurisdiction as much of the king's nonfeudal territory as possible, and extending his influence in areas where he was not the feudal suzerain. This was done especially through listening to complaints against the local administration of justice and trying to substitute an appeal to the king's justice instead of to the feudal court.

The king himself made effective use of his power of summoning his vassals, direct and titular, to his court for advice and assistance, accustoming them to regard themselves as his real vassals, and, as we have seen, he led them against the English possessions in France at a profit to themselves as well as to him. But one of his greatest titles to fame was his recognition of the importance of the towns, which were as prosperous as any in Europe in the thirteenth century. Philip was entirely willing to grant them charters giving them freedom to organize local internal government, in exchange for suitable amounts of money. The towns recognized the value to themselves of having an efficient king rather than an irresponsible feudal nobility as their protector. So they provided him not only with money but with soldiery, and in many cases guaranteed to undertake their own defense. Philip also appointed townsmen to high positions in his government.

But it was, on the whole, the conquests of Philip that made all the other successes possible. He had the nucleus of an administration which took care of very small territories; when the territories were enlarged he increased the number of his officials and maintained the same organs of government, adding only a few new officials, such as seneschals. All the officials had to be watched carefully by each king, since it was not easy to control them.

Perhaps as early as Philip Augustus the officials of the king, sometimes, in committee, tried cases under feudal law in which the king's interests were involved. This committee of the king's council ultimately developed into the Parlement of Paris, the chief law court of the realm. Another committee looked into the receipts of money that came into the king's treasury to see that the baillis and seneschals were doing their duty. But by the time of

St. Louis IX, King of France. From a Moralized Bible *(French), 1226–1234.* (COURTESY PIERPONT MORGAN LIBRARY. Ms. 240, folio 8)

Louis IX (1226–1270) the king was asserting successfully his prerogative of administering justice for the entire kingdom of France, and not only for his feudal vassals. The king had always in theory been supposed to be the protector of all and the maintainer of peace. He and his lawyers now asserted that many cases tried locally by feudal nobles came within his jurisdiction. By decree Louis forbade feudal warfare, and tried to persuade contenders in disputes that might have led to war to come to his courts, either to himself, for he often gave personal judgments, or to the Parlement of Paris, which was under his control; and he forbade also, following the example of the Church, all recourse to trial by ordeal and combat. He did not trouble, as a rule, to obtain the consent of his vassals to his decrees, as had been the previous custom; but since he was everywhere revered as a saintly person—he was later formally canonized as a saint—this addition to royal authority was generally accepted, and on several occasions he obtained the signatures of a representative selection of vassals. Louis, finding that the communal government of the towns given charters by Philip Augustus too often failed to work well because of internal quarrels between merchants and other burghers, suspended many charters and renewed them only when the towns could show that they deserved them. He made the towns have their public accounts audited by his officers, and introduced officials of his own, such as mayors, which for centuries were royal and not local appointees.

Centralization of public finance and administration It should be understood that the French kings as yet had no right to tax, and though occasionally they attempted taxes for special purposes, such as Crusades, there was always such an outcry that the attempts were abandoned immediately. Philip IV (The Fair—1285–1314) and the able corps of lawyers who formed his body of advisers recognized the importance of money in any centralized administration. They set themselves determinedly to find new sources of royal income, which was used for the purpose of enlarging the realm and controlling the feudal nobility by an increasing use of mercenary rather than feudal troops. On the towns he laid increased customs duties, forced loans, and sales taxes. He assessed the nobles highly for the privilege of avoiding military service; he expropriated the Templars, originally one of the crusading orders in the Holy Land, which by now had become extremely wealthy and had undertaken the duties of the kings' bankers. As we saw in Chapter 10, Philip also succeeded in taxing the French clergy. All accounts were carefully scrutinized by a special accounting department staffed by salaried officials.

Philip reorganized the official organs of state into what will hereafter be called the king's council, which had an inner group consulted on special occasions. This group remained the chief advisory body to the Crown until the Revolution. The Parlement of Paris, under the king's direction, became a real law court composed of trained lawyers. One branch was given the task of listening to requests that

the king rather than any other court render justice. The Parlement of Paris also assumed jurisdiction over local courts, transferring their cases, when necessary, to itself.

It may be mentioned that the king's council, made up largely of lawyers trained in the Roman law, was something new at this early period, and was found to be extremely effective in enhancing the king's authority. Looked at with suspicion by the feudal nobility, which in France throughout history remained an aristocratic military caste and made no effort to control the civil administration or even to cooperate with it, these lawyers had only one duty and one aim—to aid the monarchy which had appointed and could dismiss them. Paid in money and not in lands, they never became part of the aristocracy; even in later times, when lawyers and assistants to the king were ennobled, they became a separate nobility, known as the nobility of the robe rather than of the sword. Moreover they were in the time of Philip IV, laymen and not clergymen, and thus could be independent even in dealing with the Church. As the power of the monarchy grew, so must their own power with it; while if the monarchy's power declined, they personally would lose any authority they possessed. They therefore took every opportunity to exalt the power of the monarchy over any competitor that threatened it, and, being thoroughly educated men, took the lead even in appeals to public opinion. It was the king's counselors in particular who dominated the great appeal to national unity presented by the quarrel with Pope Boniface VIII, which has already been discussed in Chapter 10.

The States-General The calling of the States-General in 1302 by Philip IV was essentially an appeal to public opinion, and was intended by the lawyers who dominated it to be precisely this, presenting a complete contrast with the English Parliaments of the same period. Parliaments were called by the English kings in response to pressure by the barons and taxpayers, and diminished rather than increased the absolute authority of the monarchy.

The representation in the States-General was substantially similar to that of the English

Parliaments. The first estate, the clergy; the second estate, the nobility; and the third estate, the remainder, especially representatives of the towns, were the same as in England, though there was nothing in France to correspond to the crucial group in England, the knights of the shire, who gave leadership to the bourgeoisie without being dominated by their special urban interests. In Philip's assembly his policy had virtually unanimous support because the quarrel was so well calculated to appeal to all. No one was anxious to see France dominated by an authoritarian and grasping papacy. Bishops, monks, and friars were as favorable to the king's position as were lords, bourgeoisie, and university professors. If the king had called them, as later kings were compelled to call them, for the purpose of extracting funds from them, there would have been no such impressive unanimity. However, the precedent had been set for an assembly of all classes of the realm, dominated by the king and his council; and we should note in passing that the sentiment of nationality must have been growing if the well-informed and able lawyers who knew what they wanted found it worth while to couch their appeals in this vein.

FRENCH FAILURE TO ACHIEVE REPRESENTATIVE INSTITUTIONS

The end of the Capetian monarchy After the death of Philip the Fair in 1314 the feudal lords made a determined effort to regain some of their power lost to the encroachments of the monarchy. Philip's successors were forced to make a few concessions, defining the limits of the royal power and the rights of the nobles. But the nobles lacked effective means of enforcing their rights, which remained a dead letter as long as the monarchs retained the power they had acquired in the later Middle Ages under the Capetians.

Meanwhile, the Capetian monarchy was nearing its end. Louis x, who reigned only two years, left no son to inherit his throne. He was therefore succeeded by each of his brothers in succession, none of whom left any male heir. The last of the Capetian kings designated his cousin Philip of Valois, son of the brother of

Philip the Fair, as king, and he was accepted by the French nobility and duly assumed the crown. But Edward iii, king of England, whose mother was the daughter of Philip the Fair, asserted that the French throne could descend through daughters in default of sons, as had been accepted by this time in England. This was the excuse for the Hundred Years' War, which was briefly touched upon in the first part of this chapter.

Contrasting roles of French and British nobility In a very real sense the end of the Capetian monarchy in France marks the close of the consolidation of the French kingdom, much as the reign of Edward i in England marks the greatest power of the later medieval English monarchy. Thereafter both monarchies lost power to the as yet undefeated forces of feudalism, while the two countries fought with each other and with the feudal nobility. But France had developed no constitutional counterbalance to the Crown, and at the end of the period of medieval disintegration absolutism was re-established in a modern form with relatively few changes from the monarchy of Philip IV. In England the institution of Parliament had grown throughout the period of disintegration, and remained still potentially strong even during the period of absolutism that followed it. During the Hundred Years' War it seemed, for a brief period, that the French monarchy would be brought under control by the same forces that limited it in England; but the chance was missed and it never occurred again. Fundamentally, it was the failure of the nobility to accept any social responsibilities, and its insistence on remaining a privileged and irresponsible group harking back to a long-outmoded military tradition, which handed absolute power back to the monarchy. The bourgeoisie found it impossible to cooperate with the lords, and made few attempts at effective action on their own. Preferring an orderly absolute monarchy to a disorderly and irresponsible feudalism, they were willing to pay the price exacted of them.

Nothing really new came out of the struggle; the French nobles learned nothing from their disasters, and far too much of the monarchs' energies had to be spent in combating them. Throughout the sixteenth century the nobility still pursued its own interests, waging war against the monarchs, intriguing for the succession, or trying to gain the ear of the kings. The civil wars of the sixteenth century were complicated by religious struggles; but in France, unlike England, the religious struggles were not used to extract concessions from the monarchy. When the French civil wars finally came to an end with the establishment of the Bourbon monarchy at the close of the sixteenth century, the king's position was secure. Subsequent rebellions by the nobles were suppressed without great difficulty, and the absolute monarchy continued substantially unchanged until the French Revolution at the end of the eighteenth century.

Subservience of States-General to the monarchy The States-General, the germ of a French parliament, might have been used in the Hundred Years' War as an instrument for the curbing of royal power. When the monarch needed subsidies to enable him to prosecute the war, he was compelled to call the States-General. But sooner or later it granted what the king wanted, the nobles who dominated that body probably recognizing that they too constituted a privileged class, and needed the king if they were to survive. They preferred alliance with the king to an alliance with the bourgeoisie. When Paris during the war rose in revolt under a merchant named Étienne Marcel, the nobles preferred to join the king in suppressing the rebels to joining with the rebels to force concessions from the king. The peasants were always on the verge of revolt, especially after the Black Death, a plague which killed an estimated fifth of the whole population of France. Faced with a scarcity of labor, the nobles tried to act as if there had never been a plague, and proceeded to exploit the peasants as before. When they revolted, the nobles joined the king in suppressing them.

Having thus irrevocably cast their lot with the king, the nobles, through the States-General, granted him the means by which he could carry on the war and maintain his government.

Although intended to be temporary, the two important taxes thus granted—a sales tax and a tax on hearths—were made permanent by a later monarch. With these taxes and the all-important *taille,* to be described later, at his disposal, the French monarch, unlike the English, seldom had to resort to calling the States-General for money. The last time it was called before the French Revolution was in 1614. Since this meeting in fact granted notl.ing, its very failure made the monarch aware of the truth that he could do perfectly well without it.

THE HUNDRED YEARS' WAR AND THE ESTABLISHMENT OF ABSOLUTISM

The early stages of the Hundred Years' War went uniformly against France, in part because of the refusal of the French nobility to abandon its old feudal methods of warfare in face of the yeoman archery of the English. In the later years of the fourteenth century the French recovered and improved their methods of warfare. Under the Valois monarch Charles v (1364–1380) the English were almost driven out of France. Then the tide turned again soon after the accession of Charles vi (1380–1422), who was

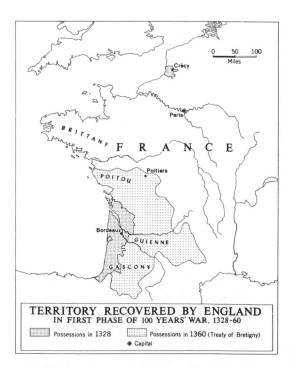

TERRITORY RECOVERED BY ENGLAND
IN FIRST PHASE OF 100 YEARS' WAR, 1328-60
Possessions in 1328   Possessions in 1360 (Treaty of Bretigny)
⊙ Capital

Portrait of Charles VII, King of France (the Dauphin, later king, to whom Joan of Arc was sent with her famous message). Painted by Fouquet.

insane for much of his reign. To understand the last phases of the war, however, it is necessary to consider what proved to be the most dangerous threat to the centralized French monarchy in the later Middle Ages. This was nothing less than the rise of a power which for a time possessed greater resources and territories than the Valois monarchy and ruled a substantial part of present-day France. This was the duchy of Burgundy, created by the Valois monarchy during the Hundred Years' War, and granted initially to a Valois prince, with the permission of the Holy Roman emperor, who was the suzerain of a part of the duchy.

Anglo Burgundian alliance The dukes of Burgundy by the early part of the fifteenth century had greatly increased their territories by marriage and conquest. Allied as they were with the French royal family, it was natural for them to try to win the French crown for themselves during the troubled years of the war; or failing that, at least to control the government of the mad king Charles VI. The easiest way to do this

was to ally themselves with the English, and hope for the opportunity in due course to oust the English. Thus the dukes entered into an alliance with Henry V of England (1413–1422). After the great victory of the latter at the battle of Agincourt in 1415, it was the Burgundians who compelled the French monarch to give his daughter in marriage to the English king, and to sign the Treaty of Troyes (1420), under which Henry was to inherit the French throne after the death of Charles VI. In fact Henry and Charles both died in the same year of 1422, and Henry's infant son was proclaimed king of France by the English and by the Burgundians, who at that time controlled much of northern France, including Paris. The dauphin Charles (later Charles VII) was thus deprived of his inheritance. Not only was much of the north and east of his country controlled by the Burgundians and their English allies, but the English possessed in their own right parts of southwestern France. It was at this unpromising moment that Joan of Arc, the Maid of Orléans, took a hand. Her aid to Charles was largely instrumental in effecting the changes that were to drive the English out of France and the Burgundians from their alliance with the English.

Role of Joan of Arc The work of Joan of Arc is sometimes minimized, but there can be little doubt that it was crucial. Her story of course is well known—how she heard voices which instructed her to go to the Dauphin, as he was still called, since his right to the throne was in doubt;

how she recognized him at once and greeted him as king; how she breathed new life into the dispirited royal forces, and led them to the great victory at Orléans, which was the first substantial check to the English and Burgundians. With a sure instinct she recognized that until the Dauphin was crowned king at Reims, like his ancestors, he would not be accepted as king by the majority of the French. So after the victory of Orléans she insisted that he be

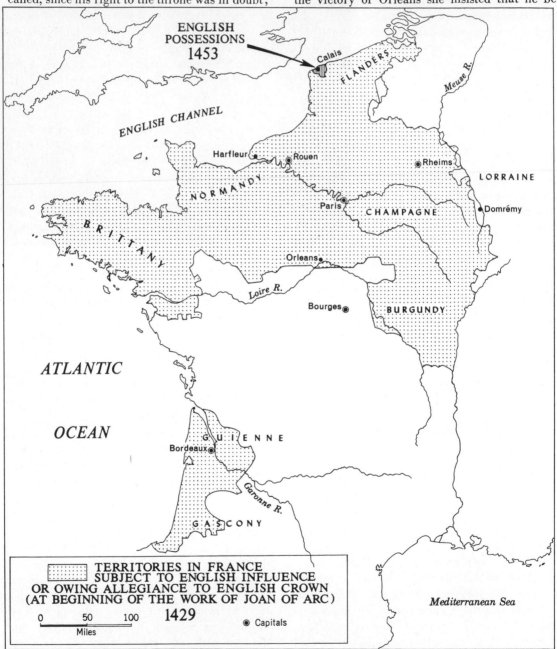

ENGLISH
POSSESSIONS
1453

Calais

FLANDERS

Meuse R.

ENGLISH CHANNEL

Harfleur   Rouen

Rheims

LORRAINE

NORMANDY

Domrémy

Paris   CHAMPAGNE

BRITTANY

Orleans

Loire R.

Bourges

BURGUNDY

ATLANTIC

OCEAN

GUIENNE

Bordeaux

Garonne R.

GASCONY

Mediterranean Sea

TERRITORIES IN FRANCE
SUBJECT TO ENGLISH INFLUENCE
OR OWING ALLEGIANCE TO ENGLISH CROWN
(AT BEGINNING OF THE WORK OF JOAN OF ARC)
1429

0   50   100
Miles

● Capitals

crowned (1429). When the ceremony was over her real work was done, but she insisted on continuing to lead a part of the French forces until she was captured by the Burgundians and sold to the English. The latter had her tried by the Inquisition in a process of very doubtful legality, since the bishop who presided was an old enemy of the Maid's, and was not authorized by the Church to hold the trial. Moreover, he was in any case not a free agent, since the English were not prepared to accept any verdict but condemnation; they wished to break Joan's influence by having her convicted as a sorceress. After her capture Charles attempted to ransom her, but he lacked power to rescue her. Thus Joan, after recanting briefly, was put to death as a relapsed heretic.

Meanwhile Charles and his chief adviser, Reginald, archbishop of Reims, patiently negotiated with the Burgundians, and were at length able to persuade them to abandon the English alliance—a negotiation which would have been unthinkable without the victories won for Charles by the Maid. The English, robbed of their allies, were unable to keep their gains; and at last Charles, with the aid of a strong army, paid for out of new taxes, was able to drive them from the country. Without the initial impulse contributed by Joan none of this would have been possible, and Charles, the dispirited dauphin, would never have won the title of Charles the Victorious that he merited before his death.

The work begun by Charles (1422–1461) was finished by his son Louis XI (1461–1483), a tireless schemer and indefatigable bureaucrat, who was able to put an end to the Burgundian menace forever by the use of bribes and shrewd diplomacy, aided by a good dose of luck. Before the end of his reign France was again united within substantially the boundaries that she has today.

THE MACHINERY OF ABSOLUTISM AS
DEVELOPED BY CHARLES VII
AND LOUIS XI

The secret of French absolutism is to be found in the financial autonomy granted by the States-General to the French kings during the Hundred Years' War, and in the efficient organization of an improved bureaucracy to collect the new permanent taxes, devised in part by Charles VII but perfected by Louis XI and his two Valois successors. Until the rise of modern Germany, France was always potentially the richest country in Europe, possessed of the finest resources and the hardest-working peasantry. When she has been well governed, prosperity has always been quick to return. In a centrally administered kingdom so many possibilities existed for corruption, so many opportunities for personal enrichment presented themselves to unwatched officials, that the kings were often ludicrously short of money in a country where ample funds were really available.

The work of Charles VII consisted in obtaining the authorization from the States-General, or the nobility and bourgeoisie, to collect taxes on a permanent basis beyond the simple receipts from the king's property which were all that a feudal king commanded. Charles was granted this in order that he might be enabled to defeat and expel the English. The taxes thus granted, however, were never abandoned by the monarchy, though the fiction was observed that some revenues were temporary and extraordinary, while others were ordinary and regular. The chief tax granted in 1439 was the *taille*, a tax imposed upon all financial and real property throughout the kingdom. A remarkably complex system was inaugurated to collect this tax, which remained the chief tax in France till the Revolution and even afterward. The total amount needed by the Crown for each particular year was assessed. This total was then divided by the officials through each unit of government down to the level of the parish, which was assessed for its portion of the whole. On tax collection day in the parish the bells were tolled and the citizens were informed what their total contribution was to be. Then they had to elect assessors, who determined what the individual share of each must be. Naturally, every peasant wished to avoid his tax, and tried to conceal his wealth—a French custom which has persisted to this day—and many were the expedients adopted. But the taille could be collected, even though large

parts of the collections found their way into
the pockets of the officials through whose
hands they passed on the way to the treasury.
Louis XI was extremely careful to check all
corruption, as in general the best French kings
were, until the later kings defeated their own
objectives by granting excessive numbers of
immunities from taxes to favorites.

The aids, or sales taxes, and the customs
duties, both interior and those collected at
the ports, and the proceeds from royal monopolies, especially the infamous *gabelle*, or
salt tax, were given into the hands of tax
farmers, who established their own collection
posts and bought the whole contract for taxes
from the king. The latter was therefore able
to command the expected income from these
taxes without having to go to the trouble of
instituting a system for collecting them himself. This task was performed by private
enterprise, which helped itself to considerably
more profit from the collection than was officially permitted by the kings. The difficulty
was the control of the tax farmers, and again,
only the most efficient kings were able to keep
them in order. With such possibilities for living
beyond their means, many French kings in later
times would persuade the tax farmers to give
them several years' income in advance, and
thus would be short of income in later years
when it might be equally needed.

With the money thus newly available, and
with the services of a great financial expert to
assist him, Charles VII reorganized the French
army. It was officially announced in 1439 that
only the king could levy and maintain troops.
Charles then proceeded to enforce this decree
by levying an army of professional troops,
with a permanent cavalry of twenty companies
(about six hundred men to a company, including bowmen and lancers). Then a further body
of bowmen was organized for the infantry, the
soldiers (free-archers) being exempted from
the taille in time of peace. They were to be
chosen by the king's officials, the baillis. They
were instructed in the use of firearms and artil-
lery, engaged in periodic maneuvers, and were
kept together according to the regions from
which they hailed—the ancestors of the modern
regiments. In addition to these French soldiers,
enormous numbers of mercenaries from all the
countries of Europe were added when necessary.

It will be seen that the basis for all this
military activity was the ability to collect the
taxes to pay for it. If the mercenaries were
unpaid, they preyed upon the country; if the
king could not establish his authority firmly,
the trained troops might just as easily join a
pretender or a feudal lord who promised to
pay them. For most of a century, or at least
until the death of Francis I in 1547, the French
kings were the masters of France through possession of an adequate income and well-paid
troops able to maintain the king's peace against
any feudal lord, and during this period France
had a growing prosperity. When the royal government again failed in the middle of the
sixteenth century, feudalism, which had only
temporarily been held in control, burst forth
anew.

The new financial regime called forth
thousands of new officials, and it is from this
time that a bureaucratic career became the
position of honor in France that it remained
until very recent times. Louis XI, a meticulous
and tireless administrator, took very great care
of all the appointments that he made, and he
watched the behavior of his nominees with the
most meticulous attention. He would stand no
communal nonsense from the towns and insisted
on appointing all the superior officials in them.
Every official in the country had to be absolutely loyal to Louis, on pain of instant dismissal. Each official felt it to be his duty to enhance
the authority of the king, his master, and incidentally his own at the same time. He received
a good salary, and there were many valuable
perquisites to be obtained from office. Thus it
came to be the custom that the positions were
actually purchased by the incumbents; and the
kings did not usually dismiss them unless they
proved exceptionally inefficient or disloyal.
The majority of the officials of whom we know
died safely in office, after designating a successor who would have to pay an indemnity
to the king for confirmation of his appointment
(as well as another to the departing official
who had selected him). When a king died, the
officials were all required to receive a confirma-

tion of their title to the office, which helped the new king over what would otherwise have been financially a difficult time.

The system worked, for the interests of kings and officials were one. The sufferers were the taxpayers who groaned, but for a long time thought that the comparative efficiency of the government was at least far better than the anarchy and civil war that had preceded it. Under feeble kings the officials paid less to the treasury than under the efficient ones, but they still paid something. The country was administered, and a high degree of stability was ensured. The law courts functioned, administering the king's justice as in the earlier medieval period; and the accounts were audited, or at least examined, by the central bureaus set up in earlier reigns for the purpose. At the top were the great officials of the king's council, appointed directly by him, usually from the ranks of the Church or the upper bourgeoisie.

When the Crown failed in the middle of the sixteenth century the system endured for a while, until it too collapsed under the recrudescence of feudal anarchy. But as soon as the centralized government was re-established by Henry IV in 1589, few indeed were the changes that had to be made. The machinery of the late-medieval *ancien régime* was the machinery in all essentials that lasted till the French Revolution of 1789; and by no means all its earlier features were changed even by the Revolution. Almost as much as in England can the structure of modern France be traced back to its medieval antecedents.

❖ The Iberian peninsula

Although Spain was not unified into a single national state until the late fifteenth century, the separate states of the Iberian peninsula were effective feudal kingdoms during the period when England and France were ruled by feudal monarchs, and similar institutions were developed to keep the feudal monarchs under some control. As the result of the long occupation by Muslims, however, the history of the Iberian peninsula has from the beginning presented certain important contrasts

with the development of other European countries. The process of driving out the Muslims took several centuries, and was not completed until the end of the Middle Ages. A kind of continuous crusade, backed by the Church, was in process during the greater part of the Middle Ages.

Not all of Spain was subjected to the Muslims. In the northwest the kingdom of the Asturias was able to defy the efforts of the Muslims to drive the Christians from the peninsula, while the Basques in the north were never subdued by them, and retained a fierce independence which drove them to attack the Franks in the eighth and ninth centuries. Eventually the kingdoms of León in the northwest and Navarre in the north became fully independent of the Muslims, while the territories which were to become the great Spanish kingdoms of Aragon and Castile were still subjected to them. But persistent effort by the Christians culminated in the capture of Toledo in central Spain in the middle of the twelfth century, while Cordova, the Muslim (Moorish) capital of southern Spain, was taken in 1236. Seville followed in 1248, leaving only the kingdom of Granada in the extreme south in Moorish hands, where it remained until 1492.

In the twelfth century León and Castile united into one kingdom, the most powerful in Spain, while Aragon was united with Catalonia and other areas in the northeast. At the end of the eleventh century Count Henry of Burgundy had been granted a fief in the west of the peninsula in exchange for help given to the ruler of Castile in the wars against the Muslims. Henry's successors, by hard fighting —which included wars against the Castilians as well as the Moors—gradually built up the kingdom of Portugal, which was to remain independent of the rest of the peninsula. In 1383, however, the throne would have gone to the Castilians, since the sole heiress was married to a Castilian prince. This the Portuguese nobles and people would not permit. They had fought too hard in past centuries against the Castilians to let the kingdom fall quietly into their hands. John I, grand master of the Order of Avis, a Portuguese crusading order whose main task had been the expulsion

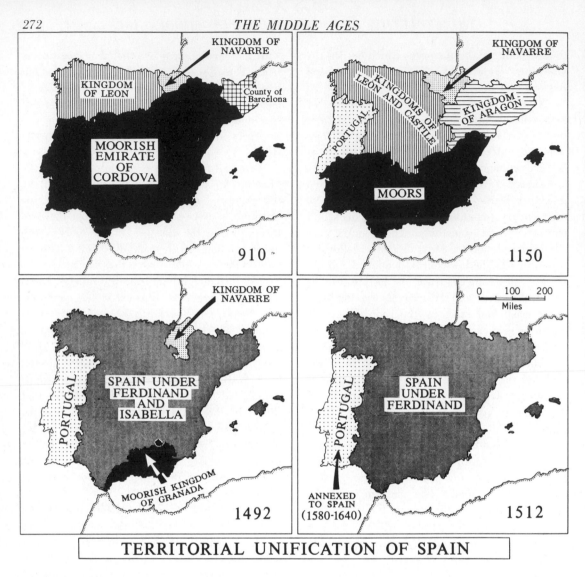

TERRITORIAL UNIFICATION OF SPAIN

of the Muslims from the country, was chosen king instead; and when he inflicted a crushing defeat on the Castilians, the independence of the kingdom was assured. The dynasty founded by John was to lead Portugal, small as she was, to her crucial role in the expansion of Europe to the East in the fifteenth and sixteenth centuries.

By the middle of the thirteenth century there were thus four well-established Christian kingdoms in the peninsula. The northern kingdom of Navarre comprised territories on the French side of the Pyrenees as well as on the Spanish side, and from 1234 was ruled by a Frenchman. Ferdinand III of Castile united León and Castile permanently in 1230. Thereafter the country was simply known as Castile.

The kingdom of Aragon was a confederation of many separate entities, each of which retained some autonomy. But it was ruled effectively by the house of Aragon and its kings, whose possessions were not confined to Spain. They possessed a number of French fiefs, and, as we have briefly noted in the last chapter, from 1282 they fell heir to the Hohenstaufen kingdom of Sicily.

In all the Spanish kingdoms the feudal monarchs had to submit to a limited control by their subjects, who fought hard for their privileges. As in France, the three estates— clergy, nobility, and townsmen—were summoned by the monarch when he was in need of money. But these Cortes, as they were called, were far more effective than in France, and obtained the right to present petitions and be consulted on taxes and legislation. On the other hand, the Spanish rulers were always more powerful than the late-medieval English monarchs, who had to call Parliament at regular intervals and who needed Parliament to finance their wars. When necessary, the Spanish rulers were always able to make their will prevail, and by the end of the Middle Ages the Cortes were clearly subordinate to them, as the States-General was subordinate to the kings of France, save in exceptional circumstances.

In 1469 a great step toward the unification of Spain was taken when Ferdinand of Aragon and Isabella of Castille, heirs to their respective thrones, were secretly married. In due course they inherited their thrones; and though the two countries were not officially amalgamated, and the union was only a personal union of the monarchs, in fact under their joint rule Spain became at last a national entity (1479). When Isabella died before her husband, a number of important Castilians tried to sever their kingdom from Aragon. But the movement quickly collapsed, and the whole kingdom was inherited by the daughter of the two monarchs, who proceeded to marry into the Hapsburg family. The son of Joanna, this first queen of Spain, was Charles v, who was elected Holy Roman Emperor, thus bringing Spain as a great power into the politics of Central Europe.

Ferdinand and Isabella brought together the commercial experience of Aragon and the great military tradition of Castile, which had been the leader in the wars against the Muslims. At once they proceeded to consolidate the entire peninsula except for Portugal. They drove the French out of that part of Navarre that was south of the Pyrenees, and they drove the Muslims out of Granada in the south, where they had been harmlessly living for centuries, paying regular tribute to the kings of Castile. For good measure, Ferdinand and Isabella then expelled the Jews, to an estimated number of two hundred thousand. This was an economic as well as a human disaster for the country, as many of these people, skilled in commerce, industry, and agriculture, could hardly be replaced. However, converted Mus-

lims (Moriscos) were permitted to remain for another century, and it was not till the expulsion of these latter in 1609 that the disastrous policy of persecution had its full effect. It is generally conceded that much of Spanish economic backwardness to this day can be traced to the systematic destruction or expulsion of those classes which had always borne such a large share of the economic activity of the country.

For the suppression of the feudal nobility the monarchs, especially in Castile, won the support of the towns, which, as usual, preferred absolutism to feudal anarchy, and by enlisting picked troops from the towns they were able to make considerable headway. But perhaps the greatest instrument for enforcing absolutism was the Spanish Inquisition, the adaptation of an established and accepted institution for new ends hardly in conformity with its original purpose.

As a "crusading" people, engaged for centuries in war against the Muslim infidels, the Spanish had a horror of heresy, and were deeply attached to militant Christianity. Moreover, the monarchs themselves were very strict Catholics and detested heresy no less than did their subjects. The relatively mild papal Inquisition, discussed in an earlier chapter, had fallen into disuse in Spain. Ferdinand and Isabella therefore requested the papacy to set up a new and more severe Inquisition, no doubt with the intention of subordinating it to the monarchy and using it for political ends. Pope Sixtus IV was reluctant to permit it, but allowed himself to be persuaded, and in 1478 the so-called Spanish Inquisition was duly established. The monarchs were indeed successful in gaining control of it, using it to establish their supremacy over the Spanish Church by driving out of the Church many of the local clergy, who were at this time rather lax in their discipline and observances, and replacing them with rigid disciplinarians. They also used the Inquisition against dissenters and their own personal enemies, and later, of course, against Protestants. They met little opposition from their own subjects, who were, on the whole, very religious and very orthodox. As long as the monarchs presented their persecutions under a religious guise they could rely upon popular support.

The result was a reformed Church in Spain which was able, in the following century, to give much-needed leadership to the Catholic Reformation, made necessary by the initial successes of the Protestants. Spain thus became dominant in Europe for a time by the use of religious as well as political and military means.

Even so, the Spanish would not have possessed enough resources to maintain this position without the aid of the riches of the New World, discovered at the end of the fifteenth century by the Italian sailor Christopher Columbus, who had taken service under the monarchs of Aragon and Castile. A few years previously, the Portuguese, from their separate and independent kingdom, had succeeded in making their way down the coast of Africa, and in 1498, six years after the first voyage of Columbus to the East, the Portuguese sailor Vasco da Gama rounded the Cape of Good Hope, and reached the town of Calicut on the west coast of the Indian peninsula.

❖ Switzerland

After a consideration of the major national states of the Middle Ages, a few words may be added on the formation of another tiny national state, which has survived to the present day. The antecedents of Switzerland are to be found in the late thirteenth century, when three peasant cantons united in a confederation. The purpose of the confederation was to escape domination by the growing power of the Hapsburgs, many of whom held the imperial crown, and whose ancestral lands bordered those of the Swiss. Several times the Swiss peasants defeated numerically larger feudal armies sent against them. Other cantons, urban as well as peasant, joined the confederation as it succeeded in its objectives. By the end of the fifteenth century they were virtually independent, and their right to this independence had been formally acknowledged by the rulers of the Holy Roman Empire. The formidable Swiss soldiers were by this time much in demand as mercenaries by all the monarchs of Europe.

In 1648, at the Peace of Westphalia, the confederation was recognized as the independent country of Switzerland—the only nation in Europe which has always been republican, and has never submitted to rule by any monarch, either native or foreign.

❖ The national state as the key political institution of modern times

The discovery of the New World, and the opening up of Asia, is as fitting a dividing line as any between the Middle Ages and the early modern era, which we are now about to discuss. Europe had been consolidated into several national states, under a form of government sometimes called the "new monarchy,"—a monarchy which was fully abreast of the times, and was in a strategic position to take advantage of the new opportunities, economic and political, which were opened up by the new discoveries. The old universal State, which had always been the ideal of the Middle Ages, was now, in reality, gone forever, or at least postponed for an unforeseeable future. In spite of this, however, the Holy Roman Empire had not yet fully abandoned its pretensions, and on at least two separate occasions came close to restoring some of its former glories.

The great political fact of the centuries since 1500 has been the rise and growth of the national state, an entity larger than the ancient city-states of Greece and Rome, but smaller than medieval Christendom. These national states have shown themselves capable of taking care of tremendous commercial and industrial expansion, and of ensuring certain basic rights, ultimately including self-government, for their particular nationals. In the process they have fought terrible internecine wars, and they have competed by war and diplomacy for the resources, not only of each other, but also of the distant lands which they have subjected to their control.

Thus an institution which grew out of the needs of men in the Middle Ages has been sanctified as the natural form of government among men, as the Roman Empire was once sanctified by Christians who had grown up beneath its shadow. It remains to be seen whether the national state can survive the trials of the present epoch, or whether, as Toynbee has urged, it is already obsolete and will give way to some other equally "natural" form of government. But it cannot be denied that from the sixteenth to the twentieth century A.D., the national state was the predominant form of governmental organization; and this, too, we owe to our medieval forebears.

Suggestions for further reading

PAPER-BOUND BOOKS

Cam, Helen. *England Before Elizabeth*. Torchbooks. Excellent survey.

Fawtier, Robert. *The Capetian Kings of France*. St. Martin's Press. One of the few useful books on medieval France to appear in English. Excellent on the growth of royal power.

Froissart, Jean. *Chronicles of England, France and Spain*. Everyman. A contemporary account of the first period of the Hundred Years' War.

Haskins, George L. *The Growth of English Representative Government*. Perpetua. Good account of the medieval development of Parliament.

Kelly, Amy. *Eleanor of Aquitaine and the Four Kings*. Vintage. Good popular account of the period covered by the life of the French duchess who later became queen of England.

Livermore, Harold. *A History of Spain*. Evergreen. Sometimes a little confusing for the beginner and lacking effective synthesis, but reliable and informative.

Maitland, Frederick W. *The Constitutional History of England*. Cambridge University Press. Peculiarly organized and difficult to find one's way about in, but well worth the effort because it introduces the student to one of the great legal historians of all time and permits the reader, as it were, to see into his workshop.

Muntz, Hope. *The Golden Warrior*. Scribner. One of the very best of medieval novels. Solidly based on the available sources, it is moving, accurate, and well written in a simple style.

Myers, A. R. *England in the Late Middle Ages*. Penguin. Valuable survey of all aspects of English life in the period.

Painter, Sidney. *The Rise of Feudal Monarchies*. Cornell University Press. Excellent survey.

Petit-Dutaillis, C. *Feudal Monarchy in France and England from the 10th to the 13th Century*. Torchbooks. Perhaps the most valuable work on the subject in English.

Sayles, G. O. *Medieval Foundations of England*. Perpetua. Best general study of Anglo-Saxon England in convenient form.

Stenton, Doris M. *English Society in the Early Middle Ages*. Penguin. Covers the period 1066 to 1307 topically in the same manner as Myers.

Trevelyan, George M. *A History of England*. 3 vols. Anchor. Vol. I covers the Middle Ages. Especially good on social history.

Trask, Willard, compiler. *Joan of Arc—Self-Portrait*. Collier. Interesting compilation from Joan's own speeches at her trial, as reported at the time.

HARD-COVER BOOKS

Adams, G. B., and Schuyler, R. L. *Constitutional History of England*. New York: Holt, Rinehart and Winston, Inc., 1934. Standard text on English constitutional history, good on the Middle Ages, though much specialized research in the years since has made some of the interpretations no longer fully acceptable.

Altamira, Rafael. *History of Spain: From the Beginnings to the Present Day*, trans. by Muna Lee. Princeton, N.J.: D. Van Nostrand Company, Inc., 1949. The standard history of Spain by a Spaniard.

Barlow, F. *The Feudal Kingdom of England, 1042–1216*. New York: David McKay Company, Inc., 1954. Useful study, especially good on the earlier period.

Brooke, Christopher. *The Saxon and Norman Kings*. New York: The Macmillan Company, 1963.

Kern, Fritz. *Kingship and Law in the Middle Ages*. Chester, Pa.: Dufour Editions, 1948. Fundamental study.

Painter, Sidney. *The Reign of King John*. Baltimore: The Johns Hopkins Press, 1949. Valuable monograph by a distinguished American scholar on this crucially important period.

Perroy, E. *The Hundred Years' War*, trans. by H. B. Wells. New York: Oxford University Press, 1951. A full political history of the relations between England and France during the period and a fair-minded account of the work of Joan of Arc.

Powicke, F. M. *King Henry III and the Lord Edward*. 2 vols. London: Oxford University Press, 1947. Outstanding study by the late dean of English medievalists. Excellent both as biography and history. By the same author is a fine study, *The Thirteenth Century* (London: Oxford University Press, 1953).

TWELVE

Medieval Culture

Up to this point in the book separate sections have been devoted to the culture of each of the peoples considered. No difficulty was experienced in following this procedure, which has become traditional. Clearly the procedure is justifiable when one can perceive, in the perspective of history, the total cultural achievement of a particular civilization. These earlier civilizations all have long ago come to an end, and their legacy has been absorbed by their successors.

The Middle Ages, on the other hand, is an arbitrary abstraction, and not a true civilization distinguishable from its predecessors and successors (as was noted in the introduction to this Part). It is merely the early period of our own Western civilization. The people of the Renaissance, who knew and admired classical antiquity, regarded themselves as "modern" in contrast to the "ancient" Greeks and Romans. The age of the Renaissance is now called "early modern," but the "Middle Ages" has persisted as a descriptive term applied to the period between the fall of the Roman Empire and the somewhat arbitrary date of 1500.

Nevertheless, although the achievements of the medieval people are the achievements of our own immediate ancestors, and although there is a recognizable continuity of culture in almost every field between the men of the Middle Ages and ourselves, there is something different about that time, even if we have difficulty in saying exactly what it is. The characteristic medieval civilization, moreover, did undoubtedly decline in the fourteenth and fifteenth centuries from its high point in the thirteenth.

Perhaps medieval culture is best thought of as a prenational European culture, produced at a period when, despite the rise of vernacular languages, the vast bulk of literary work was written in the still universal language of the educated, Latin; when Europeans did not yet recognize that there would be no restoration of an empire like Rome; when the Church still did exist as a universal institution and the concept of Christendom had some reality. In the thirteenth century the German scholar Albertus Magnus had as a pupil Thomas Aquinas, who belonged to a noble Italian family. The greatest philosophers of the next century were William of Occam, an Englishman, and Duns Scotus, an Irishman (probably). Although these men were born in different European countries, their culture was in all essentials the same; whereas the manifestations of the Renaissance, a bare century after the life of Thomas Aquinas, were noticeably different in Italy and in the northern countries. We shall therefore deal here with the Middle Ages as a whole, without attempting to distinguish between the cultures of the different nations during this period. In modern history such a procedure would no longer be valid. Even though such movements as Romanticism affected all Western Civilization, their manifestations differed markedly in the different countries.

It has already been noted that the men of the Renaissance looked upon their immediate predecessors as barbarians. They believed themselves to be the heralds of a new era, and consistently derided the achievements of the medieval people. They pictured their forebears as living in total bondage to an authoritarian Church, unable and unwilling to think for themselves, with every slightest deviation from orthodoxy punishable by a horrible death at the hands of the Inquisition.

This stereotype of the Middle Ages was accepted for so many centuries, and is, even now, dying so hard, that we do not regard medieval times frequently enough as the formative period of our own age, nor examine closely enough the immense obstacles that had to be overcome by the barbarians in a society that had collapsed as completely as the old Greco-Roman civilization. It was centuries before the static manorial feudal society was undermined deeply enough for an urban society to develop, and, as we have seen, civilized arts have hitherto never appeared in a rural society. But the medieval people did finally develop an urban civilization and an urban culture, and the cities which they founded have continued into our own times without serious breaks, excepting a few affected by external causes such as the Black Death.

What should be studied therefore in medieval culture is the struggle of the people to absorb what was left of the heritage of older civilizations, and the new creative effort to strike out on a line of their own afterward—to emancipate themselves from the static conception of life natural to a rural existence, to discover the power of reason and free themselves from the bondage to authority, and to see how in doing this they made possible the enormous scientific and political advances which have been the main glory of Western civilization as a whole. We shall understand their achievement better if we emancipate ourselves from the outworn stereotype that medieval civilization began with the barbarian invasions and ended with the Renaissance, that it was an age of faith and acceptance of authority, that reason did not begin until at least the seventeenth century, and that the all-embracing Church stifled the efforts of men to improve their lot on earth by assuring them that the next life alone was of importance. It is true enough that the last was the official teaching of the Church, but it is not true that the teaching stifled initiative and freedom of thought, nor that it succeeded in turning men exclusively to preparation for the hereafter.

The story of medieval culture is, in a sense, extraordinarily dramatic if viewed sympathetically, with a realization of the enormous obstacles to freedom of thought which were progressively overcome; if we try to see the objectives of medieval thinkers and scientists and writers, and realize how consistently they were striving to relate their actual experience to the picture of life on earth and in the hereafter presented to them by the conservative elements in their society. Progress in the Middle Ages was slow, and perhaps the total of its achievements was small in comparison with achievement in the centuries since. But preparatory and formative periods must necessarily last longer and show less spectacular results than the later flowering. It was many centuries after the Dorian invasions that the Greeks came to the height of their powers. There is no flower until the roots have taken hold; and the roots of Western civilization lie far back in the Middle Ages, when the struggle was being fought between reason and faith, between freedom and authority, between the miracle and the natural law, between the pull of the past and the urge toward the future.

❖ **Contrast between early and later periods of Middle Ages**

Medieval culture falls into two periods. The period that has sometimes been characterized as the Dark Ages is really entitled to the adjective. Outside the fold of the Church there was almost no education at all; and even within the Church only a very small percentage of men and women were literate. In some of the monasteries, manuscripts from the ancient world were diligently copied; but, as we know from the errors in copying, too often the contents were not understood. Charlemagne never learned to read or write; and when he wished to make a modest beginning toward a revival of learning in his empire, the scholars that he found, though the best in Europe in his day, would never have been considered anything but mediocre in any more enlightened age. Outside Ireland, Greek had been forgotten. There is but one creative European thinker known in more than three centuries, and he was an Irishman; yet this dark time was also the period of the flowering of the Muslim civilization. When, in the late tenth century, Gerbert became known as the most learned man in the West, and was finally elected pope as Sylvester II, we are told that he had studied every branch of knowledge available in his day. But the sum total is pitiful indeed. Except for those few who could understand Arabic and had access to Muslim works, the only reading available was the Bible, some of the works of the Christian Fathers, a few inaccurate and highly simplified encyclopedias, and some elementary textbooks.

Then, almost suddenly, the Western mind seemed to awake and ask questions, and the Dark Ages were over. On the one side, it began to learn to reason, and to apply reason to what it had hitherto received as dogma, bestowed by authority; and, on the other side, certain individuals began to become aware of and interested in the wider world of Muslim culture, and at once began to contrast this knowledge with the abysmal ignorance of the West. Bringing back knowledge to their homelands, they stimulated others to the same quest. Then, as the Western mind began to sharpen its tools for reasoning, it began also to demand more sustenance. And to satisfy this hunger, one after another the works of Aristotle were translated—an enormous fund of knowledge, gradually assimilated over a period of centuries. Bewildered and impressed by this knowledge, the Westerners in their humility at first thought him almost superhuman, and with the attitude of faith and reverence customary to them they thought he had known everything, that all they had to do was to recover for themselves what he had known, and elaborate on it. Then came the realization that Aristotle too had made mistakes; his was a master mind, but not omniscient. So they understood that it was Aris-

totle's task to train them in method, but not to give them the finished answers. Not many men had understood this, perhaps, by the close of the Middle Ages; but it was nevertheless the work done by Aristotelians at the universities of Paris and Padua that, as is now known, prepared the way for Galileo, modern mechanics, and all modern science which is based on it—as it was the thorough reworking of Aristotle by St. Thomas Aquinas that was able to make the teachings of Christianity conform to the requirements of natural reason.

From what has been said above it will be seen that it is impossible to characterize medieval culture as being of such or such a kind, for it lacked uniformity. If we say the medievals lacked intellectual curiosity, as we said of the Romans, exceptions at once spring to the mind, and we can see that acceptance of the given world without questioning it was a passing phase. If we say that they were not interested in new knowledge so much as in pondering the old, reading new meanings into it without adding to it, then this attitude too disappeared as reason began to supplant blind faith. If we say they wanted to reconcile all knowledge with the teachings of Christianity, the suggestion of intellectual dishonesty implied in this statement is unfair. Thomas Aquinas undoubtedly believed in Christianity, but he knew that if it was true it *could* not conflict with what reason told him. He did not dishonestly shirk the difficulties, and he honestly tried to resolve them. He was not trying to explain away the findings of his reason in order to bolster an unsound theology. Indeed, he was extremely scrupulous in avoiding the temptation of trying to prove by reason things which he did not think could be proved by it. Naturally, as a medieval Christian, he believed in the creation of the world out of nothing by God; but he was careful to show that Aristotle had not believed in it, and that his reasoning was justified. The story of the Creation was one of the matters which could not be proved, and so must remain in the realm of faith.

Medieval thought, like all thought, was concerned with the problems of the time, and it reflects an honest and not unsuccessful attempt to deal with them within the framework of its presuppositions and assumptions. But, more important, as these assumptions ceased to appear valid, new thinkers arose who grappled with new assumptions and new knowledge. This eagerness for new knowledge is the mark of a living culture, which, in this case, has continued to live and move forward, even into our own time. If the medieval answers no longer seem valid, this is because the compass of our knowledge has been so greatly extended. But it was the medievals who first in our civilization fought for the rights of reason, the medievals who trained us in logic and analysis and gave us our tools of inquiry, the medievals who formed the very language in which we continue to express ourselves and who gave the world the first great masterpieces in every Western European tongue. And since it was also the medievals who taught the world to use representative assemblies to limit the powers of monarchs, it is perhaps time that the word "medieval" cease to be used as a term of abuse for all that we like to think of as reactionary.

❖ Learning and education in the Dark Ages

READING MATERIAL OF THE DARK AGES

We have noted in an earlier chapter that Boethius, a scholar of the reign of Theodoric in Italy, feeling that Latin learning was about to be submerged in a sea of barbarism and that Greek would simply disappear from Western Europe, translated a number of the works of Aristotle into Latin, and wrote some simplified textbooks on a variety of subjects, including arithmetic and music. These books did indeed become a part of the staple intellectual fodder of subsequent generations. But the most widely read of all secular books in the early Middle Ages was undoubtedly the *Etymologies* of St. Isidore, seventh-century bishop of Seville. This was a kind of scrapbook of learning, much of it taken from authors no more reliable than Isidore himself, purporting to be a list of the derivations of words in general use, on which Isidore wasted

considerable ingenuity. The purpose of the good bishop, which was indeed to a large extent fulfilled in his book, was to preserve as much as possible of his own learning for posterity, while presenting it in a language which could be understood by posterity—which he confidently and correctly believed would be less learned and less well educated than he. Perhaps the most original work of this early period was the *Ecclesiastical History of England*, written by the Venerable Bede, an English monk. In this book Bede showed himself to be skilled in historical method, carefully checking his statements and explaining the nature of his sources. Bede also wrote a book on chronology, from which later was taken the method of dating years before and after the birth of Christ (B.C. and A.D.); though most modern scholars believe he made an error in his calculations by which Jesus was held to be born four years after he really was.

THE CAROLINGIAN RENAISSANCE

An important truth is concealed under the grandiloquent term Renaissance, as applied to the age of Charlemagne, for by fostering education he made possible all later advances. In the Merovingian age learning had been seriously neglected. There had been a few writers of note, especially the historian Gregory of Tours, but literacy was becoming ever more rare, and what learning and literacy existed was confined to the clergy. What Charlemagne did was to obtain the services of the few scholars that were available to him and put all the resources of the monarchy to work in improving the education not only of the clergy but of as many laymen as could be accommodated in the schools. He desired at least one cathedral school for every diocese, and he placed the man who may be regarded as his minister of education, Alcuin of York, at the head of his palace school in his capital of Aachen. The curriculum was traditional and was to remain traditional throughout the Middle Ages. What was to be taught were the seven liberal arts, consisting of the *trivium* (grammar—that is, Latin grammar, rhetoric and logic) and the *quadrivium*

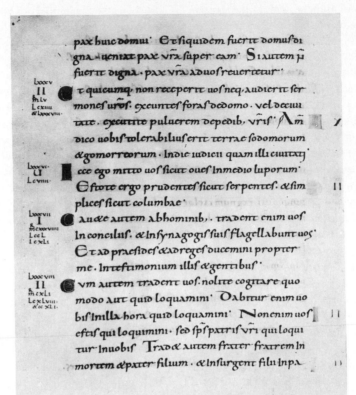

Example of the new manuscript writing which came into vogue during the Carolingian Renaissance and which is the precursor of our ordinary cursive writing. Previously all writing had been done in capital letters. From a late ninth-century manuscript, Evangelia IV (Switzerland ?). (COURTESY THE PIERPONT MORGAN LIBRARY. Ms. 1, folio 29)

(arithmetic, geometry, astronomy, and music). At this early stage of European civilization few of these subjects were actually taught, and even those only in the most simplified form. In later centuries almost any subject that it was desired to teach could be compressed within the compass of the seven arts. Carolingian education, such as it was, consisted fundamentally of a training in literacy and the Latin language. Without these tools there could have been no progress. In the time of Charles there was also an important development in the art of writing. The script known as the Carolingian minuscule, from which came the "Roman" letters used in most European writing thereafter, replaced the "Gothic" script, except in Germany. From the Carolingian script came ultimately those letters which are commonly used today, and which were adopted by printers when printing was first brought into use in Europe.

In the course of the century following the death of Charlemagne the meager advances made in his reign were unable to survive the chaotic political conditions that prevailed in Europe, especially the destructive invasions of the Vikings. The favorite target for the depredations of the Vikings was the monasteries, where the manuscripts from earlier ages were so often preserved. Some culture was to be found at the court of Charles the Bald, grandson of Charlemagne, and the monarch patronized some court poets. The most important figure of this time, however, was the Irishman John Scotus Erigena, who produced the most original work of philosophy of the early Middle Ages. John was still acquainted with Greek and able to translate a work concerning the heavenly hierarchies, or Intelligences, written by a Neoplatonist, which was commented on in later years by Thomas Aquinas and many other medieval theologians. John, in his own work, *De divisione naturae*, developed a complete system of Christian metaphysics patterned after Neoplatonism, a mystical pagan philosophy of the third century A.D., which could have been understood by few in the West in his time. The work was to enjoy some respect in the later Middle Ages, and became sufficiently influential to come for a period under the ban of the Church.

In the next century one name stands out, that of Gerbert of Aurillac, who became pope under the name of Sylvester II (999–1003), and who was in his own day reputed to have sold himself to the Devil in exchange for his learning. Skilled in mathematics and familiar with the Arabic numeral system, as well as with much of the Muslim science of his day, he taught some astronomy and constructed spheres to demonstrate the planets and constellations. Pupils taught by him continued to be interested in Muslim science, and he influenced scholars at the Cathedral School of Chartres to take up seriously for themselves the study of Latin pagan authors. But Gerbert was an isolated figure in his own time, as the legend of his pact with the Devil suggests, though his influence probably long outlasted his life and may have been influential in the growth of interest in the work being done by the Muslims.

❖ **The triumph of reason in theology**

As has been suggested earlier in this chapter, perhaps the most important contribution of the medieval thinkers to Western civilization was the reversal of the opinion held by Gregory I and by the African Fathers of the Church who preceded him, that faith is morally superior to reason, that there is no moral merit in believing what can be proved by reason, and that what God desires of man is faith, rather than knowledge. The human mind, according to these earlier thinkers, is a weak and imperfect instrument, created for man's undoing. Even in the high Middle Ages we find Pope Gregory IX (pope, 1227–1241) instructing the Dominicans not to pursue learning, for there is no merit in believing what can be shown by natural reason to be true. This formidable barrier to the pursuit of knowledge

by natural reason had to be breached before there could be any pursuit of knowledge for its own sake. It was the glory of medieval thinkers that they overcame this obstacle. The manner in which this was done deserves a section to itself even in a book which tries to cover the entire history of Western civilization in one volume, and even though other aspects of medieval thought and culture may have to be given less space than they would, in themselves, merit.

BERENGAR OF TOURS—REASON AND AUTHORITY

One of the first to announce boldly the rights of reason was Berengar of Tours in the eleventh century. Berengar had studied logic at Chartres and had come to the conclusion that it could not be ignored, even in theological discussion. Logic, he said, is nothing but the power of reasoning, and it was by virtue of his reason that man could be said to be made in the image of God. When authority and reason conflict, he added, then it is reason that must be followed. Armed with his new tool, he brashly attacked the doctrine of transubstantiation. There is no apparent difference to any of the senses in the bread and wine after the sacrament of the Eucharist, he said, and therefore no miracle has taken place. This was a remarkable use of logic, which incidentally begs all the questions involved in the difference between spiritual and physical substance and the adequacy of the senses to distinguish between them, and it was unlikely that Berengar would be permitted to announce such doctrines. He was commanded to recant or be declared a heretic. He recanted, but it was hardly a notable defeat for reason itself, for Berengar's use of it was scarcely convincing even to would-be skeptics.

ST. ANSELM OF BEC AND CANTERBURY (1034?–1109)—PROOFS FOR THE EXISTENCE OF GOD

Toward the end of the eleventh century it occurred to St. Anselm, not to *question* the existence of God, but to see whether it was possible by logical demonstration to *prove* this

existence, and so confound all atheists and unbelievers. He made his position quite clear by
explaining that no Christian should doubt any
revealed truth of his religion, but that this
truth should be capable of being made intelligible to man. Some truths were above reason
and should be accepted unconditionally; but
without losing his faith a Christian might
nevertheless seek to understand as far as his
fallible reason could take him. Anselm and all
medieval Christians believed that there could
be no contradiction between reason and the
truths of revelation; but the opening of the
whole subject to discussion was a dangerous
path, as was realized by some thinkers even
in the eleventh century. For the time might
come when an irreconcilable conflict might
occur. What, then, was to be done? Abandon
what reason seemed to demonstrate, or what
the Christian revelation had taught for centuries? For Anselm faith came first ("I do
not seek to understand in order that I may
believe, but I believe in order that I may understand"); but this position was soon to be
reversed by other Christians, as faithful and
sincere as himself.

Using his logic, Anselm tried to prove the
existence of God. His argument that every
mind can conceive of the greatest possible
being, and that this being, to be really greatest,
must also have existence, which is known as
the "ontological" argument for the existence
of God, need not detain us. But it is of the utmost significance that at this moment in the
eleventh century a Christian saint and archbishop should have thought it either possible
or valuable to be able to prove the existence
of God, and it shows that the era was passing
in which it was morally superior to believe
without seeking for proof.

ABÉLARD—"I SEEK TO UNDERSTAND IN ORDER THAT I MAY BELIEVE."

With the great teacher and critic Peter
Abélard (1079–1142), the first phase of the
struggle for the rights of reason was completed. A man of clear incisive thinking,
potentially a skeptic though remaining formally true to his Christian faith, he made a

contribution of the utmost significance to
medieval thought. Few men in the whole history of thought have been so influential as he,
in spite of the fact that he was in no way a
creative thinker. But his penetrating logic and
clear exposition attracted thousands of students to his lectures, and started them working
in a direction from which there was never to
be any return.

Driven out of Paris after an unfortunate
love affair with Héloïse, he escaped to a monastery for a while, then returned to teaching
but got into trouble with the Church because
of his divergent views on the Trinity. Even
in a desolate rural retreat, students followed
him. The significance of this extraordinary
popularity was that he was teaching them to
think, and to doubt. His most famous book,
called *Sic et Non* (*Yes and No*), is typical of
his method, and permits us to understand what
his students found so fascinating. He thought
it was the duty of a Christian to use his reason
even on the substance of theology. He was the
first to point out clearly that the Fathers of
the Church, who were accepted as authorities, had themselves been in doubt, and that
there were contradictory opinions on theological subjects even among these authorities.
Abélard did not conclude that the Fathers
did not know what they were talking about,
but rather that there were reasonable grounds
for doubting where the truth lay. What he
proceeded to do, therefore, was to list a number of important theological questions, and
then draw up the various opinions that the
Fathers had held about them. Sometimes the
contradictions could be reconciled, but more
often the only thing to do was to accept the
best authority. But, above all, the student must
work out the answer for himself, for only by
doubting could there be any inquiry, and only
by inquiry could one come to truth.

This was already a reversal of the position taken by St. Anselm. Abélard wished
to arrive at belief through the process of
doubting and trying to understand. Faith no
longer was primary, and indeed, implicitly,
was an enemy to understanding. Abélard had
firmly planted the seed of honest and disinterested inquiry, and suggested that the way to

resolve a problem was to think about it, not to see what had been thought about it by some great man in the past, whose opinion had afterward been accepted as authoritative by the Church. Only after one had tried to reason it out for oneself should one have recourse to some predecessor, whose other work had entitled him to be considered as an authority in theology.

REACTION OF THE CHURCH TO THE METHOD OF ABÉLARD

Abélard was unfortunate in being opposed, in his own generation, by so severe a critic and such a sworn foe of human reason as the mystic St. Bernard, of whom we have already spoken in an earlier chapter. Bernard at once saw the danger and pursued Abélard bitterly all his life. If human reason were to triumph, there would be no mystery left. "He thinks himself able by human reason to understand God, completely," Bernard charged. He accused Abélard of pride and arrogance in thinking that man with his puny mind could ever comprehend the mysteries of faith, and he did not hesitate to accuse him of heresy in questioning authority, and arriving at conclusions contrary to those held by the Church. By his influence he was able to have Abélard condemned to silence, although it is doubtful whether he could have sustained the conviction at Rome, whither Abélard was going to defend himself when he died.

But Bernard was already behind the times, and the victory lay with his opponent. One of Abélard's own pupils, Peter Lombard, bishop of Paris, using his master's method, became the teacher of generations of churchmen; his book of the *Sentences* became the standard text for theology for centuries and is still not altogether outmoded today. Fundamentally, any opponent of Abélard must take the untenable position that Christianity is contrary to reason. For if it is not contrary, then reason can only serve to support faith, and help to convert the doubting or the unbelievers.

Nevertheless, for centuries there was opposition to the use of even Peter Lombard's book. In the process of discussing theological questions by the use of reason, there was a natural tendency to escape from essential Christianity as it was revealed in the Gospels. Well on into the thirteenth century we find complaints that theological students were wasting their time studying logic and learning to resolve knotty points of doctrine, rather than learning to preach the way of salvation and the teachings of Christ.

THE DEVELOPED SCHOLASTIC METHOD OF PETER LOMBARD

Systematic theology in the hands of Peter Lombard became, following his master Abélard, a discussion of important theological questions. The teacher would propound a question, as, for instance, whether God created the world out of nothing himself or through "intelligences." The discussion therefore always starts with *Utrum*—Whether. The following step is to take the authorities who have spoken in favor of the proposition—*Quod sic videtur,* For it seems so. The arguments will be listed clearly, and perhaps disposed of, at once, if there is an inherent contradiction. Then the arguments on the other side will be taken. *Sed contra*—But, on the other hand. Finally, the master will try to reconcile the difficulties in his own *Solutio,* which carries no authority beyond the weight of the particular master's name. These solutions are the master's *Sententiae* or Opinions (hence the title of Peter's book, the *Sentences*). It became the custom at the universities where theology was taught for every student to dispute publicly on these questions, and to give his opinions. Thus from many masters of theology in the thirteenth century we possess *Commentaries on the Sentences*, which are usually a publication of their opinions given on disputed questions during their period of study. They thus represent something close to the doctoral dissertations of our own day.

The method is intellectually of the utmost honesty, for no one was allowed to propound opinions in this public manner which relied on anything except the best that reason could offer. Though authorities were used, the master's solution had to be his own or at least one that appealed to reason and itself reconciled the conflicting opinions. It was not, in the last analysis, the weight of authority that decided the question for the successors of Peter Lombard, but the best opinion available at the time; and this is how all questions are decided in a free world.

THE RECOVERY OF ARISTOTLE IN MUSLIM GUISE

While this new method in theology was being developed, Muslim Spain was gradually being reconquered. When Toledo was captured in the middle of the twelfth century, it was discovered that the Muslims had translated into Arabic many works of the great Greek philosophers that had hitherto been unknown to the West. In particular, the major works of Aristotle were available in Arabic, together with commentaries by Muslim philosophers. In view of the paucity of such materials in the West, the archbishop of Toledo authorized a number of translations, and for a time Toledo was the center of a considerable intellectual activity. Gerard of Cremona (died 1187) is said to have translated himself no fewer than seventy-three works from the Arabic. These new works rapidly became available in Christian centers of learning, especially in the schools that preceded the University of Paris, which was formally opened as a university in 1200.

Professors and students were evidently delighted to recover Aristotle almost in his entirety, a fact which in turn stimulated some to acquire more manuscripts of Aristotle from Constantinople. But the Church was not so content, especially when a number of teachers began to utter opinions that it deemed heretical, on the authority of Aristotle. In 1209 the archbishop of Sens, within whose archdiocese Paris was situated, condemned a number of opinions derived, as he believed, from Aristotle, and forbade public lecturing on his works in the natural sciences. The truth was not so much that Aristotle had made statements that were, or could be considered, heretical, but that his method lent itself to rational exposition. Aristotle had not believed in the creation of the world; it is doubtful whether he believed in the immortality of the soul—not, at all events, in the sense in which it was believed by Christians. Gregory IX ordered his works to be expurgated, but the commission he appointed never seems to have completed its task—in any case an impossible one, since the secular and rational method, rather than any particular conclusions, was to blame. Anyone who used the Aristotelian method was likely to come to not dissimilar conclusions.

Aristotle was already suspect because his works had been translated by the Muslims, and the Muslims were suspected of having altered him to suit their own faith. But in 1230 Michael Scotus completed a translation of the great commentary on Aristotle by Averroës, the Spanish Muslim philosopher referred to briefly in Chapter 8, who had died as late as the end of the twelfth century. Averroës' work was scarcely known to the Muslims at all. The philosopher had indeed been persecuted by his co-religionists, and had defended himself by stating that there was a "double truth," one truth accessible to reason and another to faith, which might be contradictory to one another—or apparently so. Among other things Averroës had come to the conclusion that Aristotle had believed in collective and not individual immortality, that the "active intellect" of man, his immortal part, returned to the active intellect of the world, the world mind, after death. Such a doctrine, it may be imagined, was extremely painful to Christians, although it became popular with students in the universities of Paris and Padua, who may have preferred that there should be no individual immortal soul. So Averroës and his commentaries joined Aristotle as forbidden to good Christians.

THE ESTABLISHMENT OF ARISTOTELIANISM AS FOUNDATION OF CHRISTIAN THEOLOGY —ALBERTUS MAGNUS AND THOMAS AQUINAS

The ban on Aristotle seems to have been rather indifferently observed, and to have lapsed during the period when the papacy was quarreling with the emperor Frederic II, as recounted in Chapter 10. But Averroism, as it came to be called—the doctrine of the double truth and of collective immortality—grew powerful, especially in the faculty of arts at Paris. Meanwhile the greatest scientist of the thirteenth century, Albertus Magnus, had conceived the idea that Aristotle could be used to aid the Christian faith rather than to subvert it. Though a self-taught man and not a renowned theologian, he wrote an exposition of Aristotle in which he attempted to show that Aristotle, rightly understood, would bring reason to bear on religion, and show that the basic doctrines of Christianity could in fact be *proved* by the use of natural reason. Albert's leading pupil, Thomas Aquinas, wrote a number of important works in which he used Aristotle's arguments and method to prove, as he believed, the existence of God, and the qualities of God. A work of impeccable logic if the basic premises are accepted, Thomas' *Summa theologica* represents the high-water-mark of medieval scholarship. It is perhaps the supreme achievement in human thought of a purely rational nature, without reference to observable facts in the world, but spun entirely out of the unaided human reason.

Thomas held that the vast majority of religious truths could be discovered by man by means of reason. But there must, in his view, always remain some truths that could not be discovered in this way. It was impossible, for instance, for man to arrive at the mystery of the Holy Trinity for himself; such knowledge had to be revealed by God. But Thomas wished to grant as much as possible to the reason, and reason should also be used to try to make intelligible those things which had been revealed. Man could not, according to St. Thomas, arrive for certain by natural reason at the conclusion that the world had been created out of nothing by God; but once this had been revealed to him by the Scriptures, then it was possible and proper for man to try to understand for himself the means of creation, and to see that it was reasonable. So the triumph of reason was complete. Revelation was necessary as a supplement, and this required faith from man, which faith was at once to be supplemented by reason. Medieval thought had moved a very long way indeed

from St. Bernard in not much more than a century.

Thomas was not particularly successful in his own time. The quarrels in the University of Paris continued. Even a tremendous polemic written by Thomas in 1270 against Averroism did not convince its proponents. Finally the bishop of Paris, in 1277, drew up a huge list of errors which, he declared, must not be taught in Paris. Among these were some of Thomas' own doctrines as well as those of his Averroist opponents. The University of Oxford soon afterward followed the Parisian lead, and it was clear that the attack must have been authorized by Rome. It was also widely believed that the Franciscans, perennial rivals of the Dominicans, had used their influence to condemn the teachings of Thomas, the leading light of the Dominican Order, at the same time as the Averroist doctrines.

But Thomas, Albert, and the movement they represented were not without influence at Rome. Devoted Dominicans kept the ear of successive popes, evidently impressing on them how great an aid to faith the work of the two Dominican masters could be. In 1328 they succeeded in having Thomas Aquinas canonized as a saint. His works from that time on became authoritative, and Thomas himself acquired the name of Doctor Angelicus. Every article in his works is a miracle, declared the pope in his bull authorizing the canonization.

But the Franciscans, especially those at Oxford—who, as we shall see, early took an interest in science—were far from content; and two considerable theologians and philosophers, at the end of the thirteenth century and during the next, denied the whole possibility of attaining truth by the means advocated by St. Thomas Aquinas. Like most Franciscans, they believed in divine illumination of the human mind, and, following St. Augustine, insisted on the mind's incompetence, especially in the field of religion. Duns Scotus (died 1308) denied categorically that it was possible to prove the existence of God, the immortality of the soul, and such truths of religion by reason. The only possible approach to the truths of religion was by faith and meditation. William of Occam (died 1349) took substantially the same line, denying the ability of human reason in heavenly matters but emphasizing it in earthly things. William insisted that the great universal ideas and abstractions of Thomas had no real validity, and that ideas were only names which described objects of experience in a convenient way. Ideas therefore are applicable only to things of the sense world revealed by experience, and it is only in this realm that reason and its logic are competent. William's influence in his own century was considerable, and his followers, especially at the University of Paris, for a time became interested in a number of scientific questions. They hoped to find answers to these by reason, and they to some degree neglected theology.

It will be noted that these men denied the competence of logic and reason only in religion; they did not deny its competence altogether, as St. Bernard would have done, nor did they suggest that its use was likely to lead to the deadly sin of pride. The form of their criticism therefore is the surest sign that reason had at last emerged as the greatest of human faculties, limited indeed, but powerful as an instrument for discovering the truth about the created world. The way lay open for the scientific achievements of Western civilization.

❖ Medieval science

The medievals, as is well known, were not conspicuous for their scientific interest, and few discoveries in the scientific realm can be attributed to them. Indeed, there is a characteristic medieval attitude toward the realm of nature which militated against scientific discovery in our sense. This attitude it is essential to understand if one is to have a grasp of that abstraction known as the medieval mind. Greater attention will therefore be given to it here than would be warranted if we were interested solely in listing positive accomplishments. Even so, these accomplishments are far from negligible, though pale by comparison with those of the modern age. After all, the main interests of the Middle Ages lay elsewhere.

Although there were several important scientists who obtained a fair knowledge of Muslim science as early as the twelfth century, it may be safely said that there was no really important medieval science before the recovery of Aristotle, and that medieval scientific theory was always Aristotelian, though made as far as possible to accommodate itself to Christian theology. Most medieval scientists were, indeed, more addicted to theorizing than to practical experimentation, whereas modern science is distinguished by its very lack of a comprehensive general theory. We have minor limited theories in the special sciences, but none to cover the whole field of science. Vaguely, we believe that science ought to be useful to mankind in rather obvious ways, such as prolonging life, minimizing pain, increasing pleasure; and we believe, equally vaguely, that it is a good thing to have more knowledge and understanding about the world we live in.

The medievals started from the opposite standpoint. They believed they knew why we are on earth in the first place, the relationship of the soul to the body, the relationship of man to the universe, the purposes served by the animals and plants; they had all the answers to those questions which we think it illegitimate to ask because science is incompetent to deal with them. So-called laws of nature, discovered by induction, were not interesting to them because nature itself, as a conception, was unacceptable. God was the lawgiver, and laws of nature were God's laws, which were entirely under his control, and with which he could interfere as often as he wished. At any moment a miracle might happen which would invalidate a law. A relic of a saint, or a suitable prayer offered in the right quarters, might be able to cure a dangerous disease in a moment, or rain could appear out of a cloudless sky. What was the use of trying to discover the mundane causes of a disease or of studying the science of meteorology?

Every medieval scientist had to struggle with these commonly accepted assumptions of his age; hence it was a great step forward when Albertus Magnus proclaimed that God works through natural causes which can be investigated, implying that in the ordinary

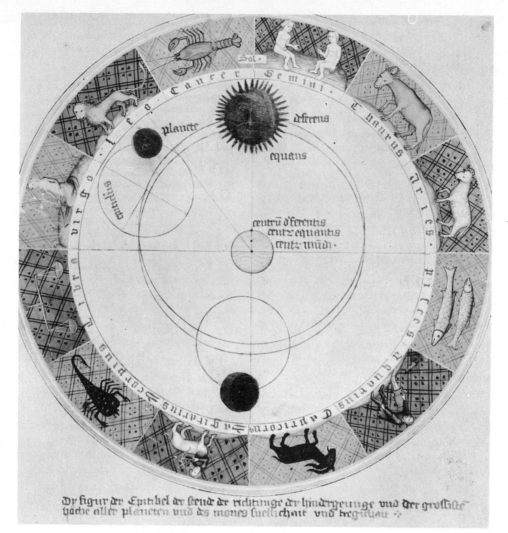

A sphere depicting the signs of the zodiac, the earth, the deferent and equant circles in which the sun and moon's epicycles move, and the epicycles of the planets. In the original, which is an illustration from the famous medieval textbook The Sphere, *by John of Sacrobosco, the signs of the zodiac are upon alternating green and rose-red grounds in the outer circle. The sun and planets are shown in gold, and the moon in silver.* (COURTESY THE PIERPONT MORGAN LIBRARY. Ms. 722, folio 18)

course of affairs God does not interfere, but allowing him freedom to do so if he wishes. Adopting such an attitude, and performing serious investigation, it would not be too long before a scientist noticed the extreme rarity of miracles, and went ahead without paying too much attention to their possibility.

But it was not so easy to escape from the leading strings imposed by the more respectable philosophy and science of the Greeks and the Muslims. Astrology was not, to the medievals, an unscientific aberration, as it is to modern scientists. It was based on the understanding (derived from Plato via Avicenna) that the relationship of man to the universe is as the microcosm (or little world) to the macrocosm (the great world). Man, in Plato's phrase, is a lesser world. Everything in the heavens is reflected in man. A planet seen in the heavens is also present in concentrated form in the organs of man—Saturn, for instance, in his spleen, and Venus in his kidneys.

The plant also is directly connected with the planets, the blue-colored flower with Saturn, the yellow with Jupiter, the red with Mars. Thus a knowledge of the heavens is essential for a true understanding of man himself, and is not just a separate science to be studied for its own sake. Astronomy might be a branch of mathematics, but it was also a part of psychology and medicine. A knowledge of the movements of the planets, and their position in the heavens, was therefore of the utmost importance for man, since, in the medieval phrase, superiors (in the heavens) ruled inferiors (on earth); and not only man but all his doings were subject to the decrees of the heavens, which themselves, according to those who remembered their Christianity, expressed the will of God (Neoplatonists and Avicenna had indeed speculated as to whether the stars were not, in fact, gods).

Moreover, every man at birth was an exact image of the cosmos at the moment of his birth; and if the cosmos could be read at that moment, then the physiology and psychology of the man could be exactly determined. Hence the importance of ascertaining the exact hour of birth and casting a horoscope. Up to this point medieval thinkers were in agreement. But there was considerable dispute on how all this affected the free will of man, and whether what was called judicial astrology was equally true and permissible. For it might also be possible to determine the path of life for man; and, as the heavens were perfect and unchangeable, this looked as if the path of man's life was likewise unchangeable and determined from his birth. After the great age of rationalism in the thirteenth century was over, judicial astrology, appealing to the superstitions of mankind then as now, became ever more popular. Philosophers produced a theory that the movements of the planets paralleled the life of man but did not determine it, thus saving free will; and horoscopes continued to be cast for centuries with only sporadic opposition, at one time being the major interest of the majority of scientists of the day, who, like Paracelsus, found as late as the sixteenth century that at the least the casting of horoscopes provided them with a living, allowing them leisure to engage in other and more worth-while pursuits.

Biology was dominated throughout the medieval period by Aristotle, whose biological theories could be made to conform to the Christian idea of divine Providence. Aristotle had produced a very comprehensive set of observations, most of them extremely accurate. But he had not been content with this; he had also tied them together with a remarkable theory whose central observation was that "nature does nothing in vain." Nothing in the living world exists without a purpose that can be understood by the unaided human mind. The phenomena themselves needed to be investigated for the purpose of adding to human knowledge (Aristotle had begun his *Metaphysics* with the dictum that "all men by nature desire to know"), but once they had been investigated, they could be understood in terms of purposes. If it were seen that a mistletoe grew on an oak tree, then the *how* of this phenomenon did not need to be investigated, though of course it could be if desired. Aristotle himself might very well also have investigated how it is nourished and how it maintains itself, and what effect it has on the tree. But in order to understand the mistletoe, one need only ask why it is there. And the answer might be, in natural terms, that it relieves the tree of some of its evil humors, or alternatively, and more probably, that it sucks the life out of the tree; or, in human terms, it might exist as an example of the evils of parasitism, and thus serve man as a moral symbol. Or it might exist because mistletoe was necessary for man and the tree was as convenient a place as any for nature to put it. But of one thing the medieval man could be certain: It must serve some real purpose in the total economy of nature, which included man. Roger Bacon was once called upon to answer the question whether plants feel. In Aristotelian terms the answer, to us insoluble, was not difficult. The purpose served by feeling, he replied, is to enable one to move either toward or away from an object exciting it (sympathy and antipathy). A plant is stationary and cannot move. Therefore feeling would be unnecessary to a plant, and nature would have given feeling to it in vain. But nature does nothing in vain. Therefore the plant cannot feel. Q.E.D.

It is clear that the supposed understanding of purposes in nature would conduce to reverence for the divine Providence which had ordered all things in this beneficent way; but it would not tend to encourage investigation of how they actually worked, and it would certainly inhibit our modern practice of manipulating natural things for human ends. As long as this attitude remained, there could be no practical or applied science.

But medieval practice in time became much better than its theory. We do not find any thinker in medieval times urging the usefulness of knowledge and encouraging scientists to investigate for the purpose of alleviating man's lot on earth, though Roger Bacon does emphasize usefulness of knowledge for theology and for helping kings to defeat their enemies. It was a later Bacon, Francis, who in the seventeenth century for the first time sounded the clarion call for scientific investigation to improve man's ordinary life. But we do find medieval scientists encouraging experiments, if only in the hopes of proving theories which they could never have proved since they were demonstrably false. We find a number of experiments being made, though as a rule in an unplanned manner. We find the spirit of criticism growing, and serious efforts to escape from the authority of Aristotle, and we find it gradually becoming natural not to take things for granted without testing by experience. We find, in short, the native curiosity of man escaping from the fetters imposed upon it by a premature belief that everything that was worth knowing was already known. It can hardly be claimed that the Middle Ages were among the great ages of science, but, as in other fields, they were preparing quietly and diligently for the future.

Among a host of names of medieval scientists only four will be discussed here— Robert Grosseteste, Albertus Magnus, Roger Bacon, and the emperor Frederic II. Robert Grosseteste (d. 1253), bishop of Lincoln in England, within whose diocese was the University of Oxford, taught at Oxford for several years and lectured, especially to the Franciscans, on scientific subjects. Grosseteste in some ways was the most important of medieval scientists, in that he devoted much of his thought to the manner in which theory, observation, and experiment are related. He set forth clearly the procedures necessary for the disproving of hypotheses by logical analysis and experimentation, a very necessary task in the medieval world; and he outlined an experimental procedure which could take account of new facts and place them within a proper conceptual framework. Grosseteste was almost the first medieval thinker who perceived the importance of mathematics for providing a rational explanation of the universe. The Platonic strand of his thought is clearly visible in the importance he gives to mathematics, as also in his belief in divine illumination as the sole means for obtaining metaphysical certainty. Yet all his work demonstrates his thorough grasp of the most difficult of the logical works of Aristotle, especially the *Posterior Analytics,* on which he wrote a commentary. Grosseteste was especially interested in the phenomenon of light, which he spoke of as the "first corporeal form."

His work as a teacher proved to be extremely influential in the centuries that followed, especially among the Franciscans. Roger Bacon was thoroughly familiar with his works, though a comparison between the two men shows Grosseteste as the more scientific, in our sense, of the two. Bacon certainly owes his understanding of the role of experience and experiment in the attainment of knowledge to Grosseteste; but Grosseteste appears to have limited the role of divine illumination more strictly than his successor. From Grosseteste through Bacon and other thirteenth-century scientists and the Averroists at Padua there is a clear line of thought down to the great theoretical and experimental scientists of the seventeenth century on the relation between thought and experimentation, which became ultimately *the* scientific method of Western civilization. In the medieval period experimentation was a new thing, quite distinct from the scientific method of antiquity. Though Bacon is often given most of the credit for it, it is to the work of Robert Grosseteste above all that we must look if we wish to discover its origin in the Middle Ages.

Albertus Magnus (1193?–1280) was a comprehensive investigator of nature, who understood the value of experiment even though he is not known to have conducted any advanced experiments of his own. His method was to be critical of everything he was told and to try to find the natural causes behind all phenomena. Aristotle, in the view of Albert, could be wrong; it was well to check what Aristotle had said, especially anything that looked like an old wives' tale. As mentioned already, much of Albert's work is related to his effort to show that Aristotle could be reconciled with Christianity. But in this work of reconciliation Albert constantly made digressions, and it is these digressions on his observations that constitute the main evidence for his scientific acumen and learning. He himself was a first-rate observer of plants, and he wrote a book on mineralogy; in both these fields he surpassed his master, who was not especially skilled in either science. It is evident that Albert, like most medieval scientists, tried to gain as comprehensive a view of nature as he could. Bacon criticizes Albert for his ignorance of mathematics and optics—a criticism which would be pointless in our time, when a botanist and mineralogist, and even a student of chemistry or alchemy such as Albert, would hardly be expected to know physics very thoroughly as well.

Roger Bacon (1214?–1292?) is best known for a famous compendium of scientific knowledge which he wrote for Pope Clement IV in the hopes of persuading the pope to take an interest in and to subsidize the study of science. It is a bad-tempered work, full of criticisms of other scientists for their failure to experiment and to check the popular superstitions of the day, for their failure to appreciate the work of the Muslims in science, and for their use of bad translations of Aristotle. Bacon's own viewpoint was both modern and typically medieval—modern in that he insisted that all theories should be tested by what he spoke of as the "science of experience," and medieval in that he believed that

all knowledge had been revealed to Seth, the son of Adam, then to Solomon, as recorded in the Bible; that it had been diluted in the process of being transmitted from these great men to the pygmies of his own time; and that a good moral character was the first prerequisite for receiving a revelation from God. Nevertheless, Bacon did a good deal of experimenting in optics, publicized the work of other investigators, and described many of the speculations and experiments of his own time. He is not now believed to have made any substantial discoveries of his own, although his alert mind and his undoubted scientific interest, combined with a talent for exposition, won him a reputation in later centuries as a magician, and, in very recent times, as the only true scientist of his age, far ahead of all others—a view which Bacon himself quite possibly shared. He gained little reputation while he was alive, and led an uncomfortable life as a Franciscan friar—probably as a result of his character and disposition rather than of any distaste or dislike for science by his order, still less as a result of any persecution for his unorthodox scientific views.

Frederic II (1194–1250) was a many-sided genius. We have already had occasion to note his long quarrel with the papacy, and have mentioned his predisposition to freethinking. This freethinking and skepticism he carried over into his scientific pursuits. He was frequently critical of Aristotle, especially of the intrusion of moral preconceptions into his observations. Many experiments are attributed to Frederic. He is said to have weighed a dying man before and after his death to see whether there was any measurable evidence for the existence of a soul that escaped at death; he was accused of having killed two men, one after exercise and one after rest, subsequently examining their intestines to see which had digested his food more thoroughly. The account of these experiments comes from his enemies; what we do know for certain is that he wrote a book *On the Art of Hunting with Birds*, which is one of the best works on falconry ever written, and contains very careful and accurate ornithological observations.

Frederic dissected birds himself and described his observations, and he used his royal resources to gather together information and specimens from beyond his own dominions. There is no sign anywhere in his book of any preoccupation with medieval scientific theory or any acceptance of unconfirmed statements or explanations. His book, even today, is entirely reliable as far as it goes. In this respect it is unique among medieval works known to us, although a small book on the magnet by Peter de Maricourt, a friend of Roger Bacon, comes close to meriting similar praise.

In the fourteenth century science made perhaps more progress than in the thirteenth, as it became more interested in the explanation of observed phenomena. For example, considerable attention was given at the University of Paris to a problem which arose out of the new use of gunpowder and projectiles. Aristotle's theory of motion (that all motion is communicated motion from an initial "mover") was soon seen to be unsatisfactory. It could not adequately explain why a projectile fired from a gun should move at a higher speed when fired than a few seconds later, nor why it should describe a parabola when falling to the earth. A scientist named Jean Buridan suggested the idea of "impetus," a step in the right direction, though the problem was not solved till Galileo solved it by a combination of theory and experiment with inclined planes. Nicholas of Oresme, a bishop, began to question the theory of the movement of the sun around the earth, accepted by nearly all medievals on the authority of the Hellenistic scientist Ptolemy. But, more important, Nicholas liked to use diagrams for the illustration of theological problems. In the process he hit upon the idea of coordinates and curves to show the relation between two variables, thus anticipating by centuries the invention of analytical geometry. At the University of Padua the Averroists, driven forth from Paris at the end of the thirteenth century after the condemnation of their philosophical findings, found a refuge under the protection of Venice. There, among much speculation on the immortality of the soul and similar dogmas, they devoted themselves to mathematics, being interested, like the Parisians, especially in the study of acceleration. It was probably at Padua that the first serious work was done in the use of Arabic numerals, which had been introduced to the West as early as 1202 by Leonardo of Pisa, but had not at first attracted much attention. It was the work done at Padua over several centuries that prepared the ground for the great advances of Galileo, which ushered in the age of modern science.

❖ **Medieval education**

It has already been noted that as early as the time of Charlemagne the curriculum of the schools was restricted to the seven liberal arts. This curriculum was carried over into the medieval university, a direct forerunner of our own universities, which have preserved even to our own time many medieval customs. The leading medieval university, though not the oldest, was the University of Paris, which had a faculty of arts where students obtained the degree of master of arts, usually about the age of 21. They could then become teaching masters or continue with higher education. The most difficult degree, and the most sought after until at least the fourteenth century, was the doctorate in theology, which could not be granted before the age of 35 and required, as a rule, about fourteen years of rigorous study, mostly in logical analysis and disputing. Medieval education was not very strong in subject matter, but the trained master was thoroughly efficient in reasoning and argument, even if, from our point of view, much of his intellectual energy was spent in the art of making fine distinctions.

The University of Paris was controlled by its own faculty. Not so the University of Bologna, which had sprung up initially as a law school for the purpose of training students in the Roman law and the canon law, which was based upon the Roman. The university owed its beginning to a lawyer who rediscovered and reintroduced to the West the *Digest* of Justinian, upon which he offered comments (glosses) and changes to bring it into accord with European custom and law.

He retained those principles of Roman law that were manifestly superior to Germanic law, which was singularly deficient in what might be termed legal principles. Most of the students who went to Bologna desired to grasp as much Roman law as they could within the limited time they had available. Probably the majority were mature men, and they were seriously interested in gaining their education so that they could find or return to good jobs within the Church or in royal chanceries, where the Roman law (which, as will be remembered, naturally tended to exalt the power of the monarch over local customs and precedents) was held in high esteem. The professors were acceptable to the students only insofar as they delivered what the students felt they needed. The university was thus largely directed by the students, the consumers of education. It was the professors who had to band together to prevent themselves from being exploited by the students, who, on occasion, did not hesitate to fine them or cut their salaries.

Probably the oldest university in Europe, outside Spain (whose University of Cordova was organized on very different lines), was Salerno in Italy, originally a medical school. In the fourteenth and fifteenth centuries the universities spread all over Europe. The color map in this chapter will give some indication of their distribution. The majority of the universities, including those of Oxford and Cambridge, were organized according to the Parisian model. The Parisian model was also used for those universities which sprang up beyond the seas, including those of the United States of America. But in a few instances where conditions were comparable to those of Bologna that model was also used with modifications.

❖ **Medieval art**

The greatest artistic glory of the Middle Ages in Europe is undoubtedly the Gothic cathedral, and the bulk of the small space we can devote to medieval art will be devoted to it. There was sculpture, mostly in the churches, since the portrayal of the human form was not forbidden to the Christian, as it was to

the Jew and the Muslim. The figures of saints had to follow an approved and customary style, but within this convention it was possible to give life and character to the figures. It was possible to decorate capitals and pillars with scenes from nature, closely observed and accurately rendered, as in the famous "vintage" capitals of the cathedral of Reims. But architecture, above all church building, overshadows all other medieval artistic achievements, although the development of church music runs it a close second.

THE ROMANESQUE

In the Dark Ages there was very little building beyond the mere provision of places of worship. The Germanic peoples had had no experience in building such edifices as churches, and skill and materials were lacking. Such building as there was consisted for the most part of wooden churches, easily destroyed by fire, and later churches built of stone but with wooden roofs, also easily destroyed by fire, as the Vikings proved. The plan of all medieval churches in early times was derived from the Roman basilica, or meeting place, modified to meet the needs of worshipers in a Christian church. The general plan was to have three aisles, the center aisle called the nave, separated from each other by arcades of arches, capitals, and columns. The walls were solid, and light was provided only by small windows set in a clerestory above the nave. At the end of the nave, where the Romans had usually built a semicircular apse in which the presiding officer had his seat, the Christians placed their altar. The apse, by religious custom, faced the East. In time it became necessary to enlarge this apse in order to contain the choir, and transepts were added by the side of the aisles, bringing the whole church into the form of a Latin cross.

The great difficulty to be overcome, as has been suggested, was the danger of fire on account of the wooden roof. The Romans had not been content with wooden roofs but built them of stone and concrete. The early medievals knew that the Romans had used vaults of different kinds for their roofs, but for many centuries the Christians were unable to build vaults in such a way that the walls were strong enough to hold them. The thrust and weight of the Roman vaults necessitated very strong walls, and if the walls were very massive, then it was dangerous to pierce them for windows. We know of many early medieval buildings which indeed did collapse while the architects experimented with different kinds of vaults. Cross vaults were used for the smaller areas; while the nave itself had to be roofed, as a rule, with a massive barrel vault. But this doomed the church to shortage of light and only the smallest of windows, owing to the great weight of the roof. Moreover, the height of the church was severely limited by the weight to be supported.

This Romanesque style was capable of modification, therefore, but only within certain well-defined limits. Many of the problems were indeed solved, especially by the Norman builders of the eleventh century, but certain fundamental changes were necessary if a church was to be able to soar to heaven, and be filled with light, as the builders themselves would have wished. It should be emphasized that such changes as took place were figured out by the architects and craftsmen actually on the job. It was impossible in medieval times to work out in advance, as do modern architects, the theoretical stresses to which the various parts of the building would be submitted, and there was much trial and error before the immense difficulties were overcome.

But there was an enormous demand for churches. Every bishop desired to have a great church in his diocese, and an enthusiasm and local patriotism amounting almost to a mania set in during the eleventh and twelfth centuries. The buildings were nearly always raised by cooperative labor, in which every person in the area joined, some yoking themselves to the cart which carried the materials needed for the church and pulling it, while priests chanted and prayed. Throughout the day psalms and canticles were sung, relics of the saints were brought along, and miracles were hourly expected. It was the same religious enthusiasm that was responsible for the success of the First Crusade.

THE GOTHIC STYLE—POINTED ARCHES AND FLYING BUTTRESSES

The Gothic style, which solved the outstanding problems of the Romanesque, was developed almost entirely in northern France, though spreading into Germany and elsewhere afterward. The use of the pointed arch, which distributes the weight differently from the rounded arch and the vault, was the key to the new style. It was soon discovered that an entirely different system of ribbing and support was possible with the pointed arch, which took the weight off the walls and gave the builder freedom to alter the shape of his church as required. The developed Gothic church is nothing but a gigantic skeleton of wall buttresses within the church, flying buttresses outside it, piers and ribbing, all in perfect equilibrium; the walls themselves now cease to be of importance and can be made even of glass. And the best Gothic churches are indeed full of glass, stained glass colored and painted to show whatever scenes the artist wished. And usually over the portal was the great rose window, which was so designed that it lighted the church in a different way at the different hours of the day. Early stained glass was always in solid colors, set into lead frames as a kind of mosaic, with figures suggested by these frames and small, lightly penciled touches. Medieval stained glass was one of the age's greatest achievements, and has never been equaled, even in modern times, with all the advantages of modern technical inventions.

The Gothic church, with its soaring arches aspiring toward heaven, has often been compared with the logical structure of the great medieval *Summae*, those works in which medieval theologians attempted to set forth the whole plan of salvation, tied together by the Aristotelian syllogism; and the comparison is not inept, for the Gothic structures are faultlessly worked out, with perfect balance, each part dependent upon the other, and, in the best examples, free of any unnecessary decoration or striving for effect. The façades of the cathedrals could be and were decorated, and it was here that the sculptor was given a chance to display his mastery—especially in and over the portals, where saints, devils, plants, and animals real and mythological could be shown, and even the Last Judgment. Inside the cathedrals, especially in the wonderful Cathedral of Chartres, the artist was free to fill the windows with scenes from the Old and New Testaments and stories from the lives of saints, with delicate pencil work touching up the solid-colored panes of glass. Even scenes of everyday life are depicted in these windows, scenes often provided by the particular guild represented. The last details of the work, whether inside and visible, or high up on the towers where no man could see them once they had been set in position, were almost invariably beautifully and honestly wrought. The medieval craftsman, like the Greek craftsman of the time of Phidias, would not have tolerated anything less than the best he could give in the service of his religion and art.

In a book of this kind it is not worth while to attempt the description of these Gothic masterpieces, since the bare words will do no justice to them, and mean little to those who have not viewed them. The accompanying pictures are inadequate, but they may suggest what the written word cannot, and the special features of the style can be picked out with the aid of the brief remarks printed under each picture. There is no perfect cathedral. Some cathedrals have features that seem to approach perfection, as the fan vaulting in Westminster Abbey, the façade and *chevet* of Notre Dame of Paris, the structural design of Amiens, the incomparable majesty of the site of Reims, and the interior of Chartres. But in every cathedral there are some dissident elements, the necessary consequence of the long time consumed in the building. The building of a cathedral might take fifty years. Yet the style was living, always growing and evolving, so that the builders who completed the edifice would be working in a different manner from their predecessors who had begun the work. The most familiar of these discords is the pair

Detail of the portal of Notre Dame de Paris.

of spires at Chartres, constructed nearly four centuries apart in time. The twelfth-century spire is simple and chaste, while the sixteenth-century one, a few feet higher, is elaborate and ornate, constructed at a time when Gothic was past its best, and structural simplicity had to some degree been sacrificed to exuberance of decoration—a tendency we have already noted in contrasting Hellenic and Hellenistic art in an earlier chapter.

The Gothic style continues to be a matter of delight and wonder to the modern architect, who marvels at the authority which the medieval architect was able to wield over his whole building, subordinating all decoration to the needs of the architecture itself, and who is constantly astonished at what his medieval forebears were able to accomplish with primitive tools, working in stone and with none of the aids he now considers essential. The artist appreciates the absolute integrity of his medieval ancestor, the truth that he built into his works of stone, and the consummate skill with which he used what was available to him to create beauty—especially his use of natural light to shed color and light over the whole interior through the medium of his stained-glass windows. Even the modern religious skeptic is made to pause before this revelation in form of a faith that was as fully experienced by the medieval artist as it is alien to himself.

For medieval Gothic really is an expression, caught once and for all time, of a compelling vision whose essence is religious. The purpose of man's life on earth was to aspire toward Heaven. For a brief period medieval man really believed this. Man was a child of God, placed on earth in a particular position of honor or servitude which was none of his fault but merely God's will. He was taught not to envy the great man but to accept his lot, whatever it might be, knowing that after death he and the great man would be equal in the eyes of God and man. Only in the house of God on earth could he know himself as an equal. In the cathedral there was a place for him as there was a place, though a different one, for the noble and the bishop. Together they made up humanity as God had ordained it, and together their souls were lifted up toward the unseen God above. This was the symbolism of the Gothic—the ribs and the vaults and the pointed arches that gave the illusion of height and aspiration toward the great world above, where saints and sinners, nobles and serfs, were together before the judgment seat of God, saved through the blood of Christ.

When for the first time in the twelfth and thirteenth centuries it was possible for the medieval man to gain a tiny surplus over and above his daily needs, a surplus of either goods or leisure, the first task, the very first task, that he set himself was the building of a church or cathedral. As the Egyptians in the early part of their civilization built pyramids for the ascent of their king-god to Heaven, as the Greeks in the halcyon early days of Pericles built their temples for the gods to live in and protect them by their presence, so the men of the Middle Ages, in the springtime of their religious fervor, built a cathedral—not for

their God to live in, for he was in Heaven, but for a place of assembly for themselves, the congregation of the faithful to worship their God and soar upward in their souls toward him.

It was no wonder that the ages of skeptical "enlightenment" that followed the great age of church building termed the architecture of medieval man Gothic, or barbarian. The vision was too great for them to comprehend. They pretended to feel at home with the classic and the simple, the art forms of this world, not the aspiration toward Heaven and the striving toward infinity that had been the glory of their rude ancestors. Not until the nineteenth century was the supreme achievement of medieval man appreciated; and now we can only visit and wonder, trying to encompass in our imagination what it was that this strange semibarbarian felt in his inner world that could drive him to such a frenzy of creation, to so many hundreds, even thousands, of magnificent buildings, while he lived his ordinary life in unrelieved squalor. The bishop who commanded the task was moved by rivalry with his fellow bishops; the bourgeois who paid out the small profits of his business was moved perhaps by civic pride. But what of the poor unnamed worker, he who dragged the cart, who climbed the scaffolding, who had nothing but his labor to give, for him did the task represent only a day's wage on a public works project? It is hard to think so. And it is certain that there will be no more Gothic cathedrals, that our poor imitations are at once seen as frauds—for even the ignoramus in all matters of art feels no doubt when he comes to distinguish the genuine Gothic from the spurious.

The church we build today is the expression of ourselves. It may have admirable qualities, but it is not an expression of that compelling religious emotion, disciplined by a clear and logical mind, that came to maturity in the twelfth and thirteenth centuries of our era and found its architectural expression in the Gothic cathedral and its literary masterpiece in the *Divine Comedy* of Dante. As the Egyptians after the Old Kingdom built no more pyramids, save a few shoddy efforts by imperial imitators, so we shall build no more such cathedrals. But for a few more years we may still hope to see those built by our ancestors, and, seeing them, pause for a few moments in respect for a vision we have lost.

❖ Medieval music

As the great medieval cathedral is not truly itself without the throng of worshipers within, so also is it to be recognized truly only when filled with song. And of course it is no accident that medieval music, which spread from cathedral and church into the outer world and ultimately gave birth to the secular instrumental music of our own day, was developed to its fullest within these cathedrals, especially in Notre Dame of Paris, which was famed in medieval times for the excellence of its music. And it is also no accident that the music thus developed fitted in perfectly with the architecture of the buildings themselves.

The voice is the first great musical instrument, and it was the use of the human voice in medieval services of worship that gave birth to the great advance of music in all its forms during the medieval age. Very early in the Middle Ages the voice was used to chant the words of the Latin Liturgy in unison, or what was called plain song. In plain song all the voices followed the melody without variation except according to the pitch of the voice, at intervals of a full octave. This Gregorian chant, so called after Pope Gregory I the Great, is still used in church worship, and never died out in spite of the many other forms of song that now supplement it. But by the ninth century other intervals than the octave were used, and the enormous possibilities inherent in these variations were increasingly realized in subsequent centuries. While one voice held the melody, another sang the same melody but at an interval of a fifth (beginnings of polyphony, or many sounds). Then other intervals were also found to add beauty and fullness to the total sound, and altogether different melodies were made to interweave with the whole (the interweaving, note by note, of separate melodies with the basic one was called counterpoint). Finally, with the motet, even different words were sung at the same time as the basic melody, which was carried by one of the parts (hence the word *tenor*, the "holder" of the melody). Naturally, during the process of development, which occupied several centuries, a musical notation had to be adopted which was conventionalized into substantially the same notation that we use today.

The organ, which had originally been invented by the Greeks, and had been developed in the Byzantine Empire, was still rather a primitive instrument when introduced into the West in the ninth century. Thereafter it was continually developed into the complex instrument that it was by the end of the fourteenth century. The late medieval organ was able to perform the same kind of interweaving of sound that human voices had already been trained to make; and in later centuries of the modern era the various instruments likewise interweave to make the whole which we call the symphony (literally, "coordinated" sound as distinct from merely many sounds, *poly*phony).

❖ Medieval literature

In order to deal with the very large quantity of extant medieval literature in a short compass, it is necessary to be ruthlessly selective. We will therefore indicate the types of medieval literature, characterizing these very briefly, while devoting our small space to rather fuller discussions of a few acknowledged masterpieces which seem to the author to illustrate best the medieval attitude to life and the different strains of medieval thought and aspiration.

The most characteristic medieval works are written in the vernacular, and not in Latin, which, though it was still a living tongue in the Middle Ages, had to be learned, and was therefore not accessible to all. The amount of space devoted in this chapter to vernacular literature should not be taken as an indication of the relative quantity of literature available in Latin and vernacular tongues.

LATIN LITERATURE

Medieval Latin went easily into poetry, and rhyming was usual. We have the stately hymns of the medieval church, many of which are still in use, either in Latin or in the vernacular. But we also have great quantities of lighthearted verse, much of it composed by students at the universities, singing cheerfully of love and the springtime and similar subjects. There is also much satire, especially on the manners and customs of the clergy. A whole series of these poems is given the name of Goliardic poems, probably from the frequent references to a certain Bishop Golias, a mythical character who was supposed to be the poets' patron.

As the Middle Ages drew on, Latin literature became more confined to the clergy and educated classes, and was the official medium of communication for those who had to appeal to a wider audience than the inhabitants of any single area in Europe. History, memoirs, philosophy, and religious and scientific work continued to be written, for the most part, in Latin, while each area began to develop literature in the vernacular tongues, the medium of expression in everyday life.

VERNACULAR LITERATURE

Heroic epic Most of the great civilizations known to us produced their first literature in the form of heroic epics, sung and recited perhaps for centuries before they were written down. Western civilization was no exception. All the Germanic peoples had their sagas, dating from very ancient times, long before the advent of Christianity. The content of these is pagan, the deeds of pagan warriors and their gods, though sometimes overlaid with Christian feeling of a later age. *Beowulf*, the great Anglo-Saxon poem, is of the former kind; other examples are the Norse and Icelandic sagas. On the other hand, the *Nibelungenlied*, transformed into an operatic

cycle by Richard Wagner in the nineteenth century, retains the pagan background, but even in the early Germanic version the ancient warrior ideals have been partly transformed by Christian tradition and chivalry.

Poetry of feudalism The early folk epics were succeeded in the eleventh century by at least three distinct types of poetry, composed for the entertainment of the feudal nobility and on subjects of the greatest appeal for them.

The first type is the *chanson de geste*, or tale of heroic deeds, for the most part of northern French origin and headed by a masterpiece, the *Song of Roland*, which concerns the heroic death of Count Roland, one of Charlemagne's knights, at the battle of Roncesvalles against the Muslims. Around the figure of Roland a whole cycle of songs sprang up, even in countries quite unconnected with the hero. The songs also tell of the marvelous deeds of Charlemagne himself and his other knights. No attempt is made to relate the poems to the actual time of Charlemagne, but all describe the feudal world of the era when they were written and recited.

In southern France there grew up a school of lyric poetry recited and sung by troubadour minstrels in the noble houses and castles of the area. The troubadours introduced the element of love into their songs, which were no longer simply a recital of heroic deeds. It was under their influence that the cult of romantic love, still with us, first entered the Western world, since the troubadour by convention addressed his songs to the great lady of the castle, whose charms he extolled endlessly, and for whose smile he was willing to endure any torture. The influence of the troubadours spread into Germany, where they were called *minnesingers* (*minne* = "love"). In the hands especially of Walther von der Vogelweide (1170?–1230?), the romantic theme is handled with great freshness and delicacy as well as greater depth than is usual in poetry of this type.

The third type of poetry is a combination of the chanson de geste with the chivalric romance. Instead of the ordinary feudal world of the warrior, we now find portrayed idealized kings and knights, as in the legends of King Arthur, originally of Celtic origin. These knights often perform deeds of heroism for the sake of fair ladies, rescuing them from enchanted castles and such. This world of perfect chivalry is best described in the poetry of Chrétien de Troyes (last half of the twelfth century).

As time went on, the Arthurian legends became suffused with Christian thought and feeling. The culmination of this process is to be found in the legendary search for the Holy Grail, the vessel in which the blood of Christ was caught, or, in another version, the vessel used for the Last Supper, or a magic stone. All were equally symbolic of Christian aspiration. The hero who alone can find the Grail is a Christian, not merely a feudal or chivalric hero, whose purity and chastity rather than his deeds as a warrior bring him to his goal. The *Parzival* of Wolfram von Eschenbach (1170?–1220?) is the most fully Christian account of the wanderings of the hero in search of the Grail, while the culmination of the Arthurian legend is to be found in the prose *Morte d'Arthur* of the Englishman Sir Thomas Malory in the fifteenth century.

It has been possible only to touch upon the varieties of medieval poetry sung and recited among the nobility, in part for reasons of space limitation, and in part because of the difficulty of making any adequate generalizations when the total is so large and of such varying quality. At their best the heroic sagas are almost, if not quite, the equal of the heroic sagas of earlier peoples; at its worst medieval epic is feeble and derivative, using stock stories from the decadent periods of Greek and Alexandrine literature. The Arthurian legends are ancient Celtic tales which have been transformed out of all recognition by sophisticated poets of a later age, writing for an aristocratic audience for whom they were quite consciously extolling the cult of chivalry.

The fantastic world depicted in these legends no doubt provided a welcome escape for their audience from the anarchic feudal world of their day. Yet it also bears a direct relationship to it; it is a world less harsh, a world softened by the application of Christian ethical teachings. The poets have a secondary purpose beyond mere entertainment; their poems are truly didactic, not spontaneous and descriptive. The virtues they extol are not the heroic and martial virtues of an Achilles; courtesy and gentleness may be rewarded better than mere valor. In the Grail legends and especially in the poem *Parzival*, this tendency comes to full fruition and is entirely explicit. It is instructive to compare such a poem as *Parzival* with the earlier "wandering" epics of Gilgamesh (see Chapter 3) and the *Odyssey*, and to see revealed one aspect of the medieval mind and the medieval attitude to life. All these poems reflect the preoccupations of their time, as such poems always must. The Sumerian hero Gilgamesh searches for the plant of immortality, but having found it, he loses it again; the gods are arbitrary and unjust, they cheat mankind, and the hero has no recourse but to plunge himself back into life and build a city. Odysseus is stripped of his possessions and loses his companion in a shipwreck. He learns humility by hard experience, and through this experience he regains his lost rights as a king and vanquishes his enemies.

But Parzival in the poem of Wolfram begins as a fool and an ingrate; he leaves his mother without a thought, and she dies of grief. He kills a knight who turns out to be his kinsman, and is so unskilled he cannot even strip the dead knight of his armor. He early reaches the Grail Castle which he is destined some day to rule, but he does not ask the crucial question which would heal the wounded guardian of the Castle. In his subsequent loneliness and suffering he seems to deny even God. Yet this folly is also simplicity; it is culpable, but it can be redeemed and changed through the growth of wisdom. The poem is the story of how through the help of suffering he at last learns wisdom, and is permitted first to meet and become reconciled to his brother, the Oriental pagan prince Feirefiz, then finally to find again the Grail Castle with the help of sages who give him advice and warning. This time he asks the right question and achieves the Grail.

The poem does not seem to be allegorical in essence; it is not a *summa* of salvation like the *Divine Comedy* of Dante, to be described later. The Church plays almost no part in it. It seems to be the pursuit of the Christian ideal through life experience rather than through the mediation of the Church, and in this aspect it is significant. Parzival as a Christian prince is pursuing a Christian ideal. It is not his valor that triumphs. His first victory is not gained through valor, but through foolhardiness and good fortune, and he is defeated in combat by the heathen Feirefiz, who spares his life after Parzival's magic sword—the sword of his kinsman whom he killed so wantonly in his youth—has broken. In the end it is the purity and simplicity of his human heart, and his ability to learn wisdom, that make him worthy of the Grail. The wisdom he has learned and the reconciliation with, and ultimate conversion of, his heathen brother lead him to his goal. Thus this German poem already looks forward to a later age of religious thought than Dante's masterpiece, although it was written almost a century earlier; and it was no doubt this element in the poem that appealed to Richard Wagner. Though medieval in setting, *Parzival* transcends the medieval thought of the age when it was written. In the homelessness and loneliness and individual suffering of its hero, it seems to picture in advance the modern man, a prototype of Faust rather than of the medieval man who was led by Vergil and Beatrice on a spiritual journey to the contemplation of God.

Literature of the towns When we enter the world of the growing towns, the life of chivalry and courtesy is left behind, for these qualities are conspicuously missing in popular urban literature. The townsman preferred raw, earthy stories which were concerned with his own experience. He liked, in particular, animal stories and fables, above all the adventures of the cunning Reynard the Fox. The *fabliaux*, especially designed for the taste of townsmen, were undistinguished by literary graces of any kind, and their sense of humor appears to us as extremely primitive. The unfaithfulness, laziness, and untidiness of housewives were pilloried, as were similar sins on the part of monks, friars, and secular clergy. Women and the clergy were the principal butts of the satire of the fabliaux, and the plots hold no surprise. In the same vein as the fabliaux, but at a far higher stage of literary accomplishment, were the fourteenth-century stories of the Italian Boccaccio (1313?–1375) in his *Decameron*. The English popular poet Chaucer (1343–1400), however, stands in a class by himself. The characters in the *Canterbury Tales* are no longer mere types; each is sharply differentiated with wit, humor, and sometimes profound insight. Most of Chaucer's plots, however, are closely related to those of the fabliaux.

It is useless to try to describe Chaucer intelligibly in a few sentences. Always when writing of him, one drops into quotations, the only way to convey his flavor. The *Canterbury Tales*, his masterpiece though by no means his only poem—he was skilled also as a translator—tells of a pilgrimage made by a group of assorted characters to the tomb of St. Thomas Becket. Each of the characters is introduced to us; his or her character is hit off with exquisite precision in a series of rhymed couplets, sometimes sympathetic, sometimes malicious. Then Chaucer allows each of them to tell a tale to while away time on the journey. No other work gives us so full a picture of the ordinary medieval man and woman. When we have taken the journey with them and listened to their tales, we feel that we have indeed met and talked for a time with fourteenth-century human beings; we feel we should recognize them if we met them in life. Though the Middle English of Chaucer is no longer comprehensible to most of us, it slips easily into modern English; and though he has not always been admired as much for his poetical and especially metrical skill as he is today, there has never been a time since his death in 1400 when he has not been read for his narrative ability, his unerring character painting, and the vitality and freshness of his picture of medieval man as he really was in the fourteenth century.

An earlier contemporary of Chaucer gives us the first piece of serious social criticism of Western civilization, the *Vision of Piers Plowman*, by one William Langland, of whom nothing else is known. In this poem the poor peasant finds his voice. The poem, though couched in the form of an allegory, is a realistic description of the hard lot of the English poor in the fourteenth century—hardships which were later to lead to prolonged revolts, perhaps in part the result of this very poem.

Perhaps the most popular of all medieval poems was a composite work known as the *Romance of the Rose*. The first part is an allegory, written by William de Lorris (early thirteenth century). It is an ingenious love poem in the conventional style of courteous poetry, but no longer directed only to the noble classes, and clearly influenced by Christian tradition. It tells the story of a youth who is pierced by an arrow sped from the bow of the God of Love, whose heart leaves his own breast to be embodied in the Rose, which is surrounded by thorns and presents a difficult obstacle to be overcome. Jealousy, Reason, Danger, and other abstractions play their part in his efforts to reach the Rose, and after over four thousand lines, when William's poem breaks off, the unfortunate lover has still not attained his goal. It is at this point that a later writer, John de Meun (second half of the thirteenth century) takes up, and the poem ceases at once to be an idyllic dream and becomes a cynical satire on all contemporary institutions. Hypocrisy (the friars) is given a chance to speak; Reason and the other characters from the earlier poem flay superstition; Nature gives a discourse on medieval science and current history. In short, the poet is able to grasp the opportunity of the unfinished poem to give an invaluable account of medieval life. With the aid of Venus, the youth is able to gain his Rose; but this is only incidental to the satire, which has been called a "guidebook to the Middle Ages." It was, however, a guidebook in an entirely different sense from the greatest of medieval masterpieces. This work, which sums up knowledge and aspiration equally, welding the whole into a perfect synthesis, unique in history, entirely inimitable, and almost untranslatable, is the *Divine Comedy* of Dante.

The *Divine Comedy* was not the name Dante Alighieri (1265–1321) gave to his own poem. He himself simply called it the *Comedy*, because it begins in sadness and ends in supreme happiness. But it was early given the epithet "Divine," which has now been incorporated in the title. No poem has ever deserved it more, both for its beauty and for the sublimity of the theme.

It is impossible to do justice to the poem in a short space; in fact, it cannot properly be described at all. It must be read and experienced, preferably in the original Italian, a language full of vowels and music which Dante himself helped to fix. The Tuscan dialect of the poet indeed became, through his work, the literary language of Italy, and it has in essentials changed very little to this day.

One aspect of the *Comedy* cannot be understood without knowledge of the poet's first work, the *Vita Nuova*, in which he tells how at the age of nine he saw Beatrice, who was herself only eight, and how thereafter she remained his ideal though he never knew her well and she married without being aware of his unspoken feelings. He tells us that he had determined to express one day his love for Beatrice in poetry. It is this human and yet unearthly love that in manhood transformed the poet's whole inner being, giving especially to the *Paradiso*, the third part of the *Comedy*, an extraordinary intensity of thought and emotion which is recognizably medieval and closely akin to the work of the medieval church builders. It is impossible to separate the poet's sublimated love for Beatrice from the Christian love which made it possible.

Beatrice is a guide to the poet in his journey through the realm of the spirit to the vision of God, a realm in which the planetary spheres are not only seen but experienced, in which thought is not only apprehended but actually perceived. Yet Beatrice is also a woman before whom Dante is tongue-tied, so that at one moment he is unable even to pronounce her name. And she represents also revelation in the sense in which Thomas Aquinas understood it, the visitor from the world of the spirit who adds to what he cannot find for himself. Vergil, the Roman poet, takes Dante as far as the summit of the Mount of Purgatory, but the pagan can go no further. Reason must be supplemented by revelation. Vergil was first sent to Dante by Beatrice as he faced the gates of Hell and feared to enter—divine grace must aid the natural reason, which then, with the help of revelation, can ascend to the full contemplation of God.

So the poem is profoundly allegorical; and yet at the same time it is real. The journey may have been the ascent of a soul to salvation, but the poet feels and perceives as a human being. The sufferings of the damned are portrayed with gruesome realism, and Dante experiences all the shock and revulsion of a healthy mortal. When Vergil leaves, Dante grieves and wishes him back; he suffers the pangs of loneliness in a deserted Garden of Eden until he recognizes Beatrice, who comes riding to him in her chariot drawn by a gryphon. If the chariot is the Church and the gryphon is the animal symbol of Christ, this symbolism does not intrude. The symbolic or allegorical and the real are so wonderfully fused that the reader is caught up with his imagination into the experience, and need know nothing of the symbolism until he feels the need for it.

Finally, it may be added that the poem has certain important political meanings. Dante was through and through a political man; he played an important part in the affairs of his native Florence, and he was a leading figure in the city's government before being forced into exile by his political enemies. He was a partisan of the empire in the struggle between the empire and the papacy. In his work *De Monarchia* he makes clear the reasons for this partisanship. He believed that the spheres of Church and State should be separate, but that the State should be a true World State, such as had been known in the early centuries of the Christian era under the aegis of Rome. The political condition of man is a consequence of sin, and leads to ever more deadly sins. Dante's choice of characters for the dwellers in his three realms of Hell, Purgatory, and Paradise is undoubtedly to some degree determined by his political views. It is significant that the Byzantine emperor, Justinian, noted by historians for his universal law code and for his reconquest of Italy, is greatly exalted

in Dante's Paradise, and is seen by the poet as having been permitted by God "the glory of avenging his wrath by the living justice that inspires me"—a line hardly equaled for concentrated thought in all literature.

The poem begins on the night preceding Good Friday; during that night the moon is to be at the full. Throughout the next day and night the poet will make his horrifying journey through Hell (the *Inferno*). For twenty-four hours more he struggles to the foot of the Mount of Purgatory (the *Purgatorio*). Then for three days he is on the Mount and at last ascends to Paradise (the *Paradiso*), where there ceases to be any time. It remains the same day (Thursday) as Dante circles the earth in company with the heavenly planets until he is over Italy and the sun is setting in Jerusalem. The journey has taken exactly a week.

In Hell, accompanied by Vergil, he passes by all the various grades of sinners undergoing punishment, till he comes to Satan himself; then he is pulled past the center of gravity by his guide. The worst is over. Those whom he will meet hereafter are souls who are saved but are not yet ready for Heaven. On the Mount of Purgatory there are many terraces, each with its different sinners, and before he even reaches the terraces the poet sees others who have for some reason not yet begun to make the ascent, though in time they will be able to undertake it. In the *Purgatorio* the whole atmosphere is different from that of Hell, where all hope has been abandoned for eternity. Here in Purgatory one first comes to the realization that though the way is long, salvation is ahead. There is hope, indeed certainty, for the sinner in Purgatory. Then at last the Garden of Eden is reached, Vergil leaves the poet, and Beatrice comes for him as his new guide.

Light, music, joy, and love are the glories of Paradise, marvelously conveyed in the liquid Italian, with its many beautiful images; the planets dance and sing as they wheel in the Ptolemaic universe, so deeply experienced by Dante that it seems impossible to doubt that this is the way the universe is in the world of imagination. ("Like the clock that calls us to prayer, in which one part draws and impels the other, chiming 'tin tin' so sweetly that the well-disposed spirit swells with love"—"Tin tin sonando con si dolce nota Che il ben disposto spirto d'amor turge.") Here are the great saints, Bernard and Thomas Aquinas, Peter, and, at last, the Virgin Mary and a momentary vision of God, which, as soon as it is experienced, cannot be remembered save as an afterglow of something indescribable. But among the blessed this vision is always there. When Dante looks into the eyes of Beatrice, the Light is reflected there, and though he turns about to discover the source of the Light, it eludes him.

In all the great medieval thinkers there is nothing abstract or arid. The Latin of Thomas Aquinas, crystal-clear and sharp, bears the reader along with him to share his enthusiasm for the adventures of the mind, the logical thrust and counterthrust corresponding to the thrust and counterthrust of the piers and buttresses of the cathedral. So the reader is pulled onward toward the summit of the vision, the "intellectual contemplation of God" in which, as Thomas experiences it, there is nothing cold—the love of the heart leading to the understanding of the divine (as, also, in Plato's *Symposium*), the love that leads to this ascent having been implanted in man as grace, the gift of God. So also in Dante. "Luce intellettual pien d'amore, Amore del vero pien di letizia, Letizia che trascende ogni dolzore" —"Light of the mind, full of love, Love of the truth, full of joy, Joy that transcends every sorrow"—this is Dante's description of that love which draws mankind to the contemplation of God. Every word in the great poem is full of the profoundest thought, often untranslatable into languages other than Italian, in which feeling and thought are fused as in no other. It lacks the extreme clarity of the cold intellect which is the genius of the French language, and the Italian itself was never again used as it was by Dante, who found in it the perfect vehicle for his experience. The whole knowledge of the world of the senses and the world of the spirit as experienced by medieval man is in the *Divine Comedy*—the deadliness of sin and the eternal punishment that it entails, the great hope held out to man

by God and the means for its attainment, and at last a vision of eternal blessedness with the saints and heavenly hosts in the spaceless, timeless kingdom of heaven.

It is sometimes claimed that Dante is a Renaissance rather than a medieval writer. It will be clear from the above that the present writer has little sympathy with this point of view. Insofar as there is a characteristic way of looking at life that we may call medieval, insofar as there is a distinctive climate of ideas and beliefs that may be called medieval, the *Divine Comedy* was the very fullest and most far-ranging expression of medievalism, and the author makes no apology for including it in a chapter on medieval culture. It is true that Dante lived in a Florence where the Renaissance was already awaking, that his political preoccupations foreshadow those of the Renaissance, and that in some respects he greatly influenced his successors in the period of the Renaissance. But in all the essentials of his work he remains medieval, and for this reason he has been included in this chapter, whereas Petrarch, who was seventeen years old when Dante died, is clearly, at least in the opinion of this writer, a Renaissance figure, and will therefore, unlike Dante, be excluded from this book.

Medieval drama In conclusion, a few words should be said on the medieval drama, which, though not one of the great dramas of the world, is nevertheless original and, in its way, characteristic of the Middle Ages. In early medieval times the drama consisted of the re-enacting of biblical scenes in the churches at times of festival. These re-enactments developed into the mystery play, which also used biblical subjects but combined them with legends and tales from the lives of the saints. Mystery plays, too, were performed in church, but quite early were presented in the vernacular since the purpose was to instruct the people. The performers were usually the clergy, though lay actors were also used. An outgrowth of the mystery play is the Passion play, which represented with deep sincerity the crucifixion of Christ. Some of the Passion plays still survive, played by village actors and joined in by the whole village community.

The Oberammergau Passion play, performed in the Bavarian village of that name every ten years, is the outstanding surviving example.

The miracle plays, which became popular by the twelfth century, usually represented some exceptional intervention of a saint or the Virgin Mary in the ordinary lives of men. Finally, with the growth of the towns, came the play we most associate with the Middle Ages, the morality play, originally of a religious nature. By far the best known of these morality plays is the famous *Everyman*, the story of the rich young man who was visited by Death and warned that he had only a few hours left to live, who first tried to bribe Death, and then to persuade his kinfolk and his friends to go with him. Refused by all, he had to die alone, with only his good deeds to help him to ultimate salvation, after repentance and absolution.

In concluding this chapter on medieval culture, it may be worth while to think briefly of the distance traversed by modern man since the Middle Ages, and try to imagine the beautiful simplicity of medieval belief—and also to consider Shakespeare, whose drama was, in a sense, not so far removed from *Everyman*. Shakespeare was still in the fullest sense a moralist. Yet he was deeply concerned with the individual and not the type—the character, deeds, and motives of man on earth, his relations with other human beings, and his actions in the face of his destiny. Such interests are our heritage from the Renaissance, and therefore lies outside the scope of this book.

With the fading of the medieval concept of the universal man as a member of the universal Church and of Christendom, and of the conviction that all the answers to the questions man has to ask are already known, the adolescence of the human being was over.

Suggestions for further reading

PAPER-BOUND BOOKS

Adams, Henry. *Mont-Saint-Michel and Chartres.* Anchor, Collier, Mentor. Though not approved by all scholars, this classic synthesis of the medieval vision by a scion of a famous American family remains one of the best books to introduce the student to medieval culture.

Aquinas, St. Thomas. *Summa Contra Gentiles* (trans. as *On the Truth of the Catholic Faith*). 4 vols. Image. One of St. Thomas' two major *opera*, this one gives proofs for the existence of God and is directed primarily to unbelievers as a polemic on behalf of Christianity. Also available are useful selections published by Galaxy and Washington Square Press.

Butterfield, Herbert. *The Origins of Modern Science.* Collier. Interesting and provocative study of several problems considered by medieval as well as more recent scientists. Some of the material is also covered in Butterfield, *et al., A Short History of Science* (Anchor).

Copleston, Frederick. *Aquinas.* Penguin. A clear summary of the work of St. Thomas by a Jesuit priest. The same author has a brief history of medieval philosophy, *Medieval Philosophy* (Torchbooks) and a more extended *History of Philosophy*, of which the medieval sections are available in an Image edition in four volumes.

Crombie, A. C. *Medieval and Early Modern Science.* 2 vols. Anchor. Detailed history, with many diagrams, especially strong on physics.

Curtius, Ernst R. *European Literature and the Latin Middle Ages.* Torchbooks. A valuable study of vernacular literature during the High Middle Ages.

Dawson, Christopher. *Religion and the Rise of Western Culture.* Image. Valuable interpretation by a leading Catholic historian.

Eschenbach, Wolfram von. *Parzival*, trans. by H. M. Mustard and C. E. Passage. Vintage. A new prose translation with a good introduction.

Fremantle, Anne. *The Age of Belief: The Medieval Philosophers.* Mentor. Useful introduction, including extracts from the originals.

Gassner, John, ed. *Medieval and Tudor Drama.* Bantam. Excellent selection in modern English, including the Everyman play and several medieval Passion plays.

Gilson, Étienne. *Héloïse and Abélard.* Ann Arbor. A serious study by a leading French writer on medieval philosophy, less vivid than Helen Waddell's novel, but places the famous romance of the two tragic lovers more within the framework of the time.

Gilson, Étienne. *Reason and Revelation in the Middle Ages.* Scribner. A short, well-written interpretation, to be supplemented by the hardcover book, *The Spirit of Medieval Philosophy*, the author's masterpiece. (New York: Charles Scribner's Sons, 1936.) A paper-bound selection is also available: *The Gilson Reader* edited by Anton Pegis (Image).

Katzenellenbogen, Adolf. *Sculptural Programs of Chartres Cathedral.* Norton. The best modern discussion of medieval sculpture.

Leff, Gordon. *Medieval Thought from St. Augustine to Ockham.* Penguin. Useful introduction.

Lorris, Guillaume de, and Jean de Meun. *Romance of the Rose,* trans. by Harry W. Robbins, Jr. Everyman. Complete poem discussed in the text.

Panofsky, Erwin. *Gothic Architecture and Scholasticism.* Meridian. Stimulating description and interpretation of Gothic architecture by an art expert.

Southern, R. W. *The Making of the Middle Ages.* Yale University Press. Especially valuable discussion of the relation between medieval religion and culture.

Temko, Allan. *Notre-Dame of Paris.* Compass. History of the famous cathedral including full description and an account of how it was built.

Vignaux, Paul. *Philosophy in the Middle Ages.* Meridian. An introduction and up-to-date interpretation; thorough, intelligent, and based on the latest material. Probably the best short work for the beginner.

Waddell, Helen. *Peter Abélard.* Compass. A fine, evocative novel written by a competent medieval scholar, which succeeds in conveying a good picture of twelfth-century intellectual life and the environment in which Abélard lived.

Waddell, Helen. *The Wandering Scholars.* Anchor. Small classic, slightly overwritten, on the medieval poets.

Williams, Charles. *The Figure of Beatrice.* Noonday. A stimulating and beautifully written appreciation of Dante by an English novelist. Severely critical of the notion that Beatrice is an allegorical figure.

Wulf, Maurice de. *Philosophy and Civilization in the Middle Ages.* Dover. A serious and interesting study by a noted Belgian historian of medieval philosophy, but should not be read .by itself as it is more a personal interpretation than a factual book on medieval philosophy. Similar comments apply in a lesser degree to the same author's *Introduction to Scholastic Philosophy* (Dover).

HARD-COVER BOOKS

Artz, Frederick B. *The Mind of the Middle Ages,* 2d ed. New York: Alfred A. Knopf, Inc., 1954.

An up-to-date survey, especially notable for its extensive and valuable bibliography, which should be consulted for further works on subjects handled in this chapter.

Crombie, A. C. *Robert Grosseteste and the Beginnings of Experimental Science.* Oxford, England: The Clarendon Press, 1953. Important scholarly work, perhaps the best single book on medieval science in English and not confined to Grosseteste.

Crump, C. G., and Jacob, E. F., eds. *The Legacy of the Middle Ages.* New York: Oxford University Press, 1926. Very good on medieval arts and crafts.

Laistner, M. L. W. *Thought and Letters in Western Europe,* 2d ed. Ithaca, N.Y.: Cornell University Press, 1957. By far the most substantial work available on the literature of the early Middle Ages, though not easy reading.

Morey, Charles R. *Medieval Art.* New York: W. W. Norton & Company, Inc., 1942. Probably the best single work on the subject.

Rashdall, Hastings. *Universities of Europe in the Middle Ages,* rev. ed. New York: Oxford University Press, 1936. Readable and usually interesting; the unevenness of this book is to be accounted for by the incompleteness of the material available to the author and his revisers. Still the only comprehensive account of the universities available.

Taylor, Henry Osborne. *The Medieval Mind,* 4th ed. 2 vols. Cambridge, Mass.: Harvard University Press, 1925. Though slightly uneven, since Taylor did not have an equal knowledge of all the writers and subjects he covered, this remains the best single work on the subject— sympathetic, eloquent, encyclopedic, and original—based on the author's own impressions of the writers he treated.

Thorndike, Lynn. *A History of Magic and Experimental Science.* New York: Columbia University Press, 1923–1941. Six vols. to the close of the Middle Ages. A mine of information on individual scientists, drawn from their own writings, but lacking any attempt at synthesis of the whole.

William of St. Thierry and others. *St. Bernard of Clairvaux,* trans. by G. Webb and A. Walker. Westminster, Md.: Newman Press, 1960. One of our best contemporary sources for the life of St. Bernard, demonstrating the impact he had on the life of his time.

INDEX

Aachen, 189, 279
Abbas, 172
Abbasid dynasty, 170, 172, 176–177
Abélard, Peter, 282–283
Abner, 202
Abraham, 44
Absolutism,
　Charles I and, 279
　French,
　growth of, under Roman Empire,
　　101
　Russian,
　See also Monarchy, absolute
Abu Bekr, 170
Abydos, 29
Achaeans, 52, 53
Achilles, 55, 70
Acre, 230, 231
Acropolis, 55
Actium, battle of, 104
Acton, Lord, 110
Acts of the Apostles, 135
Adam, original sin of, 132
Adriatic Sea, 96
Aegean civilization, 52–53
　Greek civilization influenced by,
　　52–53
　map of, 53
Aegean Sea, 52
Aegospotami, battle of, 66
Aeneas, 114
Aeneid, 114
Aeolians, 53
Aequitas, 116
Aeschylus, 70, 71
Africa,
　Egypt (*see* Egypt)
　Ethiopia (*see* Ethiopia)
　Greek colonies in, 55
African Fathers of the Church, 281
Agamemnon, 52, 55, 71, 72
Agincourt, battle of, 267
Agora, 61
Agriculture, beginnings of, 16
　See also under specific civiliza-
　　tions
Ahmed, Sultan, mosque of, 162
Ahmose I, Pharaoh, 29
Ahura-Mazda, 41, 42
Aingra-Manu (Ahriman), 41, 42
Aistulf, 185
Akhenaton, Pharaoh, 31
Akkadians, Sumerians conquered
　by, 37
Alaric, Rome sacked by, 137, 148
Albertus Magnus, 276, 284, 285,
　286, 289, 290
Albi, 235
Albigensian Crusade, 176, 235, 239,
　262
Albigensians, 42, 235
　suppression by Innocent III, 235
Alcibiades, 71, 73
Alcuin of York, 189, 279
Alemanni, 153
Alexander III, pope, 234
Alexander the Great, 42, 45
　Aristotle and, 76, 82

Egypt conquered by, 32
Greece conquered by, 75, 81
India conquered by, 81
Persia conquered by, 41, 81
polis favored by, 82
successors of, 82
Alexandria, 85, 108
Al-Farabi, 174
Alfred the Great, 155, 247
Algorism, 173
Al-Hazen, 174
Ali, 170
Al-Idrisi, 175
Al-Khwarizmi, 173
Al-Kindi, 174
Allah, 169, 170, 177
　Mahomet, prophet of, 168
Alodial, 251
Alsace-Lorraine, 189
Amalfi, 209
Ambrose, 135
Amenhotep IV, pharaoh, 31–32
Amiens Cathedral, 294
Amon-Re, 30, 31
Amorites, 35, 37
Amphorae, 62
Anagni, 242
Anatolia, 159
Anaxagoras, 76
Anaximenes, 69
Ancient world:
　chronological charts of, 22–23,
　　28–29
Andromache, 70
Angles, 150, 154
Anglo-Saxons, 155, 247
Antigone, 71
Antigonus, 82
Antoninus Pius, 112
Antony, Mark, 102
Anytus, 73
Aphrodite of Melos, 85, 86
Apollo, 55, 66, 73
Apology, 73
Aquinas, St. Thomas, 72, 276, 278,
　280, 284, 285, 302
Aquitaine, 254, 261
Arabesques, 176
Arabia, 167
Arabian Nights, 176
Arabs, 166, 167, 170, 173
Aragon, 239, 271, 272
Aramaeans, 43
Archimedes, 85
Architecture:
　Gothic, 293–296
　Greek, 79–80
　Roman, 117–119
　Romanesque, 292–293
　See also under specific civiliza-
　　tions
Arete, 70, 72
Arianism, 136, 150, 164
Arians, 164
Aristarchus, 85
Aristophanes, 71
Aristotelianism, 284

Aristotle, 50, 68, 70, 173, 278, 289
　Alexander the Great and, 76
　biological classification of, 76, 77
　condemnation of, by Archbishop
　　of Sens, 284
　Lyceum founded by, 75
　metaphysics of, 76, 288
　Muslim civilization influenced
　　by, 284
　Muslim regard for, 173
　Plato contrasted with, 76, 287,
　　288
　Politics of, 76
Arius, 136
Arles, 118
Art (*see* under specific civiliza-
　　tions and countries)
Arthur, King, 298
Arthurian legends, 298
Asia Minor, 43, 82, 91
　See also under names of specific
　　countries
Assize of Clarendon, 254
Assize of Northampton, 254
Assurbanipal, 40
Assyrians, 34, 35, 36
　Babylonia conquered by, 39
　empire of, 39–40
　Hebrews conquered by, 40
Astrolabe, 174, 177
Astrology, 287–288
　See also under names of civili-
　　zations
Asturias, 271
Ataraxia, 84
Athanasius, 136
Athena, 79
Athens, 56, 61, 63, 66, 130
　capture and sack of, 65
　Darius I, expedition against, 64
　Delos Confederation led by, 66
　Macedonia, conquest by, 64
　Marathon, campaign of, 65
　Persians, defeat of, at Mycale,
　　65
　Salamis, victory of, 65
Athens School (*see* School of
　Athens)
Aton, 31
Attalus, 82
Attica, 61
　See also Athens
Attila the Hun, 135
　Italy invaded by, 148
Augustine, St., 136, 137, 188, 285
Augustine Age, 125
Augustine of Canterbury, St., 136
　139
Augustus Caesar, 101, 102, 119
　achievements of, 109–110
　agriculture under, 109
　army under, 102, 104
　boundaries of Roman Empire
　　reset by, 107
　civil power of, permanent, 105
　Egypt under, status of, 107
　genius, cult of, in worship of,
　　106

305